EDUCATIONAL MEDIA AND TECHNOLOGY YEARBOOK

ELWOOD E. MILLER, Editor
MARY LOUISE MOSLEY, Associate Editor

EDUCATIONAL MEDIA AND TECHNOLOGY YEARBOOK

1985

VOLUME 11

Published in Cooperation with and Cosponsored by
The Association for Educational Communications
and Technology
and
The American Society for Training and Development
(Media Division)

1985

Libraries Unlimited, Inc. • Littleton, Colorado

ISBN 0-87287-446-X

ISSN 8755-2094

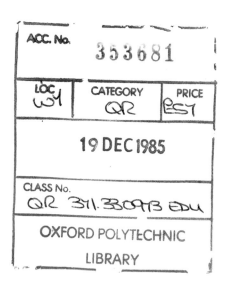

Dedication

Barbara Andrew Miller,
1928-1984
School Librarian

A late afternoon sun cast light on a woman tossing a box of books overboard into the blue waters of the South Pacific. Barbara Miller was not seeking to stock the library of Old Man Neptune, rather she was cleaning the shelves of the world's only floating university library on board the SS *Universe.*

Night and day she labored, completely reorganizing the twelve-thousand volume collection until it was a well-ordered collection of reference volumes on every subject studied by the globe-circling students.

Somewhere off Korea a typhoon bore down on the ship. The seas grew until the ship tossed back and forth so much the captain ordered everyone below decks. The ship's librarian stayed with her charges, catching books with every roll of the ship and clinging to tossing instructional aids — projectors and copy machines.

The captain found her there, scurrying madly about the upper deck library. He ordered her below, and she turned her back on the rapidly deteriorating cranium of the ship's educational function.

After a night that saw the rolling ocean liner come within mere degrees of capsizing, the librarian went back to check on her charges. She found a copy machine that had done end-overs all the way across the library. Shelves were smashed; books were everywhere. Her hours of labor to reorganize had been for naught; biographies lay with encyclopedias on top of mathematical treatises. There is no sense to a storm-sorted library. Calm night waters reflected the lights of the library as Barbara Miller worked to once again put order back into the ship's library.

Barbara Miller was, like all great librarians, the kind of person students love to turn to for guidance into the world of words, pictorial images, recorded voices, and music. A teacher takes one down a path, but the librarian opens a door into a world where the student chooses the route.

As technology introduces a myriad of new ways of storing knowledge, from microfilm to computers, many are the librarians who face typhoon-lashed libraries turned topsy-turvy. All who are worth the title of librarian roll up their sleeves and begin the task of renewal.

Barbara Miller's memorial service this past spring found a host of teachers, students, and friends filling a Boulder church to the brim. All remembered a mother, teacher, librarian, and human being who reveled daily in finding ways to begin building anew. This year's edition of the *Educational Media and Technology Yearbook* is dedicated to her spirit of searching for the best way of serving those who relied on her.

Andrew D. Miller
February 1985

Contents

Part Two
ORGANIZATIONS AND ASSOCIATIONS

Part Three
GRADUATE PROGRAMS

Part Four
DIRECTORY OF FUNDING SOURCES

Part Five
MEDIAGRAPHY
Print and Nonprint Resources

Preface

As the last quarter of the twentieth century goes roaring by, numerous authors such as Alvin Toffler in the early seventies, and more recently John Naisbitt have predicted and warned of enormous changes in American and world social and economic orders. And social and economic systems *are* changing at a breakneck pace. Books are printed by computer; newspapers are distributed first by satellite, then by computer and high-speed presses; money is managed by plastic cards; and on and on.

The American educational community, usually slow to identify and accept changing times, is now faced with a seeming avalanche as the electronic revolution imposes computers, video recorders, satellites, and a multitude of electronic devices that *almost* seem designed to make things easier, or more difficult, depending upon the educator's view of the contrivance. Technology, in the guise of the microchip with its enormous ability to store and sort information within space that is miniscule, and with power demands that are almost nonexistent, is threatening an educational order that has done little changing since monks of the Middle Ages determined that a class sitting at the feet of the teacher was the model that was most efficient (at least for the teacher).

Will the educational establishment keep to its usual 50 to 60 year lag time to adopt innovations? Or is the time such that pressures from the public to use innovative communications systems will require the establishment either to change or to loose its clientele to the private sector or some other organization that will use established information in new and better ways to insure quality learning at affordable prices? There is an audience of teachers, learners, parents, and citizens who are asked to finance public education (as well as private) and who are looking for guidance as education experiences these pressures. To those who want to lead intelligently toward the end of the century, the editors address this volume.

For these reasons, and others, the new editor of the *Educational Media and Technology Yearbook 1985* (formerly the *Educational Media Yearbook*) has assembled a team of writers and advisors to seek fresh directions for this publication that has been for over ten years the informational backbone within the media and technology establishment.

Changes in the 1985 *Yearbook* are extensive within several parts of the book, but the general organization of the book is similar to that of past volumes. As a user, you will find the same search strategies that worked in the past to secure information and ideas will continue to work.

Part 2, "Organizations and Associations," has been heavily edited. All entries were thoroughly screened, and the result is a leaner and more useful listing for the reader and researcher. Part 5, "Mediagraphy," has been changed a great deal with the hope of the editors that it, too, will be easier to use. Other sections of the book will receive a heavier scrutiny for the 1986 *Yearbook*. All sections have been reviewed and changed for this edition, however.

We hope that *Educational Media and Technology Yearbook* will remain the major tool for serious reference work and research within the profession. The information is as accurate and up-to-date as possible and is concise and easy to find; it should be most helpful to all who are interested in the contributions of both media and the media technologist to the future of education in the remainder of this century.

The editors would like to acknowledge the fine assistance of a number of professionals who have helped in the decisions and reviewing of manuscripts for the 1985 *Yearbook*. They include Mr. Ray L. Anderton of the University of Colorado; Ms. Naomi O. Story of Maricopa Community College District; Dr. Paul Welliver of Pennsylvania State University, who secured the presidential papers for section 1; Dr. Edwin "Ned" Logan of Washington, D.C., who prepared the section on graduate programs; Dr. Richard Scudder of the University of Denver, who assisted with efforts to computerize the database for the *Yearbook*; and Mr. Andrew Miller, of Winter Park, Colorado, who assisted in the preparation of the manuscript.

As was true for the 1984 yearbook, this edition is sponsored by the Association for Educational Communications and Technology, and by the American Society for Training and Development (Media Division).

In closing this preface, the editor must comment upon the major contribution to the profession that Jim Brown, along with Shirley Brown (for the past six years), has made. Only upon nearing the completion of the editing task, can one really appreciate the long hours of labor and the effort, referred to by Jim as a "labor of love," that have gone into the ten yearbooks that the Browns edited. All of us in the educational media and technology field owe the Browns a great vote of thanks for the superb job done over the years.

Thanks, too, to the authors who have written and worked with the editors, and to the hundreds of people who have rewritten their entries, and to the score or so of professionals who have made valuable suggestions for the book.

And finally, thanks to the gracious staff of professionals at Libraries Unlimited, Inc., for helping the editor and his team work their way through the process of producing *EMTY*. First journeys are always the most difficult, and you have guided us well.

Abbreviations Used

The following abbreviations are used in this yearbook:

Act. Dir.	Acting Director
admin.	administrator
ALA	American Library Association
ann.	annual or annually
approx.	approximately
Assn.	Association
Assoc.	Associate
Asst.	Assistant
AV	audiovisual
b&w	black and white (film)
bi-ann.	biannually
bi-mo.	bimonthly
bi-wk.	biweekly
Chair	Chairperson
Co-Dir(s).	Co-Director(s)
comp(s).	compiler(s)
Coord.	Coordinator
Corp.	Corporation
d.	daily
Dept. Dir.	Department Director
Dir.	Director
Div.	Division
ed(s).	editor(s)
exc.	except
exec.	executive
HB	hardbound
indiv.	individual(s)
inst.	institution(s)
irreg.	irregularly
libr.	librarian
libs.	libraries
Mgr.	Manager
Mng. Dir.	Managing Director
min.	minutes
mm	millimeter
mo.	monthly
nat.	national
n.d.	no date or date not known
n.p.	no pagination or pages not known
occas.	occasionally
Off.	Officer
organ.	organization(s)
PB	paperbound
pna	price not available
pp.	pages
PR	public relations
Pres.	President
prog.	program
Prof.	Professor
pub.	publisher
q.	quarterly
rep.	representative
rev.	revised
SASE	self-addressed stamped envelope
Secy.	Secretary
semi-ann.	semi-annually
semi-mo.	semi-monthly
spon.	sponsor
sr.	senior
Univ.	University
V.P.	Vice-President
vol(s).	volume(s)
wk.	weekly
yr.	year

Part One

Educational Media and Technology
A Time of Transition

Introduction

Since the early 1940s one educational group has been especially active in examining the multitude of possibilities in working for more efficient and cost-effective instruction. The group is generally identified as "instructional media specialists or technologists."

In 1942 the U.S. Armed Services created a group of military officers who concerned themselves with the problems of training tens of millions of young men and women for a war effort of vast and immediate proportions. In a matter of months, they designed systems using films, slides, models, and simulations that were very effective in teaching new information and skills in a sophisticated and successful manner.

The editor of *Educational Media and Technology Yearbook 1985* is the son of one of those early audiovisual pioneers, and from the early sixties he was formally involved with curriculum improvement based on the intelligent and effective use of materials and with the hardware necessary to display those materials for effective learning.

The major impediment to the speed and effectiveness of development in technology has been the rather crude and difficult machines necessary to bring about the reforms that many of us envisioned. Since 1980, however, major advancements in information management with electronic devices have removed most of these obstructions. World War II audiovisual pioneers have seen astounding advances in computers, television, and combinations of these two electronic giants that have moved education in the direction of a major breakthrough in the mid-1980s.

Thus, the editor of *EMTY 1985* and his advisory group decided to focus on *transition* as the appropriate topic for the first section of the 1985 yearbook. We believe that the changes in educational patterns and learning systems will be remarkable in the late 1980s, and that by the end of the decade, the structure and look of U.S. education will be much different from what it was in 1970.

Fifteen authors were selected to write papers addressing the transition theme. Some of their papers cluster together into subthemes. The first two papers (by Gubser and Baltzer) focus on the directions that education and educational technology seem to be going in. The next two papers are especially insightful in the new area of interactive video: Hannafin, Garhart, Rieber, and Phillips suggest a theoretical approach to the area, and Schaffer writes of the practical problems of implementing interactive education in the public school arena. The following two papers deal with training: Knab and Donnelly present an interesting story on the development of training programs for a major insurance program; Mosley and Story share some case studies on instructional development within a community college setting. Next Komoski presents a highly insightful paper on computers and computer software.

The next four papers address the general arena of television in 1985. Brock writes of the new emphasis on adult education at the Corporation for Public Broadcasting; Niemeyer shares a paper on television use in continuing education across a consortium of colleges; Binns describes the use of community antennae television for education in Florida; and Wilson suggests the effective use of satellite television at the U.S. Air Force high school at the Air Force Academy near Colorado Springs.

Grady then describes current thinking on accreditation of professionals in the field; Sinofsky shares some of her concerns with the "copyright quagmire," and Berling writes about new directions in library resource management and administration. Part 1 closes with a broad view of the media technology revolution.

The editorial board believes that within these fifteen papers there is a wealth of information that can assist the media/technology professional with his or her thinking about the direction that these transitions are taking the education and training communities.

Public Education in a
Year of Transition

Lyn Gubser
Executive Director
Association for Educational Communications
and Technology
Washington, D.C.

"Through a mixture of destiny, default, and design, virtually every important industry in the United States is becoming high-tech" (Schrage, 1985, p. E-1). That pronouncement from *The Washington Post* includes the industry of U.S. education. Whether we like it or not, the fact remains that we have entered a new age — an age in which information has become the central commodity of our trade and our culture. Inevitably, we will experience major changes in the way that society transmits to younger generations our essential cultural priorities and what we believe to be knowledge.

Meanwhile, our schools are preoccupied with problems that seem to have little to do with "becoming high-tech." In 1984 we saw the beginning of what the Council of Chief State School Officers (CCSSO) called "a national emergency" in school staffing. The CCSSO cited three primary reasons for this emergency: low economic benefits and the low status of teaching; the movement that allows modern women to become something besides housewives, nurses, and schoolteachers; and poor and violent conditions within our schools.

The Rand Corporation warned of a "Coming Crisis in Teaching," noting that

> the nation's teaching force is changing dramatically. The current highly educated and experienced staff is dwindling as older teachers retire and many younger teachers leave for other occupations. Recent evidence suggests that new recruits to teaching are less academically qualified than those who are leaving; moreover, the number of new entrants is insufficient to meet the coming demand. (Darling-Hammond, 1984, p. 1)

In addition to the problem of adequate school personnel, we find that many of our schools are in disrepair, classrooms are ill-furnished, and instructional laboratories and shops lack modern equipment. It is unlikely that sufficient monies can be diverted from other social, military, and economic programs to solve our most pressing educational problems. However, modern electronic technologies can help to reduce instructional expenditures by absorbing some of the direct costs of instruction and by helping to reduce expenditures for purchase and maintenance of equipment and facilities. If properly employed by competent teachers, new interactive media can expand the effectiveness of teachers and help improve the quality of instruction in our schools.

U.S. schools have long depended on technologies of one type or other—to one degree or another—to impart instruction. We have used print technologies (i.e., books) as classroom aids from the time the colonists used the Bible to teach children to read. Slates, chalkboards, magic lanterns, programmed texts, filmstrips, slides, tape recorders, motion pictures, television, and multimedia kits have all had an impact on instruction. Now advanced electronic technologies are entering U.S. classrooms: computer-based and computer-assisted instruction (CBI and CAI), videodisc, interactive systems, holography, robots, computer-generated graphics, and simulations offer an unprecedented array of instructional resources. These resources offer competent instructional personnel the tools necessary to improve and individualize instruction.

Former U.S. Secretary of Education Terrel Bell (1984), said that new applications of electronics to instruction "will turn American education upside-down in the years immediately ahead." Bell made this statement at the commissioning of the National Institute of Education's Task Force on Educational Technology. Assigned to determine the implications of the new technologies for the nation's schools, the Task Force's particular concern is to determine whether electronic media can help compensate for the general lack of adequate staff.

The question of whether technology can provide effective instruction is hardly a new one. To some people the answer is decidedly yes—and has been common knowledge for years.

> Our technologies of instruction were demonstrated to be effective 25 years ago. They are even more effective today. In addition to adding more technologies such as the computer, we know much more today about how students learn and how to design effective instruction. With expert teams of curricular and instructional designers planning, developing, and packaging reliable instructional systems, even the average classroom teacher can achieve superior results.... We do not need more teachers in order to improve ... instruction. (Heinich, 1983, p. 3)

This quotation from Robert Heinich of Indiana University presents clearly the position of many instructional technologists. While they recognize that the new generation of electronic media is still in its infancy, most observe that already a significant portion of instructional support can and is being assumed by new hardware and software.

A significant point often missed by critics is that subject areas of the curriculum differ widely in their susceptibility to instructional support from educational technology. Advanced instruction in the social sciences, analysis of literature, and studio art and sculpture have evaded most software producers. But in many other curricular areas the story is different. Keyboarding, for example, has replaced typing in many secondary schools, and typing teachers are now supported by software that teaches keyboard skills independently with patience, strong intermittent rewards, and no small dose of entertainment. The computer graphics firm of Evans and Southerland has created, for Mercedes-Benz, software for total automobile simulations that probably teaches driver education more effectively—and certainly more safely—than the traditional school program could ever have done, requiring fewer personnel and fewer real automobiles. Software for microcomputers and interactive video systems is now available to support the teaching of English composition, spelling, reading, arithmetic, science, foreign language, and even higher mathematics. Companies such as Videodiscovery of Seattle produce interactive videodisc programs that enable learners to acquire many concepts formerly taught only in laboratories. This reduces facility costs and creates new avenues for independent instruction.

But there are those who do not believe the new generation of media will be effective in providing a solid foundation for improved teaching. They maintain that the present quality of software, both electronic and film-based, is inferior. The film and electronics industries have acted to make fast profits from shoddy products, these critics contend, and there is no immediate solution to educational problems through technology. We simply cannot expect electronic technologies to "make teaching 'regular subjects' better and cheaper, saving money or improving test scores," says Art Luehrmann (1985), commenting in *Electronic Learning*. "Despite claims to the contrary," Luehrmann writes,

> computers have largely failed to do these things. Therefore, to promote school computers as mere educational technology is courting disaster. A naive public may believe these claims today, but it will look for results tomorrow, and, not finding much, will dismiss computers as "just one more technological fix that didn't work"—like instructional TV, language labs, and programmed instruction. (p. 22)

Unfortunately, Luehrmann and other critics miss entirely the point that we have entered a new age—an era in which none of the old circumstances, or the old rules, apply. We are moving away from labor-intensive schools as we have known them, schools that reflected the industrial nature of the society that supported them. Modern U.S. education will increasingly reflect the informational nature of the new society. If schools fail to make this change, they will perish as surely as have other industries that could not or would not adapt to changing economic and social expectations.

Labor-intensive businesses depend upon a large supply of cheap labor. Schools are no exception. As the supply of cheap industrial labor has dwindled in the United States, those industries that have depended on this supply have become extinct or moved abroad. We cannot send our children to school in Taiwan, South Korea, or Mexico as we have sent much of our industrial manufacture. So we must seek tools that will enable those talented teachers who have survived in our schools to expand their instructional competence to reach an increasing number of learners.

If we assume that interactive video systems, computers, and other new microchip-based technologies can absorb much of the burden of instruction—particularly drill-and-practice and information-dispensing tasks—what is the incentive for the average classroom teacher to learn about and apply these new technologies? Why should an overburdened teacher, facing substandard benefits, assume the additional responsibilities of learning to teach with and through new technological systems? If that teacher is fully licensed, has reached the top of the district salary schedule, and has tenure—which describes the bulk of our teaching force—what's in it for them to assume more responsibility? Worse yet, many teachers may believe that such new technologies as computers are just another fad to hit education. Some may even feel that technology will produce the automation that could replace them.

To ensure a smoother transition in our schools between the labor-intensive, industrial model of the past, and a more cost-efficient and individualized system reflective of the expectations of our informational society, we must link incentives to productivity. Presently, teachers are paid virtually the same no matter what they do or how many students they teach. If incentives were based on productivity and technological resources were abundant, teachers would readily adopt instructional technology. Trainers already have adopted computer-based instruction and interactive systems in the private sector, where a high correlation exists between productivity and compensation. If we base incentives on production, public school teachers also will adopt with enthusiasm those instructional technologies that can add to their productivity—and thus their remuneration.

As is true of any time of transition, the present offers us both the chance for growth and social advancement and the possibility of missed opportunities and social failure. The impending teacher shortage and the advent of uniquely sophisticated instructional technologies provide a happy coincidence for those who believe in the effectiveness of educational media. But we must remember that when faced with a massive teacher shortage in the 1950s, the states responded by lowering standards for teacher licensure until they could find sufficient "warm bodies" to meet staff demand. It is possible that such an irresponsible solution will be used again to solve the present crisis. It is also possible that American public schools have exhausted their utility. Some see a future of highly productive, technologically based public schools that finally achieve the old dream of individualized instruction. Others believe the present transition will see our public schools become babysitting services for poor whites and minorities, while children of affluent families are served in high-tech academies.

That instructional technology holds the potential for solving some of our most challenging educational problems appears generally accepted. Whether we will actually use this resource toward that end remains to be seen.

REFERENCES

Bell, T. (1984, October). Remarks presented to the National Institute of Education's Task Force on Educational Technology, Washington, D.C.

Council of Chief State School Officers. (1984). *Staffing the nation's schools: A national emergency.* Washington, D.C. Author.

Darling-Hammond, L. (1984). *Beyond the commission reports—The coming crisis in teaching.* Santa Monica, Calif.: The Rand Corporation.

Heinich, R. (1983). Legal aspects of alternative staffing patterns and educational technology. *Synthesis, Southwest Educational Development Laboratory, 6*(2), 3.

Luehrmann, A. (1985). The new trend: Ed-teching the computer. *Electronic Learning, 4*(4), 22.

Schrage, M. (1985, January 13). The lure of the new technologies. *The Washington Post*, p. E-1.

The Consumer and Converging Telecommunications

Jan Baltzer
Director of Telecommunications
Maricopa Community College District

Over the past few years, I have read numerous articles and papers on the future of telecommunications in which the authors list many diverse and seemingly unrelated technologies together as if there were some relationship or pattern to them, leaving the reader to devise an overall trend or direction for the future of telecommunications. This paper does not do that. There is no litany of electronic alphabet soup here. Instead, I attempt to suggest the future direction of telecommunications by presenting several concepts that I believe are fundamental to any discussion regarding telecommunications — particularly telecommunications and higher education. These concepts are:

1. Telecommunications is a *process* not an *artifact*.

2. The consumer (whether at work, at home, or at school) is the primary driving force in the acceptance and use of any new communications technology.

3. The lines that separate the various communications technologies are blurring so that there will soon be no clear-cut way to differentiate among them.

THE DEFINITION OF TELECOMMUNICATIONS

When asked to define the term *telecommunications*, many people respond with a list of technologies that are examples of telecommunications systems. They tend to look at telecommunications as an artifact, something one can see and touch and feel. I believe that there is another way of looking at this issue: telecommunications should be examined as a process — the process of sending information over a distance by using electrical or electromagnetic systems. The information that is transmitted or sent can take the form of voice, data, pictures, or text.

Telecommunications, then, is not a goal; it is a tool, which if used wisely and correctly, will assist people in achieving goals. This is an important concept to remember as we consider telecommunications and education. Buying a television or radio station, constructing a microwave network, or offering telecourses for the sole purpose of owning or using a telecommunications system and thus appearing to be innovative, should not be the goal of any educational institution. Instead, the goal of that institution should be to provide education to its target populations through the most efficient and effective means possible. For many institutions, the most efficient and effective means possible is the teacher in the classroom; for others, it is the use of communications technologies to enhance classroom teaching along with stand-alone instructional technology delivery systems.

If we think of telecommunications in this broader sense, then, as a means to an end rather than as an end in itself, we will be better able to envision the future of telecommunications and the impact of telecommunications on education in the next two decades.

THE ROLE OF THE CONSUMER

In the third edition of the *Channels Field Guide to the Electronic Media*, subtitled *Revolution at the Hearth*, Les Brown (1985), the editor-in-chief of *Channels* states:

> First came the technologies, then the large corporations with fortunes to invest. Now comes the consumer to decide what will have a place at his electronic hearth. He has entered the picture not as the passive viewer this time, but as a force to determine how the rest of the story unfolds. (p. 2)

The statistics are undoubtedly in Brown's favor. In 1964, there were 86 million telephones in service in the United States. The 1985 forecast is for 250 million. In 1964, there were 214 million radios in use in the United States. By 1985, the forecasters predict there will be 500 million. In 1964, there were 64 million television sets in use in the United States. If industry predictions are correct, there will be 205 million television sets in use by 1985. In 1984, 19 percent of all U.S. homes had videocassette recorders and experts forecast a penetration of 30 percent more by 1990. In 1984, 14 percent of all U.S. homes had personal computers. The industry prediction is a penetration of 40 percent of all homes by 1990.

The consumer is rarely considered as a primary factor in the future of telecommunications. This is particularly true in the area of telecommunications and education where educators are often more concerned with grade distributions, number of hours spent in the classroom, and the traditional way of doing things, than with the real goal of providing high-quality, relevant education for students.

If the student, as consumer, can withdraw cash from his or her checking account by entering a series of numbers into a machine on the side of a bank twenty-four hours a day, seven days a week, why should that same student be required to register for college by making an appointment weeks in advance so that he or she can stand in long lines at the local college? If the student, as consumer, can satisfactorily complete all of the class requirements at his or her own pace by watching a series of videocassettes at home and taking specified examinations in a CAI (computer-assisted instruction) mode at the college library, why should that student be required to spend a minimum of 2,400 minutes in a classroom with a certified instructor?

Students are not the only consumers in the educational area. Faculty also find themselves in the role of telecommunications consumers. In this role, faculty want the most up-to-date tools to enhance their classroom teaching and the training required to use these tools. Imagine how frustrating it is to an instructor who has wonderful teaching materials available to him or her on videodisc or videocassette but cannot use these materials in the classroom because of an insufficient amount of playback equipment or a poorly designed distribution system. Imagine the frustration of the faculty member who uses a personal computer at home for word processing and database management but who is forced at the college to use an electric, or manual, typewriter and a pencil-and-paper record keeping system.

At many educational institutions throughout the country, students, faculty, and staff are demanding that new telecommunications systems such as up-to-date telephone systems, personal computers, online registration systems, and instructional delivery systems be instituted. Colleges and universities that fail to heed these demands may soon find themselves with fewer students requiring their traditional services.

THE CONVERGING TECHNOLOGIES

In 1980, I was asked to make a presentation on the new "alternative instructional delivery systems." It was a fairly simple presentation to research and to organize with the technologies involved clearly divided into four different distribution systems: (1) electronic transmission systems—television, radio, radio subcarrier, cable television, Instructional Television Fixed Services; (2) copy delivery systems—videocassette, videodisc, audio-cassette; (3) computer delivery systems—computer-assisted instruction and computer-managed instruction; and (4) telephone delivery systems—audio teleconferencing, audio graphics, slow-scan video.

Today, however, the lines that separated these delivery systems and individual technologies are blurring so that the individual system is no longer the solution to meeting user needs; the integration of systems is the solution. Further, the three essential building blocks to the successful integration of the technologies are the computer, electronic links, and video technologies.

As a result of this new integration of technologies, we in higher education now have a number of new telecommunications systems available to us including:

- Voice response registration systems that allow the student to register by telephone twenty-four hours a day, seven days a week by entering the necessary data into the computer using a touch tone telephone.

- Online databases that are available regionally and nationally and can be accessed using a regular telephone and a personal computer.

- Videotext systems that can be used on campus and in the community to provide instant access to such information as personnel and student policies, registration dates, course descriptions, and student activities.

- Audio and video teleconferencing for the delivery of instruction as well as for meetings, staff development, and professional growth activities.

- Interactive video instruction using either videodiscs or videocassettes in combination with microcomputers.

- Radio subcarrier (SCA) for the citywide transmission of paging, downloading of data, or the delivery of instruction to specialized populations such as the blind or print-handicapped.

- Integrated voice and data terminals (the newly coined Executive Workstation) that allows the users to process data or to share textual information at the same time they are talking with other individuals.

- Digital PBX's that can handle both voice and data and can serve as local area networks for connecting microcomputers to microcomputers and microcomputers to large mainframe computers.

Making these technological applications even more astounding are the latest electronic links including satellites, microwave systems, local area networks, and fiber optics.

The merging of the technologies and the transmission systems is so complete, even now, that the educational institution that tries to evaluate a particular technology for instructional uses cannot avoid evaluating that system for administrative and student support purposes. It is impossible today to evaluate a telephone system without considering the impact that that system will have on the data processing environment of the institution and vice versa. New classroom buildings cannot be constructed without the architects and educational specialists' regarding the wiring of the buildings as vast highways for the transmission of voice, video, and data and for support of terminals and instruments that may not, as yet, have been developed. Finally, with the myriad of new telecommunications applications being developed, there is a very real temptation for institutions and individuals to discard "good enough" or workable technologies for newer or "better" technologies — to be the first on the block to own the latest technological toy. Now, being the first at something is not necessarily bad, particularly if being first means that you are better able than your competitor to meet the needs of the consumer. But, being first for the sake of being first hardly ever accomplishes this task.

As educators, our goal is to provide high-quality, relevant learning experiences for students, and we should make every attempt to provide this service in the friendliest and most convenient manner possible. Can telecommunications systems help us with this task? Yes, I believe they can. Do we all need to construct two-way video microwave networks with audio talk-back loops? No, we do not.

Not every college needs to be cabled with fiber optics. Not every college needs to own its own television or radio station. Not every college needs to invest in microwave or satellite networks. What every college and university *does* need to do, however, is to stay alert to the new telecommunications advances and carefully evaluate the new technologies as potential tools for use by the college. Only by being aware of the power and magnitude of these new tools and by incorporating them appropriately into our institutions can we insure that our institutions will survive the current telecommunications revolution and will provide us with the most efficient and effective education possible in the future.

REFERENCES

Brown, L. (1985). *Channels of communications, the essential 1985 field guide to the electronic media: Revolution at the hearth.* (p. 2). New York: Media Commentary Council, Inc.

Keeping Interactive Video in Perspective
Tentative Guidelines and Cautions in the
Design of Interactive Video

Michael J. Hannafin
Associate Professor

Casey Garhart, Lloyd P. Rieber, and Timothy L. Phillips
Doctoral Candidates
Instructional Systems Program
The Pennsylvania State University

Interest in the instructional applications of interactive video has grown significantly during the past few years. In general, instructional interactive video may be defined as "any video program in which the sequence and selection of messages is determined by the user's response to the material" (Floyd, 1982, p. 2). The potential of such a formidable instructional technology is impressive, permitting seemingly unlimited combinations of instructional stimuli, lesson pacing, lesson control, and other options.

A major problem confronting the instructional technology profession, however, is that little empirically derived information exists to guide instructional design decisions. This is not to say that little has been written concerning interactive video. Clearly, even a casual review of popular publications supports the widespread interest in interactive video. Interactive video presently lacks a meaningful context for study and development, a context that includes a grounding in accrued knowledge and a defensible articulation of the tacit assumptions of interactive video. Instead, we seem to be slipping into the hardware-dominated orientation that has plagued instructional innovations in the past, where the capability of the *instructional hardware* appears to be dominant. Our fascination with the "toys" of the trade has obscured important questions of appropriate design and use.

Although there is a paucity of research investigating the instructional design issues of interactive video, a highly developed body of related research exists. For example, studies utilizing the component technologies, computers and video, may provide insights into the design of interactive video. The study of learning and cognition has also provided useful information pertaining to both the instructional manipulations and mental processing aspects of learning. Indeed, Clark (1983) has suggested that instructional design and cognitive processing considerations are more salient than media used to deliver the instruction. In effect, although little empirically derived research has been reported specifically for interactive video, a vast body of related research exists that may be useful in evaluating present-day design decisions.

The purposes of this paper are (1) to present a series of empirically derived, tentative guidelines to be considered in the design of interactive video and (2) to identify and describe several issues in the design of interactive video where caution should be exercised.

SOME TENTATIVE GUIDELINES FOR THE DESIGN OF INTERACTIVE VIDEO

The following guidelines are based on the findings reported in the learning literature and cognitive research, as well as the research pertaining to computer-assisted instruction (CAI), video, and televised instruction.

1. *When imposing lesson control, interactive video lessons should be adaptive in nature to permit a greater level of individualization.*

   Individuals process information in different ways. The strategies used by one learner are likely to differ from those of another learner; what benefits one group of learners may actually hinder the performance of another group (Bovy, 1981; Cronbach & Snow, 1977; Salomon, 1979). Ideally, it would seem, every lesson should be individually tailored to suit the needs and abilities of each student "so as to develop, compensate for, or capitalize upon student characteristics for the optimization of subject-matter learning" (Messick, 1984, p. 69). Accomplishing this goal, however, can be difficult.

   Group instruction, given through lectures, films, and video, requires the imposition of predetermined strategies. All learners follow the same sequence at a rate judged to be of maximum benefit to most learners. With the advent of programmed instruction and CAI, greater individualization became possible. Still, most lessons continued to control the learning sequence, with pace the primary individualized variable. (Bovy, 1981; Cronbach & Snow, 1977)

   A possible solution to rigid lesson control involves the use of adaptive designs. An adaptive program tracks student progress and makes continuous revisions based on the learner's cognitive ability, prior knowledge, and task-related performance (Tennyson & Buttrey, 1980). Amount of instruction, sequence of instruction, and instructional display time can all vary depending on the unique characteristics of each learner.

   Through the use of adaptive designs, individual differences can be accommodated by considering such factors as *when* errors are made and by placing substantially greater importance on recent performance versus early performance. Responses are not simply tallied; they are evaluated based on both cumulative and current performance. In this way, the options provided by the designer can be used more intelligently, resulting in instruction that is more sensitive to individual learner differences (Tennyson, 1984).

2. *Criterion-based interactivity should be used to direct learner processing and to monitor on-going comprehension of intended learning.*

   There are two principal theories concerning learning from video: the reactive theory and the active theory. Proponents of the reactive theory suggest that students are passively involved in the learning, focusing more on reception than processing. Proponents believe that the degree to which the person attends to the video affects the level of comprehension (Bandura, 1977). Questioning, in such cases, serves to direct and to focus learners' attention on intended information.

   The active processing theory, on the other hand, suggests a type of comprehension schema derived from previous experience and modified by the induction of new information (Stein & Trabasso, 1984). Attention results from a need to fill in "slots" in this schema with expected information (Schank & Abelson, 1977). Attention either may be terminated, if the information is too unfamiliar to be effectively comprehended, or sustained by the effective integration of information (Anderson & Lorch, 1983). Criterion-based questions may be useful to monitor and to ensure ongoing comprehension, which should in turn improve the learner's ability to sustain attention. In this regard, criterion-based questions might improve learner performance by increasing the amount of invested mental effort (AIME) learners direct toward material (Salomon, 1981).

The roles of questions embedded in an interactive video lesson, therefore, could be defined compatibly with either of the dominant "learning from video" theories. Questions may encourage learners to apply greater mental effort to a formerly passive video medium, thereby increasing attention and subsequent comprehension, or, questions may monitor comprehension of intended information, resulting in increased attention. In either case, it seems that the incorporation of criterion-based questions in video instruction is likely to improve intended learning.

3. *Video stimuli should provide the primary instruction; the computer should manage and control instructional sequence decisions.*

Interactive video, as a hybrid instructional technology, has generated interest in both the computer and video fields. Most of the early designers and producers were "video people" who developed interactive video as computer-controlled video. As computer enthusiasts have become interested, the perspective of interactive video as video-enhanced CAI has also become popularized. Is interactive video primarily an extended form of video, or an enhanced form of CAI?

There is no research to support one side over the other, so we are left with logic and common-sense to form an initial hypothesis: Let each medium do what it does best. Video is good at producing complex, realistic images, at depicting a broad range of colors, at showing smooth, realistic motion, and at transmitting lifelike audio. While expensive computer systems with complex programs can do these things as well, video does them well with less effort and expense. Computers, on the other hand, are good at handling and storing large amounts of information, at accepting and evaluating user input and making conditional decisions based on that input, and at generating output that is contingent on individual user input (Roblyer, 1982).

Research suggests that combining modalities often increases learning (Fleming, 1979; Rowher & Harris, 1975). Computer-managed video, where instruction is presented through high fidelity audio and video, provides dual modality instruction. The video instruction provides both audio and pictures for dual coding (Nugent, 1982), thus increasing the memorability of information presented by video (Nasser & McEwen, 1976). The management capabilities of the computer, then, permit verification of learning and additional instruction as needed. From both practical and empirical perspectives, it makes the most sense to maximize the strengths of both components of interactive video.

4. *The fundamentals of good instruction are more likely to be appropriate to the design of interactive video than not; the processes included are more important than the technology per se.*

Although some people feel that interactive video is more than simply the merging of the parent technologies of computer and video and therefore presents unique design considerations (DeBloois, 1982), it is more likely that the fundamental elements of well-designed interactive video lessons are comparable to those of any well-designed lesson in any medium. There is evidence to suggest that no single medium is sufficiently unique to transcend the fundamental components of effective instruction (Clark, 1983). So perhaps it is more fruitful to consider how the time-tested components of good instruction can best be integrated with interactive video.

Whereas a wide range of instructional research studies and theories has been reported, perhaps the most useful synthesis has been offered by Gagné and Briggs (1979), who described "events of instruction." These events, which were subsequently applied specifically for CAI (Gagné, Wager, & Rojas, 1981), are the instructional milestones of a lesson that support the internal processes of learning (Gagné, 1977). Each external event is assumed to relate to the internal, cognitive processes of learning. Instruction is seen as providing events that promote the conditions needed to activate executive control, to retrieve information to working memory, to encode information, and to develop mechanisms to aid in subsequent retrieval. The events of instruction synthesize information into a more or less generic set of instructional components, which presumably relate to how information is presented, perceived, encoded, organized, and retrieved. From a design perspective, interactive video *may* be especially useful for different events, but it seems unlikely that the conditions of learning from interactive video will be radically different from those prescribed by Gagné.

5. *The level of difficulty of the video-based lesson should be perceived by learners as challenging and as requiring considerable effort.*

Learning from television or video is affected by the expectations of the student. If the information fits too easily into the comprehension schema or if the information is too difficult for the learner to integrate effectively, students will experience difficulty with both attention and comprehension of the lesson (Anderson & Lorch, 1983). Consequently, "difficult" video instruction has always been discouraged because there has been no way to verify en route comprehension. This problem may be ameliorated through the use of interactive video; interactive video can supplement the video by questioning, repeating, or recasting difficult concepts, as needed. As a result, more difficult information can be presented and comprehension can be verified through the interactivity.

Learning can also be influenced by student preconceptions of the learning technology itself (Meringoff, 1980). Students perceive video as much easier, more lifelike, and less demanding for comprehension than the same information in alternative forms. Such preconceptions result in reduced mental effort, which tends to reduce the level of student learning and the effectiveness of video as an instructional tool (Salomon, 1983a, 1983b).

It seems reasonable to assume that to overcome student preconceptions that result in reduced mental effort, video lessons must be perceived by the learner as challenging and requiring effort. Interactive video, with its ability to monitor student progress and to prescribe alternate instruction, can be utilized to increase student performance by fostering greater mental effort.

SOME TENTATIVE CAUTIONS IN THE
DESIGN OF INTERACTIVE VIDEO

The following cautions address some of the problem areas for which design decisions must be made. The findings from related research, however, are inconclusive and often troublesome. Each caution is described and analyzed using existing, related research.

1. *The type, level, and position of questions for interactivity will affect the type of learning.*

Questioning as an instructional strategy has been used to motivate, to review, to focus student attention, and to inform of progress. In interactive technologies, questions may also be used to increase learner involvement. Very often, however, we assume that all questions motivate or provide adequate review without considering the effect that different types, levels, and positions of questions have on learning.

Mayer (1984) discussed three processes necessary for meaningful learning: selection, organization, and integration. The first, selecting or attending, is a necessary but not sufficient prerequisite to learning. Without selection there is no learning, but if selecting is the only cognitive process in which the learner engages, learning will be unstructured and will be retrievable only as isolated facts. In order to have more structured learning, Mayer's second process, organizing, is necessary. Through organization the learner builds internal connections within the new material. With both selecting and organizing, partially meaningful learning occurs. But it is not until the learner is able to integrate the new information with what is already known that learning becomes truly meaningful. By building connections between the new information and prior knowledge structures, the new material is not only more easily retrieved but is also transferable to new situations.

In a study on mathematics concept acquisition, Mayer (1975) found that questions aimed at lower level processes aid in acquiring those processes but interfere with higher level processes. Definitional (selecting) prequestions improved scores on definitional tests, and use (organizing) prequestions helped on both definitional and use tests, but only the relationship (integrating) prequestions were beneficial for all three types of learning. In fact, on relationship questions the control group (no prequestions) scored better than either the definitional or use groups, indicating that lower level questions actually interfered with the learning relationships.

Clark (1984) has also indicated concern for the relationship between the type of questions used for practice during instruction and the resulting learning consequences. Highly specific questions that focus literally on information presented during a lesson may result in "near transfer" consequences, which provide limited generalizability. Whereas this type of practice question is likely to be both effective and appropriate for certain types of learning, it poses problems for "far transfer" skills that are to be generalized to novel, problem-solving settings. Broader-based questions, that are not lesson specific, may be more appropriate for such tasks.

These findings are also supported in numerous studies that have looked at intentional versus incidental learning (Klauer, 1984; Koran & Koran, 1975; Reynolds & Anderson, 1982; Watts, 1974). In each study, specific prequestions had a positive effect on intentional learning, but a negative effect on incidental learning. Klauer also noted that focusing attention on specifics, through questions aimed at selection, may also interfere with the student's organization of the material and general understanding.

This is not to say that prequestions are necessarily detrimental to learning. Mayer's (1975) relationship questions actually facilitated all types of learning and Klauer (1984) found that more general questions and goal statements were more likely to have a positive effect on both intentional and incidental learning. Although he did not specify the nature of these more general statements, it is probable that the more successful ones focused on higher levels of processing. These more general, integrative prequestions help learners relate the material to what they already know in an organized and meaningful fashion (Andre & Anderson, 1978-1979; Memory, 1983; Watts, 1974).

Thus far the discussion has focused on questions as motivators and organizers, but what about the role of questions in review? It is often assumed that postquestions help learners review, rehearse, and integrate new information. How well this occurs depends on the nature of the questions and whether or not the learner is able to return to the original material. Once again, high level questions requiring applications of principles and concepts to new situations are better than definitional or factual questions that focus on selecting (Andre & Anderson, 1978-1979). And, although intuition might suggest that it is beneficial for learners to refer back to the original content when they discover they do not know the answers, Schumacher, Moses, and Young (1983) found no significant difference between groups that were able to look back and groups that were not. They hypothesized that since looking back requires no mental processing there was no gain in learning.

In summary, then, it appears that both prequestions and postquestions improve learning if they involve higher level processing tasks and if they require mental effort. If factual recall is all that is intended from a learning situation, specific prequestions or postquestions aimed at these facts will suffice; if later transfer to new situations is expected, questions must be of an integrative nature.

2. *In general, it is not advisable to transfer instructional control decisions to learners unless additional prompting is provided.*

Among the general features of CAI courseware most desired by educators, the feature of learner control is highly valued (Caldwell & Rizza, 1979). Many educators would initially agree with this recommendation since learner control seems to imply individualization of instruction. However, much current research indicates several disadvantages to transferring lesson control to the learner (Hannafin, 1984; Ross, 1984; Tennyson, 1980). For instance, researchers have been fairly consistent in concluding that learners fail to make appropriate decisions during CAI instruction when relying solely on their own judgments.

This does not imply, however, that learner control should be abandoned entirely. Learner control has been found effective for CAI when paired with learner advisement or coaching. Usually, the advising consists of informing learners of ongoing progress toward performance standards, recommending the number of practice items or examples to be used, and other types of coaching that provide the learner with meaningful performance-based information upon which an informed decision can be made. Learner control with advisement was found to be as effective and more efficient (less time on task) than an adaptive design strategy (Tennyson, 1980).

Our recommendation is for designers of interactive video to be very cautious when transferring lesson control to the learner. Generally, learner control without some sort of advisement or coaching will result in ineffective learning (DiVesta, 1975; Hannafin, 1984; Rothen & Tennyson, 1978; Tennyson, 1980). When tasks require minimal prior knowledge and include a simple content structure, a learner control strategy with coaching can be appropriate (Steinberg, 1977). However, when instructional tasks consist of a complex content structure and demand greater prerequisite knowledge, the management design should provide program control (Tennyson & Rothen, 1979).

3. *There is evidence to suggest that the more explicit the imposed organizational structure of the lesson, the greater the potential for conflict with individual learner schema.*

Interactive video provides a wide range of possibilities for organizing and structuring the sequence of activities. Lessons can include any of a variety of adjunct questioning techniques, mnemonic devices, and other organizational procedures, in addition to the basic organization of the information to be presented. Of concern, however, are how, when, and whether or not such strategies *should* be used. There is considerable evidence to suggest that such procedures may be unnecessary, and even contraindicated, for many learners.

Individuals vary widely in their capacity to learn from instruction. Cognitive strategies, those processes used in selecting, organizing, and integrating information, also vary considerably. Good learners have numerous, well-developed strategies to draw upon in learning situations; poor learners generally lack either relevant strategies or the knowledge of when to use strategies they do possess (Belmont & Butterfield, 1971; Mathews, Hunt, & MacLeod, 1980; Raphael & McKinney, 1983). Clearly, some learners do not require the imposing of processing strategies, while others not only find them useful but may depend on such techniques to aid in the selection, organization, and integration of information.

The question of how to design instruction that is sensitive to the types of learners for whom it is designed is important. Bovy (1981) suggested that instruction can (1) externally model appropriate cognitive strategies, in which case strategies are imposed on the learner, (2) direct the cognitive processes of the learner, or (3) let the learner activate the appropriate processes independently. To the extent that a person possesses the appropriate strategies and can apply them, external structure is not necessary. In fact, such structure may inadvertently cause good learners to apply the less developed strategies imposed during a lesson. However, learners who lack effective cognitive strategies will likely require external assistance.

Imposed processing models may be beneficial for learners who have mediational deficiencies (Guttentag, 1984). However, they may enhance intended information material at the expense of incidental information. This, in turn, may make low level learners unnecessarily dependent on external aids, rather than bringing them to a level where they can apply strategies on their own. Of potentially greater concern is the belief that high level learners may actually suffer under imposed structure, resulting in declining performance (Bovy, 1981; Cronbach & Snow, 1977; Salomon, 1979).

Directed processing cues the learner to activate existing strategies and is especially beneficial for learners who possess the strategies but suffer from production deficiencies (Guttentag, 1984). If learners possess the necessary strategies, learning may be facilitated more by cuing than by imposing processing strategies (Bovy, 1981). Cuing also leaves room for some ambiguity, which leads to greater effort and greater learning (Kunen, Green, & Waterman, 1979).

Finally, instruction during which learner activated processes are used may be beneficial for learners once they have achieved a mature use of the relevant strategies (Guttentag, 1984). High ability learners often profit from the opportunity to use their own processing strategies, but a complete lack of structure can be disastrous for all but the best learners. Low level learners, or learners who simply lack the necessary cognitive strategies, are likely to be most handicapped by this type of instruction.

4. *Learning efficiency may suffer as a result of interactivity — especially under mastery-oriented conditions.*

The computer component of interactive video has the capability to monitor student progress as well as to access and to play the given video sequences. It is not uncommon for instructional segments to be repeated or recast during instruction, resulting in an increase in learning time. This is likely to be most obvious in mastery-based lessons.

Critics of mastery learning have contended that equalizing student achievement and reducing student learning time are nothing more than "educational rhetoric" (Glass & Smith, 1978) and "boondoggling" (Mueller, 1976). In one study, mastery learning raised achievement levels significantly, but the additional instructional time required was considerable (Arlin & Webster, 1983). Results of a different study also indicated that, contrary to mastery learning theory expectations, learning time remained at initial high levels or actually increased (Arlin, 1984a, 1984b). Wells, Whechel, & Jamison (1975) found that when the level of increased achievement was compared to the amount of additional practice needed to attain it, the results indicated positive, but diminishing returns.

Recent research with interactive video has supported these conclusions, indicating that instructional time may be an important consideration for interactive video applications. Schaffer and Hannafin (1984) reported that mastery-based interactive video increased achievement but decreased the learning efficiency when compared to linear video versions of the same instruction. As the amount of interactivity increased and the associated instructional time increased, students learned proportionately less.

Attempting to increase student performance using interactive video may actually reduce the learning rate. The time required to question the learner, to accept and evaluate input, and to branch and replay the appropriate video segment may aid in the magnitude of learning but with significant increases in instructional time. Whereas the additional time may be warranted for many tasks, it remains to be seen whether the higher levels of performance are attributable to more, rather than better, instruction, and whether or not the kinds of additional information learned through interactive video are sufficiently worthwhile.

SUMMARY AND CONCLUSIONS

Educational innovations are tempting, but they are often adopted and installed based on a misleading set of considerations. As a profession, we seem awestruck by the power and features of technology, and we often respond to the innovation at a superficial level. We focus on the capabilities of the *technology* rather than what *learners* do effectively with technology. In the past, this has hampered the installation of promising technologies because of a predictable and justifiable backlash: Instructional innovations are considered little more than high-priced fads, lacking the theoretical and conceptual bases needed to survive. If interactive video is to be perceived as more than another passing fad, these are certainly patterns that we must seek to avoid.

An important key to the long-term adoption and installation of interactive video is the effective use of the cumulative wisdom accrued through learning, cognition, and technology research. Despite claims to the contrary (DeBloois, 1982), it seems likely that a significant amount of existing research *is* relevant to the design of interactive video. It seems reasonable to assume that the principles of learning developed across instructional media will not be radically altered or redefined by interactive video. It may be more sensible to approach interactive video as an extension of our capacity to present and to manage instruction rather than as a technology that dramatically redefines the process of learning.

The purposes of this paper were to present a sampling of tentative guidelines and cautions for consideration in the design of interactive video. The discussion suggests that many issues in the design of interactive video are comparable to those of any technological innovation: What do we know about how people think and learn, and how can technology be used to effectively support the learning process? In many cases, we already possess the necessary information to make supportable decisions. In other cases, however, the issues are not nearly so clear or straightforward. This may provide an appropriate and necessary starting point for placing interactive video in perspective.

REFERENCES

Anderson, D. R., & Lorch, E. P. (1983). Looking at television: Action or reaction? In J. Bryant & D. Anderson (Eds.), *Children's understanding of television*. New York: Academic Press.

Andre, M. E. D. A., & Anderson, T. H. (1978-1979). The development and evaluation of a self-questioning study technique. *Reading Research Quarterly, 14*, 605-673.

Arlin, M. (1984a). Time, equality, and mastery learning. *Review of Educational Research, 54*, 65-86.

Arlin, M. (1984b). Time variability in mastery learning. *American Educational Research Journal, 21*, 103-120.

Arlin, M., & Webster, J. (1983). Mastery time costs. *Journal of Educational Psychology, 75*, 187-195.

Bandura, A. (1977). *Social learning theory*. Englewood Cliffs, NJ: Prentice-Hall.

Belmont, J. M., & Butterfield, E. C. (1971). Learning strategies as determinants of memory deficiencies. *Cognitive Psychology, 2*, 411-420.

Bovy, R. C. (1981). Successful instructional methods: A cognitive information processing approach. *Educational Communication and Technology Journal, 29*, 203-217.

Caldwell, R. M., & Rizza, P. J. (1979). A computer-based system of reading instruction for adult non-readers. *AEDS Journal, 12*(4), 155-162.

Clark, R. E. (1983). Reconsidering research on learning from media. *Review of Educational Research, 53*, 445-459.

Clark, R. E. (1984). Research on student thought processes during computer-based instruction. *Journal of Instructional Development, 7*(3), 2-5.

Cronbach, L. J., & Snow, R. E. (1977). *Aptitude and instructional methods: A handbook for research on interactions.* New York: Irvington.

DeBloois, M. (1982). Principles for designing interactive videodisc instructional materials. In M. L. DeBloois (Ed.), *Videodisc/microcomputer courseware design.* Englewood Cliffs, NJ: Educational Technology Publications.

DiVesta, F. J. (1975). Trait-treatment interactions, cognitive processes, and research on communication media. *A V Communication Review, 23*, 185-196.

Fleming, M. L. (1979). On pictures in educational research. *Instructional Science, 8*, 235-251.

Floyd, S. (1982). Thinking interactively. In S. Floyd & B. Floyd (Eds.), *Handbook of interactive video.* White Plains, NY: Knowledge Industry Publications, Inc.

Gagné, R. M. (1977). *The conditions of learning* (3rd ed.). New York: Holt, Rinehart & Winston.

Gagné, R. M., & Briggs, L. J. (1979). Principles of instructional design (2nd ed.). New York: Holt, Rinehart & Winston.

Gagné, R. M., Wager, W. W., & Rojas, A. (1981). Planning and authoring computer-assisted instruction lessons. *Educational Technology, 21*(9), 17-21.

Glass, G. V., & Smith, M. L. (1978). The technology and politics of standards. *Educational Technology, 18*(5), 12-18.

Guttentag, R. E. (1984). The mental effort requirement of cumulative rehearsal: A developmental study. *Journal of Experimental Child Psychology, 37*, 92-106.

Hannafin, M. (1984). Guidelines for determining instructional locus of control in the design of computer-assisted instruction. *Journal of Instructional Development, 7*(3), 6-10.

Klauer, K. J. (1984). Intentional and incidental learning with instructional texts: A meta-analysis for 1970-1980. *American Educational Research Journal, 21*, 323-339.

Koran, M. L., & Koran, J. J., Jr. (1975). Interaction of learner aptitudes with question pacing in learning from prose. *Journal of Educational Psychology, 67*, 76-82.

Kunen, S., Green, D., & Waterman, D. (1979). Spread of encoding effects within the nonverbal visual domain. *Journal of Experimental Psychology: Human Learning and Memory, 5*, 574-584.

Mathews, N. N., Hunt, E. B., & MacLeod, C. M. (1980). Strategy choice and strategy training in sentence-picture verification. *Journal of Verbal Learning and Verbal Behavior, 19*, 531-548.

Mayer, R. E. (1975). Forward transfer of different reading strategies evoked by testlike events in mathematics text. *Journal of Educational Psychology, 67*, 165-169.

Mayer, R. G. (1984). Aids to text comprehension. *Educational Psychologist, 19*, 30-42.

Memory, D. (1983). Main idea prequestions as adjunct aids with good and low-average middle grade readers. *Journal of Reading Behavior, 15*, 37-48.

Meringoff, L. K. (1980). Influence of the medium on children's story apprehension. *Journal of Educational Psychology, 72*, 240-249.

Messick, S. (1984). The nature of cognitive styles: Problems and promise in educational practice. *Educational Psychologist, 19*, 59-74.

Mueller, D. J. (1976). Mastery learning: Partly boon partly boondoggle. *Teachers College Record, 78*, 41-52.

Nasser, D. L., & McEwen, W. J. (1976). The impact of alternative media channels: Recall and involvement with messages. *A V Communication Review, 24*, 263-272.

Nugent, G. C. (1982). Pictures, audio and print: Symbolic representation and effect on learning. *Educational Communication and Technology Journal, 30*, 163-174.

Raphael, T. E., & McKinney, J. (1983). An examination of fifth- and eighth-grade children's question-answering behavior: An instructional study in metacognition. *Journal of Reading Behavior, 15*, 67-86.

Reynolds, R., & Anderson, R. (1982). Influence of questions on the allocation of attention during reading. *Journal of Educational Psychology, 74*, 623-632.

Roblyer, M. D. (1982). Courseware: A critical look at "making best use of the medium." *Educational Technology, 22*, 29-30.

Ross, S. M. (1984). Matching the lesson to the student: Alternative adaptive designs for individualized learning systems. *Journal of Computer-Based Instruction, 11*, 42-48.

Rothen, W., & Tennyson, R. D. (1978). Application of Bayes' theory in designing computer-based adaptive instructional strategies. *Educational Psychologist, 12*, 317-323.

Rowher, W. D., & Harris, W. J. (1975). Media effects on prose learning in two populations of children. *Journal of Educational Psychology, 67*, 205-209.

Salomon, G. (1979). *Interaction of media, cognition and learning.* San Francisco: Jossey-Bass.

Salomon, G. (1981). Introducing AIME: The assessment of children's mental involvement with television. In H. Gardner & H. Kelly (Eds.), *Children and the world of television.* San Francisco: Jossey-Bass.

Salomon, G. (1983a). Television watching and mental effort: A social psychological view. In J. Bryant & D. Anderson (Eds.), *Children's understanding of television.* New York: Academic Press.

Salomon, G. (1983b). The differential investment of mental effort in learning from different sources. *Educational Psychologist, 18,* 42-50.

Schaffer, L., & Hannafin, M. J. (1984, April). *The effects of systematically varied interactivity of learning from interactive video.* Paper presented at the annual meeting of the American Educational Research Association, New Orleans.

Schank, R., & Abelson, R. (1977). *Scripts, plans, goals, and understanding.* Hillsdale, NJ: Erlbaum.

Schumacher, G. M., Moses, J. D., & Young, D. (1983). Students' studying processes on course related texts: The impact of inserted questions. *Journal of Reading Behavior, 15,* 19-36.

Stein, N. L., & Trabasso, T. (1984). What's in a story: Critical issues in comprehension and instruction. In R. Glaser (Ed.), *Advances in psychology of instruction* (Vol. 2). Hillsdale, NJ: Erlbaum.

Steinberg, E. R. (1977). Review of student control in computer-assisted instruction. *Journal of Computer-based Instruction, 3,* 84-90.

Tennyson, R. D. (1980). Instructional control strategies and content structure as design variables in concept acquisition using computer-based instruction. *Journal of Educational Psychology, 72,* 525-532.

Tennyson, R. D. (1984). Application of artificial intelligence methods to computer-based instructional design: The Minnesota Adaptive Instructional System. *Journal of Instructional Development, 7*(3), 17-22.

Tennyson, R. D., & Buttrey, T. (1980). Advisement and management strategies as design variables in computer-assisted instruction. *Educational Communication and Technology Journal, 28,* 169-176.

Tennyson, R. D., & Rothen, W. (1979). Management of computer-based instruction: Design of an adaptive control strategy. *Journal of Computer-Based Instruction, 5,* 126-134.

Watts, G. (1974). Effect of prequestions on control of attention in written instruction. *Australian Journal of Education, 18*, 79-85.

Wells, S., Whechel, B., & Jamison, D. (1975). *The impact of varying levels of computer-assisted instruction on the academic performance of disadvantaged students.* Princeton, NJ: Educational Testing Service.

Is Interactive Video for You?

Lemuel C. Schaffer
Library/Media Specialist
Cherry Creek School District
Colorado

Interactive video (IV), which combines the power of computer management with the live action and accuracy of video, may be the most powerful instructional tool to date. Yet, it is one of the most complex. Interactive video multiplies design, production, and hardware requirements, and necessitates orchestrating the efforts of instructional designers, television producers, and computer programmers. Many popular articles hail IV as the instructional technology of the future: "Never before has the power of the computer been coupled with the assets of video. Add to this users being able to control the speed at which they're taught and consumers being able to select the information they receive and you begin to get the picture" (Fort, 1984, p. 39).

Interactive video instruction can be effective and can bring returns in terms of interest and content mastery. *Dragon's Lair* and other videodisc-based games have done more than anything else to demonstrate the potential of interactive video (Ottenberg, 1984). Animated segments present dangers to which the player must precisely respond in order to stay in the game. The technology in itself, however, is no substitute for good instructional design, high quality television production, and efficient programming. Although shortcuts can be used to produce interactive video programs, the power of the end product is usually sacrificed. Also, interactive video users are critical of production quality and intolerant of system failures (Lee, 1984).

WHAT IS INTERACTIVE VIDEO?

Interactive video makes possible a dialog, or interaction, between the learner and the content being presented. The learner has a degree of control over the program (Fort, 1984). The program, on the other hand, directs student time-on-task and focuses the instruction on learning outcomes. The interactive video system presents information via computer or video display and asks for a response. The viewer responds by pressing a button, touching a location on the screen, typing on a keyboard, or moving a joystick. This input may be an answer to a question, a response to a particular situation, or a request to see an item on a menu. The IV system quickly assesses the viewer's input and presents the appropriate menu, information, instruction, test, review, or simulation. The presentation can take the form of video, computer text, or computer text over video image all on a single monitor.

Some assert that the combination of computer and video technologies produces results that are greater than the sum of the components (DeBloois, 1982; Floyd, 1982). In other words, interactive video is more powerful than the combined effects of computers and video functioning separately.

Advantages and Disadvantages

Interactive video has all the potential of computer-assisted instruction (CAI) plus the advantages of high quality, live-action video. Video segments also can be used in the instruction to provide clear motion sequences that could not be readily achieved with computer graphics. Like computer-assisted instruction, interactive video is an ever-present teacher that adapts to the user. It may be self-paced, taking more time and providing reviews when the learner needs them. Instruction is consistent for all learners but each learner can progress at his or her own pace, viewing instruction as many times as necessary before progressing to the next segment. Interactive video can be designed to operate in the same way as a good teacher who changes the instruction when students are confused.

Interactive video means that instructional video need not be viewed in a linear, passive fashion. Portions of the video instruction can be presented and the student's understanding of the content can be assessed. If adequate mastery of the content has been achieved, new information is presented. If not, interactive video can review the instruction until it has been learned. If so desired, IV can rearrange the order of video segments or present just the ones for a particular student's needs.

The advantage of interactive video to designers is the almost infinite number of instructional combinations (e.g., live-action video, still-frame video, still-frame with audio, computer graphics with audio, and branches to all of these segments). The video source selection also provides options. Up to two hours of video can be accessed on a single videotape. A videodisc has 54,000 individual pictures (equal to 678 carousel slide trays) and one half hour of playing time per side. Access from first frame to last frame ranges from 2 to 6 seconds depending on the videodisc player. Still-frame audio on a videodisc can stretch the 30-minute disc playing time to 150 hours. The trade-off for this long playing time, however, is a loss of video frames ("Interactive Videodisc," 1984).

Despite the advantages of interactive video, there are some rather severe disadvantages. Lack of software and equipment standardization limit the number of programs that can be played on a particular system. Although the videotape and videodisc formats are standardized, the means of accessing the video segments are not. Different levels of interactivity use different outboard or integrated computer configurations. Computer programs may be encoded on the videotape, embedded in the videodisc, or contained on a floppy disk. Further confusing the issue are the various interface boards and drivers needed to control video players. Different model players from the same company often require a different set of computer instructions. General instructional IV materials will not be produced until a significant number of standardized IV systems are in place, and institutions will not purchase IV systems until there are a significant number of standardized software programs available.

Even if IV standardization were available, there are other costs to consider. If the same video instruction is presented in linear and interactive forms, the interactive version requires more time to complete. In addition, interaction and reinstruction aspects of IV may needlessly consume learner time if a high level of mastery is not needed. Although there are some group IV applications, interactive video is most effective with one person per work station. Individual work stations, costing from $4,000 to $20,000, may or may not be cost-effective, depending on the situation.

Design and production of IV involves integrating and coordinating the multifaceted aspects. It is not simply a matter of designing an instructional video program or computer-based instruction, but both of these working together. Development costs are high because diverse skills are needed, usually requiring the efforts of a team. Turn-around-time to complete an interactive program makes it impractical for many applications. A major cooperative effort between ABC and NEA to produce videodiscs for education was cancelled, because the development and production costs were too high and too few school districts had videodisc players (Bosco, 1984). The Alaska Innovative Technology Project for the Office of Technology and Telecommunications of the Alaska Department of Education, after a major study, advised caution in relation to videodisc technology (Hiscox & Brzezinski, 1981).

Given the cost, time, and money required for interactive video, one must ask if the instructional capabilities justify the time and expense. Granted, interactive video may be a revolutionary instructional tool, but are its capabilities truly unique? Clark (1984) has stated that all of interactive video's instructional capabilities have been available to us in one form or another. While IV represents a significant advancement in instructional technology, it only gets a little closer to the techniques of a good teacher who instructs, assesses, gives feedback, and reviews. All of these functions could be done with previous media but not as efficiently and not integrated into a single package. Now they can be done with interactive video, but for a price.

INTERACTIVE VIDEO APPLICATIONS

The applications of interactive video range from Army tank artillery simulation training to department store point-of-sale systems. Interactive video is even being used by the American Heart Association for CPR (cardiopulmonary resuscitation) training (Hon, 1982). Interactive video may help solve some of the more challenging training problems, such as teaching reluctant learners and poor readers. It seems to have great potential and it is limited more by imagination, cost, and human skills than by the medium itself.

Interactive video instruction can involve the learner in lifelike learning situations. Relatively simple IV instruction might include video instruction with checkpoints to test a learner's understanding and retention before proceeding to the next instructional segment. Simple IV instruction might repeat the same video segment or use computer text as a review. More sophisticated IV instruction would use new video segments to teach a missed concept. Applications of this technology range from a single system to teach, for example, the operation of the offset press (Sanders, 1985) to multiple work station systems (DeVelde & Frederick, 1985).

Interactive video simulations access video segments that "play out" the consequences of a learner's choice. Lifelike IV simulations can replace dangerous and costly training. For example, a chemistry student can "experience" the results of improper procedures without being harmed and without damaging costly equipment. Some simulations present rather straightforward, matter-of-fact consequences. Jeppesen Sanderson, for example, produced a simulation in 1980 to teach pilots the use of the Terminal Control Area that had them landing at a remote airstrip with no services. Other simulations are more complex and frustrating because the users must evaluate several variables, such as wind direction and velocity in the Ford Motor Company IV golf program. Poor judgment might put the ball in a sand trap just like it would in the real game. A more dramatic simulator is the Army's tank trainer. After entering the coordinates, the trainee "fires" the tank's cannon and views the dramatic results.

Although most IV instruction is individualized, there are some group applications. Science instructor Arthur Jennings had students discuss various answers and vote on the answer to be entered. Incorrect answers sent the tape back to the appropriate segment ("A Successful Classroom," 1985; "Interactive Video," 1985).

Well-designed IV information systems give the viewer control of the kinds and amount of information desired. Library of Congress is in the process of converting visual information to disc for public access ("Newsline," 1983). Computer and Technology for People have set up the MoTourist Info Center Network, a videodisc-based system to give travelers information about food, shelter, and relevant attractions ("MoTourist Network Launched," 1985).

Interactive video information systems can provide answers to numerous questions with a minimum of personnel. Library services, career information, college majors, and advisement are good candidates for future applications of interactive video. IV information systems could supplement the efforts of existing staff and give students the opportunity to explore answers to questions that they might not ask otherwise.

Interactive video is enjoying its greatest economic success in retail sales applications. Point-of-sale systems are being installed that allow you to see product demonstrations, rent a car, make hotel reservations, or purchase items with your charge card. Point-of-sale interactive video systems display menus and play the requested video and/or computer segment. Upon completion of the segment, a menu usually reappears for another selection. Point-of-sale systems are successful because they help sell products and teach people to use new products. Cuisinart, Inc. is presently using interactive video to demonstrate and sell their food processing products ("Interactive Kiosks Communicate," 1984). IBM has contracted with Cameron Communications to assemble an interactive video system to demonstrate their products in European dealerships ("Cameron Secures," 1984).

THE INTERACTIVE VIDEO SYSTEM

An interactive video system can be acquired in one of two ways: (1) by selecting and assembling the various components or (2) by acquiring an integrated system such as Sony's SMC-70 videodisc/personal computer or Panasonic's Interactive Video Training System. Whether you are assembling your own system or purchasing an integrated system, it is virtually impossible to obtain a single IV system that will play all IV programs. In addition to computer, software, and interface variables, there are three levels of interactive videodisc. Level I interactive videodisc has the least amount of interaction and can be played on almost any consumer or industrial videodisc player. It can include stop-frame menus that direct the user to go to another part of the disc. Level II videodiscs incorporate the computer program, called a digital dump, right in the videodisc itself. This program loads itself into the computer, which is built into Level II videodisc players. Pioneer and Sony use different Level II programs that are incompatible, but 3M can press discs that include both computer program formats. Level III interactive videodisc systems use the outboard computer to make possible more sophisticated levels of IV design, flexibility, and management.

Computers used in IV systems range from microcomputers to mainframe computers that can operate a number of terminals. Computer selection is affected by available computers, desired software, compatible interface cards, and cost.

The video source is either videotape or videodisc with a number of options. Players for either tape or disc must be capable of electronically connecting and communicating with the interface. Panasonic and Sony industrial videotape recorders and players, and Pioneer and Sony videodisc players have the needed interface and random search capabilities.

To operate properly, the computer, interface, and video equipment must be compatible electronically, but they must also be able to communicate via compatible computer program commands. Just as different brands and models of computer printers require different sets of commands or drivers, each video machine requires a unique set of drivers. When selecting a video player, you must be sure that it is compatible with the other components and that the computer software to be used has the needed drivers.

Videotape and videodisc formats have unique advantages and disadvantages. Videotape can be produced and changed relatively easily and inexpensively. But, tape access time from one segment to another is slow because the tape must shuttle to the new location. Videodisc, on the other hand, provides fast access of 2-6 seconds, because it can quickly skip to the new location. Unlike tape, high quality still-frame pictures, and even still-frame with audio are possible with disc. Pressing of the original disc master costs from $1,800 to $2,500. Once the discs are pressed, they can be changed only by pressing new discs. Discs do become more cost-effective over tape as the number of copies increases (Utz, 1984). The comparison in the following table shows the strengths of tape and disc.

Strengths of Tape and Disc

Item	Videotape	Videodisc
Fixed content		X
Readily changed content	X	
Fast access time		X
Total in-house production	X	
Experience with IV	X	X
Still-frame pictures		X
Still-frame pictures with audio		X

The interface card pulls the IV system together, electronically connecting the computer and the video source so that they can "talk" to each other. The interface card also switches between the computer display and the video display, sending the appropriate display to the monitor. Some enhanced interface cards enable computer text/graphics to be displayed over video images. Interactive video interface cards are available from a number of companies with different features and price tags ("Directory of V/C," 1985). When selecting an interface card, you must be sure that it is compatible with your computer, video player, and computer software.

Two kinds of software are needed for a interactive video: (1) computer software and (2) video program software. Computer software needed to direct interactive programs can be developed using an authoring system, an authoring language, or a more powerful programming language such as Pascal.

Authoring systems enable the user to develop an instructional program without any programming knowledge. Generally menu driven, they ask the user to select the instructional function (e.g., information, questions, video, graphics, etc.). Then the author uses plain English to enter the information the learner will see. The main disadvantage of this user-friendly software is the lack of design flexibility. An authoring language, however, provides more flexibility than an authoring system, because it has less structure. An authoring language, such as SuperPILOT, is a programming language modified for writing instructional programs. Interactive programs written in languages such as Pascal have the most flexibility and power, but they also require more programming skills. When selecting software, you should check for the following:

- Is it user friendly?

- Will it work efficiently and effectively with all equipment in the system?

- What are the costs and licensing agreements?

- Does it respond quickly to user input or is there a hesitation when nothing seems to be happening?

- Will it perform the desired functions?

- Is it reliable, or are there bugs that will cause the system to fail?

INTERACTIVE VIDEO DESIGN

Depending on one's perspective, interactive video can be viewed as a computer program that has been enhanced by a video database, or as video instruction that has been enhanced by a computer program. Both concepts are valid and prominent IV instruction models.

Interactive video programs range in complexity from simple information access to complex games and simulations. Simple IV designs are relatively easy to develop using an authoring system and an existing linear video program. In contrast, complex IV program development requires the combined skills of an interactive courseware team (Ittelson, 1984). The team should consist of designers, television writers, producers, and computer programmers who can work together to make a program that is dynamic, effective, and instructional.

Linear video instruction can be improved by dividing it into segments and embedding questions after each instructional segment. If the content is mastered, the program branches forward; if it is not mastered, the program recalls the video segment, or a portion thereof, for review. This technique of teach, test, and teach or reteach produces significantly greater learning than linear video instruction (Schaffer & Hannafin, 1984).

Interactive video can be used to "edit" and rearrange existing video instruction without physically editing the tape. This may provide a quick fix for a marginal video program. For example, poor or redundant video segments may be skipped. Or, if designers want to reorder the video sequence, the video segments may be accessed in a different order. In addition, video instruction can be enhanced by inserting computer text and graphics to reinforce the instruction and to present additional information. For example, if dimensions or formulas are presented in a brief video segment, they can be repeated in computer text with the learner controlling the length of viewing time.

Unlike linear video programs, complex interactive video may be designed in modules. One module can present the instruction the first time. Another module would present the concept in a different way for the learner who did not understand the first time. The final module would summarize the instruction and give a review at the end of the lesson. The video would be specifically designed and produced with a variety of segments, not to be played linearly but accessed as needed. The different video segments would teach and then reteach the same concept but with more detail or a simpler explanation.

Regardless of the complexity, IV programs should be designed on the basis of good instructional design. Designing IV instruction requires keeping track of all of the video segments, computer screens, basic instruction and assessment, as well as all the possible "if the student responds in this way, the system will do thus and so." Several schemes have been devised to facilitate interactive design (Dargan, 1982; DeBloois, 1982; Floyd & Floyd,

1982; Smith, 1985). The video portion of the instruction also must be of acceptable quality. Broadcast television has conditioned viewers to high quality television production with a certain entertainment quality. Although not always of entertaining or broadcast quality, interactive video segments must hold the learner's attention and clearly convey the content. Finally, the computer program that presents text, poses questions, branches, and manages the entire system must work efficiently and flawlessly.

Alternatives to Interactive Video

Investigating IV may cause us to reexamine other forms of instruction. There are a number of alternatives to IV, such as random access audio players attached to a computer, interactive slides (Peck & Hannafin, 1983; Wallington, 1984), and traditional media. Linear video is more efficient than IV when a lower level of mastery can be tolerated. In addition, one video player and monitor can be used with a group of people in contrast to IV, which requires an expensive work station for each person.

FUTURE OF INTERACTIVE VIDEO

Interactive video, though in its infancy, has made some rather significant contributions to information access, instruction, and even games. If interactive video follows the trends of other technology, and there is no reason to believe that it will not, it will become more sophisticated and more compact. Sony's recent introduction of a portable audio laser disc player, the D-5 Discman portable CD leads one to speculate that the future might hold a portable videodisc player and even a portable interactive videodisc system. Courseware development software will continue to improve, making interactive video programs easier to produce. An inexpensive read-after-write will allow you to record your own videodisc and will facilitate in-house production without expensive mastering costs. Interactive video has great instructional possibilities.

REFERENCES

Bosco, J. J. (1984). Interactive video: Educational tool or toy? *Educational Technology*, 13-19.

Cameron secures interactive video contract with IBM. (1984). *Videodisc & Optical Disc, 4*(2), 98-100.

Clark, R. (1984, April). Comments made in the session on interactive video at the annual meeting of the American Educational Research Association, New Orleans.

Dargan, T. (1982). Five basic patterns to use in interactive flow charts. *Educational and Industrial Television, 14*(6), 31-34.

DeBloois, M. L. (1982). Principles for designing interactive videodisc instructional materials. In M. L. DeBloois (Ed.), *Video/microcomputer courseware design*. Englewood Cliffs, NJ: Educational Technology Publications, 25-66.

DeVelde, C., & Frederick, J. (1985). Higher education sows its garden of new technology: Grove City College students receive t.l.c. *Instructional Innovator, 30*(1), 13-16.

Directory of V/C interfaces. (1985). *Educational and Industrial Television, 17*(1), 49-56.

Floyd, S. (1982). Think interactively. In S. Floyd & B. Floyd (Eds.), *Handbook of interactive video*. White Plains, NY: Knowledge Industry Publications, 1-14.

Floyd, S., & Floyd, B. (Eds.). (1982). *Handbook of interactive video*. White Plains, NY: Knowledge Industry Publications.

Fort, W. (1984). A primer on interactive video. *AV Video, 6*(10), 39-41.

Hiscox, M. D., & Brzezinski, E. J. (1981). *Structure and feasibility of group interactive disc systems: Summary technical report*. Portland, OR: Assessment and Measurement Program, North Regional Educational Laboratory.

Hon, D. (1982). Interactive training in cardiopulmonary resuscitation. *Byte, 7*(6), 108-120, 130-138.

Interactive kiosks communicate Cuisinart programs. (1984). *Videodisc & Optical Disc, 4*(2), 95-96.

Interactive video comes through. (1985). *International Television*, 70.

Interactive videodisc demonstrates new still-frame audio technology. (1984). *Videodisc News, 5*(3), 7-9.

Ittelson, J. C. (1984). Videodisc and microcomputers applications and software. *Proceedings of the COMPCON 1984, twenty-eighth IEEE Computer Society International Conference*, 62-68.

Lee, B. (1984). Interactive video: The hard goods. *AV Video, 6*(11), 30, 68.

Lindsey, J. (1984). The challenge of designing for interactive video. *Instructional Innovator, 29*(6), 17-19.

Meyer, R. (1984). Borrowing this new military technology, and help win the war for kids' minds. *American School Board Journal, 171*(6), 23-28.

MoTourist network launched. (1985). *The Videodisc Monitor, 3*(1), 3.

Newsline. (1983). *The Videodisc Monitor, 1*(3), 5.

Ottenberg, J. (1984). Discs get heavy play in the arcade. *Videography, 9*(1), 22-28.

Peck, K., & Hannafin, M. J. (1983). How to interface slides and computers. *Instructional Innovator, 28*(8), 20-23.

Sanders, M. (1985). VCR and CRT: The latest media marriage. *inCider, the Apple II Journal,* (25), 32-36.

Schaffer, L. C., & Hannafin, M. J. (1984, April). *The effects of systematically varied interactivity of learning from interactive video.* Paper presented at the annual meeting of the American Educational Research Association, New Orleans.

Smith, R. (1985). From script to screen by computer for interactive video. *Educational and Industrial Television, 17*(1), 31-33.

A successful classroom interactive tape test. (1985). *Educational and Industrial Television,* 64-66.

Utz, P. (1984). So you want to make a videodisc. *A V Video, 6*(10), 34-38.

Wallington, C. (1984). Interactive slides ... no kidding. *A V Video, 6*(10), 26-30.

Commitments
The Aetna Human Resources Television Drama Series

Bernard M. Knab
Manager of Education and Technology
Aetna Institute for Corporate Education

Julie Cotton Donnelly
Educational Consultant

INTRODUCTION

The 1980s have been widely characterized as a period of change for U.S. corporations. Whether such change refers to adapting to new business markets or to managing a rapidly changing, increasingly diverse work force, corporations countrywide are seeking ways to bring sense to this transitional period in their growth.

One such effort is *Commitments*, a six-part television drama series produced by Aetna Life & Casualty's Institute for Corporate Education. The series, based on a number of issues that address the cultural concerns of the company, is designed to assist managers and supervisors in better understanding and implementing their human resource responsibility.

PROJECT ORIGINS

The Aetna Human Resources television dramas, or docudramas, have their origins in a series of equal opportunity and affirmative action seminars that were conducted in 1980. Responding to a mandate from senior management to provide equal opportunity education to its managers and supervisors, countrywide, seventy one-day sessions were delivered in six months to approximately 1,500 people. It soon became apparent, however, that this approach was an impractical and costly one, given the numbers of people still to be reached and the time it would take to reach them. An alternative had to be found and television was selected as the probable choice.

Presented at the Presidential Session, AECT National Conference, Dallas, Texas, 1984.

Lana Wertz, then director of Equal Opportunity in the company, and Bernard Knab, who designed and conducted many of the Equal Opportunity seminars, traveled to the West Coast to explore the use of television as an alternative delivery medium. During meetings with various television producers in Los Angeles, the great potential of the medium as an educational instrument, and its power to entertain while also educating on social and cultural issues, became readily apparent.

At a wrap-up meeting at week's end, Wertz, Knab, and William Mason, a media consultant who had arranged the West Coast agenda, assessed all they had seen and heard and quickly realized that a common denominator in all of what they had viewed was *drama.* By the time the project directors returned to Hartford (Aetna's home base), they were determined to sell management on allowing them to proceed on a new and innovative project: to produce a network-quality pilot television drama through which to deliver messages to management on their equal opportunity responsibilities.

By October 1981, a pilot program, "A Promise to Keep," produced in a collaborative effort by Aetna and Rainbow T.V. Works, was completed. Much had occurred in the five months: (1) the process of bringing to life a group of believable characters in a story that would at once replicate the lives of Aetna people accurately and at the same time entertain and educate the audience on a number of issues critical to managers in the eighties; (2) endless meetings with a variety of people to assure consensus on the issues as well as on the veracity of setting and characters; (3) numerous R & D field trips to Aetna offices to gain a feel for the people and their concerns; and (4) story sessions, treatment sessions, script sessions, casting, production, and post-production. Everyone who worked on the project from Rainbow T.V. Works in Hollywood and from Aetna learned a great deal about each other and about working collaboratively in this rather unusual relationship. Wertz and Knab and a host of supporting people from Aetna and Topper Carew, Madison Lacy, Henry Johnson, and a host of supporting people from Rainbow, collaborated to produce a corporate "soap," or docudrama, that, by means of a good story, focused the audience's attention on the issue of balancing the development of people against the short-term productivity realities confronted day to day. By year's end, the pilot had been shown to a wide range of people within the company's management; they liked what they saw and encouraged production of a continuing series.

By now, too, the pilot program, and the series that was envisioned, had broadened its subject matter from equal opportunity to the whole spectrum of human resources, under which, of course, equal opportunity issues were subsumed. Also, early formative evaluation had clearly shown that producing a network-quality television drama through which to educate managers on their human resource responsibilities was an idea that was highly attractive to the audience.

But the production of further programs would be given yet another dimension; in late 1981, Badi Foster assumed the presidency of the Aetna Institute for Corporate Education and asked Lana Wertz to take on the new position of Director of Educational Research and Technology within the Institute. (Wertz subsequently asked Knab to work in this new capacity with her.) The television drama series was now to become not only a means of providing Aetna managers education in managing their human resource responsibilities, but an experiment in educational technology as well, a project through which to test the medium's general educational effectiveness.

THE CONSORTIUM

The realization that she would now be project director of five new educational television programs, coupled with the project's relocation in the Educational Research and Technology Unit of Aetna's new Educational Institute, provided Wertz with the incentive and the forum to broaden the process into a consortium effort similar in some of its major features to the highly successful Children's Television Workshop. The consortium Wertz assembled in the winter of 1982 was relatively small in comparison to those addressing educational television program needs for broadcast to a regional or even national audience. But Wertz's primary concern was the integration of production and research from the beginning on. Wertz was able to put together a group, each of whom brought a special and vital perspective and talent to the docudrama project.

The consortium was set up to function as either a whole unit or in subgroups: the entire group met on such key agenda items as deciding the issues of the programs, reviewing story lines, treatments, or scripts, or establishing learning objectives; subgroups would meet to work out the hundreds of details that needed attention and then bring recommendations to the whole body. The full consortium, which functioned from March to December 1982, consisted of the following: Harvey Brenner, story editor/writer, Rainbow T.V. Works; Topper Carew, president/producer, Rainbow T.V. Works; Julie Cotton Donnelly, consultant, Adult Development and Learning; Henry Johnson, director, Rainbow T.V. Works; Bernard Knab, project executive producer, Aetna; Madison Lacy, consultant, Project Research and Development, Lacy Associates; William Mason, consultant, Media, Research, and Development, Lacy Associates; Susan McGuiness, project coordinator, Aetna; Stanley Stephenson, consultant, Research and Evaluation, Pennsylvania State University; Lana Wertz, project executive director, Aetna.

From the beginning, Wertz sought to establish a research model that would provide a methodology for the docudrama project to follow and that would establish a paradigm for other Institute projects that shared the goal of finding efficient, alternative ways to educate at Aetna. The model that emerged kept the T.V. drama project on track; it moved from conducting a needs assessment to establishing learning objectives to considering and selecting program designs appropriate to the needs identified to production and a structured formative evaluation to implementation and finally to a summative evaluation aimed at determining if the results that were sought were in fact accomplished. From design through evaluation, the model served the effort well by providing direction and relative order to the process.

THE PROCESS

Clearly, the life blood of a consortium is the individual talents of its members pooled into a collaborative effort to achieve an agreed-upon goal. The human resources television drama consortium at Aetna wanted to produce five high-quality television dramas to comprise a series that would entertain the target audience of Aetna managers and supervisors and at the same time, and most importantly, educate them in better understanding and implementing their human resource development responsibilities in the changing world of the eighties. The process did not always run smoothly; it took time for individuals to temper egos and to learn to see the primacy of the solution arrived at collaboratively over the winning of an individual point. There was positioning and repositioning, a great deal of give and take, but ultimately there was the forging of a mindset that hammered out a product that was clearly the result of group effort and combined talent.

Wertz established an advisory panel of key managers to enlist their counsel and their criticism; she convened other ad hoc groups to help her assess and define the organization's culture and to identify and gradually reach a consensus on its issues. A *Writer's Notebook* was conceived in order to provide Harvey Brenner, who would write the series, with a detailed description of the company. To facilitate this effort, Knab guided researchers Lacy and Mason through the organization, arranging and attending numerous individual meetings with high-level managers and traveling to a number of company field offices around the country to talk in detail not only with general managers and department heads but also with an array of first- and second-line supervisors and their employees. The final *Writer's Notebook* became an even more collaborative effort when Julie Donnelly, using her expertise in adult learning, coordinated the learning objectives and designed the education program. Together with Knab, she augmented the already substantial notebook by elaborating on the book's established format of identifying a major issue, explaining it, stating the series' goal in addressing that issue, and stating and detailing a premise upon which a particular issue or program was established. In addition, Donnelly eventually developed as many as a dozen learning objectives per issue or subissue. These objectives were regarded as descriptions of the ideal behaviors and/or attitudes exhibited by highly effective supervisors and managers. Characters in the dramas would model these behaviors at various levels of competency.

Stephenson spent much of the spring and summer of 1982 designing a questionnaire for the purpose of conducting formative evaluation of the pilot program, "A Promise to Keep." Together with other consortium staff, he conducted the evaluation before selected Aetna field and home office personnel and in late July published "Evaluation of a Corporate Docudrama with Educational Implications." The document provided an excellent and essential fund of information on such things as audience response to key characters, differences in perception by race, age, sex, and so forth, and a host of details that were invaluable for designing the remaining programs. Stephenson also designed questionnaires for use in the summative evaluation. The consortium slowly reached a consensus that the television dramas and the attendant education programs should have the power to cause measurable changes in the attitudes and behaviors of managers and supervisors and that the summative evaluation would be designed to evaluate the attitudinal changes in the target audience with regard to their ability to understand and manage their human resource responsibilities.

By late summer and early fall of 1982, all these activities had resulted in the accumulation of sufficient data to proceed with the development of story. Brenner and Johnson had been soaking up all the information that they were being supplied from various sources. At a full consortium meeting in August, the group agreed to stay with and considerably augment the cast from the pilot program, and Brenner agreed to forge story lines based on all the data and details that had been gathered.

Within a few weeks, the story lines and characters had been given shape. In ensuing weeks, more life was breathed into them as they evolved into story treatments, were discussed and revised, and emerged as the first, second, and third drafts of scripts. The miracle of story transformed all the research into real, believable human dramas. Although Brenner was weighed down with goals, objectives, and dozens of directives and reminders, he applied his craft skillfully to assure stories that entertained while they presented a wealth of material that could help the target audience gain insights into the complex process of managing their people.

In late fall of 1982, Knab traveled extensively between Hartford and Hollywood, relaying responses, reactions, and suggestions back and forth between the writer and director on one coast and various subgroups of the consortium on the other coast. Remaining preproduction was completed by mid-January 1983, and the fourteen-day shoot was completed by the first of February. All five of the shows plus a thirty-minute highlight tape were completed on time in late April 1983.

THE PRODUCT

The Television Dramas

The Aetna series, entitled *Commitments*, consists of six half hour television dramas. The programs are built on six major issues that the consortium determined were the critical human resources issues within Aetna in the early 1980s. These issues are: balancing people and productivity; maximizing human resource potential; enhancing interpersonal communications; managing a diverse workforce; coping with change; and developing leadership.

From the beginning, everyone involved wanted to ensure a high-quality product that would resemble the best network television. The project is, among other things, an experiment in using television dramas as a way of sensitizing managers to a wide range of issues regarding the management of people and in turn modifying managers' attitudes and behaviors. To achieve this end, the drama consortium was formed and a production company was selected that would ensure quality in production values and content. The cast of the shows was carefully selected to ensure credibility; many of the actors and actresses in the series are well-established film and television performers.

One example of the many considerations taken into account by the consortium was the need to present stories that would allow the audience to enter the characters' personal as well as professional lives. The consortium was unanimous in believing that the programs needed to explore the myth that somehow employees leave their personal selves at the door when coming to work.

The programs that comprise *Commitments* touch on a broad spectrum of concerns, both personal and professional, that characterize the lives of the target audience. Through this medium, the audience is drawn into the dramas by briefly stepping into the lives of fictional others in positions and situations comparable to their own. Each of the programs is written to bring a vivid, human dimension to the process of managing people. All the programs probe the difficult but vital task of managing today's diverse work force, with the end in view of providing the target audience with a deeper understanding of their human resource responsibilities.

CONCLUSION

Currently *Commitments* is being implemented at Aetna through the Institute for Corporate Education. The series is being offered to company managers as one way to assist them in managing the changing environment of the 1980s. Additionally, the programs that were generically produced, in the conviction that the issues they bring to life apply across a broad spectrum of contemporary U.S. corporations, are being marketed by the Aetna Institute to audiences in other corporations and beyond, including academic, military, and government organizations.

What began in 1981 as an investigation into alternative ways to deliver equal opportunity education in a large U.S. corporation grew into an experiment in educational technology, designed to modify the target audience's attitudes and behaviors regarding sensitive human resource issues. The collaborative efforts of a great many people have made the experiment and the experience an exciting and memorable one for all involved in it.

Innovative and Exemplary Aspects
of an Instructional Development Project

Mary Lou Mosley and Naomi O. Story
Instructional Designers
Maricopa Community College District

INTRODUCTION

Howard J. Sullivan, professor at Arizona State University, received the 1985 Outstanding Practice Award from the Division of Instructional Development of the Association of Educational Communications and Technology. The Division cited Sullivan for his exemplary work as principal developer of *Energy Choices and Challenges*, the high school unit of a comprehensive, grades K-12 energy curriculum. *Energy Choices and Challenges* was released for general use in 1984 after a two-year period of development, field testing, and revision. Sullivan was also the Director of Development for the Energy Source program during its development from 1980 until early 1984.

A number of aspects that are particularly impressive and innovative about Sullivan's work in designing and developing the energy program will be described in this paper. They are the industry/education partnership, the instructional development process, the conservation and energy issues orientation, and the effectiveness and impact of the unit.

INNOVATIVE ASPECTS

A joint industry-education effort resulted in the development of the energy education program, *Energy Source*, which included four elementary, two junior high, and one high school unit. Development and field testing of the *Energy Source* program took place over a three-year period at a total cost of close to $1 million. During the 1983-84 school year, the first year of full implementation, approximately one million students across the nation used the *Energy Source* program. Not only is this industry-education partnership unusual in instructional development, but also 25 corporations and private foundations contributed from $10,000 to $150,000 each to sponsor distribution of the program to schools. In addition, more than 50 other organizations donated from $1,000 to $10,000.

Another innovative aspect of the project is the dissemination process of the *Energy Source* program. Either a corporation or a consortium of companies can sponsor the program in the local schools. The sponsor buys the program for approximately $1 per student. Current and/or retired employees of the sponsor are trained and they work with school district administrators and teachers to orient them to the materials.

EXEMPLARY INSTRUCTIONAL DEVELOPMENT TECHNIQUES

Energy Choices and Challenges, the high school unit, was developed in response to a need identified by a national survey conducted by the Education Commission of the States. Survey results indicated that high school and college age people were very poorly informed about important energy topics. In addition, more than 90 percent of those surveyed wanted more information about energy and believed that energy should be part of every school's curriculum. Nevertheless, few well-developed energy education materials were available for classroom use and teachers generally were not well informed about energy issues.

Energy Choices and Challenges emphasizes a realistic and participatory problem-solving approach to energy issues, rather than portraying a doomsday scenario that is common in school textbooks. The intent of the program is for students to believe that energy and conservation are important, they should be informed and concerned about energy issues, and they should take an active interest in energy affairs. To ensure that they acquire these behaviors, experiences are structured so that students examine and explore solutions to the major energy issues, such as radioactive waste disposal, exploration on federal lands, deregulation of natural gas prices, acid rain, and energy independence. Before they explore the sides of an issue, students learn background information about energy through structured activities. The background content, presented in an 84-page student booklet and two filmstrips, is discussed during class. One of the two filmstrips is also used as a motivator and to preview the content.

An objectives-instruction-assessment model was employed and a competency-based approach to instruction was followed. The unit was designed so that a teacher can present it by using only the teacher guide and other program materials (pretest/posttest, student booklets, filmstrips). No additional study or preparation by the teacher is necessary. The unit takes two to three weeks to complete but may take longer if the recommended enrichment activities are used.

An innovative application of an instructional development procedure was Sullivan's use of subject matter experts to ensure that the best goals, objectives, and content were identified. Sullivan consulted with members of the *Energy Source* program advisory council throughout the 3-year development of *Energy Choices and Challenges.* The advisory council consisted of representatives from energy firms and education organizations. The energy firms — including ARCO, San Diego Gas & Electric Co., and Westinghouse — supplied specialized consulting help and information about energy content as needed. Representatives of the education organizations — such as the Joint Council on Economic Education, National Council for the Social Studies, National Parent Teacher Association, and National Science Teachers Association — provided expertise on instructional methodology and checked the unit, including the illustrations, for bias.

Another exemplary application of an instructional development procedure was the field testing. The unit was field tested nationally under normal classroom conditions. About 1,500 high school students in eight separate geographic regions participated in the field testing. Slightly more than half of the classes were from middle-income areas, one-third from low and low-middle income, and about 15 percent from high income areas. Revisions were made based on field test data, and then the unit was tried out again on a smaller scale.

Results from the field tests indicated that students learned from the program and that both students and teachers liked it. The average pretest and posttest scores were 52 percent and 86 percent, respectively. Over 80 percent of the students responded positively to such items as "I liked this unit," and "I learned a lot." More than 95 percent of the teachers reported that they were satisfied with student learning, that the energy content was objective and unbiased, and that they would teach the unit again.

CONCLUSION

Unlike the other units that emphasize energy facts, Sullivan's high school unit was developed around a goal of the *Energy Source* program — to instill attitudes in students. Developing instruction that teaches attitudes is always a difficult task. It was even more so in this situation, because the attitudes to be taught are not pro or con and the content easily can be biased. The attitudes are to result in behaviors such as staying informed about economic and environmental matters related to energy, listening to and reading information about energy in mass media, and voting knowledgeably on energy issues. Sullivan repeatedly used representatives from the advisory council to review materials as he developed them. This measure was to insure that the content students would use to form opinions and behaviors was accurate, complete, and either free of bias or presenting both sides.

In summary, it is a remarkable accomplishment to develop instructional materials that meet the standards of such a diverse group as the advisory council and, in addition, enable students to learn facts and acquire behaviors. *Energy Choices and Challenges* is truly the product of an outstanding practitioner of instructional development.

Educational Computing
The Burden of Ensuring Quality

P. Kenneth Komoski
Executive Director
EPIE Institute

Snoopy said it years ago: "There's no greater burden than a great potential." Today, everyone seems to agree that the potential of educational computing is very great indeed. But it is not at all clear just who is up to bearing the burden of fulfilling that potential.

Ideally, of course, the task should be shared among school boards, educators, parents, local businesses, computer manufacturers, and software developers. And some sharing of this sort is going on in scattered communities. But even in such communities most parents are looking to the schools to make learning with computers an integral part of the educational process. This turning to the schools for a response to a new force in our lives is a well-established pattern in the United States that finds its current expression in the demands of parents that schools prepare their children for a future filled with computers.

Initially, most schools have been responding to these parental expectations by pursuing the still not-well-defined goal of *computer literacy*. Recently, however, schools have something else to respond to: multimillion dollar advertising campaigns on prime-time television, paid for by computer manufacturers, that show children using computers (at home and in school) and ostensibly becoming better students thereby. As a result, millions of parents have been buying computers for use at home. But they still expect educators to provide computer learning for their children in school as well.

One measure of the success of these advertising campaigns is the fact that many more computers were purchased by parents of school-age children during the last year than were purchased by the schools themselves. Talmis, Inc., a market research group, estimates that the parents of one out of every six school-age children have already purchased a computer for their child's use at home. Assuming that research is valid, there are currently about 5 million computers in the homes of U.S. families with children. Another Talmis estimate puts the number of computers now in the schools at 550,000. This means that computers in the homes of children outnumber computers in the schools by a ratio of almost 10 to 1.

It seems that the message the parents are buying, along with their home computers, is pretty clear: one way or another—both at school and at home—computers can help U.S. education pull itself up by its bootstraps, at a time when, according to the rash of reform

Presented at the Presidential Session, AECT National Conference, Dallas, Texas, 1984.

reports, it badly needs to do so. As a result, parental expectations for a high-tech quick fix for what ails U.S. education are rather high. But the higher such expectations go, the lower are the chances that they will be fulfilled — either by schools or by the computer companies that are peddling the message.

Educators, faced with these high parental expectations, are in a kind of high-tech catch-22. On the one hand, if they assume the full burden of fulfilling the potential of educational computing, they are undertaking a task for which, in most cases, they are ill-prepared, understaffed, and underfunded. On the other hand, if they do not commit themselves fully to the task and if the great potential of educational computing ultimately goes unrealized, those very educators will inevitably be criticized for failing to fulfill their responsibility to prepare students for the future.

Clearly, neither outcome is desirable, especially when most educators worthy of the name are already doing what they can to ensure that educational computing does fulfill its potential. But this is a difficult job, and in many schools educational computing is becoming just one more problem with which to deal — a problem that can very often be reduced to finding funds for hardware.

I must confess that I thought this mania for acquiring hardware was on the wane. However, a school computer consultant recently disabused me of that notion by telling me about what she described as a more or less typical call she received from a school principal. The call went something like this: "I need your help. We just received our first shipment of computers. But, before we take them out of the boxes, I want you to come over and tell us what we should do to get the kids on the computers as soon as possible. Come as soon as you can, because our parents helped purchase these machines, and we've got to show them that their kids are using the computers they helped us buy."

When my consultant friend explained to the principal that it would be at least a month before she could help him "get the kids on the computers," he seemed annoyed. She had been tempted, she said, to tell him, "Why don't you leave the computers in their boxes and have the kids sit on them? Then you can tell the parents that their kids were on the computers the day the computers were delivered." She didn't say that, of course.

What she did instead was talk the principal through the needs assessment he should have carried out before the school ever ordered its hardware. She directed the principal to begin by assessing those areas of the curriculum that might be effectively improved through the use of computers. She also asked him to address the task of finding high-quality software that would clearly serve the school's curriculum and teaching needs more effectively than could other, less expensive types of teaching materials. In short, she was asking the principal to face the single most important truth about educational computing: the quality of educational computing in a school depends on the quality of the software selected for use in that school and on the way in which the use of that software is integrated into the overall curriculum.

Schools must continue to acquire hardware, but they must not allow the *hardware quantity* problem to become an excuse for not facing up to the *software quality* problem. As esoteric as computer hardware may seem at first, the smaller number of hardware manufacturers now competing for the school market makes deciding on hardware a lot simpler than choosing among the seemingly countless software programs currently being offered by hundreds of educational software producers.

Purchasing computer software is clearly more confusing than purchasing computer hardware. But it is also more confusing than purchasing such familiar noncomputerized educational "software" as textbooks, workbooks, films, and tapes. Not only do the products and the companies in the computer software field far outnumber the more familiar educational media and their producers, but the products themselves are more difficult to assess and to select.

For instance, there are currently about 100 textbook publishers, but only 20 or so dominate the market and produce about 100 textbook series that are used in most classrooms across the United States. By contrast, there are currently about *700* educational software companies producing between 7,000 and 10,000 software packages, most of which are being bought by some school or parent, somewhere, for some hoped-for educational purpose. This means that, unlike the market for more traditional instructional materials, the educational software market is not dominated by a score of producers who—justifiably or not—have reputations for marketing quality products. Therefore, schools are rightly uneasy about their ability to make wise software choices.

Over the years educators have become quite confident of their ability to evaluate print and nonprint learning materials. They can readily scan print materials, examining and reexamining specific pages, chapters, or units. With a bit more effort, they can learn to examine films and tapes just as effectively. Moreover, most of these materials—especially textbooks—include teachers' guides, scope and sequence charts, and lists of instructional objectives, all of which help provide a sense of what the materials can do for children's learning.

This kind of information seldom accompanies software packages for schools. Even less often does such information accompany software aimed at the home-learning market. Yet, without such information, school people and parents are seriously hampered in their ability to select and to use software to fill the learning needs of youngsters.

Purchasers of educational software are also at a disadvantage for a number of other reasons. First, many software producers still refuse to grant previewing privileges, because they fear that their software will be illegally copied and then returned to them unpurchased. Second, even when software is available for preview, it is not as easily evaluated as print or other more familiar types of learning materials, because each software program must be examined in "real time" and should be tested with real learners. Third, even if a would-be purchaser were to make the investment of time and effort required to preview software programs and to evaluate them in relation to students' needs, the task of identifying a number of high-quality programs that meet these needs is still daunting.

The reasons for the current paucity of high-quality educational software are both numerous and complex, and the responsibility for this lack may be divided fairly equally between software companies and school and home consumers. Of course, in fairness to all the players, I should note that the present scarcity of high-quality products is to some extent a function of the tender age of the field. As developers and producers of educational software gain experience, quality should improve. It may also be true that educational software is no worse right now than a lot of other, more familiar learning materials being purchased by schools. But, as has been true of many of the noncomputerized instructional materials now available, good software may fail to drive out that which is mediocre and poor.

All of this suggests that most schools are buying software without the kind of discrimination they ought to be using, especially as consumers in an extremely complex and competitive marketplace. Consider the evidence. Today hundreds of companies somehow manage to survive in a highly competitive market, despite dire predictions of a coming "shakeout" that never seems to happen. Despite the fact that their products are almost uniformly of low quality, even the most marginal of these companies manages to sell enough to stay in business. Even the few more profitable—and usually more visible—developers of educational software are not necessarily producing products of any higher quality than their struggling competitors. Clearly, in the field of educational software, marketing has more to do with a company's success and profitability than does the quality of its product.

Now, we might like to think that educators are too savvy to be buying products of low quality just because they are marketed well. And many well-informed educators are. But such well-informed educators usually are located in the small number of school districts that have invested heavily in a substantial software selection effort, justified by an equally substantial software purchasing budget. In districts with more modest software budgets, less effective selection and purchasing practices are apt to prevail.

Even if educators were to be more discriminating in their software purchasing, there would still be ample opportunity for the hundreds of competing software companies to sell the thousands of mediocre and poor products that dominate today's market, because parents would continue to purchase an increasing amount of educational software to feed those five million computers now in homes with children. It is conceivable, therefore, that, even though educators may become increasingly discriminating about the software they purchase for children in schools, the producers may not be forced to improve the quality of their products significantly, because they can still sell lower quality products — which are cheaper to produce — to the parents of those same children.

The likelihood of this happening was dramatically driven home to me at a recent conference on school/home computer use. One of the most experienced software developers in attendance said that, when weighing all the factors that go into developing and marketing educational software for home use, educational quality was usually accorded only about 5 percent of the developer's time and attention. Packaging, advertising, market position, and a host of other factors unrelated to the educational effectiveness of the software took up the other 95 percent. I would like to think that this sad state of affairs applied only to a few of the software packages now on the market, and, indeed, other speakers claimed just that. Moreover, at a number of other recent conferences, I have heard adamant assertions that the quality of educational software is improving so rapidly that good software is now readily available in quantity.

Unfortunately, all such statements are either the result of impressionistic assessments, based on a familiarity with some very small percentage of today's educational software, or else the result of a misguided hope that the present small percentage of excellent software will somehow discourage the continued proliferation of poor programs. Such views are ill-founded and misleading because they are neither based on an understanding of the realities operating in the educational software marketplace nor based on a reliable and rigorous assessment of the quality of the software currently being marketed to home and school consumers.

During the last two years, the Educational Products Information Exchange (EPIE) — a consumer-supported evaluation agency associated with Consumers Union — has been conducting an ongoing assessment of the quality of educational software. The result of this effort is a more realistic picture of what is currently available than the picture provided by these impressionistic and hopeful assertions.

The EPIE software assessment effort was launched in 1982 with support from the Carnegie Corporation of New York, the Ford Foundation, the Geraldine R. Dodge Foundation, and the San Francisco Foundation. Continuing funding for the project is now being provided by an increasing number of state departments of education that are providing all schools in their states with the software evaluations created by the ongoing assessment effort. Recently, this growing state-supported program has been expanded to include an intrastate and interstate electronic exchange of information among school and home consumers, as well as online access for both educators and parents to all the project's independently researched information on educational software.

Two interrelated activities of the project provide a comprehensive picture of the availability and quality of today's educational software. First, for the last year and a half, the project has maintained a database that continuously monitors the production of all commercially available educational software as it enters the market and stores relevant consumer information that is constantly updated and available online to all schools in states that support the maintenance of the database. (The information is also available to school consumers outside those states in an annually updated publication.) The aim of this project activity is to provide consumers with reliable information on what software is available, what software has been taken off the market, what each program is designed to do, how much it costs, what hardware it runs on, whether it can be networked, whether it has been evaluated, and whether it is recommended for purchase.

Second, a national evaluation program uses teams of trained software evaluators to systematically assess the quality of a large representative sample of the software in the database. This activity began two years ago with the training of a national network of software evaluation teams enlisted from schools and universities. These teams were instructed in the use of a carefully researched system of software evaluation involving both a rigorous analysis and assessment of the instructional and technical design of each product and direct observation of the use of the software with learners. The process is a painstaking and expensive one, but it is producing what are recognized as the most valid and reliable software evaluations now available.

The first results of the work of these teams were described in April of 1984 at the annual meeting of the American Educational Research Association (AERA) in New Orleans. An overall analysis of the hundreds of programs that have undergone this evaluation process during the last two years demonstrates that six out of ten of those programs have been placed in the categories, "Not Recommended" or "Do Not Consider." Only three or four out of ten have been placed in the "Recommended" category, and only one out of twenty has been judged good enough to be placed in the "Highly Recommended" category. Thus, only 5 percent of these hundreds of programs have been judged to be of truly high quality, while more than 50 percent have been judged as not worth recommending to educators or parents.

A detailed analysis of a substantial subset of these evaluations was reported by the EPIE at the April 1984 AERA Meeting. This analysis revealed that only about one out of every five software programs examined by the EPIE had been learner-tested by its publisher during its development. That figure still held six months later. Moreover, the designers of most of the software made but poor use of the potential of the computer to provide learners with feedback on their performance. Thus, most of today's software developers have been ignoring two elements of software design that can greatly enhance the educational value of a program — field-testing with real learners and interactive feedback. This finding does not inspire broad confidence in the quality of the software currently being marketed to educators and parents.

Finally, and most important, our assessment of hundreds of software packages shows no increase at all during the last year in the percentage of software rated "Highly Recommended" and only a modest increase in the percentage of software receiving a "Recommended" rating (35 percent, up from 27 percent for the previous year). If this modest increase is what some people have in mind when they claim that "the quality of educational software is greatly improved," these results suggest that their claims (like the claims made by the manufacturers of most of the software) are more than a little overstated.

This is not to say that excellent software programs do not exist. They most certainly do. But for a number of reasons many of today's high-quality programs may be unknown to school and home consumers. First, the glut of glowing advertising campaigns for software, whatever its quality, makes it difficult to sort the sheep from the goats. Second, some of the best software is produced by companies that do not have the marketing dollars needed to get their message across to a large number of consumers. And third, major merchandisers and software dealers are interested in mass marketing and volume sales, and they want to stock and advertise whole lines of software. Yet, as our analysis has shown, no single line of software is consistently of high quality.

These then are the most recent findings of EPIE's independent assessment of the quality of today's educational software. Faced with this not very encouraging picture, educators might well feel that the burden of fulfilling the potential of educational computing is growing too heavy—heavy enough, perhaps, to make even the most dedicated educator retreat from the task.

But to do so would be tragic. The next two years are going to be crucial for the future of educational computing and its long-term effects on U.S. education. For this reason, retreat now is tantamount to admitting defeat. Educational computing and education itself are currently at a critical juncture, and their combined fate depends to large extent on the quality of educational software and the quality of the uses to which it is put, both in school and at home.

The question, of course, is, What can educators do to improve the quality of software? One thing, surely, is to search out and purchase only the best software available. Another thing is to provide teachers with information and training to help them make the most effective use of that high-quality software. The alternative is to put mediocre or poor products into the hands of poorly prepared teachers and let them do with them what they will.

But if all educators did search for and purchase only the best programs available, wouldn't the software industry be apt to accelerate its current trend toward targeting parents, who will inevitably be less discriminating and less persistent in their search for quality? And if the software marketers do so, what can educators hope to do about it?

I believe that educators can do quite a bit, if they are willing to look at educational computing through a broader lens than the one they now focus narrowly on—the purchase of hardware and software for in-school use during the school day. Fortunately, some educators are already using this broader vision to turn their school's involvement with educational computing into a communitywide educational effort. Although the schools are taking a leading role, a good deal of the burden is being shared with other interested forces in the community.

Educators in school districts that have taken this broader view are offering training to parents on how to make effective use of a home computer in support of school learning. Some districts are networking these trained parents and setting up hardware and software exchanges among parents. Other districts are doing this in cooperation with public libraries. Some districts are helping parents to purchase computers at significant discounts under an extension of the districts' purchasing contracts. The most advanced and socially conscious among such districts are raising money locally—or using federal or state dollars—to purchase low-cost computers that can be loaned to low-income families who participate in parent/child computer training programs.

Educators who are capable of this sort of vision—and willing to act on it—can help fulfill the potential of educational computing. That potential is both enormous and very much worth taking some risks to achieve.

PBS Tunes In to Adult Learning

Dee Brock
Adult Learning Programming
Public Broadcasting Service

PUBLIC TELEVISION'S ROLE IN ADULT LEARNING

For years PBS has asked the public to tune in to public television for the finest cultural, public affairs, informational, and general educational programming in the world. The public has tuned into that programming in growing numbers and with burgeoning enthusiasm, because PBS has kept its program mix coherent with national interests and desires.

Thus, in 1979, the increasing urgency in the demand for better quality and more convenient education for adult learners prompted PBS to mount a major study to investigate what role, if any, public television should play in meeting this national need. The study asked three main questions.

1. Is there a need for public television to take a major role in adult learning?

2. Can public television fulfill such a role in adult learning?

3. Can public television afford to take on adult learning as a major priority?

The study answered these questions *yes, yes*, and again *yes*. As a result, PBS and public television have tuned in to adult learning as a top priority.

The tune-in began with the establishment of the PBS Adult Learning Service in the fall of 1980. This bold new initiative to offer college credit courses via television to adults throughout the United States was founded on the concept of a partnership among PBS, producers of television courses, local public television stations, and the local colleges and universities.

The yearly growth has been quite astonishing. Beginning in the academic year 1981-82, some 700 colleges working with their local public television stations offered 1,400 course selections through the Adult Learning Service and enrolled about 55,000 students. In 1982-83, over 75,000 students enrolled. In 1983-84, over 100,000 students were in the courses.

Presented at the Presidential Session, AECT National Conference, Dallas, Texas, 1984.

Currently, over 800 colleges and universities, working with more than 90 percent of the nation's public television stations, have participated in the Adult Learning Service. Located in every state, these postsecondary institutions represent a real cross-section of higher education in the United States. Some 47 percent are four-year institutions; 53 percent are two-year institutions. The majority are publicly supported and about 18 percent are private colleges. Together with their local stations, these colleges have enrolled more than a quarter of a million adult learners for college credit through the PBS Adult Learning Service.

Clearly, adult learners in ever-increasing numbers have tuned in to PBS for the quality college courses they need and the convenient time schedules they demand.

READY TO COOPERATE

There are many reasons for the immediate success of this new tune-in endeavor. As Hamlet said, "Readiness is all." It appears that the public and the cooperating agencies are all ready for this national, cooperative enterprise.

In the sixties, hundreds of colleges and universities equipped their campuses with television studios. Many put television sets in every classroom and wired each room with closed circuit cable, only to lament the absence of worthwhile material to display on these monitors. Excellent educational programs were scarce, and colleges did not have the expertise or the resources to produce the kind of video they wanted to use on campus, let alone the kind that might be broadcast. Millions of dollars worth of equipment sat unused, an uncomfortable reminder that money and technology cannot in themselves solve educational problems. (Those persons who are responsible for purchasing and installing computers to deliver instruction on college campuses today might learn from this little lesson in history.) In the meantime, the adult students who could not or did not want to come to campus were home with their own television sets, waiting for some convenient way to meet their developing needs for quality college-level instruction.

During the 1970s, while some were bemoaning the failed promise of television for higher education, others were making revolutionary changes. A few innovative colleges saw that several well-produced general audience programs, such as the series *The Ascent of Man* and *Civilization*, had the potential to become fine college courses. Consequently, they created the appropriate instructional design and print materials and they proved their point.

At the same time, a group of pioneering community colleges determined to use television to help them overcome their chronically overcrowded classrooms in certain subjects and to help them bring more depth and power to their instruction in other subjects. Eschewing the old "chalk and talk" approach, they developed well-designed and carefully integrated learning systems. They used the television medium to take the student to the scene of actual events and phenomena; to introduce the greatest scholars, practitioners, and experts in their own milieu; and to illustrate, exemplify, and dramatize concepts. But the courses were far more than a series of well-produced television programs. They also included other components, such as textbooks, study guides, faculty manuals, and audio supplements. The result was such well-produced and popular college television courses as *Man and Environment* (Miami-Dade), *Dimensions of Culture* (Coast Community College in Fountain Valley, California), and *American Government* (Dallas County Community College District).

The success of these efforts was immediate. For not only did television courses help solve overcrowding, but they also attracted a new clientele to these colleges. About 20 percent of the television course students enrolled because they could not get into on-campus sections, but the bulk of the enrollees were students who would not have enrolled in those courses had they not been offered via television. These were new students—older, part-time, employed, and first time in college or returning "stop-out" students.

DISTRIBUTION AND COORDINATION

Local successes in the mid-seventies revitalized the production of and use of college courses via television. The few college pioneers developed courses for their own service areas first, but they also developed them with the idea of, to quote Bill J. Priest of Dallas County Community College, "sharing our expertise, as well as our costs, with our colleagues." Thus, for the best of these producers, the licensing of courses to other colleges also became an important source of revenue and a good way of ensuring the creation of a new series.

Although these new television courses employed good production techniques and the best instructional design, the distribution itself was slow and costly. Each licensing college or consortium was forced to buy a set of broadcast tapes and to work independently with its local public television station or other outlet to arrange for broadcast time. Throughout the seventies, as more stations and colleges used television courses, it became evident that a national coordinating effort was needed. Colleges clearly needed a central distribution channel for the television programs and a central source of information about support for television courses. They needed to know when courses would be available; how courses could be used; what experiences other institutions were having; and up-to-date details about books as well as revisions. They needed help in promotion, assistance in implementation, and guidance in faculty selection and recruitment. They needed information and services that only a national coordinating arm could provide efficiently. Further, they needed all of these at low cost.

The PBS Adult Learning Service set out to meet these college needs. Using the PBS satellite, interconnection provided central distribution and reduced costs. Courses that formerly cost $2,700 to $3,000 for the first term and $1,500 to $2,000 for each additional term (plus student fees) now cost $300 to $400 per term through the Adult Learning Service. Also, aggregating large numbers of college users meant that the Adult Learning Service could provide a wide range of important services to ensure cost-effectiveness. Services included promotional materials (press kits, ad slicks, television promo spots, etc.), professional development activities, personal consultations, national screenings, and announcements or schedules nine months prior to each term. Each public television station assigned a special Adult Learning Service person to work with local colleges to assure smooth operations.

The Adult Learning Service currently works with public television, colleges, and independent producers to develop new courses. From the seven courses offered in the first term, the PBS *Adult Learning Catalog* now includes twenty-five courses. All the courses are fine television programs that the stations are proud to broadcast. Several, such as *Vietnam, a Television History; Constitution: That Delicate Balance; Heritage: Civilization and the Jews*; and *The Brain* have been popular prime-time offerings.

Another important development in the story of college television courses is the Annenberg/CPB Project. This $150 million fund is the generous gift of former Ambassador Walter Annenberg through the Annenberg School of Communication at the University of Pennsylvania. Housed at the Corporation for Public Broadcasting, the fifteen-year-old project funds the creation of television courses and other technology-based educational resources for higher education at the rate of $10 million a year. Once again the timing was right. This remarkable gift was established just as public television tuned in to adult learning, thus ensuring interest in and space for college-level educational programming on public stations nationwide.

ADULT LEARNERS AND INCREASING
COLLEGE ENROLLMENTS

No matter how well-planned the service or how well-produced the courses, there could be no rapid growth without a real public need to be served. The fastest growing group of adult learners in this country matches the demographic make-up of television students almost point by point.

- Nearly all television students are twenty-five years of age or older.

- The largest number of students are between thirty and forty years of age.

- Almost all television students are part-time students.

- Some 60 percent have full-time jobs outside the home; most of the remaining 40 percent have part-time jobs.

- Slightly more than half are women.

- Far more than half have at least one dependent.

- Some 20 to 40 percent are first-time students; many of the remaining 60 to 80 percent have been drop-outs and are returning.

Overall, these students are ambitious, pragmatic, and busy. They want to earn college credits because they believe the resulting knowledge or degrees will advance them in their careers, assist them in career changes, or move them into the work force above the menial level.

Although some colleges worry that offering television courses will detract from their on-campus programs, enrollments in institutions participating in the Adult Learning Service have generally risen in two basic ways. First, television courses attract new students. College surveys indicate that some 60 percent of their television enrollments fall into this category. Second, when students earn more credit hours, they tend to go back to school to complete their degrees. Larry Dotolo, Executive Director of the Tidewater Consortium of Colleges in Virginia reports that 60 to 80 percent of successful television students later enroll in on-campus courses.

Even the proven need for college credit courses on television and the validated quality of the courses now offered via PBS would have been insufficient insurance for the success of this project without the strength of the overlapping partnerships upon which the service is based.

The Adult Learning Service selects courses after consultations with its participants and national cooperative screenings. Participating colleges choose their own courses and assign their own faculty to be directly responsible for adapting courses and working with students. Producers of television courses are also an important part of these overlapping partnerships and work side by side with the Adult Learning Service.

EXPANDING DESIGN AND TECHNOLOGY

Although the PBS tune-in to adult learning began first with a plan to bring college courses to the air through public television stations across the country, the effort did not stop there. Whenever possible, the Adult Learning Service acquired cable, Instructional

Television Fixed Service (ITFS), and videocassette distribution rights for courses in its catalog so that, either in conjunction with or separate from a broadcast, colleges can use courses and parts of courses in a variety of ways. Using other technologies allows stations to build in more flexibility in scheduling and to offer a wider selection of courses than broadcast alone permits.

Another expansion of the adult learning tune-in design calls for enlarging the focus of the service to include informal learners and more specialized professional development and career training needs. One ambitious strategy in the making is the National Narrowcast Service (NNS). This project incorporates both a local and a national delivery mechanism and programming service. The plan calls for several channels of national programming service to be delivered daily via satellite to public television sites. Local programmers may supplement the national schedule or develop services tailored to local educational needs. ITFS channels will initially be the backbone of the distribution system.

Capitalizing on the partnership concept already established between public television and higher education, NNS will work with local colleges to deliver television courses and specialized professional and career training directly to worksites and other places where adults congregate. In addition, informational updates on national and state legislation, trends, and developments can be a regular feature.

CONCLUSION

Alfred Rollins, President of Old Dominion University, is an enthusiastic supporter of the PBS effort. He sums up the reasons he and his institution have joined the PBS endeavor by noting that one of the nice things about television courses is that "nobody loses." His observations suggest that after many years of experimentation and debate, some grand designs, and a few flops and fizzles, the 1980s are the decade to see adult learning via television become a thriving nationwide phenomenon. And everyone benefits. For PBS and the public television stations, offering college courses is a natural extension of their commitment to public service and education. For colleges and universities, using television is a practical and effective way to reach out to the growing number of adult students. The other beneficiaries are the producers, who receive wider use of their creative work, and adults, who receive a quality product.

The result is a unique alliance that successfully blends national and local goals and efforts. PBS has tuned in to adult learning—and everybody wins.

An information packet about the PBS Adult Learning Service is available by writing the PBS Adult Learning Service, 475 L'Enfant Plaza, SW, Washington, DC 20024.

Postsecondary Consortia
and Distance Learning

Daniel Niemeyer
Acting Director
Academic Media Services
University of Colorado, Boulder

Technology is not new to postsecondary education. Various forms of print, film, and electronic media have been used to supplement and enhance instructional efforts for years.

In the past thirty years, a great deal of research has been conducted to determine the feasibility of learning from film, radio, and television. Chu and Schramm (1968) reported:

> It has become clear that there is no longer any reason to raise the question whether instructional television can serve as an efficient tool of learning. This is not to say that it always does. But the evidence is now overwhelming that it can, and, under favorable circumstances, does. This evidence now comes from many countries, from studies of all age levels from preschool to adults, and from a great variety of subject matter and learning objectives. (p. 6)

Recent events have underlined the importance of telecommunications technology in higher education. A combination of technological developments and demographic, social, and economic changes have focused the attention of administrators, legislators, and educators on telecommunications applications to postsecondary education.

Until the last few years, telecommunications technology has been limited to closed-circuit television courses used by colleges for on-campus learners. Demographic and economic developments, however, have turned attention in the 1980s to the use of open-circuit television to reach off-campus learners, as well.

POSTSECONDARY EDUCATION OFF-CAMPUS

Off-campus instruction of university students did not begin with radio and television broadcasting of instructional materials. The roots of off-campus postsecondary education, or *distance learning*, include such elements as: (1) independent study, individual projects, internships, field work, research, nontraditional study, and resource-based learning and (2) university extension, correspondence schools, home study, external degree programs, extramural tutorial, continuing education, and universities without walls.

Teather and McMechan (1981) noted:

> Teaching by correspondence began in the 1840s and by 1930 correspondence assignments were being supplemented by modern telecommunications media. By the mid-1970s many hundreds of agencies had already helped literally millions of students to overcome the barriers of space, time, social and economic status in their pursuit of learning. (p. 53).

Wood and Wylie (1977) commented:

> It matters little where a learner gets his information. What does matter is that the information be presented over an appropriate medium, that it be accurate and up-to-date, and that it be available when and where the learner needs it. (p. 232)

Potential benefits of instruction at an off-campus site reported by the California Postsecondary Education Commission (1979) included: (1) better access to instruction for the less mobile, from the severely handicapped to the full-time worker with a family; (2) energy savings from less dependence on the automobile and the classroom; (3) alternative, less costly methods for continuing professional education; (4) encounters with leading scholars and practitioners in various fields; (5) more opportunity for repetition of instruction, through replay of materials, with less reliance on note-taking and more chance of mastery learning; (6) the possibility of individualizing programs, thereby increasing student persistence; (7) a wider audience of "adjunct learners," those who are not enrolled but follow the course and perhaps become interested in later activities of the instruction; and (8) lower public cost per enrolled student.

FORMATION OF CONSORTIA

It is expensive for postsecondary educational institutions to purchase programming, and even more expensive to produce and distribute it. In order to cut costs and achieve a degree of consistency in granting credit for participation, some educational institutions in the United States have found it desirable to form regional, statewide, or area-wide consortia to deal with the distribution of educational material via television.

Simply put, a consortium is a formal organization of two or more member institutions, administered by a director, with tangible evidence of member support.

OBJECTIVES OF THIS PAPER

The objective of this investigation was to obtain baseline data on the postsecondary consortia in the United States in 1982 involving the delivery of educational material via television. Television, in this instance, includes over-the-air broadcasting, cable telecasting, instructional television fixed service (ITFS), videotape and slow scan.

The study was limited to the use of television because, as reported by the Commission on Telecommunications (1981):

> Television promises to remain the major telecommunications delivery system for off-campus education in the near future, because the medium is versatile, the receiving equipment is readily available and familiar to the user, and because television can be a cost-effective means of reaching larger numbers of students while utilizing existing faculty resources. (p. 15)

Baseline data for this survey included: (1) accurate, precise information on the name and address of the consortium; (2) organizational information; (3) the present mission and future plans of the consortium; (4) the technologies in use; and (5) funding and budgeting information.

METHODOLOGY AND PROCEDURES

This survey was conducted in two phases. Phase one involved locating the consortia throughout the United States. While it was true that many of these groups were easily found through widespread coverage of their activities in the literature, a large number of consortia exist that were not readily located. Many different strategies were employed over the course of eighteen months in order to compile a comprehensive list.

Phase two involved questioning the consortia to obtain baseline data concerning size, organizational structure, mission, technology, funding, and budget. This information was gathered by mailing questionnaires to each consortium located in phase one. Several follow-up materials were sent to organizations in order to obtain at least a 95 percent response.

SUMMARY OF THE FINDINGS

The survey located seventy-one active consortia. Data received from the survey indicated that enrollment in these consortia was strong, was increasing, and was expected to continue to increase during the next three years.

More than 100,000 students were enrolled in 1982. Enrollment had increased greatly or moderately in 61 percent of the consortia during the past three years, and 74 percent of the consortia expected enrollment to increase greatly or moderately during the next three years. More than 1,000 colleges and universities were members of telecommunications consortia, and 44 percent of the consortia expected to add members to their consortium during the next three years.

ANALYSIS OF THE DATA FROM THE QUESTIONNAIRES

Two questions, one asking about the size of the 1982 enrollment and one asking about the growth of the consortium in the past years, were used as the measures of a successful telecommunications consortium. These two independent variables — *current enrollment* and *recent growth* — were then compared with *year established, coverage area, range of services, type of membership, full-time administrator,* and *type of support* to determine any statistically significant determiners of success.

FACTORS AFFECTING ENROLLMENT

Analysis indicated that two factors are important for a consortium to have an enrollment of 1,000 students or more — a wide coverage area and a wide range of services.

It is important that the coverage area of the consortium be large — statewide or regional — as opposed to local or area-wide. It appears that a wide geographical area provides a sufficient number of college and university members in the coverage area and a sufficient market to support the cost of distributing educational materials to students via television.

It is also important that a wide range of services be available to the student, including a wide selection of courses, an assortment of degrees, up to and including an MA/MS degree, and that a large number of colleges and universities participate in the consortium.

A wide range of services seems to provide a much more appealing product for the potential student.

Four other factors were not significantly associated with a large enrollment: (1) whether the consortium was established recently or more than seven years ago; (2) whether membership was voluntary or mandated; (3) whether or not there was a paid, full-time administrator; and (4) whether the consortium was self-supporting or receiving funding from an outside source.

FACTORS AFFECTING GROWTH

Analysis indicated that four factors affect growth. One has to do with how recently a consortium had been established. Consortia formed in the past seven years were more likely to have experienced "great" or "moderate" growth in enrollment in the past three years than those established more than seven years ago. This would suggest that a consortium could expect substantial increases in enrollment during its early years, but after the large number of students who have been waiting for this service have been reached, the number of students will stabilize, and only slight increases will occur after the market has been saturated.

Three other factors are important for a consortium to achieve great or moderate increases in enrollment. Two of these factors — wide coverage area and wide range of services — are the same as factors important for a large consortium; but the third factor — funding from an outside source — is unique.

In order for a recently formed consortium to experience great or moderate growth, analysis indicates that funding must come from sources other than membership dues. The organizations that reported great or moderate increases in student enrollment during the past three years required funding from some state agency.

Two factors were not significantly associated with recent growth: whether membership was voluntary or mandated, and whether a paid, full-time administrator was present or not.

If television courses become part of the mainstream of higher education, there can be little doubt that telecommunications consortia will continue to flourish. The economics of telecourse design and production make inter-institutional cooperation and resource sharing desirable. Likewise, the economics of telecourse use make group arrangements reasonable. Certainly, telecommunications consortia are ideally suited to serve the growing needs of professional and occupational development.

REFERENCES

California Postsecondary Education Commission. (1979). *Using instructional media beyond campus.* Commission Report on Lifelong Learning.

Chu, G. C., & Schramm, W. (1968). *Learning from television: What the research says.* Washington, DC: National Association of Educational Broadcasters.

Commission on Telecommunications. (1981). Working paper. University of Massachusetts.

Teather, D. C., & McMechan, J. P. (1981). Learning from a distance: A variety of models. *International yearbook of educational and instructional technology 1980/ 1981.*

Wood, D. N., & Wylie, D. G. (1977). *Educational telecommunications.* Belmont, CA: Wadsworth Publishing Co., Inc.

A Satellite Educational Program
at Air Academy High School in Colorado

M. Lucille Wilson
Air Academy High School

In order to motivate high school students in this high tech, information-age society, new teaching techniques and new equipment are essential. In an attempt to increase the students' enthusiasm for learning, Air Academy High School in Colorado investigated new technologies and ultimately decided to purchase an earth satellite receiving system.

We realize that a satellite teaching system is not a panacea for the many educational concerns of today. Our experience, however, has been that it provides great opportunities for moving our students into the information age. Students who are exposed to this technology, the most current information, modern effective teaching methods, and dynamic teachers, can become excited, motivated learners who do not have to wait for new textbooks to be written.

SETTING UP A SATELLITE RECEIVING SYSTEM

Excited about the possibility of this new high tech equipment that would launch us more firmly into the information age, we investigated the legality of using direct satellite broadcast programs to enhance our learning system. According to Richard Brown, attorney for SPACE (Society for Private and Commercial Earth Stations), videotaping is under the "Fair Use" copyright law. In the Copyright Act of 1976, there is no provision that specifically applies to TVRO (Television Receiving Only) systems that are not used for commercial gains. Therefore, any legal restrictions are at a minimum for public school use of a satellite system. Nevertheless, we did obtain written permission from all channels to be used.

We also did a feasibility study concerning location of equipment and community services for installation of equipment, important considerations when incorporating high technology and motivational teaching/learning techniques. We are fortunate to be in a "footprint" coverage pattern, which offers us good reception for educational satellite programs. We did purchase a surge protector so that power outages would not incapacitate the equipment and cause interruptions in classroom reception or in videotaping programs. Another useful tool that can be purchased is a lockout feature on the receiver that prevents access to any inappropriate channels, such as Playboy, Pleasure, and High Life.

Students were excited about the system from the very beginning. Even the installation of the physical equipment sparked their enthusiasm. An eleven-foot compression-molded fiberglass dish was affixed to the roof of one of the school buildings, but Rampart foothill winds soon forced a move to the ground where it was anchored in cement. Cables were placed underground, installed in buildings, and connected to a power supply box, an actuator box, and a receiver. A stereo amplifier, especially good for music and drama, was added. The auditorium and all eighteen classrooms in Building D were cabled to receive audio and visual signals from the satellite dish. In addition to television sets and videotape recorders, a seven-foot RCA diagonal screen was purchased.

An integral part of implementing our earth station satellite system was communication with and orientation of faculty and administrators. Enthusiasm for the increased quality of learning was evident at all the briefings on our satellite system. Faculty meetings and special meetings with each department were held to discuss the system and its potential uses. Copies of *ORBIT*, a monthly guide for satellite programs, were ordered. Lists of relevant programs for definitive subject areas were circulated. Our media specialist worked closely with teachers so that information on system benefits and suggestions for specific programming always were available. Each department purchased videotapes so that the technician could tape requested programs.

AVAILABLE SATELLITE PROGRAMS

A skeptic may ask, "What is up there for educational use?" There are eighteen satellites and over a hundred channels. Some of the channels and programs that we have found fit with our curriculum are described below.

1. There are many programs in Spanish and French. Among these selections are the SIN (Spanish International Network), three Canadian satellites, and ANIK's that cover news, Canadian Parliament, and information about Canada and Newfoundland in French. Advertisements, sports, films, political and international affairs, as well as the language itself provide a wealth of information for foreign language classes.

2. Economics and business classes use channels that broadcast only financial and business news.

3. The physical education classes use the ESPN channel to view and evaluate professional and amateur sporting events including the winter and summer olympics.

4. The Hospital Satellite Network provides the ninth-grade health classes with programs on national health care issues.

5. Earth science teachers start off their morning classes in weather by watching the weather channel.

6. Social studies students on all levels access coverage of meetings and hearings of the U.S. House of Representatives and the Canadian House of Commons. "Why in the World" is a program that offers information and discussion on current topics. A program called "Close Up" offers three daily call-in shows, and an 800 number is used. These programs challenge students to listen effectively;

comprehend quickly; apply, analyze, and synthesize information; and compose intelligent questions in a short time.

7. Drama, performing arts, music, and art classes watch international films and performances such as opera, jazz, drama, and symphony—all in stereo from the Arts and Entertainment and BRAVO channels. Some channels offer a unique blend of musical, vocal, and instrumental jazz as well as discussion of popular sounds.

8. One channel offers a program that takes viewers behind the scenes to see things they would never see on a regular program, such as technicians adjusting equipment before a broadcast, people applying make-up, and reporters rehearsing their lines.

9. An especially valuable channel is the Learning Channel that offers a wide variety of educational programs. Biology programs enable the teacher to incorporate a close-up, in-depth look at a specific concept being taught. This has a major positive impact on subject retention. A genetic engineering teacher, who stresses laboratory techniques, can show the entire class simultaneously an expertly done procedure and can point out the pitfalls of improperly executed techniques. As a result of such programming, students receive a stronger visual image and understanding of a process and, it is hoped, will make fewer mistakes in practical application.

10. Movies such as *The Great Gatsby* and specials like "Napoleon" have been motivating introductions for U.S. literature and world history.

11. There is even a Silent Network that offers two hours of programming per week for the deaf and hearing impaired.

12. Disney Channel broadcasts films from the Disney library.

13. Alaska's channel, Aurora, broadcasts information and news about its state.

14. The program "It's the Law," is a good resource for government and law classes.

15. Counselors use some of the selective programs, such as "Stress," with their students.

BENEFITS OF A SATELLITE TEACHING SYSTEM

There are many benefits of using a satellite teaching system. Some of the primary benefits are as follows:

1. It provides an educational tool for a multiway learner-centered system that complements the one-way teacher-centered communication system.

2. It encourages learning by reinforcing concepts and ideas and by making lessons more meaningful as students examine the most current, complex, and pressing problems, such as United States-Soviet relations, energy, and the public debt.

3. It sharpens students' listening and viewing skills, which they can transfer to the real world.

4. It provides a communication tool that focuses on societal issues, literary classics, or firsthand knowledge of a subject, which encourages students to extend their global thinking or explore an issue further or read an original piece of work.

5. It provides students in the gifted and talented programs with an opportunity to use their creative abilities to assess situations, make critical judgments, solve problems, and synthesize ideas.

6. It provides an exciting way to capture attention and motivate students to effectively pursue a course of study.

There are also secondary benefits of using a satellite teaching system. Video teleconferencing can provide the school and district with another educational vehicle that can enhance in-service for teachers or provide a service to the community. Our school will be a site this year for the National Diffusion Network educational program teleconferences for teachers in the local area. Other video conferences are planned. Instructional or informational viewing by the parents in the community can be arranged. Junior college and university/college courses and credit are available for high school students and adults, providing the local higher education institution will sponsor these courses. Approximately one hundred U.S. and two Canadian universities and colleges will be offering courses for credit. (A list of these institutions offering credit is available from D. Allen Herschfield, Executive Director, International Consortium for Telecommunications in Teaching, University of Maryland, Box 438, Owings Mills, Maryland 21117.) These satellite courses are helpful to the adults in the community and for the student who wishes to gain information about a subject such as art and either does not have the time during the school day to take the course or fears a poor grade that would lower his or her grade point average. The courses are also helpful for the student who has moved to a new school in his or her senior year and needs additional credits to graduate.

FUTURE PLANS

With the aid of the satellite teaching system, Air Academy High School looks forward to providing teachers and students with basic access to interactive video teleconferencing and a dynamic student-oriented program while laying the groundwork for the fullest possible use of computers and online databases. In the "dreaming" stage is the addition of an uplink facility. Some investigative talks are taking place between the school district and local business firms. An uplink installation would provide the schools in the district and the local industry with the needed facility to broadcast courses that would enhance the education of the businesspeople, engineers, educators, and interested learners of all ages in our geographical area.

Community Antennae Television
and Education

J. Warren Binns
Florida State Department of Education

As Community Antennae Television (CATV) service began to pervade U.S. communities, speculation on its future potential, especially services for education, ran rampant. In addition to the retransmission of standard broadcast signals and nonbroadcast programming, additional services that were predicted included such things as two-way communications, wide and narrow band data links, access to massive databases, and numerous kinds of financial transactions made possible by pushing a button. Systems, as built, seldom offered these additional services. With few exceptions, all of these high technology services are possible, but the date of their becoming operational is a big question.

All communications technology is beset by the old chicken and egg problem of not being cost-effective until it is in place and used by a significant segment of the population. This is a function of time. To set in place any mass communications technology, there must be a major investment of capital, and investors want a reasonably rapid return on their investment. The few examples of CATV systems that provide the more exotic services have not produced the anticipated return on investment in a reasonable period of time and, as a result, these systems have frequently reduced their expenses and returned to their regular CATV services. The high hopes of education to improve their services by the use of this technology were therefore dealt a serious blow. There is every reason to expect the return of such services as two-way communications and data links when the mass market is ready to accept them and, more importantly, pay for them. This experience underlines the fact that public (mass) education is very dependent on the consumer market for cost-effective technology.

Educators approached the advent of cable with great and often grandiose expectations. Cable operators were optimistic, but they were also business people with an appropriate concern for the profit and loss statement. Expectations and the bottom line were often in conflict, and the water was further muddied by the franchising process. As a part of local government, educators were perceived by those seeking franchises as important allies. Frequent promises were made that were difficult to keep, and the result was disappointment on both sides. CATV, in its present configuration, has much to

Presented at the Presidential Session, AECT National Conference, Dallas, Texas, 1984.

offer education. Educators are embracing, in ever-increasing numbers, a delivery system that they can make their own. They believe that a system that can be programmed by them, configured to meet their needs, and is imminently affordable, is really their own medium. Educators who are using the present CATV technology have become a part of the system and will have the opportunity to grow with it, while simultaneously serving their clients.

There are many educational applications of CATV. A full recital of all the applications at this time is beyond the space available for this paper. To document all of the system configurations in use, much less their potential, would require a comprehensive study. The most that can be hoped for in this limited presentation will be a sampling of a variety of existing configurations serving education. It is hoped that readers will be inspired to examine the communication needs of their institution, the CATV resources available in their community(ies), and consider CATV's potential application to their problem(s).

CATV is quite simply a segment of the broadcast spectrum trapped inside a wire. Typically the spectrum includes the frequencies for both FM radio and an expanded number of VHF television channels. Whatever can be communicated on these broadcast frequencies (and more), can be done on cable, as long as the wire reaches the desired destination(s). The length and the routing of the wire appears inordinately important, although the wire is not always the limitation it might seem.

The exciting part of CATV is that it is not a mature medium. It is still growing. It is still groping for its role and potential in the world of communications. CATV is not tormented by decisions about how it can best work within its limitations but is trying to find out if there are any limits. It has few formulae or traditions to which to conform, but it is developing new formulae and is seldom overly constrained by traditions. That is not to say that CATV is the irresponsible pup it once was, but it certainly is not too old to enjoy learning new tricks.

CATV provides the opportunity to address communications problems in a manner that will be only minimally frustrated by the medium. Certainly there are constraints, but they are primarily those of common sense and those within which an educator would be constrained to operate under any circumstances. Educators have the opportunity to carefully examine needs with the reasonable assurance that there will be options available to meet or come very close to a functional solution. More and more educators are sensing this opportunity and exploiting it to the benefit of their students and communities. This is one part of the "*more* than broadcast." The other part is that many of the prohibitions imposed on broadcasters are not limitations for CATV.

CATV resolved some education problems for a Florida school system and a local community college. Transporting videotape from school to school had become an expensive and time-consuming undertaking for the school system. The local community college felt it could offer the community a broader offering of telecourses than it could afford to provide by broadcast. After a careful planning of resources and negotiations with the local CATV manager, the school system installed a cable interconnecting an origination center in the regional vocational-technical center with the CATV headend. The college and school district jointly provided programming for twelve hours a day. During the school day, programs went directly to public schools. In the evening, the focus was on college credit programs offered by the college to people at home. The demand for programs by classroom teachers grew so rapidly that the single channel was inadequate during daytime hours. Eventually, timers were attached to the school videocassette recorders, the origination center playback was automated, and programming continued until 3:00 A.M. Now, during the early morning hours the automated playback system can send programs to the automated school recorders started by timers (in true 1984 style). Later in the morning, programs are ready for local school playback. When the rural schools demanded equal services, the district also put an Instructional Television Fixed Service (ITFS) station on the air with its programming coming from the same cable feed. Neighboring school districts, faced with the same distribution problems, asked to join in the service. In 1985, the fourth school district will join the system.

CATV had more difficulty in resolving the videotape distribution problem in another school district. This problem was compounded by having seven CATV systems to serve the district schools located in different towns. Their solution was to interconnect all seven CATV installations by means of an ITFS station. Through careful negotiating, they were able to get a commitment of the same VHF channel on all CATV systems. The key to such favorable consideration by CATV operators was the assurance that the school district would faithfully provide a specified number of hours of programming and maintain excellent technical signal quality. The school district has kept its promises and kept these good relations.

A similar situation in another school district was resolved in the same way, but with an additional twist. Each secondary school has a terminal connected to its central computer. The media specialist can examine the next few weeks' schedule to see if the program he or she wants will be available in time to meet the teachers' (or students') request. If it will be available, the teachers plan to set their timer and videocassette recorder and record the program. If the program does not appear in the schedule prior to the time needed, the teachers, from their own terminal, may insert the program into an empty time slot and thus create their own schedule. There are plans to extend this service to the elementary schools in the near future.

Systems on a far grander scale are operational in both the United States and Canada. In two large neighboring cities in the United States, a cooperative operation involving several community colleges and school districts utilizes a combination of ITFS and CATV in providing educational services to homes and schools. Despite the lack of promised high-tech features on the CATV system, it is providing yeoman service to the community. In one Canadian province, a combination of satellite transmission and CATV provides access to 70-75 percent of the homes for college credit and general adult education programming. Furthermore, this system has direct video links between several hospitals and institutions of higher education with a tie into the satellite service.

The CATV technology itself seems to generate excitement and, in turn, inspire new uses. One example of this is that people seem to accept a totally different kind of programming when it is of interest to their community and themselves. Extravaganza programming techniques required to gain an audience's attention to a network show become superfluous when the content is of local interest. This does not mean that the general public will tolerate, much less view, poorly planned, poorly executed, and technically distracting programming. This type of programming will reflect the image of the producer that screams incompetency. It does mean, however, that an audience watching programs of local concern will focus attention more on content than technique. The producer of programming with local content can effectively communicate with an audience using minimal resources and still have a positive effect.

In this era of concern for quality education, many school people are eager to tell the community the story of the educational programs available in their schools. They are involving the members of the community in their institutions by informing them via CATV. Sometimes this comes about almost by accident as people encounter instructional programming aimed at students in school via standard CATV channels while scanning their cable channel. At other times, people intentionally tune in to watch cablecast school board meetings or minidocumentaries (produced by students and educators in the schools) that present school programs and activities.

In one small school system there was a major emphasis on good school/community relations. The district media specialist undertook the task of producing short documentaries about particular school programs. The district had a single portable video camera/recorder outfit. Some old photographic lights were pressed into service, and a high-quality, but inexpensive, microphone was purchased. With little experience, but abundant common sense, they undertook the project. They kept each program short; they used a lot of close camera work, and they produced creditable material within a schedule they knew they could meet. Although media services were frequently evident in the documentaries, the programming centered around all school programs. Programs were distributed over the CATV system at a regularly scheduled time each week, gaining a great deal of community interest. (Incidentally, the district media program received very good support thereafter.)

CATV operators are sensitive to community opinion—more than many business-people—since their mistakes are, by definition, communicated to all. Certainly educators are sensitive to public opinion, and if they engage in CATV programming, their mistakes will also be communicated to all. To ensure a good working relationship and a CATV system that is satisfactory to all, the educator and the CATV operator must communicate with each other. Initially they must communicate their expectations and their goals, and, on a continuing basis, they must discuss such matters as technical quality and programming policy. Anyone who has examined the bad experiences that frequently occur in the education/CATV relationship, has found a lack of understanding of each other's goals at the root of the problem. For example, a channel without continuous programming represents to the public a failure on the part of the CATV system first, and the agency responsible for programming the channel second. It is also true that empty channels do not sell CATV service, and selling service is the reason for the CATV system. These facts are bread-and-butter basics to the CATV operator and certainly must become so for the educational programmer if successfully implementing a CATV channel is a part of their media service.

The educator brings programming to the CATV operator, and programming is a salable item. Instructional programming may not be at the top of the priority list, but with multiple channels to fill, the operator can afford to offer programming for limited audiences. This is a benefit CATV offers beyond the off-air broadcast signal, and it has proven marketable.

As suppliers of low priority programming, educators may be forced to use nonstandard channels that, in some cases, will require special convertors. This is not a problem in reaching school buildings, but it is a handicap in reaching the general public. As systems are upgraded to a larger number of channels, the channel convertor becomes a regular part of the CATV installation, and the former nonstandard channel becomes one of the many channels on the expanded system. The educator therefore benefits as the CATV system expands.

Although two-way cable systems are not prevalent, many of the benefits of two-way systems can be utilized by combining technologies. One school system has provided a homework hotline via cable. During the early evening hours, teachers are present in a live studio to answer students' telephoned questions about their homework. When questions seem to have general interest, the teacher's responses are provided on camera and fed through the CATV system, providing information back to the student(s). Such use of program time would not be tolerated for the single channel broadcast, but it would fit easily within the minimal constraints of multichannel cable systems.

Even present-day cable systems need not be limited to video and audio signals. The standard video and audio band widths can readily accommodate computer data. Although some investment for hardware will probably be required, it will not be extremely expensive. Many cable operators may be reluctant to allow that unpleasant "noise" to be transmitted on standard channels during normal viewing hours. Frequently nonstandard channels are available, however, as well as early morning hours when viewers are less likely to encounter the "noise." The video channel can accommodate broad band data, such as a full school attendance report for all schools, via CATV. The telephone could be used to send the relatively short list of absent and tardy pupils from each school to the central computer.

With a little extra expense and effort, the vertical and horizontal intervals of the standard television signal can carry narrow band information along with the standard signal, and only those with special equipment will be aware of them. It would be a perfect system to activate a signal tone along with a message on a television screen in every principal's office to warn of bad weather and early school closing.

There are a multitude of questions that must be answered to the educator's satisfaction prior to venturing into the use of cable. Consideration should be given to instructional, administrative, and public relations communications. Such information must be generated through research and local study. They are beyond the scope of this paper. Let us, for a moment, consider the needs of the CATV operator. Customers are demanding large numbers of channels, and technology provides them without unreasonable expense. Once in existence, the channels must be filled with programming, and that can be quite expensive. Therefore, even low priority instructional programming on one channel (or even two channels) can be welcome to the CATV operator.

The ultimate test is the bottom line of the profit and loss statement. If the CATV operator anticipates much in the way of out-of-pocket expense required to serve education, the negative effect on the bottom line will be discouraging. If the emphasis is on in-kind services, the support of education will be much more appealing. If communications are important to the educator, valuable resources can be acquired through in-kind services. Being a partner in this growing and expanding technology has great potential value, as communications are at the very heart of education.

Accreditation of Educational Communications and Information Technology Programs

William F. Grady
*Professor of Education
and Coordinator of Educational Technology
Louisiana State University*

INTRODUCTION

On September 1, 1984, the accreditation guidelines for programs in educational communications and information technology became effective. These guidelines were developed by the Association for Educational Communications and Technology (AECT) and adopted by the National Commission for the Accreditation of Teacher Education (NCATE). Institutions undergoing NCATE accreditation review after September 1, 1984, will do so under these guidelines, which establish minimum standards for educational technology in the professional preparation of classroom teachers and specialists.

A more detailed and complete accounting of the events leading up to this can be found in reports by Grady (1983) and Wilkinson and Grady (1982).

The purpose of this paper is to report on AECT's current accreditation activities and NCATE's redesign efforts.

CURRENT ACTIVITIES

Program Folio Review

In preparation for an NCATE review, an institution develops an Institutional Report (IR) based on its self-study. This IR presents a description or folio of all programs and degrees to be considered and reviewed by the NCATE visitation team. These folios are then sent to the respective professional associations for review and evaluation. The association reviews the program folio and sends a summary report back to NCATE. NCATE then places this report in the hands of the evaluation team before the team goes to the campus to conduct its on-site review.

With the adoption of the AECT guidelines for the accreditation of professional preparation programs, the Association has developed a folio review process as called for by NCATE. NCATE forwards the folios to the AECT office. AECT in turn sends the folios to an accreditation review committee. The review committee is comprised of small subcommittees. Each member of the subcommittee reads and reviews the folios assigned to him or her. A report is written; it is then summarized and sent back to the NCATE office. NCATE then sends the summary as well as the original folio and IR to the NCATE evaluation team member responsible for reviewing the educational communications and information technology program(s) on campus. This team member then has in hand the AECT evaluation summary, the program folio, and the IR when he or she arrives on campus to conduct the on-site review.

NCATE/AECT Workshops

During the 1984 convention in Dallas, AECT and NCATE conducted a training workshop for the preparation of NCATE team chairpersons. Eleven persons completed the workshop and four have subsequently been assigned to serve as the chairperson of an NCATE visitation team. In addition to those AECT members who served as an NCATE team chairperson, there were more than fifty-five additional members who served on NCATE teams last year. When an institution with a media program is up for review, an AECT-trained person is placed on the team to review the media programs. It is to this person that the program folio and folio summaries are given as the team prepares for its on-site reviews.

NCATE and AECT conducted a training and orientation workshop at the Anaheim convention in January 1985 for individuals at institutions that are scheduled to be reviewed by NCATE within the next two years. This session was designed to assist such persons in preparing for all phases of an NCATE review, including conducting the self-study, preparing the IR, hosting the visitation team, and follow-up activities. Next year, plans call for a training workshop for AECT members that desire to serve on NCATE teams.

NCATE REDESIGN ACTIVITIES

In an effort to make the accreditation process more effective, NCATE has undertaken a study to redesign its accreditation activities. To date, six redesign principles have been adopted for further study. They represent important changes, and all NCATE constituent members are studying their implications and potential effect on all accreditation matters. The six principles are:

1. accreditation decisions are made for the teacher education unit,

2. continuing accreditation replaces the current concept of reaccreditation,

3. articulation is provided between state approval and national accreditation,

4. visiting team members are selected from a board of examiners, members of which are highly skilled in evaluation techniques and well trained in NCATE processes and standards,

5. five unit-focused standards replace the current six families for basic and advanced programs,

6. the NCATE Annual List is expanded to include a description of the unit and data that describe the support level for professional education programs.

These six principles are currently undergoing extensive review and comments are invited. Open hearings have been held and NCATE subcommittees are assigned to each principle. The results of implementing the above six principles could be far-reaching in their effect on professional associations and learned societies such as AECT. The implications are serious and worthy of your attention and comments. For example, what will be the effect of making accreditation decisions for the teacher education unit rather than the way it is now, that is program by program based on the application of professional association guidelines? Will a "unit" decision-making process render useless professional association and learned society program guidelines, since their emphasis is primarily on programs rather than on the unit per se? While there are other equally important issues, this one is raised in the hope that it will encourage you to develop your thoughts and reactions in relation to each of the six principles and share them with the author.

CONCLUSIONS

The past year has been a successful one. AECT's accreditation guidelines became effective September 1, 1984, and they are now being applied by NCATE review teams. The Association's folio review process has been instituted and is working very well indeed. Some sixty or so AECT members have served on NCATE review teams either as a chairperson or as a team member. NCATE training workshops for AECT members to serve on NCATE teams should continue.

The coming year promises to be an interesting one as NCATE's redesign study continues. The six redesign principles presented here represent very important changes and should be studied carefully by AECT and its members. If you have comments to share, please send them to the author.

REFERENCES

Grady, W. F. (1983). Accreditation of instructional technology. In J. Brown & S. Brown (Eds.), *Educational media yearbook 1983* (pp. 71-75). Littleton, CO: Libraries Unlimited.

Grady, W. F., & Bergeson, C. O. (1974). Accreditation and certification: A report. *Audiovisual Instruction, 19*(9), 10-11.

A proposed accreditation system (An alternative to the current NCATE system). (1983). An unpublished paper. Washington, DC: American Association of Colleges for Teacher Education.

Wilkinson, G. L., & Grady, W. F. (1982). AECT, NCATE and accreditation of instructional technology. In J. Brown & S. Brown (Eds.), *Educational media yearbook 1982* (pp. 64-68). Littleton, CO: Libraries Unlimited.

Copyright
Has Anything Changed?

Esther R. Sinofsky
Instructional Design Consultant
Los Angeles, CA

Chairperson of the
AECT Copyright Task Force

In January 1984, the Supreme Court handed down its 5-4 decision in favor of Sony, the maker of the Betamax videorecorder (*Universal City Studios, Inc. v. Sony Corporation of America*, 1984). Since then, one of the most frequently heard dialogs in educational circles goes something like this:

Educator A: "Hey, did you hear that the Supreme Court finally decided the 'Betamax' case in favor of off-air taping? Isn't it great! Now the school can tape off the air!"

Educator B (or producer): "Whoa! Not so fast! The decision only affected *home* off-air taping."

Educator A (in a daze): "You mean nothing's changed?!"

As far as educational and industrial settings are concerned, the copying-of-copyrighted-materials impasse remains unchanged. Whatever else the District, Circuit, and Supreme Courts may have agreed or disagreed on, they all agreed that the case "concerned the private, home use of VTRs [videotape recorders] for recording programs broadcast on the public airwaves without charge to the viewer" (*Universal City Studios*, 1984, p. 4091). Not only were educational and industrial settings *not* considered, but "no issue concerning the transfer of tapes to other persons, the use of home-recorded tapes for public performances, or the copying of programs transmitted on pay or cable television systems was raised" (*Universal City Studios*, 1984, pp. 4091-4092). In other words, the Court avoided ruling on such situations as (1) exchanging videotapes recorded off the air, (2) taping movies from subscription television, and (3) recording a program off the air at home to bring in for class viewing.

Presented at the Presidential Session, AECT National Conference, Dallas, Texas, 1984.

Disclaimer: This paper does *not* constitute legal advice.

Since the Supreme Court's Sony (also called "Betamax") decision has had no visible impact on educational and industrial settings, what affects copying rights — if any exist — in these milieus? Keep in mind that educational and industrial settings do not share the same rights. Business and industry, even in a training situation that one might think would qualify as education, have few and possibly no copying rights without the copyright owner's permission.

WHAT AFFECTS COPYING RIGHTS?

Article I, Section 8, Clause 8 of the U.S. Constitution empowers Congress to legislate copyright laws "to promote the progress of science and useful arts, by securing for limited times to authors and inventors the exclusive right to their respective writings and discoveries." The current embodiment of this constitutional power is the 1976 *General Revision of Copyright Law* (U.S. Congress, 1976). While all the Act's sections are equally important, the key ones affecting copying rights are Sections 101 (definitions), 105 (U.S. government works), 106 (exclusive rights), 107 (fair use), 110 (performances), and 117 (computer software).

The definitions in Section 101 are important in applying the remaining sections. For example, Section 101 defines *including* and *such as* as "illustrative and not limitative." This can affect whether or not situations are considered the sole instances where fair use might be applied.

Section 105 places a large body of works in the public domain by declaring copyright protection unavailable for any work of the U.S. government. For example, data from the Bureau of the Census, Department of Housing and Urban Development, and the Department of Commerce are all in the public domain. Add such publications as judicial decisions, executive documents, and legislative reports to these considerable informational sources, and an instant treasure trove of educational materials becomes available for copying (see Miller, 1983, for an in-depth treatment of public domain materials and databases).

Section 106 delineates the exclusive rights of copyright owners: to reproduce, prepare derivatives, distribute copies, perform, and display their copyrighted work. These rights are subject to the conditions set forth in Sections 107-118.

The judicial doctrine of fair use has been included for the first time in the copyright law in Section 107. This section, according to its legislative history, is not meant to change or freeze the doctrine. It is merely a restatement of the doctrine as it stands today.

Six purposes are indicated as possible fair use situations: (1) criticism, (2) comment, (3) news reporting, (4) teaching, (5) scholarship, and (6) research. Four criteria to be considered in evaluating whether or not a use is fair are as follows: (1) the purpose and character of the use, including whether such use is of a commercial nature or is for nonprofit educational purposes; (2) the nature of the copyrighted work; (3) the amount and substantiality of the portion used in relation to the copyrighted work as a whole; and (4) the effect of the use upon the potential market for or value of the copyrighted work. (See Sinofsky, 1984, for an in-depth treatment of fair use.) Despite its inclusion in the Act, fair use remains a problematic area for educators. Selected guidelines have been established to help resolve uncertainties.

Section 110 exempts certain performances and displays from copyright infringement. For example, this section states:

Notwithstanding the provisions of section 106, the following are not infringements of copyright:

(1) performance or display of a work by instructors or pupils in the course of face-to-face teaching activities of a nonprofit educational institution, in a classroom or similar place devoted to instruction, unless, in the case of a motion picture or other audiovisual work, the performance, or the display of individual images, is given by means of a copy that was not lawfully made under this title, and that the person responsible for the performance knew or had reason to believe was not lawfully made.

Section 117 is actually a 1980 amendment to the 1976 Act. It defines the limitations on Section 106 provisions apropos computer programs (see Helm, 1984, and Hoffman, 1984, for in-depth treatments of computer software copyright).

EDUCATIONAL FAIR USE GUIDELINES

Educational guidelines were established to help define fair use. Educational fair use guidelines for print materials and music were negotiated in 1976 when the current Copyright Act was passed. Educational guidelines for off-air taping were slower to appear. They were first announced in October 1981. And, guidelines for the educational use of computer software have yet to appear. The closest computer software has come to having guidelines, to date, is the International Council for Computers in Education's (ICCE) *Policy Statement on Network and Multiple Machine Software* (see Helm, 1984, for complete text of policy).

There are two basic problems with the guidelines: (1) Guidelines are part of the legislative history. They do not have the force of law. Anything can be read into the *Congressional Record.* (2) They were not endorsed by all the concerned parties. Some educational associations did not endorse the print guidelines, while many producers did not endorse the off-air taping guidelines (see Sinofsky, 1984, for a list of producers and their position on the fair use guidelines).

No one is really sure how the courts would look at the guidelines. The 1982 suit brought against New York University by members of the Association of American Publishers (AAP) was dropped when NYU agreed to adopt a photocopying policy statement reflecting the guidelines for print materials. On the other hand, in the last of the BOCES decisions (*Encyclopaedia Britannica Educational Corporation v. Crooks*, 1983), the judge denied BOCES's request to tape off the air for temporary use. (BOCES refers to the suit by Encyclopaedia Britannica Educational Corporation, Learning Corporation of America, and Time-Life Films against the Board of Cooperative Educational Services of Erie County, New York.) The judge pointed out that various licensing arrangements were available and that off-air taping, even for temporary use, would harm the potential markets for rentals, leases, and licenses.

The guidelines, regardless of the medium involved, apply to nonprofit, educational institutions. This automatically seems to exclude for-profit, business and industry educational situations. In addition to coordinating the suit against NYU, the AAP helped bring copyright infringement suits against two corporations. The issues centered on job-related research versus personal research photocopying. In both cases, agreements involving payment to the Copyright Clearance Center were negotiated. One result of these corporate suits was that two other corporations adjusted their photocopying policies and Copyright Clearance Center fee payments.

Video and computer software producers are also suing those persons who make copies of films and computer programs. According to the producers, buying a single copy of a program does not entitle the purchaser to make multiple copies for in-house use unless the proper licenses have been negotiated. Making multiple copies of a program for resale or for friends without paying the appropriate fees is piracy.

"FOR HOME USE ONLY"

The use outside the home of videocassette tapes labeled "for home use only" is another area of concern. Film/video distributors and producers do not always agree on the use of such tapes in the classroom. Social Studies School Service in Culver City, California, has issued a position statement, reviewed for accuracy by the Motion Picture Association of America (MPAA), allowing such tapes to be used in "face-to-face" teaching activities under Section 110(1) of the 1976 Copyright Act (see "Controversy Over," 1984, or contact James Bouras, Vice President, Secretary & Deputy General Attorney, Motion Picture Association of America, Inc., 522 Fifth Avenue, New York, NY 10036, 212/840-6161 for clarification of Section 110 rights). It must be noted, however, that the MPAA does not represent all producers. So this position statement probably does not apply to all producers.

This position statement on "for home use only" acknowledging Section 110(1) in direct teaching situations leaves unsettled other uses of such videos. For example, Section 110(2) seems to prohibit the transmission of copyrighted videocassettes to classrooms, via closed-circuit or educational broadcasts, without the copyright proprietor's permission. Libraries, especially public ones, and other organizations seem to be at a disadvantage unless they can meet all the Section 110(1) requirements. While screening videocassettes in carrels or special viewing rooms might seem private, a recent court decision (*Columbia Pictures v. Redd Horne*, 1984) deemed a commercial operation of this nature guilty of public performances of copyrighted works. The defendant was charged $36,000 in damages plus legal fees plus court costs. It is probably cheaper in the long run to negotiate a contract with the copyright owner (see Miller, 1984, for an in-depth treatment of this issue).

On February 5, 1982, the California Attorney General's office gave its opinion in answer to the Director of Corrections' query: "Does the showing of videocassette tapes of motion pictures to prison inmates by correctional authorities constitute an infringement of copyright?" (p. 106). The tapes in question were those sold "for home use only." The answer was: "The showing of videocassette tapes of motion pictures to prison inmates by correctional authorities without authorization from the copyright owner constitutes an infringement of copyright" (p. 106). In other words, the videocassettes should be secured through the appropriate distribution outlet. This means paying the $600 or more for a copy with public performance rights instead of the $40-70 for home use tapes. Of course, this is only the California Attorney General's opinion. But, it reflects the legal distinctions between public and private performances.

HAS ANYTHING CHANGED?

Copyright, as it applies to educational and industrial settings, has not changed in legislative or judicial terms. In fact, there has been no major restatement of the judicial doctrine of fair use since its appearance over 140 years ago.

The change seems to be in the search for equitable solutions to fair use. Negotiated guidelines are now deemed unsatisfactory. Licensing is increasing in popularity, especially for computer software. Producers are lobbying Congress for a surcharge on blank audiotapes and videotapes and computer disks. Legislative change, if it occurs, will begin its journey in 1985.

REFERENCES

California Attorney General's Office. (1982). 65 Ops. Cal. Atty. Gen. 106.

Columbia Pictures v. Redd Horne, No. 83-0016 (W.D.Pa. July 28, 1983), aff'd, No. 83-5786 (3rd Cir. November 23, 1984).

Controversy over "home use only" labeling leads to statement of clarification. (1984, January/February). *Access, 1*(2), 4. (Available from the Association for Educational Communications and Technology, 1126 16th St., Washington, DC 20036)

Encyclopaedia Britannica Educational Corporation v. Crooks, 447 F. Supp. 243, 197 U.S.P.Q. 280 (W.D.N.Y. 1978); 542 F. Supp. 1156, 214 U.S.P.Q. 697 (W.D.N.Y. 1982); 558 F. Suppl. 1247 (W.D.N.Y. 1983).

Helm, V. (1984). *Software quality and copyright: Issues in computer-assisted instruction.* Washington, DC: Association for Educational Communications and Technology.

Hoffman, P. S. (1984). *The software legal book.* Croton-on-Hudson, NY: Shafer Books. (Available from Shafer Books, P.O. Box 40, Croton-on-Hudson, NY 10520)

Miller, J. K. (1983). Copyright protection for bibliographies, numeric, factual, and textual databases. *Library Trends, 32*(2), 199-209.

Miller, J. K. (1984). *Using copyrighted videocassettes in classrooms and libraries.* Champaign, IL: Copyright Information Services. (Available from Copyright Information Services, 440 Tucker Road, Friday Harbor, WA 98250)

Sinofsky, E. R. (1984). *Off-air videotaping in education: Copyright issues, decisions, implications.* New York: R. R. Bowker.

U.S. Congress. (1976). *General revision of copyright law.* U.S. Code, Title 17, 90 Stat. 2541.

U.S. Constitution. Art. I, sec. 8, cl. 8.

Universal City Studios, Inc. v. Sony Corporation of America, 480 F. Supp. 429, 203 U.S.P.Q. 656 (C.D.Cal. 1979); *rev'd in part, aff'd in part*, 659 F. 2d 963, 211 U.S.P.Q. 761 (9th Cir. 1981); *rev'd*, 52 U.S.L.W. 4090 (1984).

The Technology of Learning Resources Services in Higher Education

John G. Berling
Saint Cloud State University

People knowledgeable in the field of technology, whether they work in education or not, would probably agree that the use of technology in the profession of teaching and learning has not reached its true potential. While external reasons for this apparent nonachievement of potential are numerous, few organizations have looked at internal adjustments as avenues for achieving a higher level of performance. A point of view on this subject that is seldom articulated or addressed suggests that each time a new technological breakthrough occurs, it is too often viewed as a separate and isolated entity and offered as a cure for all the existing educational ills. For this reason the positive impact of combining and integrating educational support technologies has seldom, if ever, been realized.

Library, audiovisual, television, instructional development, message design, telecommunications, interactive video, computer-assisted instruction – all these terms are familiar to everyone working in higher education. Standing alone, each is built on a substantial body of knowledge; each creates its own set of utilization and administrative problems. Generally speaking, current higher education practice finds that each of these technologies is utilized with only a remote awareness of the possibilities for positive interaction with the others. This interaction is the thrust of the learning resources organization, an organization that merits further investigation and analysis by higher education.

The learning resources services (LRS) model makes it possible to combine the strengths of the appropriate technologies to be applied to the solution of teaching and learning problems. This paper examines how one university has, during the last twenty-five years, attempted to implement the definition of instructional technology that was reported in the 1970 statement of the Commission on Instructional Technology:

> instructional technology goes beyond any particular medium or device. In this sense, instructional technology is more than the sum of its parts. It is a systematic way of designing, carrying out, and evaluating the total process of learning and teaching in terms of specific objectives, based on research in human learning and communication, and employing a combination of human and nonhuman resources to bring about more effective instruction. The widespread acceptance and application of this broad definition belongs to

the future. Though only a limited number of institutions have attempted to design instruction using such a systematic comprehensive approach, there is reason to believe that this approach holds the key to the contribution technology can make to the advancement of education (p. 19)

The LRS model has five program elements that will be analyzed: (1) human resources, (2) instructional materials, (3) instructional equipment, (4) preparation of the Information Specialist, and (5) program costs.

HUMAN RESOURCES

The human resources element in any organization creates many complex problems and challenges. So it follows that the most important tasks within the human resources element of the LRS model are hiring, assignment or placement of personnel, and development of personnel. Faculty entering the organization must possess a broad background. Academic preparation in library science, audiovisual education, and instructional development is required. The degree may be in any one of the disciplines, but preparation in several others will be required before tenure is granted. For example, a person entering the organization with a master's degree in library science must have in addition a required number of credits in instructional technology. All of the professional personnel are academically prepared to address service questions from the broadest possible perspective, for the learning resources concept does not establish a hierarchy among the media. Higher education with its traditional print orientation has been challenged to face information and communication problems without the prejudice that one medium has greater validity than another. It is the responsibility of LRS personnel to provide direction to this important information age challenge.

The most successful persons will be specialists able to adapt to changing situations, and they will be flexible and constantly motivated and challenged by the service needs of the user. New candidates must be carefully screened so that the emerging needs are addressed. The change in the discipline and practice covered within the LRS concept requires retraining, since LRS faculty and staff turnover is not as rapid as the change occurring within the associated technologies. Professional development programs must clearly be related to current trends. Given the need for objective measurement, academic evaluation, and professional development, the personal characteristics of the media professional should not be overlooked.

The growth of information combined with changes in communication systems compels LRS faculty and staff to be adaptable, creative, and flexible in their approach to service. The art of combining a portion of the two most rapidly growing industries in the United States (Porat, 1977) — information and service — and sharing these advances with university faculty and students is indeed a challenge. Today, most institutions of higher education have some people using the newer technologies in isolated situations, but few have a group of dedicated persons organized for the sole purpose of providing resources for learning based on the broadest perspective. LRS faculty and staff can provide a university with some assurance that all the resources and technology available within the budget constraints of that institution will be utilized to the fullest potential.

Any description of the human aspects is not complete without some discussion of the interchange necessary among faculty, staff, and users. The utilization of technology necessitates the development of "user friendly" equipment and procedures or routines. Staff assignments within learning resources are shifting away from backroom cataloging and similar support activities to a higher level of interaction with users. Consequently, job descriptions and recruiting emphases must reflect the changing service responsibilities.

INSTRUCTIONAL MATERIALS

University library budgets have been developed under stress for several years. Traditional formulas have been used to evaluate the adequacy and quality of collections, but the newer technologies have not been incorporated in the assessment. The most often used measure of the quality of a collection is still quantity, that is of counting volumes or things. This method certainly has some value, especially in the research library, as most information today continues to be stored and retrieved via the book. Its pervasive application, however, in higher education settings provides a cause for concern. Efforts should be made to use technology-based systems to assess how well the users needs are being fulfilled. This will allow for the development of libraries on the basis of need rather than current quantitative standards.

The periodical collection offers unique opportunities for cost-effective change without a deterioration in service. Communication systems assure availability of articles from periodicals that may then be dropped from a collection as a paper subscription. The displacement of a paper subscription (near and dear to the heart of some professors, who feel that no self-respecting library would be without one), even if it is unused, creates frustration and tension. This tension can be eased by the assurance that resource needs will be met; the confidence can be developed when appropriate services are provided in a timely manner by alternative methods.

Another important consideration in bringing information to persons in a cost-effective manner concerns departmental ownership. Sometimes services should and must be duplicated; but in such instances, clearly defined, functional needs should be articulated. The right of a faculty member in a department to have his or her learning resources needs met is paramount; however, the manner in which such needs are met should not be his or her decision alone. Competing and equally important needs in departments and agencies within the university must also be considered. For example, certain materials and equipment are useful only to certain departments, but a great many are seldom used and can be shared. How this sharing can be effectively and efficiently accomplished is the continuing challenge of LRS.

A goal of all educational institutions is the improvement of instruction so that learning by students will always be at the optimal level. To reach this goal, most universities will provide some level of instructional development. The LRS model provides a preferred location for developers to reside administratively, since books, films, videotapes, and so forth generally provide some of the needed background information. The model facilitates the interactions of the developer with the appropriate university faculty and the materials collections. It promotes instructional development as a continuous process with the goal of improving teaching through systematic planning and communication. A university faculty person entering any part of the system will be referred to the level of service and support most likely to fulfill his or her needs.

Requests that can be effectively and efficiently accommodated by the LRS model are those involving the production of instructional materials. Materials relating to content are easily retrieved from any one of the university owned collections. Further, the person managing such a collection may become a member of the production team. Collection development is also enhanced because weaknesses in the collections are often identified during the production process.

INSTRUCTIONAL EQUIPMENT

A key element of the LRS model is the acquisition and distribution of the instructional equipment. An online inventory provides current status information on all university owned instructional equipment. A computer-based maintenance, scheduling, and monitoring package assists in keeping the equipment serviceable and also provides information for future use. Practical, cost-effective equipment is acquired, because useful background information is available for decision making. All the components mentioned above must be present to make a centralized distribution system successful, but the system will still fail without the services of a LRS professional to negotiate and identify the functions that the equipment is expected to fulfill. Faculty and student needs must be served in a perceptive, nonjudgmental manner. The ability to say no to a request for a certain brand of equipment but at the same time show how the needed functions can be addressed is essential to the success of the program.

PREPARATION OF INFORMATION SPECIALISTS

An instructional program that prepares persons to become information specialists is readily accommodated by the LRS model. Graduates from this program enter careers in schools, government, public libraries, business, and industry. The teaching unit supports its own faculty based on full-time equivalent (FTE) production. These FTE positions are utilized in such a manner that the expertise of the entire LRS professional staff is available as needed. This ensures that students will be able to acquire both breadth and depth of content and experience in completion of their studies. A practicing cataloger teaches cataloging, a television producer teaches the television production class, and so on. In addition to the availability of quality faculty, accessibility to the university's information, production, and communications equipment is also assured. The students are able to interact with the types of systems they are studying in the classroom. Professional production capabilities, along with the latest technologies are available for exploration and instruction.

PROGRAM COSTS

Empirical evidence seems to indicate that expenditures for staff, equipment, and materials compare favorably with other models in institutions of similar size and scope. Comparisons of book, equipment, periodical, and personnel budgets over the past five years show that monetary outlays fall below that of comparable universities. On the other hand, service is rated high by the users as well as by outside evaluators. It is fair to generalize that the various services addressed in this paper bear similar costs to those located in different settings. Therefore, the sharing factor in the areas of faculty, equipment, and facilities seems to be providing a significant bonus to the campus community.

SUMMARY

Professional associations and organizations, along with educational institutions, have acclaimed the wonders of the new technology only to find that their early hopes for it were probably too optimistic. A statement attributed to Benjamin Franklin rings true. He said, "Human happiness is produced not so much by great pieces of good fortune that seldom happen, as by little advantages that occur every day." LRS faculty and staff can provide superior service through the identification and use of those "little advantages." The fact that this learning resources model provides a larger base from which creative projects can be launched is such an advantage. The model also provides for physical and organizational proximity, which should provide for better communication and, as a result, better service. In addition, partnerships with other institutions in the community and with business and industry are enhanced. An organization designed to acquire and share learning resources for a campus is well equipped to develop partnerships beyond the confines of the university.

This type of service, however, requires some centralization of budget, which of course is anathema to some. Centralization should, and indeed, must occur until the ability to serve iş reduced because of it. The establishment of this fine line between centralization and decentralization may well be the most critical undertaking in the establishment and operation of a LRS model. The entire faculty and staff must be involved in the drawing of that line; even while it is being drawn, forces are at work that may well affect the scope and breadth of that line. This is the nature of service.

Information specialists should be challenged by the changing needs of the users and try to meet them on a continuing basis. They must avoid the human urge to protect the more comfortable ways of the past when they obstruct the path of the present or the future. This should not be misconstrued as an attempt to show disrespect for past efforts; instead, it is an attempt to address the future in a positive manner. Not all universities can or should do exactly what this university has done. Each institution must address its resource problems in light of its own mission, but it is hoped that the idea of sharing the unused, the unknown, and the unidentified resources can be addressed in some way on every university campus. LRS is not a place; it is a program composed of people and equipment and collections. All of the components of this program exist on every campus. It is the responsibility of the administration at each campus to blend them in the most productive manner.

REFERENCES

Commission on Instructional Technology. (1970). *To Improve Learning, A Report to the President and the Congress of the United States* (Syst. of Docs. Y4. Ed 8/1:L47). Washington, DC: U.S. Government Printing Office.

Porat, M. (1977). *The information economy: Definition and Measurement* (Office of Telecommunications Special Publication 77-12 [1]). Washington, DC: U.S. Government Printing Office.

(Abbreviated Organizational Plan is on page 80.)

APPENDIX

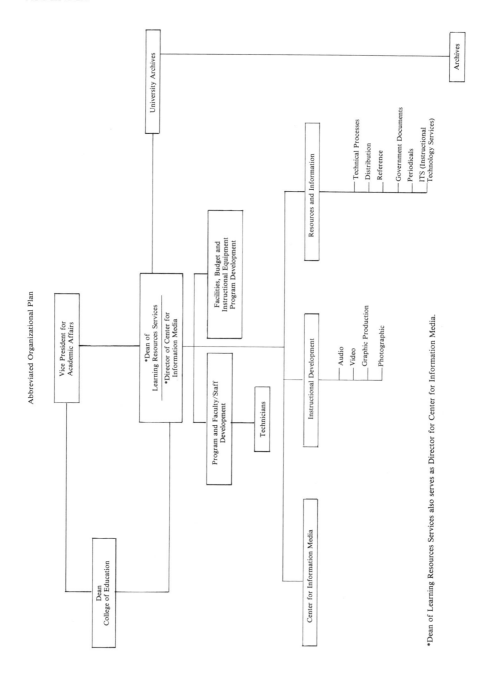

Abbreviated Organizational Plan

*Dean of Learning Resources Services also serves as Director for Center for Information Media.

The Media Technology Revolution

Ronald R. Nicoson
Director, The Media Area ASTD
Professor, Corporate/Organizational Media
Ithaca College

Have you noticed a change in media technology? It is subtle yet dynamic; gradual but certain. Our profession, media design, with its attendant implications for production, distribution, application, storage, evaluation, and more, is shifting its emphasis from the development of high technology to the provision of *service.*

We used to think of media as audiovisual materials for teaching support in education (formal) and for training support in government, industry, medicine, research, and other fields (informal). Then the information explosion of the fifties made a drastic change in how we utilized audiovisual materials.

The change was rather abrupt. Although typesetting has been around for 500 years, within relatively few years it changed from a labor-intensive effort to an instant electronic printing medium. In the past 50 years, the communication compression has taken us from our first sound movies to nearly instantaneous video satellite communication networking. And some of that communication is live interactive!

In this decade, the capacity for telephone-to-satellite transmission across the Atlantic from the United States has grown from 240 calls at any one time (in 1980), to an astounding 20,000 calls potentially possible simultaneously. By 1993, one technical projection by the satellite industry predicts a capacity of 130,000 calls globally. The "global village" is shrinking rapidly.

In the mid-eighties, nearly 100 percent of all U.S. households are equipped with at least one radio, a television, and a telephone. One video cable service predicts that approximately sixty million homes across the country will be cabled by 1990, and that 10-35 percent of those households may purchase interactive services. The estimate for home computer systems is not far behind those figures.

Technology for media communication is, therefore, reaching beyond the traditional education and industry sectors. It is an inseparable part of our home life. We speak of media systems in our homes, of media rooms designed to stimulate our senses efficiently and provide a comprehensive analysis of raw information, and of satellite computer stations away from our traditional business offices.

We involve ourselves in this media saturation in the name of quality of life. This new technology brings tangible benefits: it saves time, it is cost-effective, and it provides increased access to entertainment and education — all factors that are considered improvements in our quality of life.

And therein lies the subtle change. Our nation's economy is shifting—from manufacturing to *service*. The consumer attitude is shifting from an interest in buying products because they communicate data and create pretty graphics to a concern about finding products that provide services. Today's consumer is asking, "What will this product offer in terms of service for my business, my profession, or my leisure-time pleasures?"

Truthfully, the growth areas in education, training, and the broader spectrum of business exist in high technology "thoughtware" (as opposed to hardware). As an educator and as a trainer, are you still designing your courses and programs around the technology or hardware? Are you teaching skills limited to production and staging of the new high tech? If you are, you must change and make a generation jump into the services profession for the 1990s.

There are many associations and professions available to assist you in the generation jump to services. Among them is the American Society for Training and Development (ASTD). ASTD was established, like many of the parallel professional associations, in the 1940s, and it is dedicated to the service concept for its 23,000 national members plus another 22,000 regional and local members.

ASTD is a nonprofit educational association dedicated to serving the needs of practitioners, administrators, managers, educators, and researchers in the field of human resource development. In short, the mission of this organization is to provide service to the membership in the form of training, workshops, conferences, publications, collegial dialog in the development of competence, growth, and effectiveness of services for the human resource development field.

Within the clusters of membership are professional development groups such as Career Development, Technical Skills, International Development, Organizational Development, Sales—Marketing, and the Media Division.

The Media Division provides many services to the total membership of the society. The dominant services include:

- An annual video tape program containing excerpts from successful training programs titled *Media, Money, Results*

- An ASTD visual resource file (reference slides)

- A media resource bibliography (to be published shortly)

- A media resource directory of membership

- A growing library of resource materials including Ron Anderson's book *Selecting and Developing Media for Instruction*

- A quarterly newsletter, *Media Communicator*

- Participation in the development of a regional and eventually national computer network databank

These are some of the services of ASTD that blend well with the current media technology revolution. What are you doing in education as a teacher (or in business as a trainer) to promote interactive systems, videodiscs, computer network services, and instant graphics generated through high technology? Are you skill oriented or service oriented?

Recently, a medical media director was overheard saying, "Don't give our organization a workshop on multimedia production skills. Instead, provide us with suggestions, visual examples, abbreviated facsimiles of how we might apply this new technology effectively. Stimulate our thinking and planning. Provide us with evidence by demonstrating its effective training potential, and we will move to implement the new technologies that match our needs."

The implications of this statement are obvious for the media professional. Go beyond the skills of production and staging. Develop specific ideas or concepts for efficient information sharing and results-oriented learning. Develop content models and media formats that applied research may test in the service sector. Do this and the interactive systems, multi-image, teleconferencing, computer-generated AV materials, and *even* a well-designed flip-chart will have a permanent berth in this revolution.

REFERENCES

American Bell. (1984).

HomeServe. (1982). American Can Corporation Report.

Households TV Sets Report. (1984). *Television Digest Inc.*

Industrial Equipment News. (1983, June).

International Data Corporation Report. (1983).

Part Two

Organizations and Associations

Introduction

Section two of the *Yearbook* contains several hundred descriptive listings of media-related organizations and associations. They are organized into four general areas: the United States, Canada, the United Kingdom, and other parts of the world.

The section on the United States is preceded by a classified list with headings useful to professionals. Such a classified list is not provided for the other three sections. The subject-based classification will be useful in finding subject leads to the alphabetical listings in the United States section on organizations and associations.

Organizations listed in the United States and Canada were sent copies of the entry in the 1984 *Yearbook* and asked to update and edit the entry. Listings in this edition of the *Yearbook* reflect that extensive mailing. Listings in the United Kingdom and other parts of the world were edited by the staff. A complete review of those two sections will be done for the 1986 *Yearbook*.

Readers are reminded that changes in the communication and media arena are extensive and that information in this directory is as accurate as possible at the time of publication.

United States

This section of *EMTY 1985* includes annotated entries for several hundred associations and organizations headquartered in the United States whose interests are somehow significant to the fields of instructional technology/educational media, library and information science, communication, computer technology, training/management in business/industry, publishing, and many others.

Readers who know only the acronym for some association or organization of interest to them may refer to the index to obtain its full name.

CLASSIFIED LIST

Adult, Continuing, Distant Education
Audio (Records, Audiocassettes and Tapes, Telephone, Radio); Listening
Audiovisual (General)
Censorship
Children-, Youth-Related Organizations
Communication
Community Resources
Computers, Computer Software, Computer Hardware
Copyright
Databases; Networks
Education (General)
Education (Higher)
Equipment (Manufacturing, Maintenance, Testing, Operating)
ERIC-Related
Facilities
Films — Educational/Instructional/Documentary
Films — Theatrical (Film Study, Criticism, Production)
Films — Training
Futures

Games, Toys, Drama, Play, Simulation, Puppetry
Graphics
Health-Related Organizations
Information Science
Instructional Technology/Design/Development
International Education
Libraries — Academic, Research
Libraries — Public
Libraries — Special
Libraries and Media Centers — General, School
Microforms; Micrographics
Museums; Archives
Photography
Print — Books
Production (Media)
Publishing
Rating/Review (Materials)
Religious Education
Research
Selection, Collections, Processing (Materials)
Special Education
Training
Video (Cassette, Broadcast, Cable, Satellite, Videodisc, Videotex)

Adult, Continuing, Distant Education
Agency for International Development
American Library Association. Reference and
  Adult Services Division
Association for Continuing Higher Education
Association for Educational Communications
  and Technology
Clearinghouse on Development Communication
Continuing Library Education Network and
  Exchange
ERIC Clearinghouse on Adult, Career, and
  Vocational Education
Multinational Project in Educational
  Technology
National Adult Education Clearinghouse
National Aeronautics and Space
  Administration
National Center for Appropriate Technology
National University Continuing Education
  Association
Network for Continuing Medical Education
Non-Formal Education Information Center
Society of Manufacturing Engineers
World Radio Missionary Fellowship, Inc.

Audio (Records, Audiocassettes and Tapes,
  Telephone, Radio); Listening
American Federation of Television and Radio
  Artists
American Radio Relay League, Inc.
American Women in Radio and Television
Association for Recorded Sound Collections
Association of North American Radio Clubs
Board for International Broadcasting
Clearinghouse on Development Communication
Corporation for Public Broadcasting
Federal Communications Commission
International Tape/Disc Association
Milo Ryan Phonoarchive
Museum of Broadcasting
Mutual Broadcasting System
National Alliance of Media Arts Centers, Inc.
National Association for Better Broadcasting
National Association of Broadcasters
National Association of Business and Edu-
  cational Radio, Inc.
National Public Radio
National Radio Broadcasters Association
National Religious Broadcasters
Oral History Association
Public Broadcasting Service
Public Television Library
Radio Free Europe/Radio Liberty
Radio Information Service Unit, AFB
Recording Industry Association of America
Scanner Association of North America
United States Information Agency

Audiovisual (General)
Association for Educational Communications
  and Technology (AECT)
(AECT) Division of Educational Media
  Management

(AECT) Division of School Media Specialists
Association of Audio-Visual Technicians
HOPE Reports, Inc.

Censorship
Freedom of Information Center
Women's Institute for Freedom of the Press

Children-, Youth-Related Organizations
American Center of Films for Children
(ALA) Association for Library Service to
  Children
(ALA) Young Adult Services
Association for Childhood Education
  International
Children's Television International, Inc.
Children's Television Workshop
Close Up Foundation
Council for Exceptional Children
ERIC Clearinghouse on Elementary and Early
  Childhood Education
ERIC Clearinghouse on Handicapped and
  Gifted Children
Experience Education
Media Center for Children
National Association for Creative Children
  and Adults
National Association for the Education of
  Young Children
National PTA
Young People's Logo Association

Communication
American Newspaper Publishers Association
  ANPA Foundation
American Radio Relay League, Inc.
Communications Satellite Corporation
East-West Institute of Culture and
  Communication
EDUCOM (Interuniversity Communications
  Council)
ERIC Clearinghouse on Information Resources
ERIC Clearinghouse on Languages and
  Linguistics
ERIC Clearinghouse on Reading and Com-
  munication Skills
Freedom of Information Center
International Association of Business
  Communicators
International Communication Association
The International Communications Industries
  Association
International Friendship League, Inc.
National Council of the Churches of Christ –
  Communication Commission
Office of Communications Technology,
  American Foundation for the Blind, Inc.
Speech Communication Association
Telecommunications Research and Action
  Center
Western Educational Society for Tele-
  communications
Women in Film

Women's Educational Equity Act WEEA
Center
World Pen Pals

Community Resources
Teachers and Writers

Computers, Computer Software, Computer Hardware
Association for Computing Machinery
(AECT) Division of Information Systems and Computers
Association for the Development of Computer-Based Instructional Systems
Computer Using Educators
Digital Equipment Computer Users Society
International Council for Computers in Education
Minnesota Educational Computing Consortium
Museum Computer Network, Inc.
PLATO
Professional Software Programmers Association
RICE (Resources in Computer Education)
Society for Computer Simulation
The Society of Data Educators
SOFTSWAP
Southwest Resource (Computer) Center
Young People's Logo Association

Copyright
Copyright Clearance Center
Copyright Office
International Copyright Information Center
Television Licensing Center

Databases; Networks
American Business Network
AVLINE
DEVELOP Search Service
DIALOG Information Services
ERIC (Educational Resources Information Center) (See separate entries for the various clearinghouses.)
ERIC Document Reproduction Service
ERIC Processing and Reference Facility
NEXIS/Information Bank
OCLC, Inc.
PLATO
Project BEST
RICE (Resources in Computer Education)
SDC® Information Services
The Source
SpecialNet
(AECT) Tech Central
Video Data Bank

Education (General)
American Association of School Administrators
American Council on Education
American Montessori Society

American Society of Educators
Association for Childhood Education International
(AECT) Minorities in Media
Association for the Development of Computer-Based Instructional Systems
Association of Teacher Educators
Center for Educational Policy and Management
Center for Instructional Research and Curriculum Evaluation
Council for Basic Education
Council of Chief State School Officers
Editorial Projects in Education
Education Commission of the States
Education Development Center, Inc.
ERIC Clearinghouse on Educational Management
ERIC Clearinghouse on Elementary and Early Childhood Education
ERIC Clearinghouse on Handicapped and Gifted Children
ERIC Clearinghouse on Rural Education and Small Schools
ERIC Clearinghouse on Science, Mathematics, and Environmental Education
ERIC Clearinghouse on Social Studies/Social Science Education
ERIC Clearinghouse on Teacher Education
ERIC Clearinghouse on Urban Education
Experience Education
Institute for Development of Educational Activities, Inc.
Institute for Research on Teaching
International Reading Association
National Art Education Association
National Association for the Education of Young Children
National Association for the Exchange of Industrial Resources
National Association of State Boards of Education
National Association of State Educational Media Professionals
National Association of State Textbook Administrators
National Center for Appropriate Technology
National Clearinghouse on Bilingual Education
National Council for the Accreditation of Teacher Education
National Council of Teachers of English
(NCTE) Commission on Media
National Education Association
National Endowment for the Arts
National Endowment for the Humanities
National Institute of Education
National Science Teachers Association
Research and Development Center for Teacher Education
Social Science Education Consortium, Inc.
Southwest Regional Laboratory for Educational Research and Development

Education (Higher)
American Association for Higher Education
American Association of Colleges for Teacher
  Education
American Association of Community and
  Junior Colleges
American Association of State Colleges and
  Universities
American Council on Education
Associated Western Universities
Association for Continuing Higher Education
(AECT) Community College Association for
  Instruction and Technology
(AECT) Northwest College and University
  Council for the Management of Educational
  Technology
Association of American Colleges
EDUCOM (Interuniversity Communications
  Council)
ERIC Clearinghouse for Junior Colleges
ERIC Clearinghouse on Higher Education
University and College Designers Association
University Consortium for Instructional Devel-
  opment and Technology
University Film and Video Association

**Equipment (Manufacturing, Maintenance,
  Testing, Operating)**
(ALA) Library and Information Technology
  Association
(ALA) Resources and Technical Services
  Division
American National Standards Institute
Association of Audio-Visual Technicians
Electronics Industries Association
EPIE Institute
National School Supply and Equipment
  Association
NAVA/The International Communications
  Industries Association
Society of Motion Picture and Television
  Engineers

ERIC-Related
ERIC Educational Resources Information
  Center
ERIC Clearinghouse for Junior Colleges
ERIC Clearinghouse on Adult, Career, and
  Vocational Education
ERIC Clearinghouse on Counseling and
  Personnel Services
ERIC Clearinghouse on Educational Manage-
  ment
ERIC Clearinghouse on Elementary and Early
  Childhood Education
ERIC Clearinghouse on Handicapped and
  Gifted Children
ERIC Clearinghouse on Higher Education
ERIC Clearinghouse on Information Resources
ERIC Clearinghouse on Languages and
  Linguistics
ERIC Clearinghouse on Reading and Com-
  munication Skills

ERIC Clearinghouse on Rural Education and
  Small Schools
ERIC Clearinghouse on Science, Mathematics,
  and Environmental Education
ERIC Clearinghouse on Social Studies/Social
  Science Education
ERIC Clearinghouse on Teacher Education
ERIC Clearinghouse on Tests, Measurement,
  and Evaluation
ERIC Clearinghouse on Urban Education
ERIC Document Reproduction Service
ERIC Processing and Reference Facility

Facilities
Educational Facilities Laboratories
National Association for the Exchange of
  Industrial Resources

**Films – Educational/Instructional/
  Documentary**
Association of Independent Video and Film-
  makers and the Foundation for Independent
  Video and Filmmakers
Consortium of University Film Centers
Council on International Non-theatrical Events
Educational Film Library Association
Film Library Information Council
FILMNET: The Film Users Network
Grange Farm Film Foundation
Great Plains National ITV Library
Media Center for Children
The Media Project, Inc.
National Audiovisual Center
National Film Board of Canada
National Information Center for Educational
  Media
National Medical Audiovisual Center
Pacific Film Archive
PCR: Films and Video in the Behavioral
  Sciences
Southwestern Film Consortium
Television Licensing Center
University Film and Video Association

**Films – Theatrical (Film Study, Criticism,
  Production)**
Academy of Motion Picture Arts and Sciences
American Center of Films for Children
American Film Institute
American Society of Cinematographers
Film Advisory Board
Film Arts Foundation
Film Society of Lincoln Center
Hollywood Film Archive
International Film and TV Festival of New
  York
Motion Picture Association of America, Inc.
National Film Information Service
National Film Society

Films — Training

(AECT) Industrial Training and Education Division

Association of Independent Video and Filmmakers and the Foundation for Independent Video and Filmmakers

Consortium of University Film Centers

Council on International Non-theatrical Events

Educational Film Library Association

Grange Farm Film Foundation

Great Plains National ITV Library

National Audiovisual Center

National Film Board of Canada

National Information Center for Educational Media

Training Media Distributors Association

University Film and Video Association

Futures

Institute for the Future

Office of Technology Assessment

World Future Society

Games, Toys, Drama, Play, Simulation, Puppetry

North American Simulation and Gaming Association

Puppeteers of America, Inc.

Society for Computer Simulation

Graphics

American Institute of Graphic Arts

International Graphic Arts Education Association

Newspaper Features Council, Inc.

University and College Designers Association

Health-Related Organizations

American Medical Association, Department of Audio-Visual and Self-Learning Programs

American Society for Health Manpower Education and Training of the American Hospital Association

(AECT) Health Education Media Association

Behavioral Sciences Research Branch

Biological Photographic Association

Health Sciences Communication Association

Medical Library Association

National Association for Visually Handicapped

National Library of Medicine

National Medical Audiovisual Center

Network for Continuing Medical Education

Information Science

(AECT) Division of Information Systems and Computers

Association for Library and Information Science Education

Center for Arts Information

Information Industry Association

International Information Management Congress

National Commission on Libraries and Information Science

National Diffusion Network

National Technical Information Service

Instructional Technology/Design/Development

Association for Educational Communications and Technology

(AECT) Community College Association for Instruction and Technology

(AECT) Division of Educational Media Management

(AECT) Division of Information Systems and Computers

(AECT) Division of Instructional Development

(AECT) Women in Instructional Technology

Educational Technology Publications

Institute for Development of Educational Activities, Inc.

Multinational Project in Educational Technology

National Society for Performance and Instruction

Office of Technology Assessment

Society for Applied Learning Technology

University Consortium for Instructional Development and Technology

International Education

Agency for International Development

(AECT) International Division

Clearinghouse on Development Communication

Council on International Educational Exchange

Institute of International Education

International Friendship League, Inc.

The Society for Intercultural Education, Training, and Research

United Nations Radio and Visual Services

U.S. Advisory Commission on Public Diplomacy

United States Information Agency

Voice of America

World Pen Pals

World Radio Missionary Fellowship, Inc.

Libraries — Academic, Research

American Library Association

(ALA) Association of College and Research Libraries

Libraries — Public

American Library Association

(ALA) Audiovisual Committee (of the Public Library Association)

(ALA) Committee on Instruction in the Use of Libraries

(ALA) Library Administration and Management Association

(ALA) Library and Information Technology Association

(ALA) Public Library Association

(ALA) Reference and Adult Services Division

(ALA) Resources and Technical Services Division
(ALA) Young Adult Services Division

Libraries – Special
American Library Association
(ALA) Association for Library Service to Children
(ALA) Association of Specialized and Cooperative Library Agencies

Libraries and Media Centers – General, School
American Library Association
(ALA) American Association of School Librarians
Association for Educational Communications and Technology
(AECT) Division of School Media Specialists
(AECT) National Association of Regional Media Centers
(AECT) Northwest College and University Council for the Management of Educational Technology
(AECT) Women in Instructional Technology
Association for Library and Information Science Education
Catholic Library Association
Continuing Library Education Network and Exchange
Film Library Information Council
International Association of School Librarianship
Library of Congress
National Association of State Educational Media Professionals
National Commission on Libraries and Information Science
On-Line Audiovisual Catalogers, Inc.
U.S. Department of Education
U.S. Department of Education, Center for Libraries and Education Improvement

Microforms; Micrographics
See ERIC-related entries.

Museums; Archives
American Federation of Arts
(AECT) Archives
Association of Science-Technology Centers
Association of Systematics Collections
Computer Museum
Hollywood Film Archive
International Museum of Photography at George Eastman House
Lawrence Hall of Science
Milo Ryan Phonoarchive
Museum Computer Network, Inc.
Museum of Broadcasting
Museum of Holography
Museum of Modern Art
National Alliance of Media Arts Centers, Inc.
National Film Information Service
National Gallery of Art

Pacific Film Archive
Smithsonian Institution
Theatre Library Association
UCLA Film, Television, and Radio Archives

Photography
American Photographic Historical Society, Inc.
American Society of Cinematographers
Biological Photographic Association
International Center of Photography
International Museum of Photography at George Eastman House
Museum of Holography
National Free Lance Photographers Association
National Photography Instructors Association
National Press Photographers Association
Photographic Society of America
Society for Photographic Education
Society of Photo Technologists
Society of Photographic Scientists and Engineers
University and College Designers Association
University Film and Video Association

Print – Books
American Booksellers Association
Association of American Publishers

Production (Media)
American Society of Cinematographers
Association for Educational Communications and Technology
(AECT) Media Design and Production Division
Association of Independent Video and Film-makers and the Foundation for Independent Video and Filmmakers
Biological Photographic Association
Film Arts Foundation
The Media Project, Inc.
The NETWORK, Inc.
Southwest Alternate Media Project
Southwestern Film Consortium
Women in Film
Women's Educational Equity Act Publishing Center

Publishing
American Booksellers Association, Inc.
American Foundation for the Blind, Inc.
Association of American Publishers
Authors' League of America
Government Printing Office
Magazine Publishers Association
National Association of State Textbook Administrators
Society of Authors' Representatives
Universal Serials and Book Exchange

Rating/Review (Materials)
American Center of Films for Children
National Film Society

Religious Education
(AECT) Association for Media Educators in
Religion
National Religious Broadcasters

Research
Associated Western Universities
(AECT) Research and Theory Division
(AECT) ECT Foundation
Center for Advanced Visual Studies
Center for Educational Policy and
Management
Center for Instructional Research and Curriculum Evaluation
Center for Interactive Programs
Center for Learning and Telecommunications
Center on Evaluation, Development, and
Research
Clearinghouse on Development Communication
Computer and Information Science Research
Center
East-West Communication Institute
Education Development Center
Educational Facilities Laboratories
ERIC clearinghouses. See ERIC-related entries.
Far West Laboratory for Educational Research
and Development
HOPE Reports, Inc.
Institute for Development of Educational
Activities, Inc.
Institute for Research on Teaching
National Diffusion Network
National Institute of Education
National Science Foundation
National Technical Information Service
Nebraska Videodisc Design/Production Group
The NETWORK, Inc.
Northwest Regional Educational Laboratory
Research and Development Center for Teacher
Education
Social Science Education Consortium, Inc.
Society for Intercultural Education, Training,
and Research
Southwest Regional Laboratory for Educational
Research and Development
Telecommunications Information Center, The
Gelman Library

Selection, Collections, Processing (Materials)
Center for Teaching about China
National Information Center for Educational
Media

Special Education
American Foundation for the Blind
(AECT) Association for Special Education
Technology
Council for Exceptional Children
ERIC Clearinghouse on Handicapped and
Gifted Children
Handicapped Educational Exchange
National Association for Visually Handicapped

National Clearinghouse on Bilingual Education
Office for Communications Technology, American Foundation for the Blind, Inc.
Radio Information Service Unit, American
Foundation for the Blind
Recording for the Blind, Inc.

Training
American Electronics Association
American Management Association
American Society for Training and
Development
(ASTD) Media Division
Association for Educational Communications
and Technology
(AECT) Federal Educational Technology
Association
(AECT) Industrial Training and Education
Division
Audio-Visual Institute for Effective Communications
ERIC Clearinghouse on Adult, Career, and
Vocational Education
ERIC Clearinghouse on Tests, Measurement,
and Evaluation
Grange Farm Film Foundation
International Association of Business
Communicators
National Aeronautics and Space Administration
National Association of Business and Educational Radio, Inc.
National Cable Television Institute
National Society for Performance and Instruction
Non-Formal Education Information Center
Society for Applied Learning Technology
Society of Manufacturing Engineers

**Video (Cassette, Broadcast, Cable, Satellite,
Videodisc, Videotex)**
Agency for Instructional Television
American Federation of Television and Radio
Artists
American Women in Radio and Television
Association for Educational Communications
and Technology
(AECT) Division of Telecommunications
Association of Independent Video and Film-
makers and the Foundation for Independent
Video and Filmmakers
Center for Interactive Programs
Center for Learning and Telecommunications
Central Educational Network
Children's Television International
Children's Television Workshop
Clearinghouse on Development Communication
Close Up Foundation
Communications Satellite Corporation
Corporation for Public Broadcasting
CTIC Associates
Federal Communications Commission

Federal Communications Commission, Cable Television Bureau
Federal Communications Commission, Consumer Assistance Office
Great Plains National ITV Library
International Association of Satellite Users and Suppliers
International Tape/Disc Association
International Telecommunications Satellite Organization
International Teleconferencing Association
International Television Association
National Alliance of Media Arts Centers, Inc.
National Association for Better Broadcasting
National Association of Broadcasters
National Cable Television Institute
National Federation of Community Broadcasters
National Federation of Local Cable Programmers
National Video Clearinghouse, Inc.
Nebraska Videodisc Design/Production Group
PBS VIDEO

Prime Time School Television
Project BEST
Public Broadcasting Service
Public Service Satellite Consortium
Public Television Library
Recording Industry Association of America
Society of Cable Television Engineers
Society of Motion Picture and Television Engineers, Inc.
Telecommunications Information Center, The Gelman Library
Telecommunications Research and Action Center
Television Information Office
United States Information Agency
University Film and Video Association
Video Data Bank
Videotex Industry Association
Voice of America
Western Educational Society for Telecommunications
Women in Film

ALPHABETICAL LIST

Academy of Motion Picture Arts and Sciences (AMPAS). 8949 Wilshire Blvd., Beverly Hills, CA 90211. (213) 278-8990. An honorary, nonprofit organization composed of outstanding individuals in all phases of motion pictures. Seeks to advance the arts and sciences of motion picture technology and artistry. Presents annual film awards; offers artist-in-residence programs; operates reference library and National Film Information Service.

Agency for Instructional Television (AIT). Box A, Bloomington, IN 47402. (812) 339-2203. Edwin G. Cohen, Exec. Dir. An American-Canadian organization established to strengthen education through television and other technologies. Its primary function is to develop and coordinate cooperative instructional television projects involving state and provincial agencies. AIT also acquires and distributes television and printed materials for use as a learning resource. Board of directors consists of Americans and Canadians, and establishes areas for project exploration on the basis of needs expressed at periodic regional meetings. AIT also organizes a number of smaller cooperative efforts to finance and guide production of exceptionally promising classroom series conceived by individual agencies. *Membership:* 3,000. *Publications: AIT Newsletter; AIT Catalog;* and *Give and Take.*

Agency for International Development (AID/S&T/ED). U.S. Department of State, Bureau for Science and Technology, Office of Education, Room 609 SA-18, Washington, DC 20523. (703) 235-8980. Conducts a variety of media activities relating directly to U.S. overseas development programs. Stresses the use of media to extend the reach of educational services so that more people, particularly in remote areas, are offered learning experiences. The use of radio to deliver information is a current priority. Another activity is the rural satellite program, which is employing communications satellite technology for rural education purposes. Educational microcomputing work is beginning.

American Association for Higher Education (AAHE). One Dupont Cir. NW, Suite 600, Washington, DC 20036. (202) 293-6440. Russell Edgerton, Pres. A nonprofit, professional association organized to clarify and help resolve critical issues in postsecondary education through conferences, publications, and special projects, some of which are related to educational media and technology. Includes Center for Learning and Telecommunications. *Membership:* 6,000. *Dues:* $55.00. *Publications: Telescan; AAHE Bulletin; Current Issues in Higher Education.*

American Association of Colleges for Teacher Education (AACTE). One Dupont Cir. NW, Suite 600, Washington, DC 20036. (202) 293-2450. David G. Imig, Exec. Dir. Seeks revitalization of the preparation of professional education personnel, serves as a leadership laboratory for trainers of educational personnel through seminars, conferences and special projects in cooperation with other professional associations and government agencies. Current activities include conferences and publications on education and the human service professions, education of handicapped persons, excellence in teacher education competency assessment, bilingual and multicultural education, yearly study tours abroad in conjunction with the World International Council on Education. *Membership:* 725. *Publications: AACTE Briefs; Journal of Teacher Education; Directory.*

American Association of Community and Junior Colleges (AACJC). One Dupont Cir. NW, Suite 610, Washington, DC 20036. (202) 293-7050. Promotes two-year, community-based colleges. Sponsors an instructional telecommunications consortium. *Membership:* 883 inst.; 97 nat. assoc.; 214 indiv. *Publication: Community and Junior College Journal.*

American Association of Museums (AAM). 1055 Thomas Jefferson St. NW, Washington, DC 20007. (202) 338-5300. An organization of large and small museums as well as museum professionals. *Membership:* 7,000. *Publications: Museum News* (bi-mo.); *Aviso* (mo.).

American Association of School Administrators (AASA). 1801 N. Moore St., Arlington, VA 22209. (703) 528-0700. Offers an extensive professional development program through the National Academy for School Executives (NASE) plus an annual convention and several conferences. Leadership for Learning programs are carried out through the AASA National Center for the Improvement of Learning (NCIL). Represents educational leaders in Washington and before the national media. Members include school administrators and other educational leaders in all parts of the world. *Membership:* 18,000. *Dues:* $125.00. *Publications: The School Administrator;* Critical Issues reports and other books; audiovisual and video programs. AASA ONLINE is the association's electronic information service.

American Association of State Colleges and Universities (AASCU). One Dupont Cir. NW, Suite 700, Washington, DC 20036. (202) 293-7070. Allan W. Ostar, Pres. Provides a forum for colleges and universities to present ideas on national affairs and higher education to the public, conducts workshops, and distributes films and publications. *Membership:* 354 inst.

American Booksellers Association, Inc. (ABA). 122 E. 42nd St., New York, NY 10168. (212) 867-9060. A trade organization of large and small firms engaged in retail book sales. *Publications: ABA Book Buyers Handbook; ABA Basic Book List; A Manual on Bookselling; American Bookseller; ABA Newswire;* and *ABA Sidelines Directory.*

American Business Network (BizNet). 1615 H St. NW, Washington, DC 20062. (202) 463-5697. Doug Widner, contact person. A satellite television subscription service covering government and regulatory matters as they relate to business and industry, trade and professional associations, and chambers of commerce. News and talk show programs for cable and broadcast, video conference services. *Dues:* $5,000 U.S. Chamber of Commerce members; $3,500.00 inst.

American Center of Films for Children (ACFC). USC School of Cinema-TV, University Park, Los Angeles, CA 90089. (213) 743-8632. Shanta Herzog, Exec. Dir. ACFC is a national organization of parents, children, teachers, librarians, entertainers, film producers, and distributors whose purpose is to encourage and support the production, distribution, and exhibition of excellent films for children. ACFC represents the United States in the International Centre of Films for Children and Young People in Paris. Activities include the Los Angeles International Children's Film Festival; Ruby Slipper awards for the best children's films of the year; and sponsorship of film workshops for teachers and librarians in Los Angeles County. *Dues:* $20.00 per family. *Publication: Children's Film International: A Review Journal of the International Children's Film Festival.*

American Council on Education (ACE). One Dupont Cir. NW, Washington, DC 20036. (202) 833-4700. ACE comprises more than 1,600 higher education institutions — represented by their presidents and chancellors — and national and regional education associations. It is the major nongovernmental organization in the United States dedicated to the improvement of postsecondary education. Activities include research and policy analysis, legislative and judicial representation, coordination among the higher education associations, recommendations of credit for learning in noncollegiate settings, operation of the GED testing program, and provision of library and information services to members and media. *Publications: Educational Record* (q); and *Higher Education.*

American Dental Association (ADA). 211 E. Chicago Ave., Chicago, IL 60611. (312) 440-2659. Offers ADA-produced dental health instructional materials for rent and sale.

American Educational Research Association (AERA). 1230 17th St. NW, Washington, DC 20036. (202) 223-9485. Amy Shaughnessy, Dir. A national professional organization of educators and behavioral scientists active and/or interested in educational research and its application to educational problems. Sponsors annual meetings featuring presentations of original research findings. *Membership:* 14,000.

American Electronics Association (AEA). 2680 Hanover St., Palo Alto, CA 94304. (415) 857-9300. Kaye Storm Mesa, Mgr. National trade association of electronics companies. Involved in federal and state legislation related to technical education; compiles data on technical manpower needs within the electronics industry. Sponsors foundation to support engineering education through graduate student fellowships, faculty development grants, and equipment donations in electrical/computer engineering and computer science.

The American Federation of Arts (AFA). 41 E. 65th St., New York, NY 10021. (212) 988-7700. Wilder Green, Dir. National nonprofit museum service agency that organizes exhibitions and film programs and circulates them to museums, university art galleries, and art centers throughout the country and abroad. *Membership:* 1,200 ind.; 325 inst. *Publication:* newsletter (3/yr.).

American Federation of Television and Radio Artists (AFTRA). 1350 Ave. of the Americas, New York, NY 10019. (212) 265-7700. Sanford Wolff, Exec. Secy. A labor union representing some 54,000 professionals in the field, including announcers, actors, newspersons, dancers, and others. *Publications: AFTRA Magazine*; and local newsletters.

American Film Institute (AFI). JFK Center for the Performing Arts, Washington, DC 20566. (202) 828-4000. Jean Firstenberg, Dir. A nonprofit organization established by the National Endowment for the Arts to preserve the heritage and advance the art of film and television in America. Activities include a national conservatory for advanced filmmakers, safeguarding more than 13,000 American films for preservation in the Library of Congress, publication of the *American Film Institute Catalog of Motion Pictures Produced in the United States*, Feature Films, and a planned catalog of every film produced in the United States. Makes grants to independent filmmakers and commissions historical research projects. *Membership:* 140,000. *Dues:* $20.00. *Publications: AFI's Guide to College Film Courses in Film & TV; American Film.*

American Foundation for the Blind, Inc. (AFB). 15 W. 16th St., New York, NY 10011. (212) 620-2020. Herb Goro, Dir. of PR. A nonprofit organization providing direct and technical assistance to blind and visually impaired people and their families, and to professionals in specialized agencies, community agencies, organizations, schools, and corporations. Direct assistance includes information and referral, special consumer products, recording of talking books, a travel identification service, and general educational materials. Technical assistance includes training, consultation, professional publications, and social and technological research. *Publications: AFB Newsletter; Journal of Visual Impairment*; and others.

American Institute of Graphic Arts (AIGA). 1059 3rd Ave., New York, NY 10021. (212) 752-0813. Caroline Hightower, Dir. Conducts an interrelated program of competitions, exhibitions, publications, educational activities, and projects in the public interest to promote the advancement of graphic design. *Dues:* $30.00 student; $115.00 resident; $100.00 nonresident. *Publications: AIGA Journal; Graphic Design; Symbol Signs.*

American Library Association (ALA). 50 E. Huron St., Chicago, IL 60611. (312) 944-6780. Robert Wedgeworth, Dir. The ALA is the oldest and largest national library association. Members represent all types of libraries — state, public, school, academic, and special libraries serving persons in government, commerce, armed services, hospitals, prisons, and other institutions. Chief advocate for people of United States to achieve/ maintain high-quality library information services by protection of the right to read, educating librarians, improving services, or making information accessible to everyone. *Membership:* 39,477. *Publication: American Libraries.*

(ALA) American Association of School Librarians (AASL). 50 E. Huron St., Chicago, IL 60611. (312) 944-6780. Alice E. Fite, Exec. Dir. Seeks general improvement and extension of school library media services as a means of strengthening education. Gives special attention to evaluation, selection, interpretation, and utilization of library media. Activities and projects of the association are divided among 39 committees and two sections of school library supervisors and nonpublic school libraries. *Membership:* 5,500. *Publications: School Library Media Quarterly*; and others.

(ALA) American Library Trustee Association (ALTA). 50 E. Huron St., Chicago, IL 60611. (312) 944-6780. Sharon Jordan, Prog. Off. Interested in the development of effective library service for all people in all types of communities and in all types of libraries. Members are concerned, as policymakers, with organizational patterns of service, with the development of competent personnel, and provision of adequate financing, the passage of suitable legislation, and the encouragement of citizen support for libraries. *Membership:* 1,600. *Dues:* $45.00. *Publication: ALTA Newsletter.*

(ALA) Association for Library Service to Children (ALSC). 50 E. Huron St., Chicago, IL 60611. (312) 944-6780. Ann Weeks, Exec. Dir. Interested in the improvement and extension of library services for children in all types of libraries, evaluation and selection of book and nonbook library materials, and the improvement of techniques of library services for children from preschool through the eighth grade or junior high school. Annual conference, midwinter meeting, and summer conference with the ALA. *Committees:* Several, open to members of ALA. *Membership:* 3,696. *Publications: Top of the News; ALSC Newsletter.*

(ALA) Association of College and Research Libraries (ACRL). 50 E. Huron St., Chicago, IL 60611. (312) 944-6780. JoAn Segal, Exec. Dir. Represents librarians and promotes libraries of postsecondary, research, and specialized institutions. Has available quantitative and qualitative library standards for collection development, staffing, space needs, administration, and governance. Publishes statistics on academic libraries. *Committees:* Academic Status, Audiovisual, Continuing Education, Legislation, Publications, Standards and Accreditation. *Membership:* 9,000. *Dues:* $25.00. *Publications: College and Research Libraries News; Choice.* Free list of materials available.

(ALA) Association of Specialized and Cooperative Library Agencies (ASCLA). 50 E. Huron St., Chicago, IL 60611. (312) 944-6780. Sandra M. Cooper, Dir. Represents state library agencies, multitype library cooperatives, and libraries serving special clientele to promote the development of coordinated library services with equal access to information and material for all persons. The activities and programs of the association are carried out by over twenty committees, seven sections, and various discussion groups. Write for free checklist of materials. *Membership:* 2,000. *Publication: Interface.*

(ALA) Audiovisual Committee (of the Public Library Association). 50 E. Huron St., Chicago, IL 60611. (312) 944-6780. Shirley Mills-Fischer, Exec. Dir. Studies and promotes use of audiovisual materials in public libraries.

(ALA) Committee on Instruction in the Use of Libraries (IULC). 50 E. Huron St., Chicago, IL 60611. (312) 944-6780. Andrew Hansen, Staff Liaison. Reviews and recommends activities on instruction in the use of libraries.

(ALA) Library Administration and Management Association (LAMA). 50 E. Huron St., Chicago, IL 60611. (312) 944-6780. Roger H. Parent, Dir. Encourages the study of administrative theory to improve library administration and to foster general improvement of library administrative skills. *Publication: LAMA Newsletter.*

(ALA) Library and Information Technology Association (LITA). 50 E. Huron St., Chicago, IL 60611. (312) 944-6780. Donald P. Hammer, Dir. Concerned with library automation, the information sciences, and the design, development, and implementation of automated systems in those fields, including systems development, electronic data processing, mechanized information retrieval, operations research, standards development, telecommunications, video communications, networks and collaborative efforts, management techniques, information technology and other aspects of audiovisual activities, and hardware applications related to all of those areas. *Membership:* 5,500. *Dues:* $25.00/yr. *Publications: Information Technology and Libraries; LITA Newsletter.*

(ALA) Public Library Association (PLA). 50 E. Huron St., Chicago, IL 60611. (312) 944-6780. Shirley Mills-Fischer, Exec. Dir. Seeks to expand and improve general public library services and to emphasize and clarify their social responsibilities. *Membership:* 5,600. *Dues:* $25.00/yr., open to all ALA members. *Publications: Public Libraries* (q); *Output Measures for Public Libraries: A Manual of Standardized Procedures; Measure for Measure: Output Measures for Public Libraries* (videotape).

(ALA) Reference and Adult Services Division (RASD). 50 E. Huron St., Chicago, IL 60611. (312) 944-6780. Andrew M. Hansen, Exec. Dir. Responsible for stimulating and supporting in every type of library the delivery of reference information services to all groups and of general library services and materials to adults. *Membership:* 4,502. *Dues:* $80.00. *Publications: RQ; RASD Update;* and others.

(ALA) Resources and Technical Services Division (RTSD). 50 E. Huron St., Chicago, IL 60611. (312) 944-6780. William Bunnell, Exec. Dir. Dedicated to acquisition, identification, cataloging, classification, and preservation of library materials; the development and coordination of the country's library resources; and aspects of selections and evaluation involved in acquiring and developing library materials and resources. *Sections:* Cataloging and Classification, Preservation of Library Materials, Reproduction of Library Materials, Resources, and Serials. *Membership:* 5,800. *Dues:* $25.00. *Publications: Library Resources and Technical Services* (q); RTSD newsletter (8/yr.).

(ALA) Young Adult Services Division (YASD). 50 E. Huron St., Chicago, IL 60611. (312) 944-6780. Evelyn Shaevel, Dir. Seeks to improve and extend library services to young people, assumes responsibility within the ALA to evaluate and select books and nonbook media and to interpret and make recommendations regarding their use with young adults. *Committees:* Best Books for Young Adults, High Interest/Low Interest Reading Level Materials Evaluation, Media Selection and Usage, Publishers' Liaison, Selected Films for Young Adults, and Television. *Membership:* 3,000. *Publications: Top of the News; Best Books;* and many others.

American Management Associations (AMA). 135 W. 50th St., New York, NY 10020. (212) 586-8100. Thomas R. Horton, Pres. The largest membership organization for professional managers. AMA provides a forum for personal development, the sharing of ideas, and commitment to common goals. AMA's Center for Management Development conducts more than 4,000 courses annually, covering every area of job training and career development. Operations of the organization are conducted largely through its 12 divisions: Finance; General Management; Insurance and Employee Benefits; Manufacturing; Marketing; Information Systems; Research; Human Resources;

Packaging; Management; Purchasing and Transportation; and General Services. *Membership:* 80,000. *Publications: Supervisory Management; Personnel;* and others.

(AMA) Human Resources Division. 135 W. 50th St., New York, NY 10020. (212) 586-8100. Offers conferences, courses, and briefings in such areas as compensation, employee services and relations, human resources administration, nonunion industrial relations, management and supervisory training and development, manpower planning, career development, and others. Members of this AMA division are typically vice-presidents for personnel, industrial relations managers, safety directors, manpower planning directors, training directors, and other related positions.

(AMA) Information Systems and Technology Division. 135 W. 50th St., New York, NY 10020. (212) 586-8100. Offers training courses and seminar sessions in manual systems and computer-based systems for executives with limited systems experience, for managers with some basic experience, for practitioners, and for professionals in the field. Members of this AMA division are typically executives in the categories of vice-president for administration, vice-president for systems, vice-president for computer services, systems and procedures manager, data processing manager, and related titles.

American Medical Association (AMA), Department of Audio-Visual and Self-Learning Programs. 535 N. Dearborn, Chicago, IL 60610. (312) 751-6000. Barbara Hopper, Dir. Coordinates AMA audiovisual services to the medical profession and others.

American Medical Writers Association (AMWA). 5272 River Road, Suite 410, Bethesda, MD 20816. (202) 986-9119. An international society whose members are engaged in all media of communication in medicine and allied professions. Founded in 1940, it is the largest association dedicated to the advancement of medical communication. Aims to offer guidance in the art and techniques of medical communication and to develop courses and workshops in the field. *Membership:* 2,600. *Dues:* $55.00. *Publications: Medical Communications; AMWA Newsletter; Freelance Directory.*

American Montessori Society (AMS). 150 5th Ave., New York, NY 10011. (212) 924-3209. Bretta Weiss, Nat. Dir. Dedicated to promoting better education for all children through teaching strategies consistent with the Montessori system. Membership is composed of schools in the private and public sectors employing this method, as well as individuals. It serves as a resource center and clearinghouse for information and data on Montessori, affiliates teacher training programs in different parts of the country, conducts a consultation service and accreditation program for school members, and distributes Montessori materials and books. Sponsors four regional educational conferences per year. *Dues:* $25.00 Montessori teachers; $20.00 parents; $130.00-530.00 inst. *Publications: AMS Constructive Triangle; Annual Report.*

American National Standards Institute (ANSI), Sectional Committee on Instructional Audiovisual Standards. 1430 Broadway, New York, NY 10018. (212) 354-3000. Dorothy Hogan, Vice-Pres. Seeks to coordinate standards, recommended practices, performance specifications, nomenclature, and test methods for instructional audiovisual systems.

American Newspaper Publishers Association (ANPA) Foundation. Box 17407, Dulles International Airport, Washington, DC 20041. (703) 620-9500. Judith D. Hines, Vice-Pres. and Dir. Seeks to advance professionalism of the press, to foster public understanding of a free press, and to cultivate increased numbers of future newspaper readers. Also administers a national Newspaper in Education Program, encouraging local newspapers and school systems to cooperate in using the newspaper for various fields of study. Sponsors a minority fellowship program and supports numerous efforts encouraging freedom of the press. *Publications:* training materials for students and professionals.

American Photographic Historical Society, Inc. 520 W. 44th St., New York, NY 10036. (212) 594-5056. Provides a forum for persons interested in learning more about historical phases and technical aspects of our photographic heritage; functions as an assertive source to encourage appreciation, collection, and preservation of that heritage. *Dues:* $22.00. *Publications: Photographica; Fairs.*

American Radio Relay League, Inc. (ARRL). 225 Main St., Newington, CT 06111. (203) 666-1541. David Sumner, Gen. Mgr. A noncommercial association of radio amateurs interested in radio communication, experimentation, and the relaying of messages for the advancement of the radio art and public welfare. Supplementary curriculum materials for teachers using the amateur satellites for classroom instruction in space technology are available. *Membership:* 150,000. *Dues:* $25.00. *Publication: QST Magazine* (mo., to members).

American Shortwave Listener's Club (ASWLC). 16182 Ballad Ln., Huntington Beach, CA 92649. (714) 846-1685. Stewart H. MacKenzie, Gen. Mgr. A hobbyist organization founded to advance shortwave listening on a worldwide basis. Research and educational programs include studies of radio signals from earth satellites, relay stations, frequency interference, radio astronomy, propagation monitoring, sunspot studies, and computer communications worldwide. *Membership:* 1,000. *Dues:* $18.00/yr. *Publications: SWL; Equipment Survey; Proper Reporting Guide.*

American Society for Health Manpower Education and Training of the American Hospital Association (ASHET). 840 N. Lake Shore Dr., Chicago, IL 60611. (312) 280-6111. V. Brandon Melton, Dir. Members include health educators, patient education coordinators, education managers, human resource developers, staff development specialists, media specialists, and organization development practitioners who conduct and manage education and training programs in all types of health care institutions. *Membership:* 1,900. *Dues:* $60.00.

American Society for Training and Development (ASTD). 600 Maryland Ave. NW, Suite 305, Washington, DC 20024. (202) 484-2390. Curtis Plott, Exec. Dir. Leading professional organization for individuals engaged in employee training and education in business, industry, government, and related fields. Members include managers, program developers, instructors, consultants, counselors, suppliers, and academics. The purpose of its extensive professional publishing program is to build an essential body of knowledge for advancing the competence of training and development practitioners in the field. Several divisions are included in the organization. *Membership:* 25,000. *Publications: Approaches to Training and Development; A Checklist for Technical Skills and Other Training and Development; Competency Analysis for Trainers: A Personal Planning Guide; ASTD Directory of Academic Programs in T&D/HRD; Evaluating Training Programs; Games Trainers Play; Performance Appraisal Sourcebook; Practical Video; Training and Development Handbook;* and more.

(ASTD) Media Division. ASTD Office, Suite 305, 600 Maryland Ave. NW, Washington, DC 20024. (202) 484-2390. Jacquelyn Flowers, Staff Liaison. Sponsors activities aimed at improving and extending applications of informational/training media in training and human resource development. All members receive the *Media Resource Directory*, containing names and addresses of all division members and a resource guide offering a compilation of media program sources, conferences, how-to information, publications, and organizations. *Publication: The Media Communicator.*

American Society of Cinematographers. 1782 N. Orange Dr., Hollywood, CA 90078. (213) 876-5080. William A. Frankel, Pres. *Membership:* 273. *Publications: American Cinematographer Magazine; American Cinematographer Manual.*

American Society of Educators (ASE). 1511 Walnut St., Philadelphia, PA 19102. (215) 563-3501. Laurie Wagman, Exec. Dir. A multifaceted professional organization that serves the nation's teachers by providing information and evaluation of media resources and technologies for effective classroom utilization. *Membership:* 36,000. *Dues:* $24.00/yr. *Publication: Media and Methods.*

American Women in Radio and Television (AWRT). 1321 Connecticut Ave. NW, Washington, DC 20036. (202) 296-0009. Phyllis Tritsch, Exec. V.P. Organization of professionals in the electronic media including owners, managers, administrators, and creative positions in broadcasting, satellite, and cable, as well as advertising and public relations. The objectives are to work worldwide to improve the quality of radio and television; to promote the entry, development, and advancement of women in the electronic media and allied fields; to serve as a medium of communication and idea exchange; to become involved in community concerns. Organized in 1951. Student memberships available. *Dues:* $95.00/yr. *Publication: News and Views.*

Anthology Film Archives (AFA). 491 Broadway, New York, NY 10012. (212) 226-0010. Jonas Mekas, Exec. Off. An international organization funded by several foundations; has research facilities for use by scholars and the general public. Holds public screenings of video works. AFA library has an extensive film and video collection. *Publication: Anthology Bulletin.*

Anthropology Film Center (AFC). Box 493, Santa Fe, NM 87501. (505) 983-4127. Joan and Carroll Williams, Co-Dirs. Specializes in film communication of cultural differences. Four-year plan in progress, includes expansion of facilities and services of the center, establishing film archives, and construction of a new library building. Recently, six documentaries have been completed under center auspices and two were finalists at the 1983 American Film Festival in New York. *Publication: A Filmography for American Indian Education.*

Associated Western Universities (AWU). 142 E. 2nd S., Salt Lake City, UT 84111. (801) 364-5659. Donald I. Walker, Exec. Dir. Organization of 36 institutions of higher education offering opportunities and monetary support for individuals engaged in research at U.S. Department of Energy laboratories toward degrees in the physical sciences, involving projects that cannot normally be performed on the institutions' own campuses. It is strongly oriented to projects that permit both faculty and students to become involved in research in order to bring to the university new and revised concepts that will improve the quality of higher education at those institutions.

Association for Childhood Education International (ACEI). 11141 Georgia Ave., Wheaton, MD 20902. (301) 942-2443. Lucy Prete Martin, Ed. and Dir. of Publications. Concerned with children from infancy through early adolescence. ACEI publications reflect careful research and broad-based views and thinking about a wide range of issues affecting children. Many are media-related in nature. The journal (*Childhood Education*) is essential for teachers, teachers-in-training, teacher educators, day-care workers, administrators, and parents. Articles focus on child development and emphasize practical application. Regular departments include book reviews (children and adult); reviews on films, pamphlets, and software; research and classroom idea-sparkers. Articles address timely concerns, and two of the five issues are theme issues. *Membership:* 10,000. *Dues:* $32.00/yr. *Publications: Childhood Education; ACEI Exchange.*

Association for Computational Linguistics (ACL). c/o D. E. Walker, Bell Communications Research, 445 South St., Morristown, NJ 07960. (201) 829-4312. Dr. D. E. Walker, Pres. Founded by a group of researchers sharing common interest in problems involving both languages and computation. Promotes research and development in computational linguistics, and cooperation and exchange of information among professionals in the field. Represents the field in various ways internationally. *Dues:* $15.00 indiv.; $30.00 inst. *Publication: Computational Linguistics.*

Association for Computers in Mathematics and Science Teaching (ACMST). Box 4455-E, Austin, TX 78765. (512) 244-1771. Dr. Gary H. Marks, Ed. *Dues:* $18.00 indiv.; $36.00 libs. *Publication: Journal of Computers in Mathematics and Science Teaching.*

Association for Computing Machinery. 11 West 42nd St., New York, NY 10036. (212) 869-7440. Sidney Weinstein, Exec. Dir. Seeks to advance the science and art of information processing, including the study, design, development, construction, and application of computing techniques and languages for information storage, retrieval, and processing, as well as for automatic controls and simulations of processes. *Membership:* 70,000. *Dues:* $50.00 members; $15.00 students.

Association for Continuing Higher Education (ACHE). 432 Communications Bldg., Univ. of Tennessee, Knoxville, TN 37996. (812) 479-2472. Dr. Rogert H. Sublett, Exec. V.P. An association of institutions and individuals having a commitment to providing opportunities in higher education for adults in traditional and nontraditional programs. *Membership:* 1,300 indiv., representing 475 inst. *Dues:* $200.00 inst.; $35.00 indiv. *Publications: 5 Minutes with ACHE; The Journal of Continuing Higher Education;* and *Proceedings.*

Association for Educational Communications and Technology (AECT). 1126 16th St. NW, Washington, DC 20036. (202) 466-4780. Lyn Gubser, Exec. Dir. Concerned with learning and educational technology; established in 1923. AECT members include instructional technologists, media or library specialists, university professors and researchers, industrial/business training specialists, religious educators, government media personnel, school, school district, and state department of education media program administrators and specialists, educational/training media producers, and numerous others whose professional work requires them to improve human communication and learning. AECT members also work in the armed forces, in public libraries, in museums, and other information agencies of many different kinds, including those related to the emerging fields of computer technology. AECT serves as a central clearinghouse and communications center for its members. The Association maintains TechCentral, a national electronic mail network and bulletin board service. Through its various committees and task forces, it compiles data and prepares recommendations to form the basis of guidelines, standards, research, and information summaries on numerous topics and problems of interest to the membership. AECT professional staff members report on government activities of concern to the membership and provide current data on laws and pending legislation relating to the educational media/technology field. *Membership:* approximately 6,000, plus some 8,000 additional subscribers, 9 divisions, 12 national affiliates, 55 state affiliates, and more than 30 national committees and task forces. *Dues:* $50.00/yr. regular; $20.00/yr. full-time graduate. *Publications: TechTrends* (8/yr., with membership; $24.00/yr. nonmembers); *Educational Communication and Technology: A Journal* (4/yr., $20.00/yr. members; $24.00/yr. nonmembers); *Journal of Instructional Development* (4/yr., $20.00/yr. members; $24.00/yr. nonmembers); the bimonthly newsletter, *ACCESS*; various division publications; and a number of books, including the following recent titles: *Software Quality and Copyright: Issues in Computer Assisted Instruction* (1984) by Virginia Helm; *The Educators Handbook to Interactive Videodisc* (1985) by Ed Schwartz; *Standards for College and University Learning Resources Programs* (1985 edition); and *Learning with Microcomputers* (1983). *Using Media for Learning,* a 1983 videotape series, and other videotape programs are also produced on a range of instructional and media-related topics. AECT also maintains the ECT Foundation, through which it offers a limited number of financial grants (scholarships, special awards) to further the Association's work. Archives (see entry) are also maintained at the University of Iowa. The 1985 AECT annual conference (Anaheim, California, January 18-23, 1985) featured the nation's largest instructional media exposition, COMMTEX, held jointly with the International Communication Industries Association (ICIA). John Naisbitt, author of *Megatrends*, keynoted the conference. The next convention will be held January 17-21, 1986, in Las Vegas, Nevada.

There are nine AECT divisions:
- Division of Educational Media Management (DEMM)
- Division of Information Systems & Computers (DISC)
- Division of Instructional Development (DID)
- Division of School Media Specialists (DSMS)
- Division of Telecommunications (DOT)
- Industrial Training and Education Division (ITED)
- International Division (INTL)
- Media Design and Production Division (MDPD)
- Research and Theory Division (RTD)

Because of similarity of interests, several other organizations have chosen to affiliate with the Association for Educational Communications and Technology, as follows:
- Association for Media Educators in Religion (AMER)
- Association for Multi-Image (AMI)
- Association for Special Education Technology (ASET)
- Community College Association for Instruction and Technology (CCAIT)
- Federal Educational Technology Association (FETA)
- Health Education Media Association (HEMA)
- Film and Video Communicators (IFPA)
- International Visual Literacy Association (IVLA)
- Minorities in Media (MIMS)
- National Association of Regional Media Centers (NARMC)
- Northwest College and University Council for the Management of Educational Technology (NW/MET)
- Women in Instructional Technology (WIT)

Two additional organizations are also related to the Association for Educational Communications and Technology:
- (AECT) Archives
- (AECT) ECT Foundation

Descriptions of organizational elements under each of the foregoing three categories follow, in order.

(AECT) Division of Educational Media Management (DEMM). 1126 Sixteenth St. NW, Washington, DC 20036. Stanley E. Huffman, Pres. Seeks to develop an information exchange network and to share information such as common problems, solutions, and program descriptions of educational media management; to develop programs that increase the effectiveness of media managers; to initiate and implement a public relations program to educate the public and administrative bodies as to the use, value, and need for educational media management; and to foster programs that will help carry out media management responsibilities effectively. *Membership:* 900. *Publication: Media Management Journal.*

(AECT) Division of Information Systems and Computers (DISC). 1126 Sixteenth St. NW, Washington, DC 20036. George McNeal, Pres. Seeks to develop and promote models for the systematic design and organization of information for uniform and proper identification of educational media; and to develop systems for indexes, abstracts, and directories for effective selection of materials. Concern for the means to systematic organization of information for ordering, cataloging, classifying, and storing of media; concern for standardization of systems for retrieval of informational materials and for the training and qualifications of individuals concerned with information systems management. *Membership:* 150.

(AECT) Division of Instructional Development (DID). 1126 Sixteenth St. NW, Washington, DC 20036. Barbara Fowler, Pres. Concerned with the study, evaluation, and refinement of design processes, the creation of new models of instructional development, the invention and improvement of techniques for managing the development of instruction, the dissemination of findings, and the promotion of academic programs for preparing professional instructional developers. *Membership:* 800.

(AECT) Division of School Media Specialists (DSMS). 1126 Sixteenth St. NW, Washington, DC 20036. Evelyn Kovalick, Pres. To promote and improve communication among school media personnel sharing a common concern for the development, implementation, and evaluation of school media programs and to provide access to information on how school media programs can be developed around the functions expressed in national standards. *Membership:* 300.

(AECT) Division of Telecommunications (DOT). 1126 Sixteenth St. NW, Washington, DC 20036. Kim Nelson, Pres. Seeks to improve education through use of television and radio, video and audio recordings, and autotutorial devices and media. Aims to improve the design, production, evaluation, and utilization of telecommunications materials and equipment; to upgrade competencies of personnel engaged in the field; to investigate and report promising innovative practices and technological developments; to promote studies, experiments, and demonstrations; and to support research in telecommunications. Future plans call for working to establish a national entity representing instructional television. *Membership:* 400. *Publication:* newsletter.

(AECT) Industrial Training and Education Division (ITED). 1126 Sixteenth St. NW, Washington, DC 20036. Robert E. Holloway, Pres. Seeks to promote the sensitive and sensible use of media and techniques to improve the quality of education and training; to provide a professional program that demonstrates the state-of-the-art of educational technology as a part of the AECT convention; to improve communications to ensure the maximum utilization of educational techniques and media which can give demonstratable, objective evidence of effectiveness. *Membership:* 300.

(AECT) International Division (ID). 1126 Sixteenth St. NW, Washington, DC 20036. Robert Cox, Pres. Seeks to improve international communications concerning existing methods of design; to pretest, utilize, produce, evaluate, and establish an approach through which these methods may be improved and/or adapted for maximum use and effectiveness; to develop a roster of qualified international leadership personnel with experience and competence in the varied geographic and technical areas; and to encourage research in the application of communications processes to support present and future international social and economic development. *Membership:* 300.

(AECT) Media Design and Production Division (MDPD). 1126 Sixteenth St. NW, Washington, DC 20036. J. William Walker, Pres. Seeks to provide formal organized procedures for promoting and facilitating interaction between commercial and noncommercial, nontheatrical filmmakers and to provide a communications link for filmmakers with people of like interests; to provide a connecting link between creative and technical professionals of the audiovisual industry; to advance the informational film producers' profession by providing scholarships and apprenticeships to experimenters and students and by providing a forum for discussion of local, national, and universal issues; and to recognize and make awards for outstanding films produced and for contributions to the state of the art. *Membership:* 400.

(AECT) Research and Theory Division (RTD). 1126 Sixteenth St. NW, Washington, DC 20036. Barbara Grabowski, Pres. Seeks to improve the design, execution, utilization, and evaluation of audiovisual communications research; to improve the qualifications and effectiveness of personnel engaged in communications research; to advise the educational practitioner of utilization of the results of research; to improve research design, techniques, evaluation, and dissemination; and to promote both applied and theoretical research on the systematic use of all forms of media in the improvement of instruction. *Membership:* 250.

Association for Educational Communications and Technology (AECT)
Affiliate Organizations:

(AECT) Association for Media Educators in Religion (AMER). 1576 Glen Oak, Dubuque, IA 52001. Burton Everist, Pres. Seeks to stimulate more effective use of educational technology in churches and synagogues by providing a forum for interaction among those interested in religious communications.

(AECT) Association for Special Education Technology (ASET). 101 Carpenter Ln., Philadelphia, PA 19119. Patricia Magee, Pres. Provides a means of bringing together instructional technologists, media specialists, and special educators to improve the use of technology in special education. Aims to study, evaluate, and refine educational technology processes for handicapped persons, to disseminate findings concerning both theoretical and practical aspects of instructional technology; to foster cooperation and coordination among organizations concerned with educational technology and special education, and to develop liaison with commercial producers to assess specific needs and encourage production of educational media. *Membership:* 220.

(AECT) Community College Association for Instruction and Technology (CCAIT). Palomar College, San Marcos, CA 92069. Bonnie Rogers, Pres. A national association of community college educators interested in discovering and disseminating information concerning problems and processes of media and technology in community and junior colleges. Facilitates member exchanges of data, reports, proceedings, personnel, and other resources; sponsors regional conferences and AECT convention sessions as well as multisite conferences featuring individualized and other nontraditional learning patterns. *Membership:* 400.

(AECT) Federal Educational Technology Association (FETA). 3808 Needles Pl., Alexandria, VA 22309. Marjorie Kupper, Pres. Seeks to create an awareness of the concept of instructional technology; to provide a forum for the exchange of information and ideas related to the latest developments and programs within the field; to standardize approaches to the employment of instructional technology and to furnish guidelines for the continued pursuit of excellence in the production of educational media programs, all within the armed forces and U.S. government. Membership open to media and instructional technologists from government agencies and organizations supplying them, and to other interested persons.

(AECT) Health Education Media Association (HEMA). 1000 Bradley St., Davenport, IA 52803. Wayne Zemelka, Pres. To increase the understanding of educators regarding the potential of learning media and the vital role of instructional developers, learning resource directors, and media specialists; to assist instructional developers in improving the methods and applicability of instruments evaluating the effectiveness of media; to disseminate information regarding new developments in learning media which are applicable to the health sciences and to assist in realizing the full potential of the newer media in bringing health information to the public. *Membership:* 600. *Publication: Hemagrams.*

(AECT) International Visual Literacy Association, Inc. (IVLA). 2970 NW Hayes St., Corvallis, OR 97330. (515) 294-4476. Dennis Dake, Pres. Provides a multidisciplinary forum for the exploration of modes of visual communication and their application through the concept of visual literacy; promotes development of visual literacy and serves as a bond between the diverse organizations and groups working in that field. 1985 IVLA conference, "Making Meaning," to be held at Pomona, California, in early November. *Dues:* $25.00 regular; $35.00 comprehensive (includes *Journal*). *Publications:* newsletter; *Journal of Visual/Verbal Languaging.*

(AECT) Minorities in Media (MIMS). ECSU, Box 206, Elizabeth City, NC 27909. Ellis H. Smith, Pres. Seeks to encourage the effective utilization of educational media in the teaching-learning process; provide leadership opportunities in advancing the use of technology as an integral part of the learning process; provide a vehicle through which minorities might influence the utilization of media in institutions; develop an information exchange network to share information common to minorities in media; study, evaluate, and refine the educational technology process as it relates to the education of minorities; and encourage and improve the production of materials for the education of minorities.

(AECT) National Association of Regional Media Centers (NARMC). Heartland Ed. Agency 11, 1932 SW 3rd St., Ankeny, IA 50021. Marvin Davis, Pres. Seeks to foster the exchange of ideas and information among educational communications specialists whose responsibilities relate to the administration of regional media centers through workshops, seminars, and national meetings; to study the feasibility of developing joint programs that could increase the effectiveness and efficiency of regional media services; and to disseminate information on successful practices and research studies conducted by regional media centers.

(AECT) Northwest College and University Council for the Management of Educational Technology (NW/MET). Univ. of Calgary, SS 104-C, Calgary, Alberta, Canada T2N 2N4. Dr. Paul Morris, Manager Program Serv. The first regional group representing institutions of higher education in Alberta, Alaska, British Columbia, Idaho, Montana, Oregon, and Washington to receive affiliate status in AECT. Media managers' responsibilities include audiovisual service functions, instructional design and development, and teaching. Current issues under consideration are television technologies and copyright. Organizational goals include an effort to identify managers of campuswide educational technology service programs in higher education. *Publication: NW/MET Bulletin.*

(AECT) TechCentral. 1126 16th St. NW, Washington, DC 20036. (202) 466-4780. Cheryl Petty Garnette, Coordinator. An electronic mail service supported by AECT. Involves state departments of education and resource organizations. Open to the public at a nominal charge; sponsored by the National Public Relations Association. Bulletin boards on upcoming activities, bibliographic citations, interesting news items, funding sources, practitioner problem and message exchange on subjects related to technology and telecommunications in education. Project BEST prepared video training modules of education experiences of educators in eight schools. Teleconferences dealing with impacts of education technologies were held.

(AECT) Women in Instructional Technology (WIT). 808 4th Ave., Farmville, VA 23901. Nancy Vick, Pres. Seeks to provide education and training for women who wish to enter leadership positions within AECT and the fields of communications and educational technology; to enhance interpersonal communications among women, exchanging ideas, views, instructional materials, and information about women's concerns in communications and educational technology. Also provides career counseling and information about leadership positions and job market surveys. Sensitizes members and others to biases and stereotypes against females, males, and minorities. Offers support in attempting solutions to problems in the fields.

Other AECT-Related Organizations:

(AECT) Archives. c/o Calvin E. Mether, Univ. of Iowa, Iowa City, IA 52240. (319) 353-2121. A collection of media, projection, and reproduction equipment, photographic devices, manuscripts, and related materials representing important developments in visual and audiovisual education and in instructional/educational technology. Maintained by the University of Iowa in cooperation with AECT.

(AECT) ECT Foundation. 1126 16th St. NW, Washington, DC 20036. Robert deKieffer, Chair. This educational and charitable organization supports leadership development activities in educational communications and technology. Seeks to develop and conduct leadership training programs for professionals; to disseminate knowledge developed in the field; to conduct related research; to evaluate current programs and activities; to develop recommendations for school and college instructional design; to develop, where needed, specialized educational materials; and to conduct other appropriate activities to promote its purposes.

Association for Educational Data Systems (AEDS). 1201 16th St. NW, Washington, DC 20036. (202) 822-7845. Shirley Hammond, Exec. Dir. Provides a forum for the exchange of ideas and information on the use of computers in education; promotes a greater understanding of educational technology through its publications and activities; provides information on the impact and advancements of modern technology on the educational process. Membership comprised of educators and technical experts representing public and private schools, higher education, education departments, government and other groups interested in educational computer applications. *Membership:* 2,500. *Dues:* $55.00. *Publications: AEDS Newsletter; AEDS Monitor; AEDS Journal; AEDS Handbook;* and others.

Association for Experiential Education (AEE). Box 249-CU, Boulder, CO 80309. (303) 492-1547. Richard J. Kraft, Exec. Dir. AEE believes that the learner and the teacher have the opportunity and right to use the most powerful and effective means to interact with each other, themselves, their environments, and the tasks at hand. Experience-based education emphasizes direct experience as a resource that increases the quality of learning. AEE helps to advance, expand, conceptualize, and formalize this learning process. *Membership:* 1,000. *Dues:* $35.00 ind.; $100.00 inst. *Publications: Jobs Clearinghouse; The Journal of Experiential Education.*

Association for Library and Information Science Education (ALISE). c/o J. Phillips, 471 Park Ln., State College, Pa 16803. (814) 238-0254. Seeks to advance education for librarianship. Open to professional schools offering graduate programs accredited by the American Library Association Committee on Accreditation; personal memberships open to full-time educators employed in such institutions; other memberships available to those who qualify. *Membership:* 575 ind., 98 inst. *Publication: Journal of Education for Library and Information Science.*

Association for Living Historical Farms and Agricultural Museums (ALHFAM). Living Historical Farms MHT, Room 5035, Smithsonian Institution, Washington, DC 20560. John T. Schlebecker, Secy.-Treas. Assists U.S. historical farms and agricultural museums by providing technical research, assistance with site selection, and visitor control and interpretation; accredits such institutions; develops genetic plant pools; inventories historically accurate plants, implements, animals, utensils, and other items; and provides personnel training and scholarship opportunities.

Association for Multi-Image (AMI). 8019 Himes, Suite 401, Tampa, FL 33614. (813) 932-1692. R. Victor Lawrence, Pres.; Marilyn Kulp, Exec. Dir. A nonprofit association that brings together individuals who are actively engaged in the field of multi-image production and utilization to enhance their individual and cooperative creativity and productivity. The Association promotes the use of multi-images as a medium for education, communications, and entertainment. *Dues:* $75.00/yr. indiv.; $30.00/yr. student; $225.00/yr. corporate. *Publications:* "Multi-Images" Journal (q.); "Mini-Images" Newsletter (mo.).

Association for Recorded Sound Collections (ARSC). Box 1643, Manassas, VA 22110. (301) 424-6825. Michael Gray, Pres. Serves collectors, discographers, and others interested in classical, jazz, pop, folk, ethnic, and spoken word recordings. Offers research to assist in completing projects for publication on the history of recorded sound. *Membership:* 1,000. *Dues:* $15.00/yr. *Publications: ARSC Journal*; bulletin; newsletter; *Rules; Rigler & Deutsch Index.*

Association for Supervision and Curriculum Development (ASCD). 225 N. Washington, Alexandria, VA 22314. (703) 549-9110. Gordon Cawelti, Exec. Dir. Promotes the improvement of professional skills in supervision, curriculum, and instruction. *Membership:* 61,000. *Publications: Educational Leadership; ASCD Update;* others.

Association for the Development of Computer-Based Instructional Systems (ADCIS). 409 Miller Hall, Western Washington Univ., Bellingham, WA 98225. (206) 676-2860. Gordon Hayes, Exec. Dir. Provides a forum for the exchange of ideas, accomplishments, and plans for utilizing computers in instruction. Annual conference to be held in Philadelphia, March 25-28, 1986. *Membership:* 2,200. *Dues:* $45.00 and $75.00. *Publications:* newsletter; *Journal of Computer-Based Instruction; Conference Proceedings.*

Association of American Colleges (AAC). 1818 R St. NW, Washington, DC 20009. (202) 387-3760. Mark Curtis, Pres. AAC is the only national organization dedicated to the support and encouragement of liberal learning at all of the nation's colleges and universities. Projects focus on public understanding of the value of liberal education and redefining the meaning and purpose of baccalaureate degrees. Contact Office of Public Information. *Membership:* 560. *Publications: Liberal Education; Update; The Forum for Liberal Education.*

Association of American Publishers (AAP). One Park Ave., New York, NY 10016. (212) 689-8920. Townsend Hoopes, Pres. A group of 300 companies whose members produce the majority of printed materials sold to U.S. schools, colleges, libraries, and bookstores, as well as to homes. Range of member interests is reflected in textbooks, religious, scientific, and media books, instructional systems, audiotapes and videotapes, records, cassettes, slides, transparencies, and tests. Provides its members with information concerning trade conditions, markets, copyrights, manufacturing processes, taxes, duties, postage, freight, censorship movements, government programs, and other matters of importance. *Membership:* 300 companies. *Publication: AAP Newsletter.*

Association of Audio-Visual Technicians (AAVT). Box 9716, Denver, CO 80209. (303) 698-1820. Elsa C. Kaiser, Pres. Proposes to increase communication and to assist audiovisual technicians in their work; holds seminars in conjunction with most of the major audiovisual shows. Maintains a lending library of programs on audiovisual equipment or production. Also has a lending library of old manuals for rent by AAVT members. *Membership:* 1,200. *Dues:* $25.00 indiv.; $50.00 inst. *Publications: Fast Foreword; Annotated Directory of Parts and Services.*

Association of Independent Video and Filmmakers and the Foundation for Independent Video and Filmmakers (FIVF). 625 Broadway, 9th Floor, New York, NY 10012. (212) 473-3100. Lawrence Sapadin, contact person. The national trade association for independent video and filmmakers, representing their needs and goals to industry, government, and the public. Programs include domestic and foreign festival liaison for independents, professional screenings and seminars, health insurance for members, short film distribution through the NEA's short film showcase, and information and referral services. Recent activities include monitoring status of independent work on public TV, advocacy for cable access, and lobbying for modifications in copyright law. *Dues:* $35.00 ind.; $75.00 inst.; $50.00 libraries; $20.00 students. *Publication: The Independent.*

Association of North American Radio Clubs. 1500 Bunbury Dr., Whittier, CA 90601. Richard T. Colgan, Exec. Secy. An international association of radio listeners. *Publication: ANARC Newsletter.*

Association of Science-Technology Centers. 1016 16th St. NW, Washington, DC 20036. (202) 371-1171. Bonnie VanDorn, Exec. Dir. Supports the public understanding of science and technology through science centers and museums. Operates a traveling exhibits service; sponsors workshops; sponsors and cooperates on other projects that benefit science museum operations. Extensive exhibition on the social impact of microelectronics, "Chips and Changes," tours science museums in nine major U.S. cities through March 1986. *Membership:* 170 science museums. *Dues:* $200.00-$1,000.00, 4 categories. *Publication: ASTC Newsletter.*

Association of Systematics Collections. Museum of Natural History, Univ. of Kansas, Lawrence, KS 66045. (913) 864-4867. Stephen R. Edwards, Exec. Dir. Promotes the care, management, and improvement of biological collections; provides information on biological collections and biologists who offer taxonomic services; and publishes current information on endangered species and government permit regulations regarding the scientific use of plants and animals. *Membership:* 80 inst.; 20 scientific societies. *Publications: Pest Control in Museums; Mammal Species; Museum Collections and Computers; Biogeography of the Tropical Pacific; Amphibian Species of the World; Collections of Frozen Tissues; Controlled Wildlife (I, II, III): Guide to Federal and State Wildlife Regulations and Permits; Sources of Federal Funding in the Biological Sciences; Guidelines to the Acquisition and Management of Biological Specimens; ASC Newsletter.*

Association of Teacher Educators (ATE). 1900 Association Dr., Suite ATE, Reston, VA 22901. (703) 620-3110. Robert J. Stevenson, Exec. Dir. Annual conference and annual summer workshops. The 1985 conference was held February 18-21 in Las Vegas, Nevada; the 1986 conference will be held February 23-26 in Atlanta, Georgia. *Membership:* 3,000. *Dues:* $45.00. *Publication: Action in Teacher Education.*

Audiovisual Institute for Effective Communications. Audiovisual Center, Indiana Univ., Bloomington, IN 47405. (703) 278-7200. Terri Campbell, contact person. A one-week intensive training seminar directed toward professional, academic, and industrial personnel involved with audiovisual communications. Cosponsored by Indiana University Audiovisual Center, NAVA, The International Communications Industries Association, and the American Society for Training and Development. *Dues:* $500.00 before February 8, 1985; $550.00 thereafter.

Authors' League of America. 234 W. 44th St., New York, NY 10036. (212) 391-9198. Mary Louise Lopez, Admin. A professional organization of authors of books, magazine materials, and plays. *Membership:* 12,000. *Publications: Dramatists Guild Quarterly; Authors' Guild Bulletin.*

AVLINE. National Library of Medicine, 8600 Rockville Pike, Bethesda, MD 20209. Audiovisuals Online, an automated bibliographic database – part of the National Library of Medicine's Medical Literature Analysis and Retrieval System – contains over thirteen thousand citations to audiovisual teaching materials appropriate for college level and continuing education in the health science education field. Titles are cited with bibliographic and distribution information. In some cases, descriptive information regarding currency, content accuracy, and teaching effectiveness is included. *See also* National Library of Medicine. *Publications: National Library of Medicine Audiovisuals Catalog; Health Sciences Audiovisuals.*

Behavioral Sciences Research Branch. 5600 Fishers Ln., Room 10C-09, Rockville, MD 20857. (301) 443-3942. David Pearl, Chief. Funds basic research on the effects of television. Currently supported projects include Cultural Indicators; the Modeling of Media Violence in Children; Preschool Children's Home Television Viewing; Television's Role in Constructing Social Reality; Television Effects on Emotionally Disturbed and Learning Disabled Children; Developmental Differences in Fright from Mass Media. The Branch has also just published *Television and Behavior: Ten Years of Scientific Progress and Implications for the Eighties – Vol. 1: Summary Report; Vol. 2: Technical Reviews.*

Biological Photographic Association (BPA). #1 Buttonwood Ct., Indian Head Park, IL 60525. (312) 246-9118. Diane Jones, Exec. Dir. An organization of professionals interested in biological photographic communication, scientific research, and education. *Publication: Journal of Biological Photography.*

Board for International Broadcasting. 1201 Connecticut Ave. NW, Suite 1100, Washington, DC 80903. (202) 254-8040. Frank Shakespeare, Chair. An independent, federal agency that oversees the operation of Radio Liberty and Radio Free Europe. *Publication: Annual Report to President.*

Catholic Library Association. 461 W. Lancaster Ave., Haverford, PA 19041. (215) 649-5250. Matthew R. Wilt, Exec. Dir. Seeks to improve libraries in general and religion-oriented libraries in particular; promotes discriminating taste in literature and other communication media; encourages compilation, publication, and use of religious reference tools; seeks to attract persons into librarianship through scholarship funds; fosters research and development in librarianship and communication; and encourages cooperation with associations having mutual interests in the field. Produces continuing education programs on videotape. *Membership:* 3,000. *Dues:* $35.00-$1,000.00. *Publications: Catholic Library World* (6/yr.); *Catholic Periodical and Literature Index* (6/yr.).

Center for Advanced Visual Studies. MIT Building W11, 40 Massachusetts Ave., Cambridge, MA 02139. (617) 253-4415. Otto Piene, Dir. Founded by George Kepes, offers a unique situation in which artists can explore and realize art work in collaboration with scientists and engineers. Has done significant work on lasers, holography, video, kinetics, environmental art, and sky art.

Center for Arts Information. 625 Broadway, New York, NY 10012. (212) 677-7548. Jana Jevnikar, Assoc. Dir. Serves as an information clearinghouse for and about the arts of New York State and for the entire United States as well. The center responds to a wide range of questions about arts management and funding proposed by arts organizations, including artists and sponsors. Maintains a library of more than six thousand volumes on arts management. *Publications: Film Service Profiles; International Cultural Exchange; Video Service Profiles;* others.

Center for Educational Policy and Management. College of Education, Univ. of Oregon, Eugene, OR 97403. (503) 686-5173. Robert H. Mattson, Dir. Seeks to improve the use of human resources in schools through research and development activities that bring together scholars, educational practitioners, and community leaders. Its research focuses on the areas of administration, staff, and secondary school organization. Holds summer conferences for educators and scholars on such topics as the effects of collective bargaining and staff development for teachers. Offers scripted guides coordinating research to practice in such areas as discipline, teacher evaluation, time analysis, program evaluation, and contract management. *Publications: R and D Perspectives* (q.); *Outlook* (3/yr.); numerous research reports.

Center for Instructional Research and Curriculum Evaluation. 1310 S. 6th St., Champaign, IL 61820. (217) 333-3770. Primarily active in conducting education-related research and development projects within the College of Education, University of Illinois, but is of considerable interest to media professionals in foreign countries.

Center for Interactive Programs (CIP). Old Radio Hall, 975 Observatory Dr., Univ. of Wisconsin, Madison, WI 53706. (608) 262-2569. Christine Olgren, Assoc. Dir. Provides training programs, publications, and research in the field of teleconferencing. *Publications: Teleconferencing and Electronic Communications (I-III); Annual Teleconferencing Directory; Teleconferencing and Interactive Media; More Than Meets the Eye; Electronic Meetings; 12 Interactive Techniques for Teleconferencing; Telcoms Newsletter*; and others.

Center for Learning and Telecommunications. One Dupont Circle NW, Suite 600, Washington, DC 20036. (202) 293-6440. Marilyn Kressel, Exec. Dir. Assists postsecondary education institutions in exploring the potential of technology-based instructional programs. *Dues:* $55.00/yr. *Publication: TELESCAN.*

Center for Teaching about China. 2025 I St. NW, Suite 715, Washington, DC 20006. (202) 296-4147. Annie Wang, Dir. A project of the U.S.-China Peoples Friendship Association. The center provides assistance to educators by offering materials and ideas for including the study of China in the curriculum. Offers opportunities to visit China, exhibition samples and handouts for teacher conferences, assistance in planning teacher workshops; participates in annual meetings of the American Library Association and the National Council for the Social Studies. *Publication: China in the Classroom.*

Center on Evaluation, Development and Research (CEDR). Phi Delta Kappa, 8th St. and Union Ave., Box 789, Bloomington, IN 47402. (812) 339-1156. Established to serve PDK members as well as other educators or educational institutions. Primary goal is to help processes and their application in systematic problem solving. Continuing activities include the National Symposium of Professionals in Evaluation and Research—an annual series of three meetings on selected aspects of evaluation, development, and research.

Central Educational Network (CEN). 4300 W. Peterson Ave., Chicago, IL 60646. (312) 545-7500. James A. Fellows, Pres. Provides general audience, postsecondary programming, and ITV services.

Children's Television International, Inc. 8000 Forbes Pl., Suite 201, Springfield, VA 22151. (703) 321-8455. Ray Gladfelter, Pres. An educational organization that develops, produces, and distributes a wide variety of color television programming and television-related materials as a resource to aid children's social, cultural, and intellectual development. Program areas cover language arts, science, social studies, art, and business communications for home, school, and college viewing. *Publications:* Teacher's guides that accompany instructional TV series.

Children's Television Workshop. One Lincoln Plaza, New York, NY 10023. (212) 595-3456. Joan Ganz Cooney, Pres. An independent, nonprofit corporation that produces "Sesame Street," "The Electric Company," "3-2-1 Contact," and other educational television programs for airing on PBS stations throughout the United States and in foreign countries.

Clearinghouse on Development Communication. 1255 23rd St. NW, Washington, DC 20037. (202) 862-1900. Judy Brace, Dir. A center for materials and information on applications of communication technology to development problems. Operated by the Academy for Educational Development and funded by the Bureau for Science and Technology of the U.S. Agency for International Development. Disseminates information and serves as an international clearinghouse on information regarding communications for Third World development. Visitors and written information requests are welcome. *Publications: Development Communication Report; Project Profiles.*

Close Up Foundation. 1235 Jefferson Davis Hwy., Arlington, VA 22202. (703) 892-5400. Stephen A. Janger, Pres. An organization dealing with the involvement of citizens in government. Brings participants to Washington for a series of week-long, in-depth looks into the federal government; produces several series of television programs telecast on the Cable Satellite Public Affairs Network for secondary school and home audiences. *Publications: Perspectives; Current Issues; Special Focus.*

Coalition for Literacy. 50 E. Huron St., Chicago, IL 60611. (312) 944-6780. Violet Malone, Exec. Comm. Chair. Eleven organizations, coordinated by the American Library Association and working in cooperation with the Advertising Council, will generate public awareness of the national problem of adult functional illiteracy through a three-year multimedia advertising campaign. The campaign is focused at increasing resources from individual, corporate, and local community response. *Dues:* $10.00 assoc.; $50.00 organ.; $1,000.00 spon. *Publications:* Quarterly information sheet to dues-paying members only.

Communications Satellite Corporation (COMSAT). 950 L'Enfant Plaza SW, Washington, DC 20024. (202) 863-6000. Dr. Joseph V. Charyk, Pres. A private corporation that is an outgrowth of the Communications Satellite Act of 1962 with three of fifteen directors appointed by the president; provides worldwide satellite communication services.

Computer and Information Science Research Center (CISRC). 228 CAE Bldg., 2036 Neil Avenue Mall, Columbus, OH 43210. (614) 422-0768. Dr. Anthony E. Petrarca, Act. Dir. Research activities and fields reported on are: analysis of algorithms and data structures; artificial intelligence including expert systems; computer graphics; database systems; digital computer architecture and organization; distributed computing; very large scale integration (VLSI) man-machine interaction and human factors analysis; software engineering; systems programming and operating systems; theoretical computer science, including abstract and concrete complexity; theory and processing of programming languages.

Computer-Based Education Research Library. 252 Engineering Research Laboratory, Urbana, IL 61801. Donald L. Bitzer, Dir. Conducts research and development work primarily related to the PLATO computer-based instructional system.

The Computer Museum. 300 Congress St., Boston, MA 02210. (617) 426-2800. Dr. Gwen Bell, Dir. The Computer Museum dramatically illustrates the impact of the Information Revolution through interactive exhibits of the state-of-the-art computers, films, and recreations of vintage computer installations. A lecture series provides an oral history of the computer and its inventors. *Dues:* $30.00 indiv.; $125.00 corp. *Publication: The Computer Museum Report.*

Computer Using Educators (CUE). Box 18547, San Jose, CA 95158. Glenn Fisher, Pres. A group affiliated with the International Council for Computer Education established to promote and improve computer use in schools and colleges. CUE and the Microcomputer Center in the San Mateo County Office of Education jointly support the Softswap, a public domain library of 400+ teacher-developed educational programs for Apple, Atari, PET, and TRS-80 microcomputers. *Membership:* 6,500 from California, 44 other states, and 14 countries. *Dues:* $8.00/yr. *Publication: CUE Newsletter.*

Consortium of University Film Centers. c/o Audio Visual Services, Kent State, 330 Library, Kent, OH 44242. (216) 672-3456. John P. Kerstedter, Exec. Dir. A professional group of university film rental centers whose purpose is to improve education and training through the effective use of the motion picture; to assist the educational and training users in business in making films more accessible to renters; to foster cooperative planning among university film centers; and to gather and disseminate information on improved procedures and new developments in film and film center management. *Membership:* 200. *Dues:* Sliding scale based on collection size: $50.00-$150.00. *Publications: The Educational Film Locator; 16mm Film Maintenance Manual.*

Continuing Library Education Network and Exchange. Network of the American Library Association. 50 E. Huron, Chicago, IL 60611. (312) 944-6780. Sandra S. Stephan, Chair. Seeks to provide access to continuing education opportunities for librarians and information scientists and to create an awareness of the need for such education in helping individuals in the field to respond to societal and technological changes. *Membership:* Open to all ALA members. *Dues:* $15.00 indiv. members; $50.00 organizations. *Publication: CLENExchange* (q.), available by subscription ($20.00/yr.).

Copyright Clearance Center. 21 Congress St., Salem, MA 01970. (617) 744-3350. James J. Flanagan, Act. Pres. An organization through which corporations, academic and research libraries, information brokers, government agencies, and other users of copyrighted information may obtain authorizations and pay royalties for photocopying of copyrighted materials, in excess of exemptions contained in U.S. Copyright Act of 1976. CCC operates new Annual Authorizations Service, a flat annual photocopy program serving photocopying permissions needs of large U.S. corporations. *Membership:* 1,500 users; 950 publishers; 9,500 publications.

Copyright Office. Register of Copyrights, Library of Congress, Washington, DC 20559. (202) 287-8700. The office examines claims to copyrights for literary, musical, and artistic works, registers those claims that meet requirements of the law, and catalogs all registrations. Recently, the office has been handling one million pieces of mail and completing some 500,000 registrations a year.

Corporation for Public Broadcasting. 1111 16th St. NW, Washington, DC 20036. (202) 293-6160. Edward J. Pfister, Pres.; Sonia Landau, Chair. A private, nonprofit corporation authorized in the Public Broadcasting Act of 1967 to develop noncommercial television and radio services for the American people, while insulating public broadcasting from political pressure or influence. CPB supports station operations and funds radio and television programs for national distribution. CPB by means of a broad range of activities, sets national policy that will most effectively make noncommercial radio and television and other telecommunications services available to all citizens of the United States. *Publications: CPB Report* (wk., $10.00/yr.); *Annual Report; CPB Public Broadcasting Directory.*

Council for Basic Education. 725 15th St. NW, Washington, DC 20005. (202) 347-4171. A. Graham Down, Exec. Dir. A vocal force advocating a broadly defined curriculum in the liberal arts for all students in elementary and secondary schools. *Dues:* $45.00. *Publications: Basic Education; Issues, Answers & Facts;* reports, books.

Council for Exceptional Children. 1920 Association Dr., Reston, VA 22901. (703) 620-3660. Lynn Smarte, Prog. Dir. for Public Information. A membership organization providing information to teachers, administrators, and others concerned with the education of handicapped and gifted children. Maintains a library and database on literature on special education; prepares books, monographs, digests, films, filmstrips, cassettes, and journals; sponsors annual convention and conferences on special education; provides information and assistance to lawmakers on the education of the handicapped and gifted; coordinates Political Action Network on the rights of exceptional persons. *Membership: 50,000. Publications: Exceptional Children; Teaching Exceptional Children; Exceptional Child Education Resources.*

Council for National Library and Information Associations. 461 W. Lancaster Ave., Haverford, PA 19041. (215) 649-5251. Robert DeCandido, Pres. The council is a forum for discussion of many issues of concern to library and information groups. Current committees at work are the Joint Committee on Specialized Cataloging, the Ad Hoc Committee on Copyright and the Joint Committee on Association Cooperation. *Membership:* 21 associations. *Dues:* Inquire. *Publications:* reports.

Council for the Advancement of Science Writing. 618 N. Elmwood, Oak Park, IL 60302. (312) 383-0820. W. J. Cromie, contact person. A nonprofit educational corporation that conducts programs to increase the quality of science writing and reporting. Not open for membership. No mailing list available. *Publication: Guide to Science Writing*, available free with stamped, addressed envelope.

Council of Chief State School Officers. 400 N. Capitol St. NW, Washington, DC 20001. (202) 624-7702. William F. Pierce, Exec. Dir. Annual convention held the third week of November. Composed of the chief state school officers and leaders of education agencies in the fifty states, the District of Columbia, Guam, American Samoa, Puerto Rico, and the trust territories of the Pacific Islands, Virgin Islands, and Northern Mariani Islands. *Membership:* 57. *Publication: Stateline.*

Council on International Educational Exchange. 205 E. 42nd St., New York, NY 10017. (212) 661-1414. Jack Egle, Exec. Dir. Devoted to encouraging and facilitating educational exchange programs involving work, study, and travel throughout the world. CIEE also has offices in Paris, Tokyo, Boston, San Francisco, Los Angeles, San Diego, Berkeley, Seattle, and Austin. *Membership:* 200 coll. and univ. *Publication: 1985 Student Travel Catalog.*

Council on International Non-theatrical Events. 1201 16th St. NW, Washington, DC 20036. (202) 785-1136. Shreeniwas R. Tamhane, Exec. Dir. Coordinats the selection and placement of U.S. documentary, television, short subject, and didactic films in more than eighty overseas film festivals annually. A Golden Eagle Certificate is awarded to each professional film considered most suitable to represent the United States in international competition. A CINE Eagle Certificate is awarded to winning films in the categories of adult amateur, youth, and university student. Prizes and certificates won at overseas festivals are presented by embassy representatives at an annual awards luncheon. *Publication: CINE Yearbook.*

CTIC Associates. 1500 N. Beauregard St., Suite 205, Alexandria, VA 22209. (703) 845-1700. Harold E. Horn, Pres. A consulting group that provides technical assistance and consulting services on cable-related matters to local governments, educators, and other institutional users of cable systems. CTIC Associates assists local governments in the franchising process, attends public hearings, prepares ordinance and request for proposal documents, and evaluates franchise applications. CTIC Associates provides advice and assistance in franchise renegotiations and rate regulation. Additional consulting services include telecommunication needs assessments, institutional network research, planning and implementation assistance, and advice on cable utilization projects for noncommercial user groups.

DEVELOP Search Service. Box 10127, Denver, CO 80210. The DEVELOP database created by Control Data to serve the needs of developing agricultural and industrial countries, includes nonbibliographic information covering areas such as alternative energy, small farm agriculture, development technologies, small enterprise development, community self-reliance, and international development. For custom searches or online subscription information, write N. Miller, HQW12X, Box O, Minneapolis, MN 55440 (612) 853-4006. *Dues:* $50.00 per search; online subscription packages available.

DIALOG Information Services. 3460 Hillview Ave., Palo Alto, CA 94304. (800) 982-5838. Dr. Roger K. Summit, Pres. An online information retrieval service including more than twenty databases containing over one hundred million references from sources worldwide; includes Inspec and Compendex for microcomputer technology information; Menu-International Software Database, Computer Database, Microcomputer Index, and Magazine Index for software reviews, and evaluations; and A-V Online and NICSEM/NIMIS for information on nonprint educational materials. *Publications: Guide to DIALOG Searching; Chronolog* (mo.) newsletter.

Digital Equipment Computer Users Society. One Iron Way, Marlboro, MA 01752. (617) 467-4166. Mary B. Oskirko, Marketing Communications Specialist. Facilitates exchanges of information and programs regarding the use of Digital Equipment Corporation computers, computer peripheral equipment, and software via technical symposia, a program library, publications, and special interest groups in education, operating systems, interactive graphics, and related fields. Sponsors two national interactive symposia each year. *Membership:* 65,000. *Publications: DECUSCOPE; Proceedings; Program Library Catalog; Special Interest Group.*

East-West Institute of Culture and Communication. East-West Center, 1777 East-West Rd., Honolulu, HI 96848. (808) 944-7666. Dr. Mary G. F. Bitterman, Dir. Studies development communication, the humanities, media and international relations, and social relations; conducts research; arranges conferences; offers study grants; and publishes books, papers, and educational materials on topics related to culture and communication.

Editorial Projects in Education. 1255 23rd St. NW, Suite 775, Washington, DC 20037. (202) 466-5190. Ronald A. Wolk, Pres. *Publication: Education Week.*

Education Commission of the States. 1860 Lincoln St., Suite 300, Denver, CO 80295. (303) 830-3600. Robert C. Andringa, Exec. Dir. Formed by interstate compact in 1966 to further working relationships among state governors, legislators, and educators for the improvement of U.S. education. Its goal is to develop a partnership of public officials and education leaders within each state and among the states. Provides information on state-related education activities and, when appropriate, suggests options and alternatives to meet specific state needs. *Publications: State Education Leader* (q.); numerous papers, booklets, and reports on educational issues and topics.

Education Development Center, Inc. 55 Chapel St., Newton, MA 02160. (617) 969-7100. Janet Whitla, Pres. Seeks to improve education at all levels, in the United States and abroad, through curriculum development, institutional development, and services to schools and the community. Produces filmstrips and videocassettes, primarily in connection with curriculum development and teacher training. *Publications: Annual Report;* occasional papers.

Educational Facilities Laboratories. A Division of Academy for Educational Development, 1101 Trinity, Austin, TX 78701. (512) 474-7539. Ben Graves, Div. Dir.

Seeks to aid nonprofit, people-serving institutions in planning and managing functionally useful and practical physical facilities. Projects are supported by contracts from private and government agencies, and foundations. *Publications: Academy News; Communications Technology in Higher Education;* others.

Educational Film Library Association. 45 John St., Suite 301, New York, NY 10038. (212) 227-5599. Marilyn Levin, Exec. Dir. EFLA is recognized as the authoritative organization in assembling data about the 16mm and video fields, in encouraging quality production and appreciation of film generally, and in guiding the major segments of U.S. life in proper use of these media. Serves as a national clearinghouse of information about films; conducts workshops on a variety of film-related topics; sponsors the annual American Film Festival. *Membership:* 1,600. *Dues:* $140.00 inst. up to 250 prints; $190.00 over 250 prints; $45.00 indiv. *Publications: Sightlights; EFLA Bulletin; EFLA Evaluations; EFLA Film Evaluations Guide.*

Educational Technology Publications, Inc. 720 Palisade Ave., Englewood Cliffs, NJ 07632. (201) 871-4007. Lawrence Lipsitz, Ed. *Publications: Educational Technology: The Magazine for Managers of Change in Education; Instructional Design Library; Instructional Media Library;* and more than 150 other books and booklets, audiocassettes, and related media resources for the professional in the field.

EDUCOM (Interuniversity Communications Council). Box 364, Princeton, NJ 08540. (609) 921-7575. John W. McCredie, Pres. Promotes better use of computing, television, and other technology in higher education through research, resource sharing, and cooperative efforts of higher education institutions.

Electronics Industries Association. 2001 I St. NW, Washington, DC 20006. (202) 457-4900. Peter F. McCloskey, Pres. EIA is the full-service national trade organization representing the entire spectrum of companies involved in the manufacture and distribution of electronic components, parts, systems, and equipment for communications, industrial, government, and consumer-end uses. *Membership:* 400. *Publications: Electronic Market Trends; Publication Index; Executive Report.*

Environmental Quality Instructional Resources Center. Ohio State Univ., 1200 Chambers Rd., Rm. 310, Columbus, OH 43212. (614) 422-6717. Robert W. Howe, Dir. A subsidized service of the U.S. Environmental Protection Agency with an emphasis on water quality education and training. Maintains IRIS (Instructional Resources Information System) and an audiovisual library; offers workshops. *Publications: IRC Bulletin; IRIS* supplements; various monographs.

EPIE Institute (Educational Products Information Exchange). Box 839, Water Mill, NY 11976. (516) 283-4922. P. Kenneth Komoski, Exec. Dir. Involved primarily in assessing new educational media. Provides in-depth evaluative reports of various kinds for its members covering such topics as overhead projectors, individualized instructional materials, textbooks, and other items. Together with Consumers Union, provides evaluations of educational microcomputer software and hardware. EPIE's microcomputer product evaluations are accessible electronically via CompuServe. EPIE also provides in-service training and consultation, and microcomputer seminars on software and hardware evaluations. All of EPIE's services are made available to schools. *Publications: EPIEgram Materials; EPIEgram Equipment; MICROgram; The Educational Software Selector.*

ERIC (Educational Resources Information Center). 1200 19th St. NW, Washington, DC 20208. (202) 254-5500. Charles Hoover, Dir. Coordinates the ERIC system of sixteen clearinghouses (note following entries). ERIC's database contains citations to more than 200,000 unpublished or hard-to-find documents on various phases, levels, and subject areas of education, all of which are intended to assist professionals in locating data pertaining to classroom, administrative, and planning problems. ERIC also catalogs and announces journal articles dealing with education from over 750 educational journals. Offers a microfile of uncopyrighted materials in over 750 collections throughout the world. *Publications: Resources in Education; Current Index to Journals in Education.*

ERIC Clearinghouse for Junior Colleges. Univ. of California, 8118 Math Science Bldg., Los Angeles, CA 90024. (213) 825-3931. Arthur M. Cohen, Dir. Development, administration, and evaluation of public and private community and junior colleges; two-year college students, staff, curricula, administration, and evaluation of public and private community and junior colleges; two-year college students, staff, curricula, administration, programs, libraries, and community services. Encourages submission of papers, speeches, reports, curricula, and other materials on two-year colleges; produces bibliographies and distributes publications at workshops and conferences; computer searches of ERIC database; free newsletter and publication upon request.

ERIC Clearinghouse on Adult, Career, and Vocational Education. Center for Research in Vocational Education, Ohio State Univ., 1960 Kenny Rd., Columbus, OH 43210. (614) 486-3655. Dr. Juliet V. Miller, Dir. Career education at all levels, formal and informal, encompassing attitudes, self-knowledge, decision-making skills, general and occupational knowledge, and specific vocational and occupational skills. Adult and continuing education, correspondence study, and all areas of in-service training, relating to occupational, family, leisure, citizen, organizational, and retirement roles. Vocational and technical education, including new subprofessional fields, occupational psychology, occupational sociology, manpower economics, and vocational rehabilitation. Prepares an annual series of major publications.

ERIC Clearinghouse on Counseling and Personnel Services. School of Education, Rm 2108, Univ. of Michigan, Ann Arbor, MI 48109. (313) 764-9492. Garry R. Walz, Pres. Information on counselors and personnel workers, their preparation, practice, and supervision at all educational levels and in all settings; the use of results of personnel procedures such as testing, interviewing, group work, and the analysis of the resultant information relating to the individual and his environment, the development of counseling, the nature of pupil; descriptions of educational and occupational rehabilitation and community settings; counseling with special population groups such as the incarcerated, women, and so forth.

ERIC Clearinghouse on Educational Management. Univ. of Oregon, 1787 Agate St., Eugene, OR 97403. (503) 686-5043. Philip K. Piele, Dir. Information on educational management, including facilities at elementary and secondary levels; administration of education; management, leadership and structure of public and private educational organizations; preservice and inservice preparation of administrators; procedures of administration and educational organizations. Educational facilities; planning, financing, constructing, renovating, equipping, maintaining, operating, insuring, utilizing, and evaluating educational facilities; advancing educational programs via facilities and plant; and influences of the physical environment on learning. *Publications: The Best of ERIC*; monographs; directory; newsletter.

ERIC Clearinghouse on Elementary and Early Childhood Education. College of Education, Univ. of Illinois, 805 W. Pennsylvania Ave., Urbana, IL 61801. (217) 333-1386. Lilian Katz, Dir. Concerned with psychological, social, educational, and cultural development of children from birth through the elementary grades; parental and family behavior educational theory, research, and practice related to the development of young children. *Publications: Micronotes on Children and Computers; ERIC/EECE News Bulletin*; reviews and occasional papers.

ERIC Clearinghouse on Handicapped and Gifted Children. 1920 Association Dr., Reston, VA 22091. (703) 620-3660. Lynn Smarte, Asst. Dir. Concerned with the hearing impaired; visually impaired, mentally retarded, developmentally disabled, abused, neglected, autistic, multiple handicapped, severly handicapped, physically disabled, emotionally disturbed, speech handicapped, learning disabled, other health impaired and the gifted and the talented, behavior, psychomotor, and communication disorders. Also handles information concerning administration of special education services preparation and continuing education of professional and paraprofessional personnel; preschool learning and development of exceptional children.

ERIC Clearinghouse on Higher Education. George Washington Univ., One Dupont Circle NW, Suite 630, Washington, DC 20036. (202) 296-2597. Jonathan D. Fife, Dir. All aspects of higher education covered including student programs, conditions, and problems in colleges and universities such as faculty, graduate and professional education, governance and management of higher education institutions, legal issues, financing, planning and evaluation, curriculum and instructional problems, university extension programs, inter-institutional arrangements, related state and federal programs and policies, institutional research and statistics on higher education; higher education as a social institution, and comparative higher education.

ERIC Clearinghouse on Information Resources. School of Education, Syracuse Univ., Syracuse, NY 13210. (315) 423-3640. Donald P. Ely, Dir. Processes documents on research, development, delivery, and evaluation of information and instructional technology. It focuses on personnel, personnel development strategies, systems, procedures, materials, and equipment used in the fields of information and education. Current areas include libraries; learning resource centers; information science; instructional design, development, and evaluation; systems analysis; community information systems and instructional media; as well as strategies that follow from these topics. Also concerned with delivery of information through a host of media formats. *Publications:* A host of surveys and studies on ERIC related topics.

ERIC Clearinghouse on Languages and Linguistics. 3520 Prospect St. NW, Washington, DC 20007. (202) 298-9292. John L. D. Clark, Dir. Foreign language education, psycho-linguistics, and psychology of language learning; theoretical and applied linguistics; bilin-gualism and bilingual education; English as a second language; and uncommonly taught languages are all concerns of the clearinghouse.

ERIC Clearinghouse on Reading and Communication Skills. 1111 Kenyon Rd., Urbana, IL 61801. (217) 328-3870. Charles Suhor, Dir. Collects, analyzes, evaluates, and disseminates educational information related to research, instruction, and personnel preparation at all levels and in all institutions. The scope of interest of the clearinghouse includes relevant research reports, literature reviews, curriculum guides and descriptions, conference papers, project or program reviews, and other print material related to reading, English, language arts, educational journalism, and speech sciences. The clearinghouse also sponsors workshops, referral systems and makes available the ERIC system. *Publications:* Publishes approximately ten educational monographs per year.

ERIC Clearinghouse on Rural Education and Small Schools (ERIC/CRESS). Box 3AP, New Mexico State Univ., Las Cruces, NM 88003. (505) 646-2623. Everett Edington, Dir. Acquires, abstracts, indexes, and disseminates documents concerning American Indians, Mexican Americans, migrant workers, outdoor and rural education, and small schools. Prepares bibliographies and state-of-the-art papers, provides consultation services on the establishment and use of information centers, and conducts computer searches of the ERIC files, including both the RIE collections and CIJE articles.

ERIC Clearinghouse on Science, Mathematics, and Environmental Education. Ohio State Univ., 1200 Chambers Rd., Columbus, OH 43212. (614) 422-6717. Robert W. Howe, Dir. Includes all levels of science, mathematics, and environmental education materials; development of related curriculum and instructional materials; media; applications to science, mathematics, and environmental education with related methodological studies; impact of interest, intelligence, values and concept development upon learning related to science, mathematics, and environmental education; related preservice and in-service teacher education and supervision. *Publications:* activity manuals; monographs; directories; and indexes to ERIC materials.

ERIC Clearinghouse on Social Studies/Social Science Education. 855 Broadway, Boulder, CO 80302. (303) 492-8434. Irving Morrissett, Dir. The clearinghouse acquires, selects, and processes significant documents and journal articles on all levels of social studies/social science education. Documents are indexed and abstracted in the monthly ERIC publicatication *Resources in Education* and journal articles are indexed and annotated in *Current Index to Journals in Education.* In addition, the clearinghouse commissions or writes publications analyzing and synthesizing ideas in the field of social studies science education. It also responds to visitor and letter requests for information by drawing on the ERIC base. *Publications:* newsletter; write for free publications catalog.

ERIC Clearinghouse on Teacher Education (ERIC/SP). One Dupont Circle NW, Suite 610, Washington, DC 20036. (202) 293-2540. Specializes in acquiring, evaluating, abstracting, and indexing literature in the following areas: education personnel preparation; education theory and philosophy; health education, physical education, and recreation education (HPER). *Publications:* monographs and fact sheets; explanatory and promotional materials; training and reference services; computer searches of the ERIC database; and *Bulletin* — an information packet to mailing list subscribers.

ERIC Clearinghouse on Tests, Measurement, and Evaluation (ERIC/TM). Educational Testing Service (ETS), Rosedale Rd., Princeton, NJ 08541. (609) 734-5181. S. Donald Melville, Dir. Collects, evaluates, processes, and disseminates information in six areas of interest: tests and information about tests; all types of measurement techniques; evaluation procedures and theory; research methodology; human development; and learning theory, in general. *Publications:* publications list available upon request.

ERIC Clearinghouse on Urban Education (ERIC/CUE). Box 40, Teachers College, Columbia Univ., New York, NY 10027. (212) 678-3437. Erwin Flaxman, Dir. Scope of interest includes the academic, intellectual, and social performance of urban and minority young people from third grade on; the education of blacks, Puerto Ricans, Asian and Pacific Americans, immigrants and refugees in urban, suburban, and rural areas, as well as the education of all other ethnic groups in urban and suburban areas only; learning experiences designed to meet the special needs of the diverse populations served by urban and minority schools; structural changes in classrooms, schools, districts, and communities that directly affect urban children; economic and ethnic discrimination; educational equity for all population groups; the education of groups in other countries; the social life, conditions, and services that affect children. *Publications:* monographs; bibliographies; short reports; and a newsletter (bi-ann.).

ERIC Document Reproduction Service (EDRS). Computer Microfilm International Corp., 3900 Wheeler Ave., Alexandria, VA 22304. (800) 227-3742. Operates the microfiche reproduction service for the ERIC system. Address purchase orders to the above address.

ERIC Processing and Reference Facility. ORI, Information Systems Division, 4833 Rugby Ave., Suite 301, Bethesda, MD 20814. (301) 656-9723. Receives and edits abstracts from sixteen ERIC clearinghouses for announcement in *Resources in Education* (*RIE*) and monitors changes in the *ERIC Thesaurus.*

Experience Education. 103 S. Broadway, Red Oak, IA 51566. (712) 623-4913. William Horner, Dir. A course of study in the mass media built around concepts of individualized instruction and learning by doing. Includes fifty learning packages dealing with media hardware, production, genre, evaluation, interpretation, aesthetics, and presentation. The broad goal of "Media Now" is to point out the ways in which the media affect buying habits, leisure time, family life, and personality. The program can be used to help students become aware of the purpose and effects of advertising. It provides a course of study for the analysis of the media's impact on interpersonal communication. Built around the concepts of individualized instruction, performance objectives, and learning by doing, the course has been tested and validated in the classsroom. *Publications: The Student Learning Activity Guide; Student Learning Activity Book; Media Dictionary; Teacher Activity Book.*

Far West Laboratory for Educational Research and Development (FWL). 1855 Folsom St., San Francisco, CA 94103. (415) 565-3000. William G. Spady, Dir. Contributes to the improvement of the quality of learning experiences that support the values and functions of a humanistic society. FWL carries out its mission by producing new knowledge through research; conducting programmatic development leading to new, high-quality products or processes that will serve the needs of all learners; providing technical assistance in support of quality education for those who seek it; and by confronting and assessing educational issues in an impartial environment. FWL maintains a library with a complete ERIC microfiche collection and conducts information searches. *Publications:* books; newsletters; curriculum guides; pamphlets; and reports.

Federal Communications Commission (FCC). 1919 M St. NW, Washington, DC 20554. (202) 632-7000. An agency that regulates radio, television, telephone, and telegraph operations within the United States. Allocates frequencies and channels for different types of communications activities; issues amateur and commercial operators licenses; and regulates rates of interstate communication services of many different kinds. *Publications:* bulletins pertaining to educational broadcasting.

Federal Communications Commission, Cable Television Bureau. 1919 M St. NW, Washington, DC 20554. (202) 632-9703. Develops, recommends, and administers policies and programs with respect to the regulation of cable television systems and related private microwave radio facilities.

Federal Communications Commission, Consumer Assistance Office. 1919 M St. NW, Rm. 258, Washington, DC 20554. (202) 632-9703. Special assistance to communications services customers.

Film Advisory Board (FAB). 1727 N. Sycamore, Hollywood, CA 90028. (213) 874-3644. Elayne Blythe, Pres. Previews and evaluates films and film-type presentations in all formats, recommends for improved family entertainment fare; presents awards of excellence to outstanding motion pictures and TV programs and innovations in these industries. Technical awards also presented as well as awards for outstanding contribution to the entertainment industry and to the most promising young newcomers. *Publications:* monthly film list distributed to studios, PR firms, youth groups, PTA, clubs, and colleges ($20.00/yr.).

Film Arts Foundation (FAF). 346 Ninth St., 2nd Floor, San Francisco, CA 94103. (415) 552-8760. Gail Silva, Mng. Dir. Service organization designed to support and promote independent media production. Services include: low cost postproduction facility, skills file, festivals file, resource library, group legal plan, seminars, workshops, work-in-progress screenings, proposal consultation, nonprofit sponsorship of selected film and video projects, and advocacy for independent film and video. *Membership:* 800. *Dues:* $25.00. *Publication: Release Print.*

Film Library Information Council (FLIC). Box 348, Radio City Station, New York, NY 10101. (212) 956-4211. William Sloan, Ed. Organized to improve the quality of public library film and other new media services. Voting membership open to staff members of libraries, museums, and other nonprofit organizations that provide community film services.

Film Society of Lincoln Center. 140 W. 65th St., New York, NY 10023. (212) 877-1800, ext. 489. Joanne Koch, Exec. Dir. Programs include annual New York Film Festival; "New Directors, New Films" cosponsored by the Museum of Modern Art; Film in Education program. *Publication: Film Comment.*

Film/Video Arts, Inc. 817 Broadway, New York, NY 10003. (212) 673-9361. Encourages media production as educational, vocational, and artistic experience. Provides an equipment resource center that includes equipment loans, a video synthesis studio and postproduction facilities; film and video training workshops including a scholarship program for minorities and women; a directors project for film and television professionals in the process of directing actors; and a film bureau that provides film rental and speaker subsidies to New York nonprofit community organizations. *Dues:* $25.00 indiv.; $50.00 org. *Publications: A Guide for Film Teachers; Filmmaking with Young People; Young Animators; Equipment Loan Handbook: A Guide to the Equipment Loan Services of YF/VA;* and *Selected Issues in Media Law.*

FILMNET: The Film Users Network. c/o Cine Information, 330 W. 42nd St., Suite 2410, New York, NY 10036. (212) 873-1331. Recently established to assist film users in locating resources needed for their programs. Provides a free information service to film/video users and a targeted mailing list to film/video makers and distributors; offers other film-related mailing lists and a computerized service for an organization's mailing lists (on a contractual basis).

Freedom of Information Center (FoI). Box 858, Univ. of Missouri, Columbia, MO 65205. (314) 882-4856. Collects and disseminates material on action by government, media, and society affecting the flow of information at international, national, state, and local levels. The center answers questions on how to use the federal FoI Act, censorship issues, access to government at all levels, privacy, ethics, bar-press guidelines, and First Amendment issues. *Dues:* $15.00 indiv.; $25.00 inst. *Publications: FoI Digest; FoI Center Report.*

Government Printing Office (US GPO). N. Capitol and H Sts. NW, Washington, DC 20401. (202) 275-2951. The GPO prints and binds materials from Congress and federal departments and agencies, furnishes printed materials to all government activities, and distributes and sells government publications (through the Superintendent of Documents Office). *See also* Superintendent of Documents.

Grange Farm Film Foundation (GFFF). 1616 H St. NW, Washington, DC 20006. (202) 628-3507. Judy T. Massabny, Exec. Dir. Dedicated to the creation of better understanding between rural and urban Americans through audiovisual education.

Great Plains National ITV Library (GPN). Box 80669, Lincoln, NE 68501. (402) 472-2007. Paul H. Schupbach, Dir. Dedicated to the utilization and sharing of education television courses produced by organizations across the country. Present offerings of more than one hundred videotaped courses and related teacher utilization materials. Users may lease or purchase, some available on 16mm film. *Publications:* newsletter; annual catalog; occasional flyers and brochures.

Handicapped Educational Exchange (HEX). 11523 Charlton Dr., Silver Spring, MD 20902. (301) 593-7033. Richard Barth, Dir. A free national computer network devoted to the exchange of ideas and information on the use of advanced technologies to aid handicapped individuals. Access is available through a telephone/modem or the Telecommunication Device for the Deaf (TDD).

Health Sciences Communication Association (HeSCA). Rte 5, Box 311F, Midlothian, VA 23113. (804) 794-0363. Richart Torres, Pres. Seeks to draw together people with a wide variety of knowledge, professions, and experience in work toward the common goal of improved education in all areas of the health sciences. *Membership:* 732. *Dues:* $65.00; $32.50 students. *Publications: Feedback* (newsletter); *Journal of Biocommunication.*

Hollywood Film Archive. 8344 Melrose Ave., Hollywood, CA 90069-5420. (213) 933-3345. D. Richard Baer, Dir. Archival organization for feature films produced worldwide, from the early silents to the present. Offers comprehensive movie reference works for sale.

HOPE Reports. 1600 Lyell Ave., Rochester, NY 14606. (716) 458-4250. Thomas Hope, Pres. Provides publications for the audiovisual/video communication field covering statistical and financial status, salaries, trends, and predictions. Calendar-scheduling service of national/international events. Also makes private contract surveys, consulting.

Information Industry Association (IIA). 316 Pennsylvania Ave. SE, #400, Washington, DC 20003. (202) 544-1969. Paul G. Zurkowski, Pres. The IIA is a full-service trade association providing members with programs in government relations, conferences and conventions, publications and studies, and public relations. The association is organized into three core service councils comprised of member volunteers who direct and develop program activities during the year. These councils include Business Operations, Technology & Innovation, and Public Policy and Government Relations. In addition, two divisions were organized in 1984 — Videotex and Database Publishing. *Membership:* Over 300 companies that create, store, manage, and distribute information electronically or through traditional publishing means. *Publications: Information Sources 1985; The Business of Information Survey; Artificial Intelligence: Reality or Fantasy?; So You Want to Be a Profitable Database Publisher; Compensation Practices in the Information Industry; How to Succeed in the Electronic Information Marketplace.*

Institute for Development of Educational Activities, Inc. 259 Regency Ridge, Dayton, OH 45459. (513) 434-6969. Investigates, designs, and tests new approaches to improving elementary and secondary schools; implements school improvement programs through universities, school districts, and other cooperating groups; explores, assesses, and reports on emerging educational trends; and reports on research efforts through films and publications. Supports experimental efforts that have come to be known as IGE (Individually Guided Education) and, more recently, a School Improvement Project.

Institute for Research on Teaching. College of Education, Michigan State Univ., East Lansing, MI 48824. (517) 353-6413. Andrew Porter and Jere Brophy, Co-Dirs. Funded primarily by the National Institute of Education, conducts research on the enduring problems of practice encountered by teaching professionals and publishes numerous materials detailing these projects. *Publications:* research series; occasional papers; newsletter; annual catalog.

Institute for the Future. 2740 Sand Hill Rd., Menlo Park, CA 94025. (415) 854-6322. Roy Amara, Pres. IFTF helps organizations plan long-term futures, take advantage of opportunities in markets for emerging technologies, and use new information for improved management productivity. Research and consulting include forecasting and strategic planning, teleconferencing and office systems, and videotex and home information services. IFTF has innovative planning techniques combining quantitative and qualitative analysis and experience in practical application of new technologies.

Institute of International Education. 809 United Nations Plaza, New York, NY 10017. (212) 883-8200. Richard Krasuo, Pres. A private, nonprofit organization administering public and private grants to enable U.S. students to study abroad and foreign students to study at universities in this country. *Membership:* 500 U.S. colleges and universities. *Dues:* vary. *Publications:* reference guides to educational exchange; *The Learning Traveler Series: U.S. College-Sponsored Programs Abroad; Academic Year, Vol. 1; Vacation Study Abroad, Vol. 2; Open Doors: Report on International Educational Exchange; Costs at U.S. Educational Institutions; English Language and Orientation Programs in the U.S.; Summer Learning Options;* plus numerous publications and directories for foreign nationals interested in U.S. study.

International Association of Business Communicators. 870 Market St., Suite 940, San Francisco, CA 94102. (415) 433-3400. Norman Leaper, Pres. An association of some 12,000 business, industrial, and association/organization personnel engaged primarily in communication and public relations. IABC has 126 chapters in Canada, the United States, and the United Kingdom. It also has affiliates in 46 countries including Australia, Belgium, Denmark, France, India, Japan, Mexico, the Netherlands, Norway, South Africa, and Sweden. The largest group of IABC members works for insurance companies, followed by manufacturing, medical/hospital, finance, banking, utilities, food/beverage, petroleum, and computer technology. *Dues:* $100.00. *Publication: IABC Communications World.*

International Association of Satellite Users & Suppliers. P.O. Box DD, McLean, VA 22101. (703) 759-2094. A. Fred Dassler, Pres. A nonprofit, international trade association of corporations representing the entire spectrum of the satellite industry promoting the interests of private and commercial electronic satellite users and suppliers. *Membership:* 200. *Dues:* $195.00 to $790.00 depending on the size of company. *Publications: Transponder* (newsletter); special reports; annual meeting audiotapes.

International Association of School Librarianship (IASL). P.O. Box 1486, Kalamazoo, MI 49005. (616) 343-5728. Jean E. Lowrie, Exec. Sec. Seeks to encourage development of school libraries and library programs throughout the world; to promote professional preparation of school librarians; to achieve collaboration among school libraries of the world; and to facilitate loans and exchanges in the field. *Membership:* 800. *Dues:* $10.00. *Publications: IASL Newsletter; Annual Proceedings; Persons to Contact; Directory of National School Library Association;* and occasional papers.

International Center of Photography. 1130 5th Ave., New York, NY 10028. (212) 860-1777. Cornell Capa, Dir. A comprehensive photographic institution whose exhibitions, publications, collections, and educational programs embrace all aspects of photography — from aesthetics to technique, from the eighteenth century to the present, from master photographers to newly emerging talents, from photojournalism to the avant-garde. Changing exhibitions, lectures, seminars, workshops, a museum shop, and screening room make ICP a complete photographic resource. *Membership:* 3,500. *Publications: Library of Photography; Encyclopedia of Photography.*

International Communication Association. Box 9589, Austin, TX 78766. (512) 454-8299. Robert L. Cox, Exec. Dir. Established to study human communication and to seek better understanding of the process of communication. Engages in systematic studies of communication theories, processes, and skills; disseminates information. *Membership: 2,400. Dues: $50.00. Publications: Journal of Communication; ICA Newsletter; Human Communication Research.*

The International Communications Industries Association (ICIA). 3150 Spring St., Fairfax, VA 22031. (703) 273-7200. Harry R. McGee, Exec. V.P. An international association of media hardware and software producers and manufacturers, dealers, representatives, and others involved with educational, communications, and information activities, services, and products. Maintains close liaison with Congress in matters pertaining to media legislation. Annual convention and exhibit held each January. Recent media-related activities have included meetings and other programs with Audio-Visual America, National School Board's Association, American Society for Training and Development, Visual Communications Congress, Video East and Communications Day. *Publications: Audio-Visual Equipment Directory; Communications Industries Report.*

International Copyright Information Center (INCINC). c/o Association of American Publishers, 2005 Massachusetts Ave. NW, Washington, DC 20036. (202) 232-3335. Carol A. Risher, Dir. Assists developing nations in their efforts to translate and/or reprint copyrighted U.S. published works.

International Council for Computers in Education (ICCE). Univ. of Oregon, 1787 Agate St., Eugene, OR 97403. (503) 686-4414. Bobby Goodson, Pres. ICEE is a nonprofit organization dedicated to promoting instructional and creative uses of computers in education and teacher training. *Membership: 15,000. Dues: $21.50/yr. Publications: The Computing Teacher* (mo. journal); 17 booklets including *School Administrator's Introduction to Instructional Use of Computers; Teachers Guide to Computers in Elementary School; Parents' Guide to Computers in Education; Logo in the Classroom; Precollege Computer Literacy; Computers in Composition Instruction.* Catalog available on request.

International Film and TV Festival of New York. 246 W. 38th St., New York, NY 10018. (914) 238-4481. Gerald M. Goldberg, Chair. An annual competitive festival presenting examples of professional film and video productions and television shows. Includes TV, cinema, and commercials. *Dues:* various.

International Friendship League, Inc. 55 Mount Vernon St., Boston, MA 02109. (617) 523-4273. Edna R. MacDonough, Exec. Secy. Organized in 1948 in 129 countries; aims to promote a better understanding of the world among young people through regular exchanges of personal letters. The largest percentage of mail matched is with secondary school students, although students of college age as well as adults also participate. Send envelope for complete details. *Dues: $3.00 7-19 yrs.; $5.00 over 19 yrs.;* one time fee.

International Graphic Arts Education Association (IGAEA). 4615 Forbes Ave., Pittsburgh, PA 15213. (412) 682-5170. John T. Pagels, Pres. President's address is 28144 Newport Dr., Warren, MI 48093. An organization of professionals in graphic arts education and industry, dedicated to promoting effective research and disseminating information concerning graphic arts, graphic communications, and related fields of printing. *Membership: 800. Dues: $10.00 regular; $7.50 assoc.; $3.00 student; $25.00-$10.00 sustaining. Publications: The Communicator* (newsletter); *Visual Communications Journal.*

International Information Management Congress (IMC). Box 34404, Bethesda, MD 20817. (301) 983-0604. Don M. Avedon, Exec. Dir. An educational association supporting education in the information management field; exchange of information and publications. Organizes yearly conferences and exhibits in different parts of the world. *Membership: 37 assoc.; 100 sustaining company members. Publications:* quarterly journal; monthly newsletter.

International Museum of Photography at George Eastman House. 900 East Ave., Rochester, NY 14607. (716) 271-3361. Robert A. Mayer, Dir. World-renowned museum of photographic history established to preserve, collect, and exhibit photographic materials and to present a variety of services and programs to promote a better understanding and appreciation of photographic art and science. Services include archives, traveling exhibitions, regional center for the conservation of photographic materials, photographic print service. Educational programs, symposia, and internship stipends offered. *Dues:* $30.00; $20.00 student. *Publications: IMAGE; Microfiche Index to Collections;* newsletter.

International Reading Association (IRA). 800 Barksdale Rd., Box 8139, Newark, DE 19714-8139. (302) 731-1600. Ronald Mitchell, Exec. Dir. Seeks to improve the quality of reading instruction at all levels; to develop awareness of the impact of reading; to sponsor conferences and meetings planned to implement the Association's purposes, and to promote the development of reading proficiency that is commensurate with each individuals unique capacity. *Membership:* 60,000. *Dues:* $30.00 and up. *Publications: Reading Research Quarterly; Journal of Reading; The Reading Teacher.*

International Tape/Disc Association (ITA). 10 Columbus Circle, Suite 2270, New York, NY 10019. (212) 956-7110. Henry Brief, Exec. V.P. World's largest international audio/video trade association; acts as a clearinghouse for information about the industry; holds seminars in audio and video technology, marketing, merchandising, distribution, and programming. *Membership:* over 450 companies. *Publications: ITA News Digest; ITA Source Directory.*

International Telecommunications Satellite Organization (INTELSAT). 490 L'Enfant Plaza SW, Washington, DC 20024. (202) 488-2683. Gavin Trevitt, Pub. Info. Off. Dedicated to the design, development, construction, establishment, operation, and maintenance of the global, international telecommunications satellite system, which currently provides two-thirds of the world's international overseas telecommunications links. *Membership:* 109 countries.

International Teleconferencing Association (ITCA). 1299 Woodside Dr., Suite 101, McLean, VA 22102. (703) 556-6115. J. Robert Brouse, Exec. Dir. Seeks to provide a clearinghouse for the exchange of information between users, researchers, and providers in the field of teleconferencing. *Membership:* 450. *Dues:* $65.00 indiv.; $30.00 student; $180.00 corporations; $1,500.00 sustaining. *Publication: Insiders Newsletter.*

International Television Association (ITVA). 3 Dallas Communications Complex, 6309 N. O'Connor Rd., Suite 110, Irving, TX 75039. (214) 869-1112. Edward Sheehy, Exec. Dir. Aims to develop, share, disseminate information about the use of television for communication, both in the United States and abroad. *Membership:* 6,000. *Dues:* $60.00. *Publications: International Television; The International Television Journal.*

Lawrence Hall of Science. Univ. of California, Berkeley, CA 94720. (415) 642-3167. A center for research and public education. Its Math and Computer Education Project introduces visitors, school groups, and teachers to computers through classes, workshops, exhibits, and the publication of software packages. *Publications: Teaching Basic Bit by Bit; Creative Play; What's in Your Lunch?; Micros for Micros.*

Library of Congress. Washington, DC 20540. (202) 287-5108. The research arm of Congress and the national library. The library provides materials on interlibrary loan and prepares traveling exhibits of photographs, posters, artworks, and prints. Cataloging data available in card, book, and machine-readable formats. The American Folklife Center provides for the preservation and dissemination of folklife through research, performances, exhibits, publications, and recordings. The Copyright Office catalogs copyright entries. Many other divisions are of interest to media specialists. *Publications:* All publications are listed in *Library of Congress Publications in Print.*

Magazine Publishers Association (MPA). 575 Lexington Ave., New York, NY 10022. (212) 752-0055. William F. Gorog, Pres. MPA is the trade association of the consumer magazine industry, with 198 publisher-members representing over 700 magazines. MPA promotes the greater and more effective use of magazine advertising – with ad campaigns in the trade press and in MPA member magazines, presentations to advertisers and their ad agencies, and magazine days in cities around the United States. MPA runs seminars for its members to help them better understand and manage their magazines; conducts surveys of its members on a variety of topics; represents the magazine industry in key state capitals; and carries on other activities. *Membership:* 198 publishers representing over 700 magazines. *Publication:* newsletter.

Media Center for Children (MCC). 3 W. 29th St., New York, NY 10001. (212) 689-0300. Maureen Gaffney, Exec. Dir., Robert Braun, Info. Dir. A resource for professionals who make or use media with children. Institutional services include ongoing evaluations of short nontheatrical 16mm films and videotapes with children and documentation of children's responses in various publications; programming consultation is available for libraries, museums, schools, hospitals, and community organizations; production consultation available to individuals and institutions; and workshops and courses for teachers, librarians, art and museum educators, cable programmers, and filmmakers or videomakers. *Publications: Young Viewers* (q. review/newsletter); *What Do We Do When the Lights Go On* (handbook).

The Media Project (MPI). Box 4093, Portland, OR 97208. (503) 223-5335. Linda Stovall, Exec. Dir. MPI is a nonprofit membership organization designed to foster public awareness of independent film and video artists and their work, and it serves as a noncommercial distributor for the best of Northwest work. Publications, workshops, and seminars on technical aspects of filmmaking are offered; public exhibitions are held; a speakers bureau and fiscal administration of film projects are also available. *Dues:* $10.00 student; $25.00 indiv.; $100.00 business. *Publications: Program Catalog; Printed Matter; Oregon Guide to Media Services; Copyright Primer for Film and Video.*

Medical Library Association (MLA). 919 N. Michigan Ave., #3208, Chicago, IL 60611. (312) 266-2456. Phyllis Mirsky, Pres. MLA members are professionals in the health sciences library field dedicated to excellence in health information services and fostering medical and allied scientific libraries. MLA offers an institutional exchange list, annual meeting, librarian certification, continuing education courses, job placement, and mailing list rentals. *Membership:* 5,000. *Dues:* $60.00 indiv.; $100.00 inst.; $200.00 sustaining. *Publications: MLA News; Bulletin of the Medical Library Association; Current Catalog Proof Sheets.*

Milo Ryan Phonoarchive. National Archives and Records Service, Washington, DC 20408. Les Waffen, GSA. A collection of tapes recorded from several thousand acetate recordings, chiefly of news reports of the late 1930s and the 1940s, developed under a grant from the Columbia Broadcasting System and the Saul Haas Foundation. Contains nearly five thousand tape-recorded radio programs that are cataloged and annotated; listings have been computerized to aid in research. Sets of *History in Sound* available from Instructional Media Services, Univ. of Washington, Seattle, WA 98195 and Archives Branch, Federal Archives and Records Center, 6215 Sand Point Way NE, Seattle, WA 98115. *Publications: History in Sound; History in Sound II.*

Minnesota Educational Computing Consortium (MECC). 3490 Lexington Ave. N., St. Paul, MN 55112. (612) 481-3500. Ken Brumbaugh, Exec. Dir. An organization that coordinates and provides computer services to students, teachers, and educational administrators in Minnesota, other states, and throughout the world. MECC is comprised of a Documentation Center providing written materials and assistance along with two thousand computer terminals and five thousand microcomputers in statewide schools and colleges. MECC provides training for teachers, support staff, and administrators in the use of MECC courseware products. *Publication: MECC Network.*

Motion Picture Association of America, Inc. 6464 Sunset Blvd., Suite 520, Hollywood, CA 90028. (213) 464-3117. Supported by memberships of major U.S. feature film producers. Seeks to develop the educational and entertainment values of films.

Multinational Project in Educational Technology. Dept. of Educational Affairs, OAS, 1889 F St. NW, Washington, DC 20036. (202) 789-3301. Dr. John S. Clayton, contact person. Maintains support, information, and personnel exchanges among educational technology centers in Brazil, Argentina, Chile, and Mexico, with tie-ins to other Latin American countries. Emphasizes development of human resources through a variety of programs, seminars, short courses, on-site training, and technical assistance. Also disseminates information through its journal. *Publication: Revista de Tecnologia Educativa.*

Museum Computer Network, Inc. (MCN). Dept. of Computer Science, State Univ. of New York, Stony Brook, NY 11794-4400. (516) 246-6077. David Vance, Pres. A nonprofit corporation, voting members of which are museums and similar nonprofit organizations that maintain records of interest to museums and their publics. *Membership:* 50 inst.; 100 indiv. *Dues:* $25.00 to $350.00/yr. *Publications:* quarterly newsletter; irregular supplements.

Museum of Broadcasting (MB). 1 E. 53rd St., New York, NY 10022. (212) 752-7684. Robert M. Batscha, Pres. Founded to collect, preserve, make accessible, and interpret curatorially selected radio and television broadcast programming from the 1920s to the present. The Museum's program of ten exhibitions a year is complemented by informative program notes and by seminars and lectures. The collection of over twenty thousand programs is available for research and viewing through the Museum Library's catalog at individual monitors. The Museum is supported by daily contributions, membership fees, and grants by corporations, foundations, and government agencies. *Dues:* $30.00 indiv.; $40.00 resident double, $50.00 family; $25.00 student; $125.00 contrib. *Publications: MB News; Members Schedule; Exhibition Program Notes.*

Museum of Holography. 11 Mercer St., New York, NY 10013. (212) 925-0526. David Katzive, Exec. Dir. The Museum is an international center for understanding and advancement of this revolutionary medium. It is the focal point for art, science, and technology of holography and is the foremost exhibitor of holography. The Museum is a nonprofit cultural institution, located in New York's SoHo district. It receives more than sixty thousand visitors annually. *Dues:* $30.00/yr. domestic; $35.00/yr. Canada and Mexico; $40.00/yr. overseas. *Publications: Holosphere; Holography Directory.*

Museum of Modern Art. 11 W. 53rd St., New York, NY 10019. (211) 708-9613. Sponsors film study programs, shows films daily at the museum, and provides film rentals. *Publication: Circulating Film.*

Mutual Broadcasting System (MBS). 1755 S. Jefferson Davis Hwy., Arlington, VA 22202. (703) 685-2000. Jack Clements, Exec. V.P. and Gen. Mgr. Organized in 1934, today the nation's largest commercial radio network, serving some 850 station affiliates from coast to coast. MBS is the only commercial radio network based in Washington, DC, emphasizes national news coverage in its broadcasts. A pioneer in spoken-word broadcasting techniques.

National Adult Education Clearinghouse (NAEC). Center for Continuing Education, Montclair State College, Upper Montclair, NJ 07043. (201) 893-4353. Fran M. Spinelli, Dir. A nonprofit organization promoting easier access to information useful in the education, training, and retraining of clients in all areas of adult continuing education. Products and services for sale include a monthly newsletter available in domestic and international editions. On-site archival and current collections of commercial and noncommercial literature. *Publication:* newsletter.

National Aeronautics and Space Administration (NASA). Washington, DC 20546. (202) 755-2320. NASA's prime responsibility is to implement congressional policy with regard to the peaceful purposes of space exploration and research. It has overall charge of the total U.S. space program. A portion of NASA's activities includes the development of training and demonstration programs, a wide-ranging information dissemination program on NASA activities, and media and educational programs for elementary and secondary schools. NASA educational office service centers (seven in all) are located in various parts of the United States.

National Alliance of Media Arts Centers (NAMAC), Inc. 2388 University Ave., St. Paul, MN 55114. (612) 646-6104. Melinda Ward and Richard Weise, Co-Dirs. Interested in the organization, production, exhibition, preservation, teaching, and advocacy of independently produced film or video. Management assistance project offers grants to organizations to hire administrative consultants. *Membership:* 75 org.; 150 indiv. *Dues:* $100.00 inst.; $10.00 indiv. *Publications: Media Arts; The Media Arts in Transition.*

National Art Education Association (NAEA). 1916 Association Dr., Reston, VA 22091. (703) 860-8000. Thomas A. Hatfield, Exec. Dir. A professional association of art educators, elementary school through university and continuing education. Its purpose is to improve and expand visual art education at all levels of instruction. *Membership:* 10,000. *Publications: Art Education; Studies in Art Education.*

National Association for Better Broadcasting (NABB). 7918 Naylor Ave., Los Angeles, CA 90045. (213) 641-4903. Frank Orme, Pres. Promotes the public interest in broadcasting through the development of greater awareness of the public's rights and responsibilities in broadcasting. *Dues:* $15.00/yr. *Publications: Better Radio and Television* ($60.00/yr.); *You Own More Than Your Set!*

National Association for Creative Children and Adults (NACCA). 8080 Springvalley Dr., Cincinnati, OH 45236. (531) 631-1777. Ann Fabe Isaacs, Chief Exec. Off. Seeks to encourage the development of creativity in the general public and especially among gifted persons. Sponsors workshops, field terms and in-service training. *Dues:* $50.00/yr. *Publications: Creative Child and Adult Quarterly; Common Sense Creativity.*

National Association for the Education of Young Children. 1834 Connecticut Ave. NW, Washington, DC 20009. (800) 424-2460. Docia Zouitkovsky, Pres. Provides educational resources to adults who are committed to improving the quality of group programs for children from birth through age 8. *Membership:* 43,000 in 280 local and state groups. *Dues:* $45.00; $20.00. *Publications: Young Children*; numerous books and booklets.

National Association for the Exchange of Industrial Resources (NAEIR). 550 Frontage Rd., Northfield, IL 60093. (312) 446-9111. Norbert Smith, Pres. The organization operates as a clearinghouse for excess materials gathered from industrial sources and donated to participating member schools. Materials are stored in a new 320,000-square-foot warehouse in Chicago prior to distribution to member schools. *Membership:* 4,000 schools with representation in every state. *Dues:* $350.00. *Publication: NAEIR News.*

National Association for Visually Handicapped (NAVH). 305 E. 24th St., New York, NY 10010. (212) 889-3141. Lorraine H. Marchi, Pres. Publishes and distributes large-print books for pleasure reading; textbooks and testing material; newsletters at irregular intervals — *Seeing Clearly* for adults and *In Focus* for youth; informational literature, most of which is in large print; available to visually impaired individuals, their families, and the professionals and paraprofessionals who work with them; maintains a loan library (free) of large print books; offers counsel and guidance to visually impaired adults and their families and to the parents of visually impaired children. *Membership:* 8,000. *Dues:* minimum $25.00 indiv.; $75.00 org. *Publications: Catalog of Large Print Material; Selected List of Large Print Material for Adults; Loan Library Listing.*

National Association of Broadcasters (NAB). 1771 N St. NW, Washington, DC 20036. (202) 293-3500. Edward O. Fritts, Pres. A trade association that represents the country's radio and television stations and national networks. Encourages development of broadcasting arts, seeks to protect its members and to strengthen the standards of the industry. *Membership:* 4,500 radio stations and 700 television stations. *Publications: NAB Highlights; Radioactive.*

National Association of Business and Educational Radio, Inc. (NABER). 1330 New Hampshire Ave. NW, Washington, DC 20036. (202) 887-0920. Emmet B. "Jay" Kitchen, Exec. Dir. Represents individuals licensed in the business radio service whose business and professional needs interest them in uses of TV-shared, UHF, and 800 MHz channels for two-way radio communication and 929 MHz one-way paging. *Dues:* $35.00; $75.00 for professional mobile radio service section membership. *Publications: Business Radio; Shoptalk.*

National Association of Secondary School Principals (NASSP). 1904 Association Dr., Reston, VA 22091. (703) 860-0200. Thomas F. Koerner, Ed. Provides a national voice for secondary education; supports promising and successful educational practices; conducts research; examines issues and represents secondary education at the federal level. *Membership:* 35,000. *Dues:* $85.00/yr. *Publications: NASSP Bulletin; NASSP Newsleader; Curriculum Report; Legal Memorandum, News Technology; Schools in the Middle; Student Activities Practitioner.*

National Association of State Boards of Education (NASBE). 701 N. Fairfax St., Suite 340, Alexandria, VA 22314. (703) 684-4000. Phyllis L. Blaunstein, Exec. Dir. Conducts policy research and analysis; exchanges information regarding national and state educational policy; provides technical assistance publication information; provides educational programs and activities; and serves as a liaison with other educator's groups. *Membership:* 562. *Publication: The State Board Connection.*

National Association of State Educational Media Professionals (NASTEMP). Ed. Innovation & Support, Illinois State Board of Education, 100 N. 1st St., Springfield, IL 62777. (217) 782-3810. Marie Sivak, Pres. Formed in 1975 through the merger of two former organizations, the Association of Chief State School Audio-Visual Officers and the State School Library/Media Supervisors, with the objectives of improving staffing and financial support of expanded educational media programs within state departments of education; cooperating with other organizations in promoting improved media programs; providing information about state media programs; advancing professional standards in the field; improving preservice and in-service education of teachers with respect to media utilization; and encouraging research. *Membership:* 105. *Dues:* $7.00. *Publication: Aids to Media Selection for Students and Teachers.*

National Association of State Textbook Administrators (NASTA). Division of Textbooks, Dept. of Public Education, Educ. Bldg., #389, Raleigh, NC 27609. Claude C. Warren, Pres. The purposes of the association are: (1) to foster a spirit of mutual helpfulness in adoption, purchase, and distribution of textbooks; (2) to arrange for study and review of textbook specifications; (3) to authorize special surveys/tests/studies; (4) to initiate action leading to better quality textbooks. NASTA is unaffiliated with any parent organization. It does work with the Association of American Publishers and the Book Manufacturers' Institute. Services provided include a working knowledge of text construction, monitoring lowest prices, sharing adoption information, identifying trouble spots, and discussions in the industry.

National Audiovisual Center (NAC). National Archives and Records Service, General Services Admin., Washington, DC 20409. (301) 763-1872. John H. McLean, Dir. Clearinghouse for information about audiovisual materials produced by or for the federal government and as a central distributor for those materials. A master data file of audiovisual information, catalogs, and brochures are maintained. Buying and rental program available. Materials offered on a cost-plus basis. *Publications: NAC; Catalog of U.S. Government Produced Audiovisual Materials;* films and so forth.

National Cable Television Institute (NCTI). 3301 W. Hampden Ave., Englewood, CO 80110. (303) 761-8544. Roland Hieb, Exec. Dir. Provides technical educational materials and services for the upgrading of professional and technical competencies of cable television personnel. *Publications: Signal Level Meters: Use, Care and Maintenance; Cable Tech.*

National Center for Appropriate Technology. 815 15th St. NW, Washington, DC 20005. (202) 347-9193. Joseph F. Sedlak, Exec. Dir. NCAT produces and distributes publications and training materials on appropriate technologies; conducts workshops and training. Publications can be used as teaching materials. Provides NATAS, a free technical assistance service for U.S. Dept. of Energy. *Publications: Connections*; and forty other publications.

The National Clearinghouse for Bilingual Education. 1555 Wilson Blvd., Suite 605, Rosslyn, VA 22209. (703) 522-0710/(800) 336-4560. Dr. Daniel Ulibarri, Dir. The functions of NCBE are to collect, analyze, and disseminate information about bilingual education and related fields; to establish, maintain, and provide access to a computer-searchable database in these areas; to develop and make available information products written by experts in the field; and to coordinate information sharing among educators working with minority language students. *Publications:* free bi-monthly newsletter; monographs and papers.

National Commission on Libraries and Information Science (NCLIS). Government Services Administration Bldg., 7th and D Sts. SW, Suite 3122, Washington, DC 20024. (202) 382-0840. Toni Carbo Bearman, Exec. Dir. An agency in the Executive Branch of the U.S. government charged with advising Congress and the president in the entire field of library and information services. The commission has four major roles: (1) to serve as a resident expert for both the executive and legislative branches; (2) to be an honest broker bringing together agencies in both branches to focus on problems of common interest; (3) to serve as a forum for the entire library/information community; and (4) to be a catalyst to help get programs implemented.

National Council for the Accreditation of Teacher Education (NCATE). 1919 Pennsylvania Ave. NW, Washington, DC 20006. (202) 466-7496. J. T. Sandefour, Chair. A consortium of professional organizations interested in the self-regulation and improvement of standards in the field of teacher education.

National Council of Teachers of English (NCTE) Commission on Media. 223 Fulton St., Berkeley, CA 94720. Deborah Ruth, Dir. An advisory body that identifies key issues in teaching of media; reviews current projects and recommends new directions and personnel to undertake them; monitors NCTE publications on media and suggests program ideas for the annual convention.

National Council of the Churches of Christ – Communication Commission. 475 Riverside Dr., New York, NY 10115. (212) 870-2567. Ecumenical agency for cooperative work of nineteen Protestant and Orthodox denominations and agencies in broadcasting, film, cable, and print media. Offers advocacy to government and industry structures on media services. *Services:* Liaison to network television and radio programming; film sales and rentals; distribution of information about syndicated religious programming; syndication of some programming, news, and information to broadcast news media regarding work of the National Council of Churches, related denominations, and agencies; and cable television and emerging technologies information services.

National Diffusion Network (NDN). 1832 M St. NW, Rm. 802, Washington, DC 20036. (202) 653-7000. David Moursand, Ed. The NDN is composed of: (1) exemplary educational programs, products, and practices that have been rigorously evaluated and approved by the Joint Dissemination and (2) projects in fifty states, the District of Columbia, Puerto Rico, and the Virgin Islands that serve as a link between local educational agencies, other providers of educational services, and colleges and universities that wish to install the approved exemplary programs and the original developers of these programs who are funded to provide technical assistance. *Publications: Educational Programs That Work; Guide to Packaging Your Educational Program.*

National Education Association (NEA). 1201 16th St. NW, Washington, DC 20036. (202) 833-4000. Don Cameron, Exec. Dir. The world's largest advocacy organization of teachers, other school employees, and college faculty. Seeks to improve U.S. public education; conducts research on school problems and professional teacher welfare; maintains lobby relationships with the federal government; and provides informational media to inform the public about education and educational needs.

National Endowment for the Arts (NEA). 2401 E St. NW, Washington, DC 20506. (202) 634-6028. Offers Artists in Education project. Applications for it and for their projects providing limited support funds in arts fields are accepted, including those involving artist-teacher collaboration and projects that develop materials related to other goals of the office. For further information, contact the Artists in Education office.

National Endowment for the Humanities (NEH). 1100 Pennsylvania Ave. NW, Rm. 426, Washington, DC 20004. (202) 786-0278. Offers limited support for the planning, scripting, and production of radio, television, and cable TV projects pertaining to the humanities. Grants are available for children's as well as adult programming. The program has two deadlines each year, in January and July. For further information contact Media Program, Division of General Program, NEH.

National Federation of Community Broadcasters (NFCB). 1314 14th St. NW, Washington, DC 20005. (202) 797-8911. Carol E. Schatz, Pres. NFCB represents its members in public policy development at the national level, provides a wide range of practical services, and distributes programs to all noncommercial stations. *Membership:* 70 stations; 100 assoc. stations and production groups. *Dues:* based on income, from $75.00 to $200.00 for assoc. *Publications: Legal Handbook; Audio Craft;* newsletter.

National Federation of Local Cable Programmers (NFLCP). 906 Pennsylvania Ave. SE, Washington, DC 20003. (202) 544-7272. Sue Miller Buske, Exec. Dir. An organization that seeks to ensure citizens television access privileges and participation in the medium. Hosts regional and national conferences on community uses of cable television. Offers consulting services. *Membership:* 2,000. *Publications: Community Television Review;* newsletter.

National Film Board of Canada (NFBC). 1251 Ave. of the Americas, New York, NY 10020. (212) 586-5131. Mary Jane Terrell, Non-Theatrical Rep. Established in 1939, the NFBC's main objective is to produce and distribute high quality audiovisual materials for educational, cultural, and social purposes. *Publication: U.S. Film Resource Guide.*

National Film Information Service (NFIS). 8949 Wilshire Blvd., Beverly Hills, CA 90211. (213) 278-8990. James M. Roberts, Exec. Dir. Provides an information service on films, library, and archives films listed.

National Film Society (NFS). 8340 Mission Rd., Suite 106, Shawnee Mission, KS 66206. (913) 341-1919. Allyn M. Miller, Pres. Organized to protect and preserve the heritage of the motion picture industry and to honor and recognize those who have contributed to the American motion picture both behind the scenes and before the cameras. Annual convention in Hollywood in October; offers awards and seminars. *Dues:* $15.00. *Publication: American Classic Screen.*

National Free Lance Photographers Association. 60 E. State St., Doylestown, PA 18901. (215) 348-2990. H. Jeffrey Valentine, Pres. An organization of amateur and professional photographers in all parts of the world. Cooperates with newspapers and other news media in obtaining emergency photographic coverage and maintains members' photographic file data. *Publication: Freelance Photo News.*

National Gallery of Art (NGA). Dept. of Extension Programs, Washington, DC 20565. (202) 842-6273. Ruth R. Perlin, Head. This department of NGA is responsible for the production and distribution of art educational audiovisual programs. Materials available (all loaned free to schools, community organizations, and individuals) include films, videocassettes, and color slide programs. A free catalog of programs is available upon request. A videodisc on the National Gallery and its collection is available for loan.

National Information Center for Educational Media (NICEM). P.O. Box 40130, Albuquerque, NM 87196. (800) 421-8711. J. C. Johnstone, Pres. NICEM, in conjunction with the Library of Congress, is a centralized facility that collects, catalogs, and disseminates information about nonbook materials of many different kinds. Its mission is to build and expand the database to provide current and archival information about nonbook educational materials; to apply modern techniques of information dissemination that meet user needs; and to provide a comprehensive, centralized nonbook database used for catalogs, indexes, multimedia publications, special search services, machine-readable tapes, online access, and statistical analysis.

National Institute of Education (NIE). 1200 19th St. NW, Washington, DC 20208. (202) 254-5740. NIE is part of the Office of the Assistant Secretary for Educational Research and Improvement within the U.S. Department of Education. NIE was created by the Congress in 1972 as the primary federal agency for educational research and development. The institute supports research that improves the quality of education; provides assistance to states and localities; and encourages educators, policymakers, parents, and other citizens to exchange views on educational issues of national significance. The ERIC (see directory listing) program, supported by NIE, offers information dissemination.

National Library of Medicine. 8600 Rockville Pike, Bethesda, MD 20209. (301) 496-6308. Donald A. B. Lindberg, M.D., Dir. Collects, organizes, and distributes literature on biomedicine; seeks to apply modern technology to the flow of biomedical information to health professionals; and supports development of improved medical library resources of the country. Responsible for MEDLINE, SDILINE, CATLINE, SERLINE, CANCERLIT, AVLINE, and TOXLINE. Maintains a collection of twelve thousand health science audiovisual materials and supervises the Lister Hill National Center for Biomedical Communications. Maintains seven regional medical libraries. *Publication: National Library of Medicine Audiovisuals Catalog.*

National Medical Audiovisual Center (NMAC) of the National Library of Medicine. 8600 Rockville Pike, Bethesda, MD 20209. (301) 496-4441. William G. Cooper, Act. Dir. Efforts to improve the quality and use of biomedical instructional materials that teach basic instruction in health professions schools will be included with research and development programs to apply knowledge representation, information science, computer sciences and technology, communications engineering, and other fields of biomedical communications to problems of the health sciences in practice, education, and research. Many ongoing programs to share teaching programs; offers in-service programs to health sciences administrators, all employing a variety of approaches through the Lister Hill National Center.

National Photography Instructors Association. 1255 Hill Dr., Eagle Rock, CA 90041. (213) 254-1549. Nonprofit organization dedicated to the advancement of photographic education.

National Press Photographers Association (NPPA). Box 1146, Durham, NC 27702. (919) 489-3700. Charles Cooper, Exec. Dir. An organization of professional news photographers who participate in and promote photojournalism in publications and through television and film. Sponsors workshops and contests and maintains a tape library and a collection of slides in the field. *Membership:* 8,000. *Dues:* $40.00 professional; $25.00 student. *Publications: News Photographer;* membership directory.

National PTA. 700 N. Rush St., Chicago, IL 60611. (312) 787-0977. Elaine Stienkemeyer, Pres. A child advocacy association dedicated to improving the lives of our country's children through the school, home, community, and place of worship. Strengthens the laws for the care and protection of children and youth. A drug and alcohol project seeks to strengthen parent-child communication in order to prevent use and or abuse. Several media-related activities. *Publications: Looking In on Your School; Single Parents and Their Families; Children and Television; What Parents Can Do; Home Fire Safety; Protecting Our Children; Alcohol: A Family Affair; PTA Today;* and *What's Happening in Washington.*

National Public Radio (NPR). 2025 M St. NW, Washington, DC 20036. (202) 822-2000. Douglas J. Bennet, Pres. The first satellite radio network. It provides programming and support services to stations in forty-seven states, Puerto Rico, and Washington, DC. NPR stations are independent broadcast entities, licensed to a variety of nonprofit organizations and institutions. Its leadership in broadcast journalism is shown by its two news programs, "All Things Considered" and "Morning Edition." A full range of performance programming is offered, along with presentations for specialized audiences, including Enfoque Nacional, a nationally broadcast Spanish-language radio newsmagazine. Funding from listeners, foundations, and corps. *Membership:* 309 stations. *Dues:* average dues $6,200.00.

National Radio Broadcasters Association (NRBA). 2033 M St. NW, Suite 506, Washington, DC 20036. (202) 466-2030. Peter Ferrara, Exec. V.P. Represents radio stations and broadcast-related companies such as equipment manufacturers and program syndicators. Sponsors the only all-radio convention. *Membership:* 2,000 orgs.

National Religious Broadcasters (NRB). CN 1926, Morristown, NJ 07960. (201) 428-5400. Ben Armstrong, Exec. Dir. Sponsors an annual Summer Institute of Communications and holds an annual national convention and five regional conventions. *Membership:* 1,007 stations, indiv., and agencies. *Publications: Religious Broadcasting Magazine; Annual Directory of Religious Broadcasting; Sourcebook for Religious Broadcasting;* and *Religious Broadcasting Cassette Catalog.*

National School Supply and Equipment Association (NSSEA). 1500 Wilson Blvd., Suite 609, Arlington, VA 22209. (703) 524-8819. John Spalding, Exec. V.P. A service organization of six hundred manufacturers, distributors, and retailers of school supplies, equipment, and instructional materials. Seeks to advance the interests and image of education, to find solutions to problems affecting schools, and to encourage the development of new ideas and products for educational progress.

National Science Foundation. Washington, DC 20550. (202) 357-9498. Primary purposes are to increase the nation's base of scientific knowledge; to encourage research in areas that can lead to improvements in economic growth, productivity, and environmental quality; to promote international cooperation through science; and to develop and help implement science education programs that will aid the nation in meeting the challenges of contemporary life. Grants go chiefly to colleges and other research organizations. Applicants should refer to *NSF Guide to Programs.* To help the public learn of NSF-supported programs, scientific material and media reviews are available.

National Science Teachers Association (NSTA). 1742 Connecticut Ave. NW, Washington, DC 20009. (212) 328-5800. Bill Aldridge, Exec. Dir. International nonprofit association of science teachers ranging from kindergarten through university. *Publications: Science and Children; The Science Teacher;* and *Journal of College Science Teaching.*

National Society for Performance and Instruction (NSPI). 1126 16th St. NW, Suite 315, Washington, DC 20036. (202) 861-0777. Kay Schaeffer, Exec. Dir. NSPI is a professional organization of more than five thousand practitioners who seek to learn more about and to improve applications of human performance and instructional technologies. The society offers an award program recognizing excellence in the field. Awards are presented at an annual conference. *Membership:* 5,000. *Dues:* $80.00. *Publications: Performance & Instruction Journal;* member directory; more.

National Software Exchange. 38 Melrose Pl., Montclair, NJ 07042. (201) 783-6000. Samuel E. Bleeker, Founder. Members can exchange original software programs for a $5.00 handling fee after paying an annual fee of $75.00 for individuals and $250.00 for institutions. For more information write to above address.

National Technical Information Service (NTIS). U.S. Dept. of Commerce, 5285 Port Royal Rd., Springfield, VA 22161. (703) 487-4600. Information Center Bookstore in room 1067 in the Dept. of Commerce main building at 14th St. and Constitution Ave. NW, Washington, DC 20230. A central source for public sale of government-sponsored research, development, and engineering analyses prepared by federal agencies. Also maintains federally generated machine-processable data files. *Publications: Abstract Newsletters; Tech Notes; Government Reports Announcements and Index; Selected Research in Microfiche; Published Searches*; and scientific, technical, and engineering reports (more than a million) available on paper and microfiche.

National Telemedia Council. 120 E. Wilson, Madison, WI 53703. (608) 257-7712. Susan Dreyfus Fosdick, Pres.; Marieli Rowe, Exec. Dir. An organization of local, state, and national groups and individuals working to improve the quality of radio and television programming by educational means. Acts as a sponsoring organization for KIDS-4, the Sun Prairie, Wisconsin, Children's Channel – a dedicated cable channel of TV by and for children. Activities include annual conference, Look Listen Opinion Poll; Notable Programs guide; bimonthly newsletter; Telemedium; special projects. *Dues:* $20.00 and up. *Publications: Better Broadcast News; Annual Look Listen Opinion.*

National University Continuing Education Association (NUCEA). One Dupont Circle NW, Suite 420, Washington, DC 20036. (202) 659-3130. Harvey J. Steadman, Pres.; Kay J. Kohl, Exec. Dir. An association of public and private institutions concerned with making continuing education available to all population segments. Many institutional members offer university and college film rental library services.

National Video Clearinghouse (NVC). 100 Lafayette Dr., Syosset, Long Island, NY 11791. (516) 364-3686. Harvey Seslowsky, Pres. and publisher. A comprehensive, computerized reference center for information about prerecorded video programs in all video formats.

NAVA. *See* The International Communications Industries Association (ICIA)

Nebraska Videodisc Design/Production Group (VD-PG). KUON-TV, Univ. of Nebraska, Box 83111, Lincoln, NE 68501. (402) 472-3611. Ron Nugent, Project Dir. A group of designers and producers concerned with the development and production of programs that exploit the unique capabilities of the videodisc. *Publication:* newsletter.

The NETWORK. 290 S. Main St., Andover, MA 01810. (617) 470-1080. David P. Crandall, Exec. Dir. A research and service organization providing consultation, training, assistance, and materials to schools and other educational institutions. *Publications: Administering Writing Programs: A Training Package for the Coordination of Writing Programs; The Cumulative Writing Folder; Nutrition Education* (curriculum); and *Sex Equity* (curriculum).

Network for Continuing Medical Education (NCME). 15 Columbus Cir., New York, NY 10023. (212) 541-8088 or (800) 223-0272. Jim Disque, Dir. Produces and distributes videocassettes to hospitals for physicians' continuing education. *Membership:* by subscription. *Dues:* $1,620.00 to $1,820.00/yr.

The Newspaper Features Council, Inc. Ward Castle, Comly Ave., Port Chester, NY 10573. (914) 939-3919 and (203) 329-7927. Joseph F. D'Angelo, Pres. The Newspaper Features Council, Inc., formerly The Newspaper Comics Council, Inc., is a professional organization whose membership consists of newspapers, syndicates, editors, columnists, writers, syndicated cartoonists, and editorial cartoonists. Its purpose is to provide a forum for membership to exchange views, discuss common problems and mutual opportunities, and improve the content of newspapers for the betterment of the general public and the industry. A small library, not cataloged, is available to professional researchers. *Membership:* 125-150. *Dues:* $75.00/yr. creator (writer, artist, columnist); $160.00/yr. newspaper; $1,250.00/yr. syndicate. *Publications: Career for You in the Comics* ($2.00); *Cavalcade of American Comics* ($1.50 ea.); *Comics in the Classroom* ($1.00 ea.); and *Grapevine* (newsletter to members only).

NEXIS/Information Bank. Mead Data Central, 9393 Springboro Pike, Box 933, Dayton, OH 45401. (513) 864-6800. A computer-assisted information service with access to newspapers, magazines, newswires, and various reference works. The New York Times Information Service has recently been integrated with NEXIS; also included are the *New York Times*, the Advertising and Marketing Intelligence, Deadline Data on World Affairs and the Information Bank. The database is in English and printouts can be had in Kwick or Full format. For prices contact the above address for referral to regional representatives.

Non-Formal Education Information Center (NFEIC). College of Education, Michigan State Univ., 237 Erikson, East Lansing, MI 48824. (517) 355-5522. Kathleen Collamore Sullivan, Dir. The center assists those working on behalf of persons in the developing world; maintains a reference library and depository for reports on nonformal education; and provides a research and information exchange service to assist planners and practitioners of nonformal education for development. *Publications: NFE Exchange;* bibliographies; and occasional papers.

North American Simulation and Gaming Association (NASAGA). Box 96, Westminster College, New Wilmington, PA 16172. (412) 946-8761. Bahram Farzanegan, Exec. Dir. Provides a forum for the exchange of ideas, information, and resources among persons interested in simulation and games; assists members in designing, testing, using, and evaluating simulations and/or games, and in using these as research tools. A computerized mailing list and cross-referencing service is available through National Headquarters and UNC-Asherville. Sponsors various conferences. *Membership:* 800. *Dues:* $35.00 regular; $10.00 students. *Publication: Simulation and Games.*

Northwest Regional Educational Laboratory (NWREL). 300 SW 6th Ave., Portland, OR 97204. (503) 248-6800. Robert R. Rath, Exec. Dir. Assists education, government, community agencies, business, and labor in bringing about improvement in educational programs and processes by developing and disseminating effective educational problems, providing technical assistance in educational problem solving, and evaluating effectiveness of educational programs and processes. Sponsor of RICE (Resources in Computer Education) program. *Membership:* 812. *Dues:* none. *Publication: Northwest Report* (newsletter).

OCLC, Inc. (Online Computer Library Center). 6565 Frantz Rd., Dublin, OH 43017. (614) 764-6000. An active, computerized library network providing print and nonprint reference data, including information about audiovisual material; provides online access to local input and LC-MARC II cataloging information and online location listing of materials for interlibrary loan. Over 3,400 libraries in 50 states, Canada, Great Britain, and Mexico participate; online catalog contains more than ten million bibliographic records.

Office for Communications Technology, American Foundation for the Blind, Inc. 15 W. 16th St., New York, NY 10011. (212) 620-2051. John C. DeWitt, Nat. Consultant Communications Technology. Collects and disseminates data regarding radio reading and information services for print-handicapped persons. Works with Congress, federal agencies, and private organizations on legislative and regulatory matters affecting print-handicapped persons and provides consultation to existing and potential radio reading and information services and individuals and organizations developing computer technology for print-handicapped persons.

Office of Technology Assessment. 600 Pennsylvania Ave. SE, Washington, DC 20510. (202) 226-2115. John Gibbons, Dir. Established by Congress to study, report on, and assess the significance and probable impact of new technological developments upon U.S. society and to advise Congress on steps that should be taken with respect to new legislation pertaining to them. *Publication: Information Technology and Its Impact on American Education.*

On-line Audiovisual Catalogers (OLAC). 3604 Suffolk, Durham, NC 27707. Catherine Leonard, Treas. Formed as an outgrowth of the ALA conference, it seeks to permit members to exchange ideas and information and to interact with other agencies that influence audiovisual cataloging practices. *Publication: On-Line Audiovisual Catalogers.*

Oral History Association. North Texas State Univ., Box 13734, Denton, TX 76203. (817) 387-1021. Seeks to develop the use of oral history as primary source material and to disseminate oral history materials among scholars. *Publications: Oral History Newsletter; Oral History Review; Bibliography; Evaluation Guidelines;* and membership directory.

Pacific Film Archive (PFA). Univ. Art Museum, 2625 Durant Ave., Berkeley, CA 94720. (415) 642-1437. Sponsors the preservation, study, and presentation of classic, international, documentary, animated, and avant-garde films. Provides media research and a service to locate film sources, books, and addresses.

PBS VIDEO. 475 L'Enfant Plaza SW, Washington, DC 20024. (800) 424-7963. Dan Hamby, contact person. Markets and distributes PBS programs to colleges, libraries, schools, government, and other organizations and institutions. Top-selling programs include the series *Hard Choices; Creativity with Bill Moyers; Odyssey;* and Leo Buscaglia's *Art of Being Fully Human* and *Speaking of Love. Publication: PBS VIDEO Program Catalog.*

PCR: Films and Video in the Behavioral Sciences. AV Services, Special Services Bldg., Pennsylvania State Univ., University Park, PA 16802. (814) 863-3102. Thomas McKenna, Mng. Ed. Collects and makes available to professional users 16mm films and video in the behavioral sciences judged to be useful for university teaching and research. A free catalog of the films and video in PCR is available from AV Services. The PCR catalog now contains some 1,600 films on the behavioral sciences (psychology, psychiatry, anthropology, animal behavior, sociology, teaching and learning, and folklife). Some seven thousand professional people now use PCR services. Films are available on loan for a rental charge or may be purchased. Films may be submitted for possible international distribution through PCR. *Publication: PCR: Film and Video in the Behavioral Sciences* (1985).

Photographic Society of America (PSA). 2005 Walnut St., Philadelphia, PA 19103. (215) 563-1663. Frank Pallo, Pres. A nonprofit organization for the development of the arts and sciences of photography and for the furtherance of public appreciation of photographic skills. Its members, largely amateurs, consist of individuals, camera clubs, and other photographic organizations. Division includes color slide, motion picture, nature, photojournalism, travel, pictorial print, stereo, and techniques. Sponsors national, regional, and local meetings, clinics, and contests. *Membership:* 14,000. *Dues:* $25.00 indiv. *Publication: PSA Journal.*

PLATO: Computer-based Education Research Library (CERL). Univ. of Illinois, 252 Engineering Research Laboratory, 103 S. Matthews Ave., Urbana, IL 61801. (217) 333-6210. Dr. Donald Bitzer, Dir. CERL is a research laboratory dedicated to the development of hardware, software, and courseware for the delivery of cost-effective, interactive, computer-based education. Delivery is via a large-scale system (PLATO) linking more than 1,400 terminals to a central computer, a cluster system, and stand-alone terminals. Delivery to thousands of users by a satellite; cable television network is planned for the near future. The development of the PLATO system originated at the University of Illinois in 1960.

Prime Time School Television (PTST). 40 E. Huron St., Chicago, IL 60611. (312) 787-7600. During the school year supplies teachers, librarians, and parents with study guides including program synopses, activities, and resources as well as curriculum units based on quality commercial, public, and cable broadcasts.

Professional Software Programmers Association (PSPA). 100 W. Rincon Ave., Suite 103, General Services Admin., Campbell, CA 95008. (408) 374-8070. David Marshall, Exec. Dir. Professional organization to assist in obtaining contracting and consulting work for computer programmers; assists small businesses in locating programmers to modify or prepare packaged computer programs to meet particular needs. Conducts impartial review and tests products in the software industry. *Publication: Software Programmers News.*

Project BEST. c/o AECT, 1126 16th St. NW, Washington, DC 20036. (202) 466-4780. This project, which terminated in 1983, was funded by the U.S. Dept. of Education to enhance the capacity of state departments of education to prepare local education agency and school personnel to effectively use technology in basic skills programs. The acronym BEST stands for Basic Educational Skills through Technology. Through Project BEST, AECT established a computer network and electronic mail and bulletin board services. The public satellite system has been used for teleconferences among various school districts, state departments, and national offices. Inquire about videotape BEST programs available from AECT.

Public Broadcasting Service (PBS). 475 L'Enfant Plaza SW, Washington, DC 20024. (202) 488-5000. It serves as a distributor of national public television programming (obtaining all programs from the stations or independent producers; PBS is not a production facility). Owned and operated by the licensees through annual membership fees. Funding for technical distribution facilities in part by the Corporation for Public Broadcasting. PBS services include national promotion, program acquisition and scheduling, legal services, development and fund-raising support, engineering and technical studies, and research. PBS is governed by a board of directors elected by licensees for three-year terms. *Membership:* 169 licensees; 300 stations.

Public Service Satellite Consortium (PSSC). 1660 L St. NW, Suite 907, Washington, DC 20036. (202) 331-1154. Louis A. Bransford, Pres. Represents the telecommunication interest of nonprofit organizations; provides members with information, consultation, educational briefings, and representation to federal agencies and other organizations; assists members in contracting for operational functions such as systems engineering and networking; conducts workshops on new technologies and telecommunications issues.

Public Television Library (PTL). 475 L'Enfant Plaza SW, Washington, DC 20034. (202) 488-5000. Rental and sales outlet for Public Broadcasting System productions, available to individuals and organizations. *Publication: PTL Catalog.*

Puppeteers of America, Inc. 5 Cricklewood Path, Pasadena, CA 91107. Gayle Schulter, Membership Chair. Founded in 1937 to promote and develop the art of puppetry. It has a large collection of films and videotapes for rent in its AV library and offers books, plays, and related items from the Puppetry Store. Puppeteers is a national resource center that offers regional festivals, workshops, exhibits, and a puppetry exchange.

Radio Free Europe/Radio Liberty (RFE-RL, Inc.). 1201 Connecticut Ave. NW, Washington, DC 20036. (202) 457-6900. William A. Buell, V.P. U.S. Operations. An independent radio broadcast service funded by federal grants. Broadcasts to the Soviet Union, Bulgaria, Czechoslovakia, Hungary, Poland, and Romania.

Radio Information Service Unit, American Foundation for the Blind (AFB). 15 W. 16th St., New York, NY 10011. (212) 620-2068. John C. DeWitt, Nat. Consultant. Collects and disseminates data regarding radio reading and information services for print-handicapped persons; works with Congress, federal agencies, and private organizations on legislative and regulatory matters affecting print-handicapped persons; and provides consultation to existing and potential radio reading and information services.

Recording for the Blind. 20 Roszel Rd., Princeton, NJ 08540. (609) 452-0606. Stuart Carothers, Exec. Dir. Trained volunteers with technical backgrounds operating from twenty-eight recording studios located in fifteen states and the District of Columbia record approximately four thousand new volumes annually. Their Master Tape Library currently contains sixty thousand recorded textbooks—making RFB the largest free circulating educational library resource of its kind in the world. *Membership:* visually, physically, and perceptually handicapped students and professionals. *Dues:* free recorded textbooks to certified registered borrowers. *Publications:* tri-annual newsletter.

Recording Industry Association of America (RIAA). 888 7th Ave., 9th Floor, New York, NY 10106. (212) 765-4330. Stanley M. Gortikov, Pres.; James D. Fishel, Exec. Dir. Compiles and disseminates U.S. industry shipment statistics by units and wholesale/retail dollar equivalents; establishes industry technical standards; conducts audits for certification of Gold and Platinum Records and Video Awards; acts as the public information arm on behalf of the U.S. recording industry; provides anti-piracy intelligence to law enforcement agencies; presents an RIAA cultural award for contributions to recording industry research projects. *Membership:* 50 audio members; 16 video members. *Publications: Activity Report; Industry Sourcebook;* newsletter; press releases.

Research and Development Center for Teacher Education (R&DCTE). Univ. of Texas at Austin, Education Annex 3.203, Austin, TX 78712. (512) 471-1343. Gene E. Hall, Dir. Designs and conducts research and related activities at all levels of teacher education; aims to increase the validated knowledge bases underlying effective teaching and learning and successful implementation of research-based practices in a variety of settings. The center is a member of the Council for Educational Development and Research (CEDaR). *Publications: Annual Catalog of Publications; R&DCTE Review* (newsletter).

RICE (Resources in Computer Education). NW Regional Educational Laboratory, 300 SW Sixth Ave., Portland, OR 97204. (503) 248-6800. Robert R. Rath, Exec. Dir. Online database developed by MicroSIFT project. Database is accessible through BRS Inc. of Latham, NY. RICE provides access to information about educational applications of the microcomputer. Four files included: Software (educational software); Producers (of educational software); Project (uses of microcomputers in K-12 classrooms); and Computer Literacy (instruction). Searches of RICE available from many sources. Contact the Computer Technology Program of NWREL for further information. *Membership:* accessible through BRS Inc., Latham, NY.

Scanner Association of North America. 240 Fend Lane, Hillside, IL 60162. (312) 822-0622. Robert A. Hanson, Exec. Dir. An organization for people using scanner radios either professionally, such as in the public safety services, or as a hobby. Provides interface between government, law enforcement, scanner users, and program reception. *Membership:* 30,000. *Dues:* $12.00. *Publication: SCAN Magazine.*

SDC Information Services. System Development Corp., 2500 Colorado Ave., Santa Monica, CA 90406. (800) 421-7229. Via its ORBIT information retrieval system, SDC provides access to comprehensive online information in a large number of databases in fields such as chemistry, patents, and energy. In California toll free (800) 352-6689 or (213) 453-6194.

Smithsonian Institution. Washington, DC 20560. (202) 357-1300. Robert McCormick Adams, Secy. Independent trust establishment that conducts scientific and scholarly research, administers the national collections, and performs other educational public service functions, all supported by Congress, trusts, gifts, and grants. Includes the National Museum of Natural History/National Museum of Man, National Museum of American History, National Air and Space Museum, Freer Gallery of Art, National Museum of American Art, National Portrait Gallery, National Museum of African Art, Cooper-Hewitt Museum of Design and Decorative Arts, Renwick Gallery, Hirshorn Museum and Sculpture Garden, Anacostia Neighborhood Museum and Sculpture Garden, and others.

Social Science Education Consortium, Inc. (SSEC). 855 Broadway, Boulder, CO 80302. (303) 492-8155. Irving Morriset, Exec. Dir.; Kay Cook, Pub. Mgr. Major goal of SSEC is to improve social studies instruction at all levels of education. SSEC disseminates information about social studies materials, instructional methods, and trends; assists educators in identifying, selecting, and using new ideas and methods in social studies; provides forum for social scientists and educators to exchange ideas and views. Sponsoring organization for ERIC Clearinghouse for Social Studies/Social Science Education. Free catalog of publications/services, available on request. *Membership:* by invitation.

Society for Applied Learning Technology (SALT). 50 Culpeper St., Warrenton, VA 22186. (703) 347-0055. Raymond G. Fox, Pres. Seeks to advance the development of highest standards and practices in the application of technology to learning; to foster wide dissemination of understanding and knowledge in actual and potential uses of technology in learning; and to provide an effective educational channel among scientists, managers, and users of training and learning technology. SALT conferences held periodically. *Membership:* 400. *Dues:* $30.00. *Publications: Journal of Educational Technology Systems; Microcomputers in Education and Training; Interactive Videodisc in Education and Training; Technology of Training Evaluation and Productivity Assessment.*

Society for Computer Simulation (SCS). Box 2228, La Jolla, CA 92038. (619) 459-3888. Charles A. Pratt, Exec. Dir. A technical society devoted to the art and science of modeling and simulation. Its purpose is to advance the understanding, appreciation, and use of all types of computer models for studying the behavior of actual or hypothesized systems of all kinds. Sponsors local, regional, and national technical meetings and conferences such as National Computer Conference, Summer Computer Simulation Conference, National Educational Computing Conference and others. *Membership:* 2,500. *Dues:* $35.00. *Publications: Simulation; Simulation Series; Transactions of the Society for Computer Simulation.*

The Society for Intercultural Education, Training, and Research. 1414 22nd St. NW, Washington, DC 20037. (202) 862-1990. Diane L. Zeller, Ph.D., Exec. Dir. Seeks to increase awareness of the cross-cultural imperative inherent in global society and to work toward the solution of intercultural problems. Holds an annual conference in the spring, summer institutes on intercultural training, workshops, seminars, and regional meetings. *Membership:* 1,500. *Dues:* $25.00 student; $50.00 regular; $195.00 inst. *Publications:* quarterly newsletter; quarterly journal.

Society for Photographic Education (SPE). Box 1651 FDR Station, New York, NY 10150. An association of college and university teachers of photography, museum photographic curators, writers, and publishers; promotes higher standards of photographic education. *Membership:* 1,600. *Dues:* $40.00. *Publications: Exposure;* newsletter.

Society of Authors' Representatives. Box 650, Old Chelsea Stn., New York, NY 10013. (212) 741-1356. Susan Bell, Exec. Secy. A voluntary association of authors' agents whose members subscribe to a specific code of ethics for the conduct of their work.

Society of Cable Television Engineers (SCTE). Box 2389, West Chester, PA 19830. (215) 692-7870. James Emerson, Pres. SCTE is dedicated to the training and further education of members. A nonprofit membership organization for persons engaged in engineering, construction, installation, technical direction, management, or administration of cable television, broad band, microwave, broadcasting or closed-circuit television systems and suppliers of goods and services to these businesses. Also eligible for membership are students in communications, educators, government and regulatory agency employees, and affiliated trade associations. *Membership:* 3,000. *Dues:* $40.00 indiv.; $250.00 sustaining.

The Society of Data Educators (SDE). School of Business, James Madison Univ., Harrisburg, VA 22801. (703) 433-6189. Ben M. Bauman, Treas. A professional organization for administrators, users, and teachers of computer information systems and data processing courses. Members teach and work in schools in the public and private sector. Junior high school, secondary, college, and university teachers and industry professionals make up the membership. 1985 convention to be held in Las Vegas, NV; 1986 in Hollywood, FL. SDE names Data Educator of the Year. *Dues: $25.00/yr. Publication: The Journal of Data Education.*

Society of Manufacturing Engineers (SME). 1 SME Dr., Box 930, Dearborn, MI 48121. (313) 271-1500. Bill Hilty, Gen. Mng. A technical society that, among many other services, distributes films and videotapes for rent or purchase; covers a wide range of manufacturing technology, including robots, lasers, microcomputers, manufacturing productivity, material processing, finishing, and product design. *Membership:* 70,000 members. *Dues:* $50.00/yr. *Publications:* free catalog of videotapes on manufacturing.

Society of Motion Picture and Television Engineers, Inc. (SMPTE). 862 Scarsdale Ave., Scarsdale, NY 10583. (914) 472-6606. Lynette Robinson, Exec. Dir. Fosters the advancement of engineering and technical aspects of motion pictures, television, and allied arts and sciences; disseminates scientific information in these areas; sponsors lectures, exhibitions, classes, and conferences. Open to those with clearly defined interest in the field. *Membership:* 8,500. *Publications:* booklets and reports related to nonbook media, such as *SMPTE Journal; Special Effects in Motion Pictures; Magnetic Video Tape Recording Glossary; The ABC of Photographic Sound Recording*; and test films and slides.

Society of Photo Technologists (SPT). Box 9634, Denver, CO 80209. An organization of photographic equipment repair technicians. Improves and maintains communications between manufacturers and independent repair technicians; specialty tool company; computer bulletin board. *Membership:*, 1,200. *Dues:* $35.00-$160.00. *Publications: SPT Journal; SPT Parts and Information Directory; SPT Newsletter.*

Society of Photographic Scientists and Engineers (SPSE). 7003 Kilworth Ln., Springfield, VA 22151. (703) 642-9090. Vivian Walworth, Pres. Seeks to advance the science and engineering of imagery materials and equipment and to develop means for applying and using imagery in all branches of engineering and science. *Membership:* 3,400 in 17 chapters. *Dues:* $50.00 United States. *Publication: Photographic Science and Engineering: Journal of Applied Photographic Engineering.*

SOFTSWAP. San Mateo County Office of Education, 333 Main St., Redwood City, CA 94063. (415) 363-5472. Ann Lathrop, Library Coord. SOFTSWAP is a public domain library of some four hundred teacher-developed educational programs for use in the Apple, Atari, PET, and TRS-80 microcomputers. These programs, contributed by educators, are organized onto disks that are sold for a nominal charge, with permission to copy and distribute freely. Programs will also be sent free in exchange for original programs donated to the collection. *Publication:* catalog.

The Source. 1616 Anderson Rd., McLean, VA 22102. (703) 734-7500. A business-related, fee-charging computerized videotex database. Provides electronic mail service; United Press International news; stock and bond quotes; financial news; shopping; airline schedules; games; Information on Demand; the Media General Financial Service; Commodity World News. Hourly rates, $20.75 on weekdays, $7.75 evenings and weekends. Access through terminal or personal computer and modem. Parent company Readers Digest Association. *Membership:* 60,000 subscribers.

Southwest Alternate Media Project (SWAMP). 1519 W. Main, Houston, TX 77006. (713) 522-0165 or 522-8592. Edward Hugetz, Pres. A media arts center for the advancement of independent productions and exhibitions in the regions of Arizona, New Mexico, Oklahoma, Texas, and Arkansas. Provides information and equipment access, media arts workshops and courses, production consultation, grant writing aid, exhibition, and distribution. Gives yearly grants to southwest regional media artists, holds yearly showcase of southwest media art, sponsors a thirteen-week regional PBS series on KUHT-TV, Houston and coordinates a year-round Rice Media Center Film Series. *Dues:* $10.00/yr. indiv. *Publication: Southwest Media Review.*

Southwest Regional Laboratory for Educational Research and Development. 4665 Lampson Ave., Los Alamitos, CA 90720. (213) 598-7661. Richard E. Schutz, Pres. Conducts a number of media-related activities, including 16mm and television production, audio recordings, filmstrip/slide units, graphics design, print, and electronic information processing configuration. SWRL uses the media capability for the development and implementation of instructional product systems, educational planning systems, training systems, and information processing systems. *Publication: Technical Report Series.*

Southwest Resource (Computer) Center. Univ. of New Mexico, Albuquerque, NM 87131. (505) 277-0111. Affiliated with the University of New Mexico; provides information about computer applications in work with minorities and low-income families.

Southwestern Film Consortium (SWFC). 1139 E. 6th St., Tucson, AZ 85719. (602) 792-9202. Mark Headley, Exec. Dir. A nonprofit arts group that specializes in motion picture education through seminars, workshops, screenings, visiting artists programs, and film premieres. Service is provided throughout Arizona and the work is closely aligned with the Academy of Motion Picture Arts and Sciences. Film production by students at a reasonable cost is the primary goal of ongoing workshops.

SpecialNet. 2021 K St. NW, Suite 315, Washington, DC 20006. (202) 296-1800. A computerized fee-charging information database emphasizing special education resources.

Speech Communication Association (SCA). 5105 Backlick Rd., #E, Annandale, VA 22003. (713) 750-0533. William Work, Exec. Secy. A voluntary society organized to promote study, criticism, research, teaching, and application of principles of communication, particularly of speech communication. *Membership:* 5,500. *Dues:* $35.00. *Publications: Quarterly Journal of Speech; Communication Monographs; Communication Education; Critical Studies in Mass Communication; Spectra* (monthly newsletter).

Superintendent of Documents. U.S. Government Printing Office, Washington, DC 20402. (202) 783-3238. Functions as the principal sales agency for U.S. government publications. Has over 16,000 titles in its active sales inventory. For information on the scope of its publications, write for the free *Subject Bibliography Index* listing of over 250 Subject Bibliographies on specific topics. Of particular interest is SB-258, *Grants and Awards,* which lists 25 publications. Others are SB-114, *Directories and Lists of Persons and Organizations,* SB-73, *Motion Pictures, Films and Audiovisual Information;* and the publication (available at $36.00/yr.) *Catalog of Federal and Domestic Assistance* — designed to identify types of assistance available.

Teachers and Writers (T&W). 5 Union Square West, New York, NY 10003. (212) 691-6590. Nancy Larson Shapiro, Dir. Sends writers and other artists into New York public schools to conduct long-term projects in collaboration with classroom teachers. *Publications: Teachers and Writers Magazine; Journal of a Living Experiment: A Documentary History of the First Ten Years of Teachers & Writers Collaborative; The Whole Word Catalog; Just Writing; Exercises to Improve Your Writing; Teaching and Writing Popular Fiction;*

Writing as a Second Language; The Writing Workshop (vols. 1 and 2); *The Point: Where Teaching and Writing Intersect; Reading Your Students: Their Writing and Their Selves; How to Make Poetry Comics; Personal Fiction Writing.*

Telecommunications Information Center, The Gelman Library. George Washington Univ., 2130 H St. NW, Rm. 610, Washington, DC 20052. (202) 676-5740. Cathy Haworth, Libr. Supports research in the area of telecommunication policy; collects information in the areas of broadcasting, cable communications, common carrier, communications satellites, teletext-videotext services, electronic mail, mobile communications, and computer communications interface. Although graduate students are expected to be the principal users, the printed collections are open to the general public and the interlibrary loan service is available.

Telecommunications Research and Action Center (TRAC). Box 12038, Washington, DC 20005. (202) 462-2520. Samuel Simon, Exec. Dir. Seeks to improve broadcasting and to support local and national media reform groups and movements. *Dues:* $20.00. *Publications: Access; Citizens Media Directory; New Communication and Information Technologies and Their Application; Reverse the Charges—How to Save $$ on Your Telephone Bill*; and *The Teleconsumers and the Future: Manual on the AT&T Divestiture; Tele-Tips.*

Television Information Office (TIO). 745 5th Ave., New York, NY 10022. (212) 759-6800. Provides a two-way bridge between the TV industry and its many publics. Provides a continuing information service to educators, students, government agencies, the press, the clergy, librarians, allied communications professionals, and the public as well as broadcasters. Library includes five thousand volumes, ninety thousand documents, and information-retrieval equipment. Commissions Roper studies of public attitudes toward TV and produces video spots emphasizing positive aspects of TV. *Membership:* 3 commercial TV networks; NAB; broadcasting groups; commercial and public TV stations. *Publications:* pamphlets; speeches; paperbacks; more.

Television Licensing Center (TLC). 1144 Wilmette Ave., Wilmette, IL 60091. (800) 323-4222. Michael Stickney, Dir.; Brenda Coto, Asst. Dir. Offers licensing services for off-air videotaping of television programs from PBS, CBS, NBC, and others. *Dues:* no cost membership. *Publication: TLC Guide.*

Theater Library Association (TLA). 111 Amsterdam Ave., Rm. 513, New York, NY 10023. (212) 870-1670. Richard M. Buck, Secy.-Treas. Seeks to further the interests of collecting, preserving, and using theater, cinema, and performing arts materials in libraries, museums, and private collections. *Membership:* 500. *Dues:* $25.00 indiv.; $20.00 inst. *Publications: Broadside; Performing Arts Resources.*

Training Media Distributors Association. 1258 N. Highland, Suite 102, Los Angeles, CA 90038. (213) 469-6063. Cally Curtis, Pres. An organization dedicated to the protection of film and videotape copyright and copyright education. *Membership:* 45. *Dues:* based on number of employees. *Publication: The Monthly.*

UCLA Film, Television and Radio Archives. Univ. of California at Los Angeles, 405 Hilgard Ave., Los Angeles, CA 90024. (213) 206-8013. A communication arts archive of film, television, and radio features and productions that support the institution's programs in cinema, theater arts, and communications.

United Nations Radio and Visual Services. Dept. of Public Information, New York, NY 10017. (212) 754-1234. Produces and distributes films, still pictures, charts, posters, and audio materials about the United Nations. Distribution is worldwide and is accomplished through a network of approximately sixty United Nations information centers. Items provided in a number of different languages, including English, French, Spanish, and Arabic.

U.S. Advisory Commission on Public Diplomacy. 301 Fourth St. SW, Rm. 600, Washington, DC 20547. (202) 485-2457. Dr. Edwin J. Feulner, Jr., Chair. Established by Congress in 1978 to advise the president, Congress, and the director of the U.S. Information Agency on the formulation of U.S. Information Agency policies and programs concerning international information education and cultural activities and on the effectiveness with which those programs are conducted. Issues periodic reports. *See also* U.S. Information Agency, Office of Public Liaison.

U.S. Department of Agriculture. 14th St. and Independence Ave. SW, Washington, DC 20250. (202) 447-2791. The USDA acquires and disseminates agricultural information; is involved with research, education, conservation, regulation, and rural development. Makes available 16mm films (write Video and Film Division, Office of Government and Public Affairs, USDA, Washington, DC 20250). Filmstrips and slide sets may be purchased (write Photography Division at same address). Has as a resource the two million volume National Agricultural Library. The department's Forest Service carries on basic research, as does the Agricultural Research Service.

U.S. Department of Education, Center for Libraries and Education Improvement (CLEI). Washington, DC 20202. (202) 254-6572. The center is responsible for the coordination and implementation of strategies designed to link educational research and development with educational practice; to improve information instructional resources. These goals are accomplished through (1) the management of dissemination, technology, and library programs contained within the center, and (2) the development, testing, and implementation of innovative assessment and dissemination throughout the department to eliminate unnecessary duplication of effort and thus improve program operations. The center is under the supervision of a director who reports directly to the Assistant Secretary for Educational Research and Improvement. The director provides overall direction, coordination, and leadership to the following major elements: the Division of Library Programs; the Division of National Dissemination Programs; and the Division of Technology, Resource Assessment and Development.

U.S. Information Agency (USIA). Office of Public Liaison, 301 Fourth St. SW, Washington, DC 20547. (202) 485-2355. Charles Z. Wick, Dir. Legislation states the purpose of the USIA is to increase mutual understanding between the people of the United States and the people of other countries. The USIA is prohibited from distributing overseas material in the United States. The agency maintains 202 posts in 124 countries. Its director, deputy director, and four associate directors are appointed by the president and subject to conformation by the Senate. The agency employs radio broadcasting, information centers, libraries, personal contact, lectures, book publication and distribution, press placement, magazines and other publications, motion pictures, television, exhibits, and English-language instruction. The agency also advises the president and other government officials as to implications of foreign opinion with respect to present and contemplated U.S. policies, programs, and official statements.

Universal Serials and Book Exchange (USBE). 3335 V St. NE, Washington, DC 20018. (202) 636-8723. Joseph M. Dagnese, Pres. USBE is a nonprofit cooperative vehicle for redistribution of original information resources between libraries and other educational and scientific organizations. Receives, organizes, and supplies resources, in units as small as one issue of a serial or one copy of a monograph. Holdings total four million items. *Membership:* 1,000. *Dues:* $200.00/yr. *Publications: USBE/News* (mo. catalog and newsletter); *7,000 Most Available Titles* (microfiche list of core serials).

University and College Designers Association (UCDA). Umberger Hall, Kansas State Univ., Manhattan, KS 66506. (913) 532-5804. Garon Hart, Pres. Comprised of individuals and institutions interested in better visual design to improve higher education communication through graphics, photography, signage, films, and other related media. *Membership:* 550. *Dues:* $45.00 regular; $175.00 inst.; $60.00 assoc.; $15.00 student. *Publication: Designer* (q. newsletter).

University Consortium for Instructional Development and Technology (UCIDT). School of Education, Syracuse Univ., Syracuse, NY 13210. Donald P. Ely, Nat. Dir. Promotes participation of six U.S. institutions of higher learning in instructional design and development activities for colleges and universities, school systems, schools and other institutions, and foreign countries. *Members:* Arizona State Univ., Florida State Univ., Indiana Univ., Michigan State Univ., Syracuse Univ., and the Univ. of Southern California.

University Film and Video Association. Dept. of Cinema and Photography, Southern Illinois Univ. at Carbondale, Carbondale, IL 62901. (618) 453-2365. Richard Blumenberg, Pres. People in the arts and sciences of film and video. Promotes film and video production in educational institutions; fosters study of world cinema and video in scholarly resource centers; and serves as central source of information on film/video instruction, festivals, grants, jobs, production, and research. *Membership:* approximately 800. *Dues:* $35.00 indiv.; $15.00 students; $75.00 inst.; $150.00 commercial firms. *Publications: Journal of Film and Video; UFVA Digest*; and a membership directory.

Video Data Bank. School of Art Institute of Chicago, Columbus at Jackson, Chicago, IL 60603. (312) 443-3793. Lyn Blumenthal and Kate Horsfield, Co-Dirs. Has been producing video interview tapes with prominent artists since 1974; new tapes are constantly being added. Since 1981 the bank has also been publishing *PROFILE*, an idea-oriented publication devoted to the exploration of artists' conceptions and ideas by the artists themselves. The organizations Video Tape Review, another of its projects, is a collection of videotapes produced by artists who seek to explore the possibilities of the electronic medium. The bank also maintains a study center that includes numerous resources in the field of art.

Videotex Industry Association. 1901 N. Fort Myer Dr., Suite 200, Rosslyn, VA 22209. (703) 522-0883. William W. Seelinger, Pres. VIA was established to create interest in the videotex market; to educate the public about the benefits and applications of videotex technology; to serve as a catalyst for the exchange of information; and to represent the industry in establishing policy in legislative and regulatory matters. *Membership:* over 130 corporate members.

Voice of America (VOA). United States Information Agency, International Broadcasting Service, 330 Independence Ave. NW, Washington, DC 20547. (202) 755-4744. Ernest Eugene (Gene) Pell, Dir. Designate. The Voice of America is the global radio network of the United States Information Agency, which seeks to promote understanding abroad for the United States, its people, its culture, and its policies. Voice of America seeks: (1) to serve as a consistently reliable and authoritative source of news; (2) to represent America—not any single segment of American society; and (3) to present the policies of the United States clearly and effectively and to present responsible discussion and opinion on these policies. VOA broadcasts in 42 different languages over 980 hours each week. It maintains thirty-two studios in Washington, DC, two in New York, and one each in Chicago, Los Angeles, and Miami. It operates thirty-one domestic and seventy-four overseas transmitters.

Western Educational Society for Telecommunications (WEST). KAET Arizona State Univ., Tempe, AZ 85287. (602) 965-3506. Ted Christensen, Pres. A regional association of telecommunications practitioners. WEST offers workshops and conferences in the western United States; offers WEST awards for radio, television, and graphics productions; and sponsors annual WEST conference. *Membership:* 200. *Dues:* $20.00 *Publications: Telemo; Proceedings.*

Women in Film (WIF). 8489 W. 3rd St., Los Angeles, CA 90048. (213) 651-3680. Johnna Levine, Pres. For women in film, television, cable, and so forth. A communications network, an educational resource, and a lobby to support women and women filmmakers. The purpose of Women in Film is to serve as a support group and act as clearinghouse and resource of information on qualified professional women in the entertainment industry. WIF conducts ongoing workshops, a series of lectures, and open discussions by leaders in the industry who share their expertise with small groups of members. Areas include directing, producing, contract negotiation, writing, production development, acting, and technical crafts. The Crystal Awards Luncheon is an annual event honoring outstanding women and men for their contributions toward improving the image and increasing participation of women in the industry. Women in Film Foundation has been instituted to offer grants, scholarships, and film finishing funds to qualified recipients. *Dues:* $86.00/yr. *Publication:* newsletter ($115.00/yr. subscription).

Women's Educational Equity Act (WEEA) Publishing Center. Educational Development Center, 55 Chapel St., Newton, MA 02160. (800) 225-3088; or in MA, (617) 969-7100. Libby Wendt, Admin. Coord. Over three hundred print and audiovisual materials developed nationwide to promote educational equity for girls and women. Includes curriculum guides for all subject areas; teacher training and inservice staff development programs; educational policy and administration handbooks; informational materials; career development manuals; and workshop guides. Some designed specifically for minority groups, displaced homemakers, ex-offenders, low income, and rural women. Materials sold at cost. Funded by U.S. Dept. of Education. *Publications: Resources for Educational Equity; Resources for Working Women.*

Women's Institute for Freedom of the Press. 3306 Ross Pl. NW, Washington, DC 20008. (202) 966-7783. Dr. Donna Allen, Dir. Conducts research and publishes reports on communications media and women. Annual conference held on restructuring the communications system and expanding communications for women nationally and internationally. Annual directory of women's media available with annotated index since 1972. *Membership:* nonmember associate structure. *Publications: The 1985 Index/Directory of Women's Media; Bimonthly Media Report to Women; Five Year Index to Media Report to Women; Women in Media: A Documentary Source Book; Syllabus Sourcebook on Media and Women.*

World Future Society (WFS). 4916 St. Elmo Ave., Bethesda, MD 20814. (301) 656-8274. Edward Cornish, Pres. Organization of individuals interested in the study of future trends and possibilities. *Membership:* 30,000. *Dues:* $25.00. *Publications: The Futurist: A Journal of Forecasts, Trends and Ideas about the Future; Futures Research Quarterly*; and *Future Survey.* The Society's bookstore offers audiotapes, books, films, and other items.

World Pen Pals (WPP). 1690 Como Ave., St. Paul, MN 55108. (612) 647-0191. Loni Fazendin, Secy. Cultivates appreciation of other cultures and customs through encouraging personal letter writing activities. The service charge is $2.00 for group or class orders (minimum of six names) and $1.75 for each single applicant. *Publication: Write in There.*

World Radio Missionary Fellowship, Inc. 20201 NW 37th Ave., Opa Locka (Miami), FL 33055-0401. (305) 624-4252. Ronald A. Cline, Pres. Engaged in international broadcasting. Owns and operates radio station HCJB La Voz de los Andes and Hospitals Vozandes in

Ecuador, South America; involved in production of radio programs in Italy; affiliated with HOXO, Panama and KVMV, KOIR, KBNR, United States.

Young People's Logo Association (YPLA). Box 855067, Richardson, TX 75085. (214) 783-7548. James H. Muller, Pres. and Founder. A multinational educational association of children, parents, and teachers organized to share the fun and excitement of personal computing. Monthly publications feature programming tips in Logo, Pilot and BASIC for all popular personal computers. Other services include a member software exchange, bulletin board, contests, programming challenges, and workshops. YPLA books and software provide practical guides to the learning and teaching of Logo and other languages. The YPLA is affiliated with similar groups in England, Australia, Canada, the Netherlands, and Japan. For those interested in special education, the YPLA offers support through C-CAD, the center for Computer Assistance to the Disabled. *Dues:* $25.00; group discounts available.

Canada

This section includes data regarding 11 Canadian organizations whose principal interests lie in the general fields of educational media, instructional technology, and library and information science. Entries have been checked for accuracy, edited, and returned to *EMTY* by the organizations concerned.

ALPHABETICAL LIST

Access Network. Alberta Educational Communications Corporation, 16930 114 Ave., Edmonton, AB T5M 3S2, Canada. (403) 451-3160. Chris Jones, Dir., Marketing Development. Established in 1973 to serve the educational needs of Albertans; responsible for producing television and radio programs, multimedia kits, microcomputer-based programs, and learning support materials for educational use.

Association for Media and Technology in Education in Canada (AMTEC). Box 1021, Station B, Willowdale, ON M2K 2T7, Canada. Promotes applications of educational media and technology in improving education and the public welfare. Fosters cooperation and interaction in the field; seeks to improve professional qualifications of media practitioners; organizes and conducts media meetings, seminars, yearly conferences, and clinic; and stimulates media-related research and publication. *Membership:* 550. *Publications: Canadian Journal of Educational Communication* (4/yr., with membership); listings of media courses in Canada; and directory of educational media personnel in Canada.

Canadian Association of Broadcasters (CAB/ACR). Box 627, Station B, Ottawa, ON K1P 5S2, Canada. (613) 233-4035. G. G. E. Steele, Pres. A nonprofit, trade association representing privately owned Canadian AM and FM radio stations and television stations as well as various associate organizations and networks. Encourages exchanges of programs among members.

Canadian Book Publishers' Council (CPBC). 45 Charles St. E., 7th Floor, Toronto, ON M4Y 1S2, Canada. (416) 964-7231. Jacqueline Hushion, Exec. Dir. CPBC publishes and distributes an extensive list of Canadian and imported materials to schools and universities, bookstores, and libraries. Provides exhibits throughout the year and works through a number of subcommittees and groups within the organization to promote effective book publishing. *Membership:* 50 companies, educational institutions, or government agencies who publish books as an important function of their work.

Canadian Broadcasting System. 1500 Bronson Ave., Box 8478, Ottawa, ON K1G 3J5, Canada. (613) 724-1200. The Canadian Broadcasting Corporation (CBC) is a publicly owned corporation established in 1936 by an Act of the Canadian Parliament to provide the national broadcasting service in Canada in the two official languages. The CBC is financed mainly by public funds voted annually by Parliament.

Canadian Education Association. 252 Bloor St. W., Toronto, ON M5S 1V5, Canada. (416) 924-7721. Robert E. Blair, Exec. Dir. The Canadian equivalent of the U.S. National Education Association. *Publications: Recent Developments in Native Education* (1983, $6.00); *School and the Workplace: The Need for Stronger Links* (1983, $6.00); and *CEA Handbook* (ann., $34.00).

Canadian Film Institute (CFI). 75 Albert St., Suite B-20, Ottawa, ON K1P 5E7, Canada. (613) 232-6727. Frank Taylor, Exec. Dir. Established in 1935, the institute promotes the study of film and television as cultural-educational forces in Canada. It distributes over seven thousand films on the sciences and the visual and performing arts through the National Film Library. *Publications: The Guide to Film, Television, and Communications Studies in Canada; Canadian Film Series* (monographs).

Canadian Library Association (CLA). 151 Sparks St., Ottawa, ON K1P 5E3, Canada. (613) 232-9625, Paul Kitchen, Exec. Dir. A national organization devoted to improving the quality of library and information service in Canada and developing higher standards of librarianship. Comparable in purposes and activities with the American Library Association. *Publications: Canadian Library Journal* (bi-mo.); *CM: Canadian Materials for Schools and Libraries* (6/yr.); *Canadian Periodical Index; Feliciter* (11/yr.); various reference books for librarians; and microfilm program.

Canadian Museums Association/Association des Musées Canadiens (CMA/AMC). 280 Metcalfe St., Suite 202, Ottawa, ON K2P 1R7, Canada. (613) 233-5653. John C. McAvity, Exec. Dir. Seeks to advance public museum service in Canada. *Membership:* 2,200. *Publications: Museogramme* (mo. newsletter); *Muse* (q. journal); *Directory of Canadian Museums* (listing all museums in Canada plus information on government departments, agencies, and provincial and regional museum associations); and *CMA Bibliography* (an extensive listing of published material on the subjects of museology, museography, and museum and art gallery administration). CMA offers a correspondence course that serves as an introduction to museum operations and philosophy through selected readings.

National Film Board of Canada (NFBC). 1251 Ave. of the Americas, 16th Floor, New York, NY 10020. (212) 586-5131. Canadian address: Box 6100, Montreal, PQ H3C 3H5, Canada. Mary Jane Terrell, Marketing Mng. Established in 1939, the NFBC's main objective is to produce and distribute high quality audiovisual materials for educational, cultural, and social purposes. Main source of reference in the United States is the 1983-84 publication *U.S. Film Resource Guide* (available free in the United States from the above address).

Ontario Film Association, Inc. Box 366, Station Q, Toronto, ON M4T 2M5, Canada. (416) 429-4100. Promotes the use of film and video and fosters awareness of them as a source of information, cultural expression, and enjoyment. Sponsors the annual Grierson Documentary Seminars on film and video subjects, bringing together users, makers, and students interested in production and utilization. *Publication: A Newsletter Called FRED* (bi-monthly).

The United Kingdom

This section lists 47 organizations within the United Kingdom (England and Scotland) whose principal interests lie in the general fields of educational media, instructional technology, and library and information science. Entries have been checked for accuracy, edited, and returned to *EMTY* by the organizations concerned.

ALPHABETICAL LIST

Aslib — The Association for Information Management. 3 Belgrave Sq., London SWIX 8PL, England. Tel. (01) 235-5050. Dr. Dennis A. Lewis, Cir. Formerly the Association of Special Libraries and Information Bureau. Provides information on all aspects of information management and use. In addition to library and consultant services, Aslib publishes extensively on a wide range of information issues; organizes topical meetings, conferences, and courses. The Aslib research program includes projects on the use of information technology in information handling, as well as the use of computers in schools and the exploitation of viewdata systems for providing community and other information. *Membership:* open to any organization concerned with information; entitles the member to use any of Aslib's services, details of which can be obtained from the above address. *Publications: Aslib Proceedings* (mo. proceedings); *Aslib Information* (mo.); *Journal of Documentation* (q.); *Forthcoming International Scientific and Technical Conferences* (q.); others include directories, reports, conference proceedings, and books concerned with all aspects of information management.

Association for Educational and Training Technology (AETT). BLAT Centre, BMA House, Tavistock Sq., London WC1H9JP, England. Lord Howie of Troon, Pres. Formerly Association for Programmed Learning and Educational Technology (APLET). Strives to increase knowledge and use of educational technology in education and industry. Organizes regional, national, and international conferences. International conference at London, 1985. *Publications: Ed Tech News; Aspects of Educational Technology* (series); *Journal of Programmed Learning and Educational Technology; Yearbook of Educational and Instructional Technology; A Systems Approach to Education and Training* (A. J. Romiszowski, ed.); and *Microteaching: Analysis and Appreciation* (A. J. Trott, ed.); *Selected Readings in Computer-Based Learning* (N. J. Rushby, ed.).

BLAT Centre for Health and Medical Education. BMA House, Tavistock Sq., London WC1H9JP, England. Tel. (01) 388-7976. Margaret C. Jones, Information Off./Libr. Probably the largest medical film library in Europe, BLAT is recognized as a useful source of advice on teaching methods. Founded in 1966 by the British Medical Association, the Life Offices' Association, and the Associated Scottish Life Offices, BLAT works through educational technology, defined in the broadest terms, to promote the further education of the medical profession. It is a collaborating center of the World Health Organization (WHO) and thus has a special interest in the enhancement of health education in various developing countries throughout the world. The BLAT staff is grouped in five sections: information, administration, film library, audiovisual, and research and development. Its medical film library currently includes some nine hundred titles that are widely distributed to users within the United Kingdom.

British Association for Commercial and Industrial Education (BACIE). 16 Park Crescent, London W1N 4AP, England. Tel. (01) 635-5351. Chris Watkins, Information Off. A voluntary educational charity group that serves the interests of vocational educators through its training, information, and publications departments. Offers short courses and conferences on training-related subjects. *Publications: BACIE Journal*; various manuals and handbooks, some dealing with applications of new media in training.

British Broadcasting Corporation (BBC). Broadcasting House, London W1A 1AA, England. Tel. (01) 580-4468. Alasdair Milne, Dir.-Gen. A public corporation that operates two national television networks (with plans for two additional channels in 1986), four national radio networks, several regional services, and some thirty local radio stations in the United Kingdom, as well as an extensive worldwide radio service. The BBC seeks to inform, educate, and entertain its television and radio audiences. Educational broadcasts (excluding those for the Open University) are provided out of license revenue under guidance of the School Broadcasting Council and the Continuing Education Advisory Council. They differ from general programming in that they often have specifically defined educational goals, are often planned as a progression supported by print and other media, and are aimed at achieving progress toward mastery of a body of knowledge. For additional information, write to: The Education Secretary, British Broadcasting Corporation, The Langham, Portland Place, London W1A 1AA, England.

British Council. 10 Spring Gardens, London SW1A 2BN, England. Tel. (01) 930-8466. Aims to promote enduring understanding and appreciation of Great Britain in other countries through cultural and educational cooperation. Offers services abroad and cooperative services in Britain in various areas: teaching English and helping others to teach it; encouraging mutual acquaintance and communication of professionals in Britain with those abroad; maintaining offices, libraries, and information centers throughout the world; organizing exhibitions of British art, books, drama, dance, and music abroad; recruiting teachers and others for professional, educational, and cultural assignments abroad; and others. Much of its work is performed through efforts of the British Media Council (*see* entry). *Publications: The British Council* (ann. report); *Catalogue of Radio and Television Training Materials from the United Kingdom*; and *Film and Television Training*.

British Educational Equipment Association (BEEA). Sunley House, 10 Gunthorpe St., London E1 7RW, England. Tel. (01) 247-9320. Promotes and safeguards interests of its members who, somewhat like the U.S. National Audio-Visual Association, include manufacturers, distributors, and suppliers of media-related products and services. Seeks to maintain and develop educational and media services for the benefit of school children at all levels. *Publications: Export Pointers* (wk. newsletter); occasional manuals, leaflets, and brochures.

British Federation of Film Societies (BFFS). 81 Dean St., London W1V 6AA, England. Tel. (01) 437-4355. David Watterson, Gen. Secy. Seeks to extend the range and availability of all types of visual media to the community at large, chiefly through local film societies. *Membership:* open to members of all local film societies in England, Scotland, Wales, and Northern Ireland. *Publication: Film* (10/yr., $27.50/yr.).

The British Film and Television Producers Association, Ltd. Paramount House, 162-170 Wordour St., London W1V 4LA, England. Tel. (01) 437-7700. Similar in purpose to the Motion Picture Association of America.

British Film Institute. 127 Charing Cross Rd., London WC2H 0EA, England. Tel. (01) 437-4355. Anthony Smith, Dir. A government-funded but autonomous body whose major functions are to encourage development of the art of film; to promote its use as a record of contemporary life and manners; and to foster public appreciation and study of it from these points of view. Since 1961, the institute has similarly concerned itself with television. BFI is composed of the National Film Theatre, the National Film Archive, Production Division, Distribution Division, and Information Division. *Dues:* $14.00/yr. *Publications: Sight and Sound* (q.); and *Monthly Film Bulletin* (mo.).

British Industrial and Scientific Film Association (BISFA). 120 Long Acre, London WC2E 9PA, England. Tel. (01) 249-1073/4. Jane Mitchell, Assoc. Secy. An association of companies and individuals in industry, commerce, government, science, education, and in the film industry (including video, slide, filmstrip, and other areas). Aims to assist in the achievement of effective internal and external communications through the use of audiovisual techniques and media. Organizes annually the Sponsored Film and Video Festival (BISFA), which includes sixteen categories; also organizes the Competition for Slide and Filmstrip Programs (Slide/Strip) with seven categories. Provides information and advice as well as contacts within the United Kingdom. Internal groups include those for the construction industry, training media, slide/tape, filmstrip, and video. *Publication:* a mo. magazine for members.

British Institute of Recorded Sound. 29 Exhibition Rd., London SW7, England. Tel. (01) 589-6603. The principal objectives of this national sound archive are to preserve for the future sound recordings of all kinds and to serve as the national center for the study of recorded sound; includes The International Music Collection and The British Library of Wildlife Sounds. Also holds major collections of drama and recorded literature. *Membership:* approx. 1,000. *Dues:* $17.50/yr. *Publication: Recorded Sound* (2/yr.).

British Kinematograph, Sound, and Television Society. 110-112 Victoria House, Vernon Pl., London WC1B 4DJ, England. Tel. (01) 242-8400. William Pay, Secy. Organizers of the biennial International Technology Conference and Exhibition; courses and seminars; test films and slides; audio test cassettes. *Membership:* 2,500. *Publications: BKSTS Journal*; and technical manuals.

British Media Council. 10 Spring Gardens, London SW1A 2BN, England. Tel. (01) 930-8466. A. B. Edington, Head. The Media Council is charged with the promotion of the more effective use of radio, television, audiovisual media, distance learning systems, and information technology for developmental and educational purposes. This is done through (1) the identification and provision of British specialists to undertake short- and long-term assignments in various aspects of media advice, training, and application; (2) the advising on and the arranging of training at British institutions in the various disciplines of media work; and (3) the provision of information on all aspects of media hardware and software. *Publication: Media in Education and Development* (formerly *Educational Broadcasting International*, q. journal concerned with all aspects of media use).

British Universities Film and Video Council, Ltd. (BUFVC). 55 Greek St., London W1V 5LR, England. Tel. (01) 734-3687/8. Elizabeth Oliver, Dir. A representative body fostering use of audiovisual media for teaching and research in universities and similar institutions throughout the United Kingdom and elsewhere. Provides an information service on availability and suitability of audiovisual materials for degree teaching as well as for general applications of media in higher education. Offers preview service of university-produced materials through its Audio-Visual Reference Center. *Membership:* 64 indiv.; 14

inst. *Dues:* $25.00/yr. information service subscription. *Publications: BUFVC Newsletter* ($6.00/yr.); *BUFVC Catalogue 1983* ($24.00); *Researcher's Guide to British Newsreels* ($24.00); and *Researcher's Guide to British Film and Television Collections* ($25.00).

Commonwealth Broadcasting Association (COMBROAD). CBA Secretariat, Broadcasting House, London W1A 1AA, England. Tel. (01) 580-4468 ext. 6023. Alva Clarke, Secy.-Gen. An association of fifty-five public service broadcasting organizations in fifty Commonwealth countries that seeks to improve through collective study and mutual assistance all aspects of broadcasting in member countries. *Publications: COMBROAD* (q.); *CBA Handbook*; and *Who's Who in Commonwealth Broadcasting* (ann.).

Council for Educational Technology for the United Kingdom (CET). 3 Devonshire St., London W1N 1BA, England. Tel. (01) 636-4186. Established by the British government to replace the former National Council for Educational Technology (NCET); financed mainly through government funds. Council members represent educational and training organizations, authorities, and interests. All regions of the United Kingdom have a voice in its government. CET promotes appropriate applications of educational and information technology at all levels of education and training throughout the United Kingdom. *Publications: British Journal of Educational Technology* (3/yr.); *Annual Report*; and many other books, monographs, and leaflets including *Interactive Video: Implications for Education and Training, Objectives Model of Curriculum Planning and Evaluation, Information Technology and the School Library Resources Centre,* and *Wordprocessing and the Electronic Office.*

Educational Foundation for Visual Aids (EFVA). 2 Paxton Pl., Gipsy Rd., London SE27 9SR, England. Tel. (01) 670-4247/9. HRH The Duke of Gloucester, Patron; G. C. Marchant, Dir. Provides services to education that are chargeable (i.e., sale of audiovisual equipment and materials); servicing of equipment and rental of films; training courses on equipment utilization and materials production; and publication of catalogs and books. Training and publications departments are located at the National Audio Visual Aids Centre and Film Library in South London; regional and area sales servicing centers in ten other localities.

Educational Publishers Council (EPC). 19 Bedford Sq., London WC1B 3HJ, England. Tel. (01) 580-6321. J. R. M. Davies, Dir. A division of the Publishers Association that acts as the representative body for British publishers of school books. Provides exhibitions of books and conferences throughout the United Kingdom on a regularly scheduled basis. EPC has established a software committee that is now producing information and advice to publishers developing computer software for schools, and it is organizing exhibitions of these products.

Educational Television Association. The King's Manor, Exhibition Sq., York Y01 2EP, England. Tel. 0904-29701. Patricia Kelly, Admin. Brings together institutions and individuals using television and other media for education and training. In addition to regular regional meetings arranged for United Kingdom members, the association holds an annual conference that attracts delegates and speakers from various countries. *Membership:* over 300; includes universities, polytechnics, colleges, schools, local education authorities, training boards, broadcasting organizations, and the armed services, as well as commercial and industrial organizations in the United Kingdom and elsewhere. Send all inquiries concerning membership to the administrator. *Publications: Journal of Educational Television* (3/yr., free to members; £34 by subscription); *Directory of Members*; and *Quarterly Newsletter* (issued to members only).

Film Library for Teacher Education. Paxton Pl., Gipsy Rd., London SE27 9SR, England. Tel. (01) 670-4247/9. H. Knowlson, Chair., Mgmt. Committee. Holds over three hundred specialized films from various parts of the world. The film library was established in 1972;

membership open to institutions of higher learning and local boards of education. Subjects held include: child development, psychology, the educational system and its history, comparative education, and methods of teaching.

Independent Broadcasting Authority (IBA). 70 Brompton Rd., London, SW3 1EY, England. Tel. (01) 584-7011. B. N. Hosking, Head of Information. Created by Parliament in 1954 as the Independent Television Authority (ITA) to provide a comprehensive television service in addition to that of the British Broadcasting Corporation (BBC). The authority was renamed to its present title and its functions extended to cover the provision of Independent Local Radio (ILR) as well. The IBA now selects and appoints companies that produce its programs and those of ILR and others (e.g., the Channel Four Television Company). Fifteen ITV companies provide programs in fourteen Independent Television regions of the United Kingdom. The IBA requires that specific times be allocated to special classes of programs (education, religion, news, documentaries, and programs serving local tastes and interests). Both ITV and ILR are financed mainly through the sale of advertising.

Industrial Council for Educational and Training Technology, Ltd. (ICETT). Leicester House, 8 Leicester St., London WC2H 7BN, England. James Wright, Exec. Dir. Sponsors National Education & Training Exhibition & Conference. This association includes the Association of Consultants and Practitioners in Education and Training; Association of Video, Information Systems, and Technology Producers; Engineering Training Equipment Manufacturers' Association; and the Project Contractors and Suppliers Association.

Information for International Development. Denmas, Aller, Langport, Somerset TA 10 0QN, England. Aims to gather, use, and share information for international development and to offer training, editing, and publishing services for the field. *Publication: Network IFID* (newsletter).

Institute of Medical and Biological Illustration. 27 Craven St., London WC2N 5NX, England. Coordinates and assists the work of audiovisual professionals in the field of life sciences communication.

Institute of Scientific and Technical Communicators, Ltd. (STC). 17 Bluebridge Ave., Brookmans Pk., Hatfield, Herts AL9 7RY, England. Tel. Potters Bar 55392. E. N. White, Pres.; Eileen Parkinson, Secy. This group is composed of professional communicators who work in defense, industry, and educational institutions as technical writers, journalists, illustrators, and publicists. It establishes standards for the field, promotes education and training, and offers awards and certificates. *Publication: The Communicator of Scientific and Technical Information* (q., $8.00/yr.).

The Institute of Training and Development. 5 Baring Rd., Beaconsfield, Bucks HP9 2NX, England. A professional association of individuals conducting training and vocational education at all levels, with special reference to industry, commerce, administration, and public services.

Intermediate Technology Development Group (ITDG). 9 King St., London WC2E 8HN, England. Seeks to facilitate and widen the choice of technologies suitable for small-scale applications in developing countries, in a wide range of technical fields. *Publications: Appropriate Technology* (q. journal); *Watchlines*; and many practical manuals, economic studies, and others. Complete catalog of publications available from above address. Contact Information Officer for general inquiries.

International Association for Mass Communication Research (IAMCR). Centre for Mass Communication Research, Univ. of Leicester, 104 Regent Rd., Leicester LE1 7LT,

England. Tel. (0533) 555557. James D. Halloran, Pres. *Membership:* about 1,000 from 63 countries. *Publications:* reports and papers.

International Extension College (IEC). 18 Brooklands Ave., Cambridge CB2 2HN, England. Tel. (0223) 353321. London office: 42 Store St., London WC1E 7DB, England. Tel. (01) 580-4372. Cambridge personnel: Hilary Perraton/Tony Dodds/Solomon Inquai/ Janet Jenkins, Dirs.; London personnel: Michael Young, Chair. *Publications:* a series of broadsheets on distance learning giving advice and information on teaching in Third World countries including *Secondary Education at a Distance* (1983, Hilary Perraton); *Mass Media for Health Education* (1983, Janet Jenkins); and *Basic Education for Adults* (1983, IEC).

International Federation of Film Archives (FIAF). 90-94 Shaftesbury Ave., London W1V 7DH, England. Tel. (01) 734-4221. *Publications: International Index to Film/Television Periodicals* (ed. Michael Moulds). New in 1983: monthly microfiche for film and television periodical indexing services.

The Museums Association. 34 Bloomsbury Way, London WC1A 2SF, England. Tel. (01) 404-4767. Promotes interests of museums and art galleries; offers educational qualifications for museum and art gallery staff; promotes liaison with other museum associations; offers a range of publications; organizes seminars on current museum-related topics; and holds an annual conference on a museum-related topical theme. *Publications: Bulletin* (mo.); *Journal* (q.), and *Museums Yearbook* (ann.).

National Association for Staff Development in Further and Higher Education. Redgrave House, Prestbury, Macclesfield, Cheshire SK10 4BW, England. Coordinates the professional development work of staff development and in-service education officers of further education and higher education units.

National Audio Visual Aids Centre and Library (NAVAC). 2 Paxton Pl., Gipsy Rd., London SE27 9SR, England. Tel. (01) 670-4247/8/9. B. Mullet, Mgr. Run by the Educational Foundation for Visual Aids (EFVA). Offers information and advice on audiovisual equipment and materials; reference library; equipment sales and servicing; training courses; and publications per EFVA. Distributes some ten thousand educational 16mm films for rental throughout the United Kingdom. Provides a full range of for-purchase visual aids for many U.K. suppliers. *See also* Educational Foundation for Visual Aids.

National Extension College (NEC). 18 Brookland Ave., London CB2 2HN, England. Tel. (02) 235-1093. Founded in 1963 to develop improved methods of home-based adult education. Its activities include correspondence courses, study packs, flexistudy courses, television-based courses, outreach education with young unemployed persons, and basic skills materials. Publishes a catalog of its materials.

National Film Archive (NFA). 81 Dean St., London W1V 6AA, England. Tel. (01) 437-4355. Established in 1935 to acquire, preserve, and make available for study a national collection of films and, later, television programs. In the archive there are now approximately fifty thousand titles ranging from 1895 to the present, as well as a large collection of related stills, posters, and set designs.

National Reprographic Centre for Documentation (NCRd). Hatfield Polytechnic, Bayfordbury, Hertford, Herts SG13 8LD, England. Tel. Hatfield 66144. A service agency for individuals and organizations interested in reprographic and micrographic techniques and equipment, word processing, videodiscs, and videotex. Worldwide membership of library, educational, and commercial organizations. Activities include research, equipment, evaluation, and advisory and inquiry services. *Dues:* $70.00/yr. *Publications: Reprographics Quarterly* (with membership); *The Archival Storage Potential of Microfilm, Magnetic Media and Optical Data Discs* (1983); *Automated/Computer Retrieval of Microforms: A Guide and a Directory* (2d ed., 1983).

The Open University (OU). Walton Hall, Milton Keynes MK7 6AA, England. Tel. 0908-74066. Established by Royal Charter in 1968 as an independent and autonomous institution authorized to confer its own degrees. Offers three study programs: (1) undergraduate, (2) graduate, and (3) associate student. It seeks to advance and disseminate learning and knowledge by teaching and research through use of a variety of methods, including broadcasting, correspondence study, residential courses, in-person seminars, and others. Offers nondegree short courses, some specifically designed to help individuals in their day-to-day affairs. Makes wide use of educational media and of distance-teaching techniques. Many of The Open University's teaching materials, developed within the institution itself, are used in other situation at home and abroad. Plans call for the annual production of some four hundred television programs and four hundred radio programs each year. Departments of note that are a part of the Open University and whose work relates closely to fields treated in the *Educational Media Technology Yearbook* include: (1) Committee on Communications Technology, (2) the Institute of Educational Technology, and (3) the International Documentation Centre on Distance Learning. (*See* entry below.)

(OU) The Committee on Communications Technology. J. K. Hargreaves, Secy. Promotes developments in the use of communication/information technology for distance learning. The committee's projects include "Cyclops" — an audiovisual system based on a television set, standard audiocassettes, and microcomputer technology; "Optel" — a viewdata system having such features as page names, keyword retrieval, and automated help for information providers; and two projects involving tutoring by telephone.

(OU) The Institute of Educational Technology. David Hawkridge, Dir. Advises course teams, carries out course evaluations, and conducts various studies on the Open University's operations. Maintains a staff of about one hundred to do educational research, development, and evaluation work. Of special interest to educational media/communications specialists are the Institute's evaluative and policy-related studies of broadcasts produced for the British Broadcasting Corporation, of videocassette productions, of interactive videotex ("Cyclops") utilization, of videodisc productions, of computer-assisted learning, and of textual communication projects. *Publications:* The *Institute Bibliography* containing details of publications and other information is available (£7, surface mail). Other recent publications by staff members are: *New Information Technology in Education* (Hawkridge, £11.95 plus p&p, 1983, from Croom, Helm, Beckenham, Kent or Johns Hopkins University Press, Baltimore); *Learning and Teaching with Computers* (O'Shea and Self, £6.95 plus p&p, 1983, from Harvester Press, Brighton, Sussex); *The Effective Use of Television and Radio in Education* (Bates, about £15, 1984, from Constable, London); *Independent Learning in Higher Education* (Henderson and Nathenson, pna, 1984, from Educational Technology Publications, New Jersey); *The Role of Technology in Distance Education* (Bates, pna, 1984, from Croom, Helm, Beckenham, Kent).

(OU) International Documentation Centre on Distance Learning. K. W. Harry, Documentation Off. Collects documentation and disseminates information on distance learning. The United Nations University sponsors the Centre, which from January 1, 1984 operates an information service based on a computerized database on distance teaching institutions worldwide.

Royal Photographic Society of Great Britain. RPS National Centre of Photography, The Octagon, Milsom St., Bath BA1 1DN, England. Tel. 0225-62841. Kenneth R. Warr, Secy. Promotes all aspects of photography; awards distinctions of licentiateship, associateship, and fellowship to those achieving required standards. Open to both professional and amateur photographers.

School Library Association (SLA). Victoria House, 29-31 George St., Oxford OX1 2AY, England. Mrs. M. Curtis, Secy. Promotes the use of the library and library resources in education. *Membership:* 4,500.

Scottish Central Film Library. Dowanhill, 74 Victoria Crescent Rd., Glasgow G12 9JN, Scotland. Tel. (041) 334-9314. Supplies educational and training films throughout the United Kingdom. Managed by the Scottish Council for Educational Technology.

Scottish Council for Educational Technology. Dowanhill, 74 Victoria Crescent Rd., Glasgow G12 9JN, Scotland. Tel. (041) 334-9314. T. R. Bone, Chair; R. B. Macluskie, Dir. Promotes and encourages the understanding and application of educational technology throughout education.

Scottish Film Council. Dowanhill, 74 Victoria Crescent Rd., Glasgow G12 9JN, Scotland. Tel. (041) 334-9314. A division of the Scottish Council for Educational Technology. Promotes the use of films and related media as instructional and cultural resources.

Society for Education in Film and Television, Ltd. (SEFT). 29 Old Compton St., London W1V 5PL, England. Tel. (01) 734-5455/3211. Concerned with films, television, and other media, including their applications in visual literacy or cultural studies. Distributes a number of photoplay exercises. *Publication: Screen* (incorporating *Screen Education*, bi-mo.).

Society for the Advancement of Gaming and Simulation in Education and Training (SAGSET). Centre for Extension Studies, University of Technology, Loughborough, Leicester LE1 3TU, England. Founded in 1970 to encourage and develop uses of games and simulations in areas of education and training to which they are suited. Seeks to encourage communication between simulation/gamers working in various subject areas and at different levels, between theoreticians and practitioners, between research workers and producers, and computer-based and "manual" simulation/gamers. Also offers courses and workshops. *Publications: Simulation/Games for Learning* (q. journal); *Sagset News* (newsletter); various leaflets and manuals.

Training and Educational Systems Testing Bureau. National Committee for Audio-Visual Aids. Vauxhall School, Vauxhall St., London SE11 5LG, England. Tel. (01) 735-2904. A. M. Crocker, contact person. Evaluates and tests audiovisual equipment; provides advisory and technical consultancies. *Publications: Technical Reports* (irreg.).

World Association for Christian Communication. 122 King's Rd., London SW3 4TR, England.

Other Parts of the World

ALPHABETICAL LIST BY COUNTRY

Argentina

Associación Latinoamericana de Educación Radiofónica (Latin America Association for Radio Education). Corrientes 816, Buenos Aires, Argentina. Conducts research and promotes and publicizes Argentine and Latin American radio education.

Center for Studies on Media, Education, and Communication (CEMEC). Casilla 137, Sucursal 2, 1402, Buenos Aires, Argentina. A center for information on nontraditional higher education in Latin America; collects studies, reports, and other documents in the fields of educational technology, nonconventional educational systems, cooperation in distance education programs at the university level, and academic research. *Publication: Media Education Communicacion* (journal).

Centro Nacional de Tecnologia Educativa (National Center for Educational Technology). Tinagasta 5268, Capital Federal, Argentina. Promotes the use and improvement of television, videocassettes, and radio for educational purposes throughout Argentina.

Australia

Association of Teachers of Media (ATOM). 234 Queensberry St., Carlton 3053, Australia. Assists educators in enriching their curriculum with the study of media and popular culture. Also offers services to Australian producers and distributors and users of educational films. *Publications: Metro: Media and Education Quarterly; Filmnews* (mo. newsletter on Australian independent film).

Australian Broadcasting Commission (ABC). GPO, Box 487, Sydney, NSW 2001, Australia. Tel. 339-0211. E. D. Hetherington, Act. Dir. of Education. The national broadcasting service of Australia. It provides an extensive service of radio and television programs and support publications for preschool, school, and certain adult audiences.

Australian School Library Association (ASLA). Box 287, Aderley, Qld 4051, Australia. Roy Lundin, Secy. Provides seminars and publications on media relating to school librarianship. Holds a national biennial conference. *Publications: School Media Centres; Being Resourceful; Teacher-Librarian — Curator or Innvoator;* and *Planning for Quality.* Order from Mrs. J. Stevens, Box 140, Elizabeth, S.A. 5112.

Australian Society for Educational Technology (ASET). c/o R. Bishop, 24 Albion St., Pennant Hills, NSW 2120, Australia. Tel. (02) 8489278. A fellowship of persons interested in educational technology. It provides a forum to discuss matters of interest to members; publishes materials; and cooperates with professional organizations in related fields. *Dues:* $15.00/yr. indiv.; $5.00/yr. student; $10.00/yr. corporation. *Publications: ASET News* (news of the society's activities); *The Yearbook* (a major publication containing articles by members); *Proceedings* (of the 1982 conference "Telecommunications in Education and Training").

Curriculum Development Centre. Visual Education Curriculum Project. Box 52, Dickson, ACT 2602, Australia. Tel. (062) 43-3011. A national center for curriculum and materials development that develops books, videotapes, and other materials for teachers that stress the potential of visual learning throughout the curriculum.

Austria

Bundesstaatliche Haupstelle für Lichtbild und Bildungsfilm, Zentrum für Audiovisuelle Medien in Unterricht und Bildung (SHB). Plunkergasse 3-5, A-1152 Vienna, Austria. Tel. (0222) 92 26 16. Hofrat Dr. Franz Hubalek, Dir. An audiovisual center for Austrian schools and a member of ICEM (International Council of Educational Media), which produces films (16mm, Super 8mm), slide series, overhead programs, magnetic tapes, and video for use in schools.

Institute of Educational Technology, Media Didactics, and Engineering Education of the Austrian Universities. Universitätstrasse 65-67, A-9010 Klagenfurt, Vienna, Austria. Conducts educational technology research focused on media didactics and engineering education; provides assistance in the production of media resources for such purposes.

International Institute for Children's Literature and Reading Research. Mayerhofg. 6, A-1040 Vienna, Austria. Tel. 65 03 59. Lucia Binder, Dir. Seeks to promote children's reading and children's literature and to conduct research on problems relating to reading—the concept and technique of reading, the significance of reading in society, reading instruction, individual reading, reader personality, readability of texts, and school and classroom libraries. *Membership:* 700, open to interested individuals or groups. *Publications: Bookbird* (q., in English, in cooperation with the International Board on Books for Young People); professional literature and recommendation list; *Jugend und Buch* (q., in cooperation with the Austrian Children's Book Club); and others.

Bangladesh

Audio-Visual Education Center. Dhanmandi, Dacca-5, Bangladesh. Trains teachers in the use and care of audiovisual equipment; promotes improved utilization of AV equipment; conducts planning and research exercises.

Belgium

Centre National de Documentation Scientifique et Technique. Blvd. de l'Empereur 4, B-1000 Brussels, Belgium. Tel. 513 61 80. H. K. deJaeger, Reviewer. Develops reviews and abstracts of information science and related materials for publication in its institution-related journals.

Dienst Didactische Films en Audiovisuele Media (Film and Audiovisual Media Education Service). Ministerie van Nationale Opvoeding en Nederlandse Cultuur. Handelskaai 7, 1000 Brussels, Belgium. Provides a national film library and serves as a national center for Belgian audiovisual resources and services.

International Association for the Study and Promotion of Audio-Visual Methods (AIMAV). Univ. of Ghent, Faculty of Philosophy and Letters, Blandijnberg 2, B-2000,

Ghent, Belgium. Tel. 25 75 71. Marcel DeGrève, Pres.; Eddy Rosseel, Sao Paulo, Gen. Secy.; Corinne Merlin, Joint Gen. Secy. Studies theoretical and practical aspects of communication; publishes results; performs interdisciplinary research in applied linguistics; provides grants to underwrite media research in several European universities; offers colloquia; and forms working teams. *Membership:* 850. *Publications: Langues et Culture; Études Linguistiques; Sciences de la Communication et de la Diffusion;* and *Degres* (q.).

International Federation of Film Archives (FIAF). Secretariat, 70 Coudenberg, 1000 Brussels, Belgium. Robert Daudelin, Secy.-Gen. Seeks to encourage the creation of archives in all countries for the collection and conservation of the film heritage of each; to facilitate cooperation and exchanges among these film archives; to promote public interest in the art of the cinema; to aid research in this field and to compile new documentation for it. Recent activities: compilation of a card index (in English) of articles and reviews published on the cinema, with articles drawn from eighty leading international film periodicals. *Membership:* 70. Limited to film libraries, archives, or museums devoted to the history of aesthetics of the cinema and accessible to the public, without any commercial purpose. *Publications: Handbook for Film Archives; Manual for the Preservation of Color Film; Manual for Film Cataloging; International Index to Film and Television Periodicals* (cards service or annual cumulative volume); study on the usage of computers for film cataloging; *Cinema 1900-1906* (800 pp.); and others.

Bolivia

Accion Cultural Loyola (ACLO). Calle Loa 682, Casilla 538, Sucre, Bolivia. Tel. 22230-23201. Contact: Padre Jorge Trias, S.J.; P. Javier Velasco Suárez, S.J., Dir.-Gen.

Brazil

Associação Brasileira de Tecnologia Educacional (ABT). (Brazilian Association of Educational Technology). Rua Jornalista Orlando Dantas, 56 - CEP: 22.231, Rio de Janeiro, Brazil. José Manuel de Macedo Costa, Exec. Dir. An independent organization that seeks to improve Brazilian education and training through increased use of educational technology. Operates an information service, organizes short courses and services, and offers several distance-education programs in educational technology, some of them at postgraduate level. *Publications: Tecnologia Educacional* (6/yr.); and *Série Estudos e Pesquisas* (research reports).

Associação Brasileira de Treinamento e Desenvolvimento (Brazilian Association for Training and Development). Rua João Adolfo 118/11, Andar, São Paulo, Brazil. Concerned with industrial training and human resources management; promotes applications of instructional technology in business and industry training. Works closely with American Society for Training and Development.

Bulgaria

Board of the Media of Educational Technology. Boulevard 9 Septemvri, 224 Sofia, Bulgaria. Conducts educational media-related research, with special attention to vocational education.

Bulgariafilm. 96 Rakovsky St., Sofia, Bulgaria. Tel. 87-66-11; 88-41-83.

Institute for Scientific Planning of the Development of the Technological Basis of Culture (NIPIRMTBK). 2 rue Budapeste, Sofia, Bulgaria. Eng. Nickola Velchev, Mng. Dir. Organized to establish a separate and unified group of qualified engineers for creative work; functions are designing and creating technical sets of documents concerning the equipment of cultural sites.

Chile

Centro Latinoamericano de Educación de Adultos (CLEA). Casilla Postal 16417, Correo 9, Avenida Providencia 2093, 29 Piso, Santiago, Chile. Tel. 239375. Sergio Jaramillo Jara, contact person. *Publication: Boletin Informativo SEDECOS/CLEA* (Secretariado de Communicacion Social/Centro Latinoamericano de Educación de Adultos, 3/yr., $12.00).

Multinational Project in Educational Technology. Dept. of Educational Affairs of the Organization of American States, Casilla 16162, Correo 9, Santiago, Chile. Clifton Chadwick, Ed. Publishes *Revista de Technologia Educativa*, which reviews educational technological developments and trends in Latin America. Maintains supportive relationships and information and personnel exchanges among educational technology research and development centers in Argentina, Brazil, Colombia, Chile, Mexico, and Venezuela.

China

National Audio-Visual Centre (NAVC). Ministry of education, Beijing, China. Guo Houdeng, Dir. Established in August 1978 to organize the compilation, manufacture, collection, collation, cataloging, distribution, and exchange of all kinds of audiovisual teaching materials; to publish an audiovisual magazine; and to make studies on audiovisual information, teaching methods, their effects, and their characteristics, using models of the audiovisual equipment and training audiovisual technical personnel for modernization of the educational media and the improvement of the instructional quality.

Colombia

Accion Cultural Popular (ACPO). Carrera 39A No. 15-81; Apartado Aéreo 7170, Bogotá, Colombia. Tel. 45623. Jose A. Rodriguez, Dir. A basic education program begun some thirty years ago; now utilizes one of the largest broadcasting networks in Latin America, publishes quantities of excellently visualized materials correlated with programs, trains community leaders, and keeps a large network of participant groups throughout the country's rural areas.

Ministerio de Educación Nacional. Division de Documentaciḱon Informacion Educativa, Apdo. 80359, Bogotá, Colombia. Organizes school libraries and documentation centers throughout Colombia; offers teacher education courses, including those for improved use and local production of audiovisual resources.

Congo

Institut Nacional de Recherche et d'Action Pedagogiques. BP 2128, Brazzaville, Congo. Conducts national program of research in pedagogical techniques and resources, including those involved with instructional technology.

Costa Rica

Instituto Centroamericano de Extensión de la Cultura (CECU). Box 2948, San Jose, Costa Rica. Tel. 255338. Eduardo Yglesias Tinoco, Gen. Secy. A nonprofit, private institution dedicated to adult education and information in Central America. Produces a daily radio program entitled "School for All," (one half hour, transmitted by forty stations); maintains active correspondence with listeners.

Cuba

Radiotelevisión Educativa del Ministerio de Educación. Ministeria de Educación, Havana, Cuba. An organization that promotes the use of radio broadcasting in the economic and social development of Cuba.

Cyprus

Educational Broadcasting Service. Ministry of Education, Nicosia, Cyprus. Responsible for all activities within Cyprus that pertain to educational technology.

Czechoslovakia

International Radio and Television Organisation (OIRT). Skokanské 1, Prague 6, 16956, Czechoslovakia. An international organization that deals with practical and theoretical questions connected with broadcasting and television programs and technique; encourages cooperation among broadcasting and television organizations. Includes twenty-three members in Europe, Africa, Asia, and Latin America. *Publications: Radio and Television International Review* (in English-French, Russian, and German, bi-mo.); and *OIRT Information* (in English, German, and Russian, mo.).

Denmark

Danish Association of School Libraries. Frankrigsgade 4, 2300 Kobenhavns, Denmark. Established in 1933, gives special attention to Danish school libraries; publicizes new media generally; provides lectures and workshops for school library personnel. *Publications: Børn & Bøger* (Children and Books) (8/yr., pna, written in Danish with English summaries).

National Institute for Educational Media. G1 Kongevej 164-4, DK-1850, Copenhagen V, Denmark. Registers and catalogs educational media; provides information regarding the production and supply of educational media; serves as liaison between media users and producers; and related services.

National Library of Education (DPB). Lerso Parkalle 101, DK-2100, Copenhagen 0, Denmark. Tel. (01) 29-82-11. A national library of media dealing with education and child and youth psychology.

Nordic Documentation Center for Mass Communication Research (NORDICOM). State and Univ. Library, Universitetsparken, DK-8000, Aarhus C, Denmark. Tel. (06) 12-20-22. Claus Kragh Hansen, Secy. Seeks to develop and perfect Nordic mass media research through making national and Nordic efforts more widely available to Nordic researchers and the interested general public.

Statens Filmcentral (SFC). (Danish Government Film Office). Hovedkontoret, Vestergade 27, 1456 Copenhagen, Denmark. Tel. (01) 13-26-86. Axel Jepsen, Dir. Production and distribution of 16mm films for nontheatrical purposes in educational institutions, libraries, social institutions, kindergartens, and other locations. Catalog available in English.

Dominican Republic

Mujer-Tec. Apartado Postal 284-9. Los Rios, Santo Domingo, Dominican Republic. Sonia Andujar, Co-Dir. and Intl. Coord. A nongovernmental advocacy group devoted to promoting community action through the use of media. Objectives of the group concentrate on developing women's technical and leadership roles in the media to benefit and improve women's status. Productions include community reports, TV documentaries, and radio programs involving women in the technical aspects of media work. *Membership:* 75 (primarily women and students actively involved in media work). *Publications: Working Children* (a TV special report); a pamphlet on women in prisons; and other articles on women's contributions to various media projects.

Radio Educativo Communitario Project (RADECO). Apartado Postal No. 57, Barahona, República Dominicana. Andrew Hanssen, Admin. Coord. Uses radio to teach basic reading and writing skills to seven- to fourteen-year-olds who have no access to formal schooling. This nonformal educational project aims to be cost-effective and a model for similar strategies in a variety of settings. Contact persons are James Olsen, Chief-of-Party in the Dominican Republic and Donald Foster-Gross, Project Monitor, S&T/ED, Room 609-J SA-18, Agency for International Development, Department of State, Washington, DC 20523.

Radio Santa Maria. Apartado de Correos 55, La Vega, Dominican Republic. A government-sponsored radio station that produces programs for primary and secondary schools; used by students in small groups and by individuals at home as well.

Ecuador

Centro Internacional de Estudios Supériores de Communicacion para America Latina (CIESPAL). Ave. Almagro y Andrade Marin, Aptd. 584, Quito, Ecuador. Founded cooperatively by the Ecuadorean government, UNESCO, and the Central University of Ecuador. Promotes the development of communication, educational, and scientific journalism, and communication for development.

Finland

Valtion AV-Keskus (VAUK). Hakaniemenkatu 2, 00530, Helsinki 53, Finland. Miss Aino Toivonen, Dir. National audiovisual center, film library, and distributor of software and other audiovisual materials.

France

Center for Educational Research and Innovation (CERI). Organization for Economic Cooperation and Development, 2 rue Andre Pascal, 75775 Paris, France. Promotes and supports, or undertakes development of, research activities in education; supports pilot experiments to test educational innovations in educational systems. *Publication: Innovation in Education* (newsletter).

Centre Audiovisuel—Ecole Normale Supérieure. 2 Ave. du Palais, 92210 Saint-Cloud, France. A research laboratory in audiovisual education and educational technology, with a special interest in higher education.

Fédération Nationale des Industries Techniques du Film, Cinéma, et Télévision. 19 rue Fauborg Saint-Honore. Paris 75008, France. Tel. 359-10-11. Jean G. Noel, Pres. An association of cinema equipment manufacturers, cinematographic laboratories and studios, and sound laboratories.

Institut National de Recherche de Pédagogique (National Institute of Educational Research). 29 rue d'Ulm, Paris 75005, France. Contains two special divisions of interest to educational/instructional technologists: (1) Groupe de Recherche sur les Applications Éducatives de la Télématique et des Télécommunications, which studies educational applications of telematics and telecommunications, and (2) Division Informatique et Enseignement, which studies computer-assisted instruction and micro data processing in relation to education.

International Council for Educational Media (ICEM). Secretariat, 29 rue d'Ulm, 75230 Paris Cédex 05, France. Robert LeFranc, Dir. Promotes worldwide contacts among professionals responsible for various aspects of educational/instructional media programs in their respective countries; provides an international channel for exchanges of views and data; promotes integration of media in modern education, especially with respect to the training of teachers and future teachers; improves the world supply of educational media by practical cooperative projects; advises industrial personnel in the field; informs members of significant media developments in the field of educational technology; and cooperates with other international organizations in the promotion of educational technology.

International Council of Museums (ICOM). Maison de l'Unesco, 1 rue Miollis, 75732 Paris Cédex 15, France. Tel. 734-05-00. Cable: ICOM PARIS. M. Hubert Landais, Pres.; M. Luis Monreal, Secy.-Gen. International organization for museum professionals; operates through its national committees located in seventy countries throughout the world, and twenty-one international committees covering the following specialized topics: archaeology and history, architecture and museum techniques, applied art, modern art, conservation, costume, documentation, education and cultural action, ethnography, international art exhibitions, training of personnel, musical instruments, literature, museology, regional museums, public relations, natural history, science and technology, museum security, glass, fine arts. Triennial General Conference: next to be held in London, England, Summer 1986. *Membership:* 7,300 (indiv. and inst.). *Publications: ICOM News* (q.); and *International Museological Bibliography* (ann.).

International Film and Television Council, UNESCO. 1 rue Miollis, 75732 Paris Cédex 15, France. Enrico Fulchignoni, Pres. An international organization actively consulting thirty international organizations in UNESCO in support of the extended use of films and television in training and education. *Publications: Information Letter*; and special reports.

International Union of Cinematographic Technical Associations (UNIATEC). 11 rue Galilée, 75016 Paris, France. Tel. 720-55-69. Constituted in 1957 at the Third International Congress on Film Techniques (in Warsaw). Seeks to develop the spirit of cooperation among its members in twenty-eight countries; to encourage development of improved film techniques through exchange of information; to encourage the development of national associations of film technicians; and to encourage studies for the advancement of film techniques.

Syndicat National de l'Edition. Cercle de la Librairie, 117 Blvd. Saint Germain, Paris 75279, France. Tel. 329-21-01. M.J.-L. Pidouc-Payot, Pres. Maintains a commission on literary and artistic properties; promotes French cultural works, encourages audiovisual education.

Germany, Federal Republic of

The Central Organization for Programmed Learning and the Computer in Education. Schertlinstrasse 7, 8900 Augsburg, Federal Republic of Germany. A Bavarian Ministry of Education and Culture organization that disseminates information regarding programmed learning and computer uses in schools.

Institut für den Wissenschaftlichen Film (IWF). Nonnenstieg 72, D-3400 Göttingen, Federal Republic of Germany. Tel. (0551) 2020. The central scientific film institute of the Federal Republic of Germany produces and/or publishes annually about 120 research and higher education films and maintains a lending archive for universities with, at present, 5,500 films in 22,000 copies. It also represents the FRG in the Scientific Film Association (ISFA, Paris).

Institut für Film und Bild in Wissenschaft und Unterricht (FWU). Bavaria-Film-Platz 3, 8022 Grünwald, Federal Republic of Germany. Tel. 089-64971. Prof. Walter Cappel, Dir. A nonprofit organization of the eleven Länder of the Federal Republic of Germany, including (West) Berlin. The institute produces audiovisual materials for the educational areas of preschool to college for teacher education; produces AV materials for youth and adult education; and promotes educational technology through its advisory services, testing of equipment, and sale of materials to audiovisual centers, schools, and other educational institutions. The FWU is a member of the International Council for Educational Media (ICEM). *Publications: A V Forschung; A V Technik; A V Pädagogik;* and *A V Unterricht.*

University of Tübingen, Center for New Learning Methods. Institute of Education 11, Muenzgasse 11, D-7400 Tübingen 1, Federal Republic of Germany. Offers courses and training programs in instructional media and technology, including those in computer-assisted instruction, simulation and modeling, interactional analysis, and others.

Ghana

Ghana National Audiovisual Aids Center. Information Services Department, Box 745, Accra, Ghana. Produces audiovisual materials for various government ministries, departments, and institutions; offers instructional courses in the media field.

Guatemala

Audiovisual Centre of the University of San Carlos. Ciudad, Universitaria, Zona 12, Guatemala City, Guatemala.

Federation Guatemalteca de Escuelas Radiofonicas (Guatemalan Federation of Radio Schools). 8a Calle 11-13, Zona 1, Oficina 303, Guatemala City, Guatemala. Studies ways to improve basic education in rural areas and poor urban areas, principally through uses of radio.

Haiti

Projecto de Radio Escolar y Educativa. Damien, Port-au-Prince, Haiti. Provides educational radio programs for a large portion of the country.

Hong Kong

Chinese University of Hong Kong. Shatin, New Territories, Hong Kong, H. K. Prof. Timothy Yu, Dir. of Center for Communication Studies. *Publications: The Asian Messenger* (q. journal); *Circulation of News in the Third World: An Asia Case* (Wilbur Schramm and Erwin Atwood; Timothy Yu, ed.).

Visual Education Section. Education Department, Lee Gardens, 3/F, Hysan Ave., Hong Kong. Tel. 5-8392359. W. S. Chan.

Hungary

Hungarian National Committee for ICEM. National Technical Information Centre and Library-OMIKK, H-1428 Budapest, P.O.B. 12, Hungary. János Dúzs, Hungarian member of the International Council for Educational Media (ICEM), contact person.

National Technical Information Centre and Library, Technical Film Information Centre. H-1428, P.O.B. 12, Budapest, Hungary. Tel. 336-330. Ivan Arkos, Ed., contact person.

Publications: *Audiovizualis Közlemények: Oktatástechnikai, tájékoztatastechnikai és szervezéstechnikai szakfolyóirat/Audio-Visual Review: Journal for Education Technology, Information Technology, and Organizational Technique* (Dr. Janos Duzs, ed., bi-mo., $12.50); *Müszaki És Tudomanyos Filmek/Technical and Scientific Films* (filmography, Anna Volant, ed., q., $16.50).

Optikai Akusztikai és Filmtechnikai Egyesület (Optical, Acoustical, and Filmtechnical Society) (OPAKFI). Ankerköz 1, Budapest, Hungary H-1061. Information gathering and dissemination for professionals in fields of optics, acoustics, motion picture engineering, audiovisual techniques, research film techniques, photography, and stage engineering in Hungary, through papers, courses, workshops, conferences, and film festivals. *Membership:* approx. 2,000.

India

Central Institute of Educational Technology (CIET). National Council of Educational Research and Training (NCERT) Aurobindo Marg, New Delhi, 110016, India. Specializes in the utilization of mass media for educational purposes. Conducts training programs for ETV and educational radio producers/Scriptwriters and on educational technology for teacher educators. Produces prototypes and modules of educational films as well as audio and video prototypes. Has completed a Radio Pilot Project for teaching Hindi as the first language to primary school children. Produces educational TV programs for rural primary schools being telecast via satellite. Has carried out research on the effectiveness of educational programs on radio and television. Produces educational films, tapes, slides, and so forth.

Centre for Development of Instructional Technology (CENDIT). DI Soami Nagar, New Delhi, 110 017, India. Tel. 65-2236/4291. Anil Arivastava, Dir. The center is a research and development center for communication technology that offers training in production and use of film and video for education/training; serves as a clearinghouse on communication, development, education, and technology; runs NIBIT, a computer-based nonbook media databank; and has an ongoing rural development project where, at present, a Community Education Media Experiment is being conducted.

Indian Institute of Mass Communication. D-13, South Extension, Part II, New Delhi, 110049, India. A national center for advanced training and research in communication, with special emphasis upon the socioeconomic growth of the country.

Open School. Central Board of Secondary Education, H-24 Green Park Extension, New Delhi, 110016, India. Tel. 661744. H. R. Sharma, Dir. Designs and operates distance learning facilities and programs, with heavy emphasis upon multirack, multimedia instructional systems and packages, primarily for secondary and senior school students, including women and working adults.

Indonesia

Centre for Communication Technology for Education and Culture. Ministry of Education and Culture, J1 Cenderawsih, Ciputat, Iromolpos 7/KBYCP, Jakarta Selatan, Indonesia. Carries out projects aimed at improved use of media for instruction; emphasizes learning modules and radio production.

Ireland

The Communications Center. Booterstown Ave., County Dublin, Ireland. Trains individuals from various parts of Ireland and the world at large in broadcasting techniques, audiovisual and other media production, and systematic educational planning.

Computer Education Society of Ireland (CESI). Vocational School, Wexford. Brendan Mackey, Chair. Tel. 053/22753. A voluntary organization established in 1973 for those interested in promoting computer education. CESI is an affiliate member of the International Council for Computers in Education (ICCE). *Membership:* 700. *Dues:* $30.00/yr. *Publication: Riomhiris na Scol* (3-4/yr.).

National Film Institute of Ireland. 65 Harcourt St., Dublin 2, Ireland. Primarily an industrial and educational film lending library; also offers audiovisual courses; operates mobile film units.

Israel

Centre for Educational Technology. 16 Klausner St., Tel Aviv, Israel. Concerned with applications of computers as instructional tools; promotes activities intended to promote better use of various educational technology resources at all levels of education; also engaged in the production of needed vocational courses.

Institute for Teaching Aids. 43 Brodetsky St., Box 17168, Tel Aviv, Israel. Designs various types of teaching software and hardware, including books, for use in Israeli schools.

Israel Association for Instructional Technology. 12 Zamenhoff St., Tel Aviv, Israel. An association of professional educational technologists as researchers, planners, designers, producers, distributors, or users.

State of Israel. Ministry of Education and Culture, Pedagogic Centers, 8, King David St., 91 911 Jerusalem. Tel. (02) 238328. Zion Amir, Dir. A network of thirty-eight regional instructional materials centers serving the educational media requirements of cities and towns of Israel. The centers are continuing in their effort to decentralize by changing over to a Teachers Centers system in many of the local branches. They will continue their loan and workshop services and especially emphasize the local production of curriculum and learning materials. The national center supports and guides activities of more than seven hundred school-level resource centers and engages in limited software production and distribution.

Italy

Associazione Tecnica Italiana per la Cinematografia (ATIC). Viale Regina Margherita 286, Rome, Italy 00198. Ing. Antonio Appierto, Pres. A society of technicians of motion pictures in Italy. *Publication: Note de Tecnica Cinematografia* (6/yr.).

Istituto di Pedagogia, Sezioni Audiovisivi (Institute of Education, Audio-Visual Section). Via San Francesco 33, Padua, Italy. Conducts research and training institutes in the field of educational technology.

International Center for Advanced Technical and Vocational Training. 201 Via Ventimiglia, 10127, Turin, Italy. Offers advanced training opportunities for trainers, instructors, directors, and supervisors, middle and senior management personnel, and those involved in the production of training packages and multimedia materials; offers other related services.

Japan

Asia-Pacific Broadcasting Union (ABU). Secretariat, c/o NHK Broadcasting Centre, 2-2-1 Jinnan, Shibuya-ku, Tokyo 150, Japan. Roku Ito, Secy.-Gen. Formed in 1964 to assist in the development of radio and television in the Asia-Pacific area, particularly its use for educational purposes. *Membership:* 28 full members; 10 additional full members; and 28 associate members in 46 countries of the Asia/Pacific region and other parts of the world.

Officers: President, Dr. Sumadi (Indonesia); Vice-Presidents, Abdulla Mohamad (Malaysia) and Tomokazu Sakamoto (Japan); Secretary General, Roku Ito (Malaysia: Box 1164, Angkaspuri, Jalan Pantai Bharu, Kuala Kumpur 22-10, Malaysia); Deputy Secretary General, Ichiro Matsui (Japan). *Publications: ABU Newsletter; ABU Technical Review* (both in English).

Association for the Diffusion of Japanese Films Abroad. 9-13 Ginza 5-chome, Chuo-ku, Tokyo, 104 Japan. Tel. (03) 572-5106. Cable address: UNIJAPANFILM TOKYO. Toyoji Kuroda, Mng. Dir. *Publications: Selected Japanese Feature Films* (ann.); *UniJapan Film Report.*

Japan Audio-Visual Education Association (JAVEA). 1-17-1, Toranomon, Minato-ku, Tokyo 105, Japan. Tel. 591-2186/7. Jiro Arimitsu, Pres. Established in 1928 as a film education research society whose members were mostly elementary school teachers. Amalgamated in 1943 with a similar organization that had been working in the same field since 1937. Although at one time under the minister of education and government-subsidized, JAVEA is now a public nonprofit organization. Among its principal international functions are those of serving as the Japan Audio-Visual Information Centre for International Service, involving the preparation of catalogs and other publications about the field; managing and promoting an annual International Cultural Film Festival; serving as a full member of the International Council for Educational Media (ICEM); and organizing and managing the Japan Educational Materials Exhibition (JEMEX). Domestically, JAVEA offers an annual National Convention on the Use of Educational Aids; conducts an annual audiovisual education prize competition to schools and institutes that achieve distinction in their uses of audiovisual materials; conducts an annual competition to select prize-winning, representative educational film and slide productions; plans and promotes the production of teaching films whose themes have been selected by the ministry of education; and publishes a number of periodicals, catalogs, and handbooks (in the Japanese language) related to the field.

Japan Library Association (JLA). 1-10, Taishido 1-chome, Setagaya-ku, Tokyo 154, Japan. Tel. 03-410-6411. Hitoshi Kurihara, Secy.-Gen. Encourages Japanese library development and improvement of librarians' social position; conducts surveys concerning the status of Japanese libraries. *Membership:* 7,000 (personal). *Publications: Toshokan Zasshi (Library Journal)* (mo.); *Gendai no Toshokan (Libraries Today)* (q.); *The Library Yearbook* (ann.); *Nippon Decimal Classification; Nippon Cataloging Rules*; and *Librarian's Handbook.* JLA also produced two 16mm films in color, entitled "Libraries and Books" and "A Library and Children."

Japanese Council of Educational Technology Centres. c/o Japanese National Commission for UNESCO, 2-2 Kasumigaseki-Sanchrome, Chiyoda-ku, Tokyo 100, Japan. Provides consulting assistance to Asian countries with respect to instructional/educational technology; invites professionals to study in Japanese institutions; promotes media-related research; and offers information exchanges. *Publications: Journal of Educational Technology* (q., in Japanese); and *Educational Technology Research* (2/yr., in English).

Jordan

Ministry of Education, Directorate of Curricula and Teaching Aids. Box 1979, Amman, Jordon. Produces educational materials for schools; conducts media-related research; produces educational radio and television programs; and offers in-service instruction in areas of instructional technology.

Kenya

Kenya Institute of Education, Educational Media Service. Box 30231, Nairobi, Kenya. A division of the Kenya Institute of Education; its media specialists work with curriculum personnel in developing curriculum materials. Maintains production facilities for television, films, and other media.

Kuwait

Arab States Educational Technology Center. Box 24017, Safat, Kuwait. Tel. 448130/31. A. Jabbar Wali, Act. Dir. Established by the Arab League Educational Cultural and Scientific Organization in 1976, this center serves to develop modern educational technology to aid Arabs in contributing to progress in their society. Conducts research and studies, documents training and production efforts of the center, and promotes the use of educational media and materials in the Arab states. *Publications: Instructional Technology* (Arabic/English); and *Information Newsletter* (mo., Arabic); and some reports and studies about educational technology in Arabic.

Educational Technology Department. Ministry of Education, Box 7, Safat, Kuwait. Salman M.D. Al-Humaidan, Dir. General.

Luxembourg

Office du Film Scolaire, Centre Audiovisuel. BP 2, Walferdange, Luxembourg. Maintains an audiovisual lending library; produces selected audiovisual materials for educational uses; and conducts teacher training activities in the educational technology field.

Malaysia

Ministry of Education, Malaysia. Pesiaran Duta, Kuala Lumpur, Malaysia 11-04. Maintains an Educational Media Service that plans and produces radio and television programs for schools, trains teachers in media utilization, and produces selected audiovisual materials.

Mauritius

Audio Visual Centre. 6 Thomy Pitot Street, Rose Hill, Mauritius. Produces and broadcasts radio and television programs for school use.

Mexico

Centro Nacional de Tecnologia Educativa (National Center for Educational Technology). Avenida Acueducto S/N Ampliacion Tepapan Xochimilco, Mexico 23 DF. Conducts educational research and produces selected educational media to back up educational programs of the country.

Dirección General de Educación Audiovisual. Calz Circunvalacion Esq. Tabiqueros, Col. Morelos, Mexico 2, DF. Active in televised education and educational technology generally. Produces instructional materials and programs mainly for secondary education.

Instituto Latinoamericano de la Comunicación Educativa (Latin American Institute for Educational Communication). Apdo. Postal 94-328, Mexico 10, DF. Seeks regional Mexican cooperation in research, experimentation, production, and distribution of audiovisual materials and other resources; conducts research; trains professionals and others in the field; and maintains an extensive library.

Netherlands

Foundation for Film and Science (SFW). Hengeveldstraat 29, Box 9550, 3506 GN, Utrecht, Netherlands. Tel. 30-716816. J. J. D. Konyn, Interim Dir. Production and distribution of audiovisual programs for higher education in the Netherlands; information and advice on programs; audiovisual historical documents; and technical equipment. Institute is nonprofit, government subsidized.

International Federation of Library Associations and Institutions (IFLA). Box 95312. The Hague, 2509 CH, Netherlands. Tel. (070) 140884. Margreet Wynstroom, Secy.-Gen. Established "to promote international understanding, cooperation, discussion, research and development in all fields of library activity, including bibliography, information services and the education of personnel, and to provide a body through which librarianship can be represented in matters of international interest." Annual conference in Nairobi, Kenya, August 1984. *Membership:* 160 member assoc.; 760 inst. members and affiliates; and 107 personal affiliates. *Publications: IFLA Journal* (q.); *International Cataloguing* (q.); *IFLA Annual*; and *IFLA Directory; Series "IFLA Publications."*

Nederlands Instituut voor Audio-visuele Media (NIAM). Sweelinckplein 33, Postbus 63426, 2502 JK Den Haag, Netherlands. H. J. L. Jongbloed, Dir. Produces and distributes audiovisual programs on behalf of primary and secondary education; provides education/ technological information.

Netherlands Scientific Film Association (NVWFT). Box 9550, 3506 GN Utrecht, Netherlands. Dr. A. Smit, Pres.; Aad van der Hoeven, Information Off. Holds two meetings yearly to view the latest audiovisual productions of its members. NVWFT is a member of the International Scientific Film Association (SFA). *Publication: Newsletter* (q., for members).

Radio Nederland Training Centre (RNTC). Box 222, 1200 JG, Hilversum, Netherlands. Tel. 035-16151/47779. J. R. Swart, Gen. Mgr.; Jan G. Kinket, Deputy Mgr. A nonprofit institute supported by the Dutch government and the Dutch World Broadcasting System— Radio Nederland. Offers training and financial support for nationals of developing countries involved in planning, writing, and producing informative and educational radio and television programs in their areas and to journalists of the written press in those countries.

Technical Film Centre of the Netherlands. 17 Arnhemsestraatweg, 6881 NB Velp, Netherlands. Promotes the use of audiovisual resources in industry and education.

New Zealand

New Zealand National Film Library. Private Bag, Cubewell House, Kent Terrace, Wellington, New Zealand. Tel. 849-890. Mrs. K. C. Dear, Mgr. Holds 47,000 films and manages an annual distribution of 352,482. *Membership:* 3,137 schools and 3,759 organizations. Also distributes audiotapes and phonograph records.

Nigeria

National Educational Technology Centre. Ministry of Education. PMB 2027, Kaduna, Nigeria. Designs, produces, and distributes a variety of new educational media; trains media specialists and broadcasting personnel; organizes media instruction for classroom teachers; and provides other related services.

Norway

Statens Filmsentral (SFS). Schwensengate 6, Box 2655, St. Hanshaugen, Oslo, Norway. The National Filmboard of Norway under the auspices of the Educational Dept. is responsible for the production, distribution, and proper use of films, filmstrips, and other optical and electronic educational media for use in schools and for other educational and informative purposes; it also operates a film laboratory, distributes films to communities without permanent cinemas, and participates in international film and media events.

Pakistan

Ministry of Education, Instructional Technology Section. Sector H-9, Islamabad, Pakistan. Provides training in new media production, distribution, and utilization techniques and procedures, with emphasis upon the public schools.

Peru

National Institute of Teleducation. Ministry of Public Education. Parque Universitaria, Lima, Peru. Promotes the planning, production, distribution, and utilization of new educational media throughout the country.

Proyecto Latino Americano de Teleducación del Instituto de Solidaridad Internacional (Latin American Teleducation Project of the International Solidarity Institute). Apdo. Postal 4951, Miraflores, Lima 18, Peru. Tel. 410440. Higo Osorio, contact person. Cooperation in integral formation of people through training, technical assistance, and publications in teleducation throughout Latin America.

Philippines

Regional Center for Educational Innovation and Technology (INNOTECH). College of Education, University of the Philippines, Quezon City, Philippines. A research and training center concerned with the identification of educational problems and the development of plans, materials, and personnel to solve them. Offers special assistance with new educational media resources development.

Poland

Instytut Pedagogiki. Ul. Gorozewska 8, Warsaw, Poland.

Polish Scientific Film Association. Al. Ujazdowskie 45, Warsaw, Poland.

Polskie Stowarzyszenie Filmu Naukowego (PSFN). 00-534 Warszawa, ul. Mokotowska 58, Poland. Tel. 45-51-13 or 29-08-32. Jan Jacoby, Pres. An organization of individuals and institutions producing and using scientific films in Poland; coordinates work connected with audiovisual techniques in this country. Member of International Science Film Association in Paris.

Portugal

Instituto de Tecnologia Educativa (Institute of Educational Technology). Rua Florbela Espanca-1799. Lisbon, Portugal. Part of the Portuguese Ministry of Education; provides new media technology assistance to schools, including loans of resources; offers training courses in audiovisual education.

Senegal

Demonstration Center for Educational Technology. The UNESCO Regional Office for Education in Africa, BP 3311, Dakar, Senegal. Provides information about new materials, methods, and techniques in education; collects and shares audiovisual media; promotes and helps to support local efforts to produce educational materials; performs other catalytic services in the field of educational technology.

Singapore

Asian Mass Communication Research and Information Centre (AMIC). 39 Newton Rd., Singapore 1130, Republic of Singapore. A nonprofit regional documentation center disseminating information about mass communication under the aegis of UNESCO. Seeks to raise the quality of teaching and training through conferences, refresher courses, and similar means. Jointly sponsored by the government of Singapore and the Friedrich-Ebert-Stiftung, an independent foundation of the Federal Republic of Germany. *Membership:* 750 indiv.; 64 inst. *Publications: Media Asia* (q.); *Asian Mass Communication Bulletin.*

Institute of Education (IE). 469, Bukit Timah Rd., Singapore 1025. Tel. 2560451. Dr. Ho Wah Kam, Deputy Dir./Academic; Chan Weng Cheong, Head/School of Educational Services; and Mrs. Chong Lay Leng, Head/Dept. of Instructional Technology.

South Africa

University of Cape Town, Teaching Methods Unit. Rondebosch 7700, Cape Town, South Africa. Provides expert staff assistance in designing, improving, and evaluating the results of instruction in university courses; assists in the design and production of new educational media resources for such purposes.

South Korea

Korean Educational Development Institute (KEDI). 20-21 Woomyondong, Kang Nam, Seoul, South Korea. Monitors a "High School of the Air" project and other projects, most involving high-level use of principles and products of educational technology, to provide opportunities for dropouts and adults to obtain a high school education. KEDI provides instructional planning, produces instructional media, and evaluates results of their use.

Spain

Instituto de Ciencias de Educación. Universidad Complutense, Campus de Somosaguas, Madrid 23, Spain. Maintains four departments, one of which specializes in Instructional Technology.

Radio ECCA. Avda, Mesa y López, 38, Las Palmas de Gran Canaria, España, Apartado 994. Tel. 27-54-54. Luis Espina Cepeda, Dir. Education of adults for a three-part system including radio, print materials, and personal presentations.

Sweden

Dag Hammarskjöld Foundation. Övre Slottsgatan 2, S-752 20 Uppsala, Sweden. Sven Hamrell, Exec. Dir. Tel. (018) 12 88 72. Conducts, among other things, international seminars and workshops related to education with production and educational communications in Third World countries. *Publications: Filmmaking in Developing Countries* (by Andreas Fuglesang, SEK 40); *Doing Things Together; Report on an Experience in Communicating Appropriate Technology* (by Andreas Fuglesang, SEK 50); *About Understanding: Ideas and Observations on Cross-cultural Communication* (U.S.,

$12.00); and *Towards a New World Information and Communication Order* (Development Dialogue 1981:2).

Swedish Educational Broadcasting Company. Utbildningsradio, Fack, S-11580, Stockholm, Sweden. Produces educational television and radio broadcasts for the country's entire educational system — preschool through adult and university levels.

Utbildninsforlaget. Fack S 104 22, Stockholm, Sweden.

Switzerland

Communauté d'Action pour le Développement de l'Information Audio-Visuelle. 10, av. d'Epenex, 1024 Ecublens, Switzerland. Also maintains the Film et Video Collectif at the same address.

EURODIDAC. Jagerstrasse 5, CH-4058, Basle, Switzerland. Tel. 061/26 50 52 or 26 50 53. Alois Kappeler, Dir. A world association of manufacturers and distributors of educational equipment whose members exchange information, mediate between members and international organizations, and promote worldwide exhibitions (Didacta) of educational equipment. *Membership:* 450. *Publication: Forum* (mo., with membership).

European Broadcasting Union (EBU-UER). 17A Ancienne Route, Box 193, CH-1211 Geneva 20, Switzerland. Tel. 987766. Telex 289193. Dr. Regis de Kalbermatten, Secy.-Gen. EBU Technical Centre, 32 ave. Albert Lancaster, B-1180 Brussels, Belgium. Tel. 375 59 90; Telex 21230. The EBU, founded in 1950, is a system of international broadcasting cooperation that includes the Eurovision news and program exchanges. It supports interests of members and assists generally the development of radio and television worldwide. The Administrative Council, elected by the members, channels activities through the legal, technical, and radio and television program committees. *Membership:* 110 in 78 countries. *Publications: EBU Review* (in English and French; Geneva edition, bi-mo., program, administrative, and legal aspects; Brussels edition, bi-mo., technical part); information sheets; monographs; and reports of seminars and workshops for producers and directors of educational television and of programs for children and young people.

International Publishers Association. 3 av. Miremont, 1206 Geneva, Switzerland. Tel. 46-30-18. Established to uphold and defend complete freedom of publishers to distribute works of the mind; to secure mutual international cooperation; to overcome illiteracy, the lack of books, other means of learning and teaching; and to promote protection of authors' and publishers' rights through national and international copyright legislation.

International Telecommunication Union (ITU). Place des Nations, 1211 Geneva 20, Switzerland. Tel. (022) 99-51-11. Mohamed E. Mili, Secy.-Gen. A union of 157 countries with a General Secretariat, the International Frequency Registration Board (IFRB), the International Radio Consultative Committee (CCIR), and the International Telegraph and Telephone Consultative Committee (CCITT). Seeks to maintain and extend international cooperation for improved and rational use of telecommunications; to promote the development of technical telecommunications facilities throughout the world; and to harmonize the actions of all nations in achieving these ends.

World Intellectual Property Organization (WIPO). Chemin des Colombettes 34, 1211 Geneva 20, Switzerland. Tel. 999-111. A specialized agency of the United Nations system, responsible for promotion of protection of intellectual property throughout the world. Protected under this agency's work are: industrial property (inventions, trademarks, and designs) and copyright in literary, musical, photographic, cinematographic, and artistic works. Administers a number of general and specialized treaties in this field. *Membership:* 121.

Taiwan

Audiovisual Education Center. National Taiwan University. E. Hoping Rd., Taipei, Taiwan.

Instructional Technology Department, National Chengchi University. Taipei, Taiwan.

National Audiovisual Education Association of China (NAEAC). Taipei, Taiwan.

Tanzania

Audio-Visual Institute (AVI). Box 9510, Dar es Salaam, Tanzania. Tel. 44601/4. J. P. Mahiga, Dir. The institute produces 16mm films for educational and developmental purposes; it maintains a national film library to distribute films to all parts of the country; it operates an electronic workshop to repair and service audiovisual equipment; and it maintains a film archive for the preservation of films and other audiovisual materials. Future plans include production of slides, filmstrips, and other visual aids and establishment of a research unit.

Thailand

Asian Programme of Educational Innovation for Development (APEID). UNESCO Regional Office for Education in Asia and the Pacific. Box 1425, General Post Office, Bangkok, Thailand. Tel. 391-0879; 391-0880. Raja Roy Singh, Asst. Dir.-Gen. APEID aims are to encourage member states to promote the involvement and participation of people on a broad basis in making relevant changes in education; to contribute to efforts to identify innovations and transformations as needed by member states; and to promote understanding and appreciation of differing educational practices and approaches. There are 22 member countries with 124 associated centers. *Publications: Directory of Educational Media Resources* (1983, free); *Inventory: Low-Cost Educational Materials; How to Make, How to Use, How to Adapt Vol. II* (1982, $3.00); *Guidelines for Repackaging Multi-Media Resources* (1982, $1.00); and *Minicourse Approach: What It Is and How It Works* (1982, $2.00).

Ministry of Education, Centre for Educational Technology. Bangkok, Thailand. Responsible for school television and radio production and broadcasting, and the design, production, and distribution of related materials.

UNESCO Regional Office for Education in Asia and the Pacific. P.O. Box 1425, Bangkok G.P.O., Bangkok, Thailand. *Publications: Bulletin of the Unesco Regional Office for Education in Asia and the Pacific* (ann.); *Education in Asia and the Pacific — Reviews, Reports, and Notes* (ann.).

Turkey

Department of Educational Aids, Ministry of National Education. Milli Egitim Bakanligi, Egitim Araclari Dairesi Baskanligi. Ankara, Turkey. Maummer Sert, Dept. Head. The Center of Education through Films, Radio, and Television (FRTEM) is attached to the Department of Educational Aids of the Ministry of Education. Its film producing unit plans, develops, and produces software for schools of all levels; imports raw materials and hardware not produced in Turkey; distributes materials to provincial agencies; offers training courses for teachers, scriptwriters, producers, and other personnel; conducts research; evaluates the production and use of audiovisual materials; prepares exhibitions and publications pertaining to the media field. The Center also produces radio and television programs, films, filmstrips, wall charts, maps, photographs, language and music cassette tapes, large transparencies, flash cards, figurines, media guides, and other materials for educational purposes.

USSR

Association of Film Makers of the USSR. 13, Vassilievskaya ul. Moscow, D-56, USSR.

Venezuela

Comisión Coordinator de Sistema Nacional de Bibliotecas y Información Humanística: Información Cientifica y Tecnologica, de Archivos, e Informatica (SINASBI). Av. Vincente Lecuna, Parque Central, Edif. San Martin, Nivel Mezzanina (Norte), Local No. 5, Caracas 101, Venezuela. Tel. 572-3623.

West Indies

JAMAL Foundation. 47b S. Camp Rd., P.O. Box 60, Kingston 4, Jamaica, West Indies. Eric M. Brown, Dir. Tel. 92-84832-4. Seeks to operate a basic adult education program in Jamaica to eradicate illiteracy, improve literacy skills of the adult population, and develop human resources to effect meaningful social participation in affairs of the country. Produces weekly motivational radio and television programs (ten instructional radio broadcasts and nine instructional television programs weekly).

Yugoslavia

Educational and Cultural Film Center. Maršala Tita 2, Belgrade, Yugoslavia.

Filmoteka 16. Savska 9, 41000 Zagreb, Yugoslavia. Tel. (041) 445-800. Vera Papić, Head/Commercial Dept. Produces and distributes media for educational purposes.

Institute for Improvement of Education. Marsala Tita 2, 11000 Beograd, Yugoslavia. Tel. (011) 327-207. Gardana Zindović-Vukašinovic, Counsel for Innovations and Educational Technology.

Yugoslavia Film. 11000 Beograd, Knez Mihailova 19, Yugoslavia. Milómif Marinović, contact person. An association of film producers, distributors, and cinemas. Yugoslavia Film exports Yugoslavian films and imports foreign films for the associated companies; organizes Yugoslavian entries for the international film festivals; exchanges information; and establishes terms of cooperation with Yugoslavian television.

Part Three

Graduate Programs

Doctoral Programs in
Instructional Technology

Edwin (Ned) Logan
Professor Emeritus of Instructional Technology
Towson State University
Baltimore, Maryland

This directory presents data for 60 doctoral programs (Ph.D. and Ed.D.) in instructional/educational communications/technology currently being offered in the United States. New programs from three universities have been included in this directory—Kent State University, Kent, Ohio, The Johns Hopkins University, Baltimore, Maryland, and the University of North Carolina at Greensboro. The University of Southern Mississippi has been deleted from this directory edition.

Listings in this section were updated by institutional chairpersons themselves in response to clipped copy and questionnaires mailed to them in the fall, 1984.

Entries provide the following data: (1) name and address of the institution; (2) chairperson or other individual in charge of the doctoral program; (3) type(s) of degree(s) offered, with specializations, including information regarding positions for which candidates are prepared; (4) special features of the degree program; (5) admission requirements, including minimal grade point average; (6) number of full-time and part-time faculty engaged in the program; and (7) details of available financial assistance, doctoral program trends, and doctorates awarded 1983-84.

Directors of programs for advanced professional preparation of media specialists will find the information provided by this directory useful as a means of comparing their own offerings and requirements with those of other institutions. Individuals seeking an institution in which to undertake advanced graduate work should be helped by this list to locate those that best fit their interests and requirements.

Because users are likely to be interested in locating information about doctoral programs in their own or nearby states, the institutions in this section are arranged alphabetically by state and then alphabetically by the names of the institutions.

It should be noted that while considerable effort has been expended to ensure completeness of the listings, there may be institutions within the United States or its territories that have been omitted. Readers who know of such omissions are invited to provide information leads to the editors who will follow up on them for the next edition of *EMTY*.

ARIZONA

Arizona State University. Tempe, AZ 85287. Karen Beyard-Tyler, Chair, Dept. of Educational Technology and Library Science, College of Education. *Specializations:* Arizona State University offers programs of study leading to both the Ph.D. and the Ed.D. degrees in Educational Technology. The primary content focus of the Ph.D. and Ed.D. programs is on instructional design and development. Students may complement this focus with concentrated work in such areas as instructional media, computer-based education, and training and development. Preparation is for work as university faculty; instructional designers and trainers in business and industry; instructional designers in higher education. *Features:* Instructional development internships in public and higher education, or in business and industry. Research emphasized. *Admission Requirements:* Submit the following (two months prior to enrollment): all university application forms; two transcripts from each institution in which previous academic work has been completed; three letters of reference; a score report on either the Miller Analogies Test or the GRE; statement of professional goals. Admission standards are described in information packets for applicants. *Faculty:* 9 full-time. *Students:* 5 full-time; 15 part-time. *Assistance:* Graduate Assistantships – $2,700-$5,400 per academic year; summer teaching opportunities; fellowships, scholarships; loans administered through the university Financial Aid Office. *Doctoral Program Trends:* About half of program graduates obtain faculty positions in universities; number of placements in higher technology firms is increasing. *Doctorates Awarded 1983-84:* 5.

CALIFORNIA

United States International University. San Diego, CA 92131. Dale G. Hamreus, Dean, School of Education. *Specializations:* Ed.D. program in instructional technology prepares individuals to serve as assistant superintendents of schools for instructional planning; deans of instruction; school district coordinators of learning resources; specialists in designing learning strategies; and university directors of learning resources as well as change agents in industry and the military having learning or teaching as a primary concern. *Features:* The program involves training in human behavior and specialization in instructional technology based on negotiated performance outcomes and field-centered learning experiences. An emphasis on the use of computers in education and training has recently been made available in both the master's and doctoral programs. *Admission Requirements:* Admission to graduate program by the School of Education; evidence of interest in and commitment to studying and utilizing technology to improve instruction. *Faculty:* 4 full-time; 5 part-time. *Students:* 75 full-time and part-time. *Assistance:* A limited number of graduate assistantships offered in conjunction with research and development work being undertaken at the university. *Doctoral Program Trends:* Increasing enrollments of students interested in position placements in instructional design/development and computer education. *Doctorates Awarded 1983-84:* 5.

University of California at Los Angeles. Los Angeles, CA 90024. Aimee Dorr, Prof. of Education, Dir. of Educational Technology, Learning and Instruction Specialization, Dept. of Education. *Specializations:* Offers Ph.D. and Ed.D. programs. Ph.D. program prepares graduates for research; teaching educational technology; and consultancies in the development of instructional materials. Ed.D. program prepares graduates for leadership roles in the development of instructional materials and educational technologies. *Features:* The program addresses the design and utilization principles and processes underlying all effective uses of instructional technologies and their products. Television- and microcomputer-based systems are featured. On- and off-campus practical experiences in the design of actual products are encouraged. *Admission Requirements:* Superior academic record; combined GRE score of 1,200 or better; and master's degree in a relevant area. For the Ed.D. program, two or more years of relevant field experience is desirable. *Faculty:* 8 faculty participate in Learning and Instruction, of whom 2 teach full-time in instructional technology and the remaining 6 (all with full-time academic appointments) teach part-time in instructional technology and the remaining time in other areas in the department. *Students:* 6 full-time; 1 part-time. *Assistance:* Includes fellowships, tuition remission, and some paid research and teaching assistantships. *Doctoral Program Trends:* Doctoral applications from high-quality students have increased in recent years, and more students are interested in the instructional uses of computers in education. *Doctorates Awarded 1983-84:* 1.

University of Southern California. Los Angeles, CA 90007. Robert L. Baker, Chair, Dept. of Educational Psychology and Technology, School of Education. *Specializations:* M.A., Ph.D., Ed.D. to prepare individuals to teach instructional technology; manage educational media/training programs in business or industry, research and development organizations, and higher education institutions; perform research in instructional technology; and design instructional media. *Features:* Special emphasis upon systematic analysis and design. *Admission Requirements:* A bachelor's degree; satisfactory performance (combined score of 1,100) on the GRE aptitude test. *Faculty:* 11 full-time; 7 part-time. *Students:* 35 full-time; 100 part-time. *Assistance:* 2 graduate assistantships available as per special grant funds; part-time work available (instructional technology-related) in the Los Angeles area and on the university campus. *Doctoral Program Trends:* Increasing enrollments of students seeking position placements in business/industry, instructional design/development, media production, and computer education. *Doctorates Awarded 1983-84:* 5.

COLORADO

University of Colorado. Boulder, CO 80309. Richard E. Turner, Dean of Education. *Specializations:* Ph.D. and master's degree designed for individuals interested in the concept of educational technology as a way of solving today's instructional problems. The purposes of the program are to prepare individuals to design, develop, and validate instructional materials and systems using the concepts of instructional design and development; to assist individuals in conducting research in instructional problems and the extension of educational theory; to prepare individuals to use the computer as an instructional device by designing, developing, and producing CAI, CMI, and interactive video instructional programs; and to provide individuals with internship experiences that deal with applications of instructional design and development in education, industry, business, health sciences and other agencies that provide education and training. *Admission Requirements:* Submission of application for admittance to graduate school by deadline (March 1, summer and fall; September 1, spring); favorable action on the application by the graduate school and the School of Education (write for brochure). *Faculty:* 2 full-time; 3 part-time. *Students:* 40 full-time; 40 part-time. *Assistance:* Scholarships, fellowships, and graduate assistantships (all competitive), usually after completion of the first year of course work. *Doctoral Program Trends:* Increasing enrollments of students interested in position placements in business/industry, instructional design/development, and computer education. *Doctorates Awarded 1983-84:* 2.

CONNECTICUT

University of Connecticut. Storrs, CT 06268. Phillip J. Sleeman, Dir., University Center for Instructional Media and Technology, and Prof. of Education. *Specializations:* Ph.D., sixth year, and master's degree programs involving advanced instructional media and technology to prepare individuals for instructional technology positions of major responsibility in universities, colleges, community colleges, large school systems, state departments of education, government and industry, and other educational and media organizations of national scope. *Features:* The program seeks an optimum mix of competencies involved in solving instructional media and technology problems with competence in several fields of professional education (psychological foundations, social foundations, research and evaluation, business administration, curriculum and supervision, instructional media and technology, and data processing). *Admission Requirements:* Admission to graduate school; undergraduate GPA above 3.0; filing of transcripts of all undergraduate and graduate work; satisfactory scores on the GRE; the Miller Analogies Test; evidence of scholarly attainments, interests, and potential for growth; the strength and validity of career motive; previous significant experience in the instructional media field; and at least five years of highly successful teaching experience (of which one or more of administrative or supervisory experience would be desirable). *Faculty:* 2 full-time; 6 part-time. *Students:* Data not available. *Assistance:* a number of graduate assistantships, predoctoral fellowships, research fellowships, and federal and minority fellowships available competitively. *Doctoral Program Trends:* Information not available. *Doctorates Awarded 1983-84:* 6.

DISTRICT OF COLUMBIA

Catholic University. Washington, DC 20064. Carol Walker, Asst. Prof. of Education Curriculum Instruction and Technology, School of Education. *Specializations:* Doctorates available for individuals seeking to specialize in managerial, academic, and research-oriented phases of educational technology. *Features:* Strong emphasis on individually designed, competency-based studies using microcomputer technology. Strong capability, in formative and summative evaluation. Opportunity for students to integrate competency in educational technology with curriculum, educational psychology, and other professional and/or academic disciplines such as library science and health sciences. *Admission Requirements:* Apply for further information. *Faculty:* Data not available. *Students:* Data not available. *Doctoral Program Trends:* Increasing enrollments of students interested in position placements in business/industry, government, instructional design/development, and computer education. *Doctorates Awarded 1983-84:* 4.

FLORIDA

Florida State University. Tallahassee, FL 32306. Program of Instructional Systems, Dept. of Educational Research, Development and Foundations, College of Education. *Specializations:* Ph.D. program in Instructional Design and Development. Graduates have taken positions in universities, industry, government, military, and research and development centers. Master's degrees are offered in instructional design, which emphasizes the design and development of instructional materials, and in media education, which stresses design of mediated instruction and media management. Both master's programs can serve as entry points to the doctoral program. *Features:* Core courses include systems and materials development, analysis of media, project management, psychological foundations, and current trends in instructional design. Local internships are also required. *Admission Requirements:* Total score on the verbal and quantitative sections of the GRE of 1,000 or a GPA of 3.0 for the last two years of undergraduate study. International students must provide TOEFL scores and indication of financial support. *Faculty:* 14. *Students:* 96. *Assistance:* University and college fellowships; grant and contract-funded assistantships. *Doctoral Program Trends:* Increased enrollments of students interested in position placements in program administration, instructional design/ development, and computer education. *Doctorates Awarded 1983-84:* 4.

University of Florida. Gainesville, FL 32611. Lee Mullally, Chair. Educational Media and Instructional Design Program, College of Education. *Specializations:* Ph.D. and Ed.D. programs that stress theory, research, training, teaching, evaluation, and instructional development. *Admission Requirements:* A composite score of at least 1,100 on the GRE; an undergraduate GPA of 3.0 minimum and a graduate GPA of 3.5 minimum; three letters of recommendation. *Faculty:* 2 full-time; 1 part-time. *Students:* 5 full-time; 10 part-time. *Assistance:* 2 to 3 graduate assistantships. *Doctoral Program Trends:* Increasing enrollments of students interested in position placements in business/industry, instructional design/development, and computer education. *Doctorates Awarded 1983-84:* 0.

GEORGIA

Georgia State University. University Plaza, Atlanta, GA 30303. Rosalind Miller, Assoc. Prof. of Library Media. *Specializations:* Ph.D. in instructional technology, instructional development, media management in schools, special libraries, or business. *Admission Requirements:* Three letters of recommendation; handwritten autobiographical sketch; admission tests; and acceptance by department. *Faculty:* 3 full-time. *Students:* Data not available. *Assistance:* Graduate research assistantships. *Doctoral Program Trends:* Enrollment has decreased slightly, budget has remained about the same, facilities including space, hardware, and software have remained about the same while faculty and staff have decreased slightly. *Doctorates Awarded 1983-84:* 1.

University of Georgia. Athens, GA 30602. Kent L. Gustafson, Chair, Dept. of Educational Media and Librarianship, College of Education. *Specializations:* Ed.S. and Ed.D. for leadership positions as specialists in instructional design and development. The program offers advanced study for individuals with previous preparation in instructional media and librarianship, as well as preparation for personnel in other professional fields requiring a speciality in instructional systems/instructional technology. Representative career fields for graduates include designing/developing/evaluating new courses, tutorial programs, instructional materials in a number of different settings: military/industrial training, medical/dental/nursing professional schools, allied health agencies, teacher education/staff development centers, state/local school systems, higher education teaching/research, and publishers/producers of instructional products (textbooks, workbooks, films, etc.). *Features:* Minor areas of study available in a variety of other departments. Personalized programs are planned around a common core of courses; practica, internships, and/or clinical experiences. Research activities include special assignments, applied projects, and task forces, as well as thesis and dissertation studies. *Admission Requirements:* Applications to graduate school; satisfactory GRE aptitude score; other criteria as outlined in *Graduate School Bulletin*. *Faculty:* Data not available. *Students:* Data not available. *Assistance:* Graduate assistantships available. *Doctoral Program Trends:* Increasing enrollments of students interested in position placements in business/industry, instructional design/development, and computer education. *Doctorates Awarded 1983-84:* 3.

ILLINOIS

Northern Illinois University. DeKalb, IL 60115. James Lockard, Assoc. Prof., Chair, Instructional Technology Programs, 219 Gabel Hall, College of Education. *Specializations:* Ed.D. in instructional technology emphasizing instructional development, media administration, production, and preparation for teaching in higher education. *Features:* Considerable flexibility in course selection, including advanced seminars, internships, individual study, and research. Program is highly individualized. A total of 60 courses offered by several departments, including Library Science, Radio/Television/Film, Art, Journalism, Educational Psychology, and Research Planning. *Admission Requirements:* 2.75 undergraduate GPA; 3.50 M.S. GPA; combined score of 1,000 on GRE; three references. *Faculty:* 7 (5 full-time, with courses in other departments taught by several members of the graduate faculty). *Students:* 65 part-time. *Assistance:* 9 assistantships available involving laboratory supervision, instruction, and instructional development activities on and off the campus. Some additional fellowships and grants possible. *Doctoral Program Trends:* Increasing enrollments of students interested in position placements in business/industry, health, instructional design/development, and computer education. *Doctorates Awarded 1983-84:* 4.

Southern Illinois University. Carbondale, IL 62901. Billy G. Dixon, Prof., Chair, Div. of Curriculum, Instruction and Media, School of Education. *Specializations:* Ph.D. Specialist, and M.S. in Education with special areas of concentration in: educational technology, instructional development, computer-based education, and school library media. *Features:* All specializations are oriented to multiple education settings. *Admission Requirements:* M.S. — 2.40 GPA or better. Ph.D. — 3.25 GPA or better; MAT or GRE score; letters of recommendation; and writing sample. *Students:* 5 full-time; 5 part-time. *Assistance:* 6 graduate assistantships available, university fellowship program. Assistance has increased 30 percent during 1984 academic year. *Doctoral Program Trends:* Graduate student enrollment has increased more than 25 percent in past year. *Doctorates Awarded 1983-84:* 6.

Southern Illinois University. Edwardsville, IL 62026. Gary L. Hull, Prof., Chair, Dept. of Education Administration and Instructional Technology, School of Education. *Specialization:* Ed.D. (all-school degree) in instructional processes, emphasizing theory and research, teaching, evaluation, and instructional systems design and development. *Admission Requirements:* Miller Analogies Test; undergraduate GPA of B + . *Faculty:* 6 full-time; 1 part-time. *Students:* 4 full-time; 10 part-time. *Assistance:* 4 graduate assistantships; 2 fellowships. *Doctoral Program Trends:* Increasing enrollments of students interested in position placements in business/industry, health, government, instructional design/development, and computer education. *Doctorates Awarded 1983-84:* 2.

INDIANA

Indiana University. Bloomington, IN 47405. Dennis Pett, Prof., Chair, Dept. of Instructional Systems Technology, School of Education. *Program Features:* Four major emphasis areas: instructional design and development, message design and production, institutional and organizational change, and systems design and management of learning resources programs. Students draw on all emphasis areas when planning their academic programs. Virtually all students are full-time residents. Many opportunities for students to combine practice with study by working in the AV Center and other appropriate agencies on and off campus. *Admission Requirements:* Satisfactory GPA. Doctoral students must take verbal, quantitative, and analytical sections of the GRE. *Faculty:* 17 full-time, 3 part-time. *Students:* 74. *Assistance:* Graduate assistantships, associate instructorships, fellowships, scholarships, and fee remissions. *Doctoral Program Trends:* Increasing enrollments of students interested in position placements in business/industry, health, instructional design/development, and computer education. *Doctorates Awarded 1983-84:* 7.

Purdue University. West Lafayette, IN 47907. James D. Russell, Prof. of Education, Dept. of Education, Matthews 118. *Specializations:* Ph.D. programs to prepare individuals to direct instructional development in school districts, community colleges, industry, and the armed forces. *Admission Requirements:* GPA of 3.0 (B) or better; three recommendations; scores of at least 1,000 on the GRE; statement by the applicant concerning his proposed goals and time schedule; and acceptance by the Department of Education. *Faculty:* 6 full-time. *Students:* Data not available. *Assistance:* Graduate teaching assistantships and graduate laboratory assistantships. *Doctoral Program Trends:* Increasing enrollments of students interested in position placements in business/industry, health, instructional design/development, and computer education. *Doctorates Awarded 1983-84:* 15.

IOWA

Iowa State University. Ames, IA 50010. Michael Simonson, Prof. of Secondary Education, College of Education. *Specializations:* Master's or Ph.D. in education with an emphasis on media, computers, curriculum, and instruction, for public school, college, and university supervision of media use, operation of an instructional materials center, and instructional development; higher education research and teaching, and teacher education programs; and positions in business, industry, or public and private agencies concerned with communications and teaching processes. *Features:* Practicum experiences related to professional objectives; supervised study and research projects tied to long-term studies within the program; experience in teaching basic media courses in the teacher education program, development and implementation of new techniques, teaching strategies, and operational procedures in Instructional Resources Centers and tour computer labs. *Admission Requirements:* Admission to graduate school; master's degree in a field appropriate to the specialization; top half of undergraduate class; successful professional and/or related experience relevant to the program, such as work or instructional activities. *Faculty:* 5. *Students:* 10 full-time; 10 part-time. *Assistance:* Graduate assistantships. *Doctoral Program Trends:* Increasing enrollments of students interested in position placements in business/industry and computer education. *Doctorates Awarded 1983-84:* 1.

University of Iowa. Iowa City, IA 52242. Lowell A. Schoer, Instructional Design and Technology, College of Education. *Specializations:* Instructional Development, Computer Applications, Health Sciences Education, Media Center Administration, Training and Human Resource Development. *Features:* Flexibility in planning to fit individual needs, backgrounds, and career goals. The program is interdisciplinary, involving courses within divisions of the College of Education, as well as in the schools of Journalism, Library Science, Radio and Television, Linguistics, Art, and Psychology. *Admission Requirements:* A composite score of at least 1,000 in the GRE and a 3.0 (B) GPA on all previous graduate work for regular admission (conditional admission may be granted). Teaching or relevant experience may be helpful. *Faculty:* 6 full-time; 7 part-time. *Students:* Data not available. *Assistance:* 15 assistantships ($6,500 to $1,900); special assistantships (in the College of Education) for which students in any College of Education program may compete. Application deadline for the special assistantships is February 1. *Doctoral Program Trends:* Increasing enrollments of students interested in position placements in business/industry, instructional design/development, and computer education. *Doctorates Awarded 1983-84:* 5.

KANSAS

Kansas State University. Manhattan, KS 66506. John A. Hortin, Prof., Dept. of Curriculum and Instruction, College of Education. *Specializations:* Ph.D. and Ed.D. program. NOTE: This program is offered on a semester basis; requires 90 credit hours, including 60 in media and technology; one year of residency; and a dissertation. *Faculty:* 4 full-time; 4 part-time. *Students:* Data not available. *Doctoral Program Trends:* Increasing enrollments of students interested in position placements in business/industry, health, college teaching, instructional design/development, and computer education. *Doctorates Awarded 1983-84:* 5.

University of Kansas. Lawrence, KS 66045. Walter S. Smith, Assoc. Prof. and Chair, Curriculum and Instruction, Dir., Instructional Technology Center. *Specializations:* Ph.D., Ed.D., Ed.S., and M.S. to prepare instructional technologists to serve in leadership roles in a variety of educational settings. Emphasis is on the use of research-based data to guide decisionmaking in the various roles required of instructional technologists. Special attention is given to the principles and procedures of instructional development. *Features:* The Instructional Technology Center provides a laboratory setting to assist in research projects and in the acquisition of production, instructional development, and media management skills. The department's microcomputer laboratory provides an up-to-date facility in which to explore facets of that field. Students are encouraged to work with faculty on appropriate projects. In addition to a common core, flexibility is built into the program so students may pursue their own areas of interest. *Admission Requirements:* Regular admission — 3.5 GPA and 900 GRE; Provisional — 3.25 GPA and 900 GRE or 3.5 GPA and less than 900 GRE. *Faculty:* 2. *Students:* 5 full-time; 12 part-time. *Assistance:* 2 graduate teaching assistantships (apply by March 1). *Doctoral Program Trends:* Increasing enrollments of students interested in position placements in college teaching, program administration, and computer education. *Doctorates Awarded 1983-84:* 0.

KENTUCKY

University of Kentucky. Lexington, KY 40506. Frank Bickel, Prof., Chair, Dept. of Curriculum and Instruction, College of Education. *Specialization:* Ed.D. program emphasizing instructional design/instructional technology, research, and teaching. *Admission Requirements:* A composite score of at least 1,000 on the GRE; minimum undergraduate GPA of 2.5; minimum graduate GPA of 3.4; letters of recommendation. *Faculty:* 2 full-time. *Students:* 8 M.A. candidates; 5 Ph.D. candidates. *Assistance:* Assistantships and fellowships available. *Doctoral Program Trends:* Increasing enrollments of students interested in position placements in business/industry, college teaching, instructional design/development, and computer education. *Doctorates Awarded 1983-84:* 2.

LOUISIANA

Louisiana State University. Baton Rouge, LA 70803. Wm. F. Grady, Coord., Educational Technology, and Prof. of Education. *Specializations:* Ph.D. or Ed.D. and M.Ed. or M.A. in Education Technology to prepare professional personnel for positions in teacher education, educational media administration, instructional materials production, instructional development, and research and evaluation. Program offered by College of Education. *Features:* Courses in the specialty area (instructional television, educational computing, photography, instructional development, and educational facility planning); humanistic and behavioral studies; theory and direct experiences in professional practice; and research, both general education research and educational media research. *Admission Requirements:* Satisfactory GPA; GRE score (general aptitude and advanced education); three letters of recommendation; undergraduate and graduate transcripts; and completed application forms. *Faculty:* 8 full-time; 5 part-time. *Students:* 10 full-time; 40 part-time. *Assistance:* Graduate assistantships and university fellowships. *Doctoral Program Trends:* Increasing enrollments of students interested in position placements in business/industry, health, government, instructional design/development, media production, and computer education. *Doctorates Awarded 1983-84:* 3.

MARYLAND

The Johns Hopkins University. Baltimore, MD 21218. Marion Panyan, Assoc. Prof., Div. of Education, School of Education. *Specializations:* Ph.D. or Ed.D. — a dual major degree requiring 99 semester hours beyond the baccalaureate; 27 hours in computers and related educational technology required. (A certificate of advanced study program is also offered; this certificate is similar to a specialist degree.) *Features:* nine computer courses, interactive video, adaptive devices, educational software development, and selection and evaluation are also emphasized. *Admission Requirements:* Data not available. *Faculty:* 2 full-time; 1 part-time. *Students:* 4 full-time. *Assistance:* Information not currently available. *Doctoral Program Trends.* New program. *Doctorates Awarded 1983-84:* 0.

University of Maryland. College Park, MD 20742. Claude E. Walston, Prof. and Dean, Educational Communications Program, College of Education. *Features:* Program is broadly conceived and interdisciplinary in nature, using the resources of the entire campus. The student and the advisor design a program of study and research to fit the student's background interests and professional objectives. The Ph.D. and Ed.D. programs prepare individuals for administering and designing programs in education and training for schools, school systems, colleges and universities, business, industry, and government. *Admission Requirements:* Bachelor's degree with a 3.0 GPA or better. (The majority of students enter with a master's degree in educational technology, library science, or other relevant discipline.) GRE general tests, 3 letters of recommendation, and a statement of purpose are also required. *Faculty:* 13 full-time. *Students:* 46 full-time. *Assistance:* Some assistantships starting at $4,500 for ten months and 20 units of tuition per year. *Doctoral Program Trends:* Data not available. *Doctorates Awarded 1983-84:* 1.

MASSACHUSETTS

University of Massachusetts. Amherst, MA 01003. Chair pending replacement, Media Area of Concentration, School of Education. *Specializations:* Ed.D. and M.Ed. programs for media management/administration, materials production, utilization/application, college teaching, evaluation, and instructional development, plus state certification as media specialist. *Admission Requirements:* GRE. *Faculty:* 4 full-time; 1 part-time. *Students:* 15 full-time, 5 part-time M.A. candidates; 4 full-time, 8 part-time Ph.D. candidates. *Assistance:* 2 teaching assistantships; some fellowships, scholarships, and tuition waivers. *Doctoral Program Trends:* Communication and information transfer along with information storage and retrieval are being stressed. The student must also select three areas from the following: computer science, linguistics, media, psychology, and philosophy. *Doctorates Awarded 1983-84:* 2.

Boston University. Boston, MA 02215. Gaylen B. Kelley, Chair, Program in Educational Media and Technology, School of Education, 605 Commonwealth Ave. *Specializations:* Ed.D. for developing and teaching academic programs in instructional technology in community colleges, colleges, and universities; or specialization in such application areas as Business and Industrial Training, Biomedical Communication, or International Development Projects. Program specializations in instructional development, media production and design, and instructional facilities design for media and technology. Students participate in mandatory research sequence and may elect courses in other university schools and colleges. *Features:* Doctoral students have a great deal of flexibility in program planning and are encouraged to plan programs that build on prior education and experience that lead to specific career goals; strong faculty participation in this process. *Admission Requirements:* Three letters of recommendation; Miller Analogies Test score; copies of undergraduate and graduate transcripts; completed application form with statement of goals; and a personal interview with the department chairman (which can be waived). Minimum GPA for graduate admission is 2.7 with a Miller Analogy Score of 50 or above. *Faculty:* 3 full-time; 6 associated (full-time staff who teach part-time); 12 part-time or adjunct faculty. *Students:* 10 full-time; 57 part-time. *Assistance:* A numbezr of assistantships and part-time instructor positions for qualified doctoral candidates. *Doctoral Program Trends:* Increasing enrollments of students interested in position placements in business/industry, health, government, program administration, instructional design/development, media production, and computer education. *Doctorates Awarded 1983-84:* 10.

MICHIGAN

Michigan State University. East Lansing, MI 48824. Joe L. Byers, Prof. of Education, College of Education, Erickson Hall. *Specializations:* Ph.D. and Ed.D. to prepare individuals to improve the quality and effectiveness of instruction and to facilitate learning at all educational and training levels; serve as instructional development specialists; and improve theory and practice of Educational Systems Development. Emphasis is given to systems design and analysis; evaluation and use of instructional media; design, production, and validation of graphic and pictorial instructional materials; and research pertaining to pedagogical and cost-effectiveness attributes of teaching strategies and instructional materials. *Features:* Individually designed doctoral programs; guided field experiences in instructional design projects; major work in a cognate area (such as Communications Theory); graduate assistantships as instructional development specialists; and advanced seminars in instructional development and technology.

Admission Requirements: Master's degree in appropriate field; 3.0 GPA in last two years of undergraduate work and subsequent graduate work; teaching credentials (preferred); three letters of recommendation; performance above fiftieth percentile in the verbal portion of the GRE aptitude test or in the Miller Analogies Test; two years of teaching or related experience (desirable); statement of professional goals and indication of perception of ways the doctoral program may contribute to their achievement; and a personal interview. *Faculty:* 6 full-time; 4 part time; 3 adjunct professors. *Students:* 19 full-time; 26 part-time. *Assistance:* Graduate assistantships in many departments are available to Educational Systems Development doctoral students. *Doctoral Program Trends:* Increasing enrollments of students interested in position placements in business/industry, instructional design/development, and computer education. *Doctorates Awarded 1983-84:* 7.

University of Michigan. Ann Arbor, MI 48109. Warren G. Palmer, Assoc. Prof., Dept. of Curriculum and Instruction. *Specializations:* Innovations in ways to improve teaching and learning; development of research skills in instructional technology; development of insights and skills related to effecting curriculum changes in educational institutions. *Features:* An internship component that is based on a "medical" model offering on-the-job experience in the management and operation of an educational media center; close affiliation with clinical professors throughout the period of matriculation. *Admission Requirements:* Identical with those for admission to the School of Education. *Faculty:* 1 full-time; 1 part-time; 4 part-time faculty on Advisory Committee. *Students:* 5 full-time; 30 part-time. *Assistance:* Through the School of Education; competitive for students in all departments. *Doctoral Program Trends:* Information not available. *Doctorates Awarded 1983-84:* Data not available.

Wayne State University. Detroit, MI 48202. John Childs, Dir., Instructional Technology Programs, Division of Administrative and Organizational Studies, College of Education. *Specializations:* Ed.D. and Ph.D. programs to prepare individuals for leadership in business, industry, health care, and the K-12 school setting as instructional development specialists; media or learning resources managers; media or learning resources consultants; specialists in instructional television; computer-assisted or computer-managed instruction; teachers in higher education; or research specialists. *Features:* Guided field experience and on-the-job training; participation in teaching and instructional development activities within various colleges and departments of the university and in business and industry. *Admission Requirements:* Master's degree, graduate honor point average of 3.5 or better; strong positive professional recommendations; and an interview. *Faculty:* 3 full-time; 7 part-time. *Students:* 440 full-time and part-time. *Assistance:* Graduate and teaching assistantships; graduate assistant positions open to qualified candidates; also contract industrial internships. *Doctoral Program Trends:* Increased enrollments of students seeking position placements in college teaching, instructional design/development, and computer education. *Doctorates Awarded 1983-84:* 5.

MINNESOTA

University of Minnesota. Minneapolis, MN 55455. Robert D. Tennyson, Chair, Instructional Systems, College of Education, 130 Peil Hall, 178 Pillsbury Dr., SE. *Specializations:* M.A. and Ph.D. in Education and Educational Psychology are offered through the graduate school. Areas of study include instructional design, educational technology, computer-based instruction, curriculum systems, and curriculum and instruction research. *Features:* Internships and special field experiences. *Admission Requirements:* General requirements for admission to either master's or doctoral program of the graduate school. *Faculty:* 8 full-time; 4 associate. *Students:* 84 M.A. candidates; 32 Ph.D. candidates. *Assistance:* Teaching fellowships, research, project assistantships, and internships are available. *Doctoral Program Trends:* Increasing enrollments of students interested in position placements in business/industry, college teaching, program administration, instructional design/development, and computer education. *Doctorates Awarded 1983-84:* 5.

MISSOURI

University of Missouri-Columbia. Columbia, MO 65211. Arni T. Dunathan, Prof. of Education and Library Science, 313 Education Bldg. *Specializations:* Ph.D. or Ed.D. for teaching, research, administration, and instructional development in colleges and universities or education agencies; also a strong media/library science interdisciplinary major. *Features:* School librarian and learning resources director certificate can be elected. Variety of related areas in education and other divisions. Diverse internship-for-credit opportunities in ITV, ETV, cable TV, LRC, medical education, library, and college teaching. *Admission Requirements:* Apply to Dir. of Graduate Studies, Dept. of Curriculum and Instruction, Education Bldg., 209. GRE required; for other requirements, see *Bulletin* and *Graduate Catalog. Faculty:* 5. *Students:* 19. *Assistance:* Graduate assistantships in teaching, instructional television; LRC; other on-campus, media-related employment. *Doctoral Program Trends:* Highly selective admissions. Increasing enrollments of students interested in position placements in LRC management and administration; curriculum and instruction; and a departmental emphasis upon training technology employing cable TV. Considerable use of internships rather than formal courses. *Doctorates Awarded 1983-84:* 2.

NEBRASKA

University of Nebraska. Lincoln, NE 68588-0447. Gordon F. Culver, Prof., Instructional Media: Design and Theory, Teachers College. *Specializations and Features:* Program develops competencies for work in such positions as media specialists and directors of media programs or systems, media specialists in business and industry, and instructional design specialists and researchers. Ed.D. and Ph.D. programs are in Administration, Curriculum, and Instruction with an emphasis in educational technology. (NOTE: program should be operational by fall, 1985. For further information, contact Gordon F. Culver at the aforementioned address.)

NEW JERSEY

Rutgers—The State University of New Jersey. New Brunswick, NJ 08903. Brent D. Ruben, Prof. and Dir., Educational Technology Doctoral Program, The Graduate School. *Specializations:* Ph.D. program with emphasis on technology, communication, and information processes and communication and information organizations. *Admission Requirements:* Standards determined by the Graduate School, including GREs plus completion of a master's or equivalent degree. *Faculty:* 27 full-time. *Students:* Data not available. *Assistance:* Financially supported positions vary from year to year, but approximately 8 teaching or research assistantships are available per year. *Doctoral Program Trends:* Data not available. *Doctorates Awarded 1983-84:* 3.

NEW MEXICO

University of New Mexico. Albuquerque, NM 87131. John T. Zepper, Chair, Dept. of Educational Foundations. *Specializations:* Ph.D. and Ed.D. programs in Educational Foundations with departmental and interdepartmental work in Library/Media and courses in other departments. *Features:* Flexible program which can lead to Library/Media state certification. Emphasis on research, library media, instructional design, and use of computers. *Admission Requirements:* Write Dept. Chair. *Faculty:* 2 full-time; several part-time. *Students:* 8. *Assistance:* Some part-time opportunities. *Doctoral Program Trends:*

Increasing enrollments of students interested in positions in health fields and industry. *Doctorates Awarded 1983-84:* 0.

NEW YORK

Columbia University, Teachers College. New York, NY 10027. Robert E. Holloway, Assoc. Prof. of Education. *Specifications:* Ed.D. for individuals seeking careers in instructional technology; programs in instructional technology (in a department that also includes communication and computing in education). *Features:* Part-time employment is available and encouraged as part of the course work of 90 semester hours (in addition to the dissertation). Programs are individually planned, interdisciplinary, and based on prior and present interests and anticipated future developments in instructional technology. Up to 45 credits of relevant course work may be transferred. *Admission Requirements:* A record of outstanding capability; potential for leadership and creativity as indicated from academic records; recommendations; score on the GRE or the Miller Analogies Test; statement of expressed interests and future plans. *Faculty:* 1 full-time; 5 part-time. *Students:* 15 full-time; 45 part-time. *Assistance:* Limited scholarships (applications must be received before January 1 for the following September semester) and work-study financial aid for qualified applicants. *Doctoral Program Trends:* Increasing enrollments of students interested in position placements in business/industry, instructional design/development, and computer education. *Doctorates Awarded 1983-84:* 5.

New York University. New York, NY 10003. Francine Shuchat-Shaw, Dir., Educational Communication and Technology Program. *Specializations:* Preparation of individuals to perform as instructional media designers, developers and producers in education, business and industry, health and medicine, community services, government, and other fields; to coordinate media communications programs in educational television centers, museums, schools, and corporate, health, and community organizations; to serve as directors and supervisors in audiovisual programs in all settings listed; and to teach in educational communications and instructional technology programs in higher education. *Features:* Emphasizes theoretical foundations in instruction and information-processing and interactions of learners, symbol systems, learning environments, and socio-cultural contexts; participation in special research and production projects in photography, multi-image, television, and microcomputers. *Admission Requirements:* Combined score of 1,000 minimum on GRE; interview related to academic and/or professional preparation and career goals. *Faculty:* 2 full-time; 6 part-time. *Students:* 60. *Assistance:* Some financial aid and work-study programs. *Doctoral Program Trends:* Increasing enrollments of students interested in position placements in business/industry, health, instructional design/development, media production, and computer education. *Doctorates Awarded 1983-84:* 3.

State University of New York at Buffalo. Buffalo, NY 14214. T. A. Razik, Prof. of Education, Dept. of Educational Organization, Administration and Policy. *Specializations:* Ph.D., Ed.D., and Ed.M. to educate graduate students in the theories, resources, and dynamics of instructional communications. Emphasis is on the systems approach, communication, and model building, with stress on efficient implementation of media in instruction. *Features:* The program is geared to instructional development, systems analysis, systems design, and management in educational and noneducational organizations; emphasis is placed on research in communication and information theory. Laboratories are available to facilitate student and faculty research projects in educational and/or training settings. Specifically, the knowledge and skills are categorized as follows: planning and designing; delivery systems and managing; and evaluating. *Admission Requirements:* Satisfactory scores on the Miller Analogies Test and/or GRE; master's degree or equivalent in field of specialization; and minimum 3.0 GPA. *Faculty:* 3 full-time; 3 part-time. *Students:* 36 full-time; 53 part-time. *Assistance:* 3 graduate assistantships (apply by March 15). *Doctoral Program Trends:* Increasing enrollments of students interested in position placements in business/industry, health, college teaching, instructional design/development, and computer education. *Doctorates Awarded 1983-84:* 4.

Syracuse University. Syracuse, NY 13210. Philip Doughty, Prof., Chair, Instructional Design, Development, and Evaluation Program, School of Education. *Specializations:* Ph.D., Ed.D., and M.S. degree programs for instructional development (administration of personnel and resources, instructional design of programs and materials, educational evaluation, human issues in instructional development, and media production including computers and videodisc); and educational research and theory (learning theory, application of theory, and educational and media research). Graduates are prepared to serve as curriculum developers, instructional developers, program and product evaluators, researchers, resource center administrators, communications coordinators, trainers in human resource development, and instructors in education in higher education. *Features:* Field work and internships; special topics and special issues seminars; student and faculty initiated minicourses; seminars and guest lecturers; faculty-student formulation of departmental policies; and multiple international perspectives. *Admission Requirements:* A bachelor's degree from an accredited institution. *Faculty:* 7 full-time; 4 part-time. *Students:* 60 full-time; 40 part-time. *Assistance:* Some fellowships (competitive); and graduate assistantships entailing either research or administrative duties in instructional technology. *Doctoral Program Trends:* Increasing enrollments of students interested in position placements in business/industry, program administration, instructional design/development, and computer education. *Doctorates Awarded 1983-84:* 8.

NORTH CAROLINA

University of North Carolina – Greensboro. Greensboro, NC 27412. David H. Jonassen, Assoc. Prof., Dept. of Pedagogical Studies, Dept. of Ed. Administration and Research, School of Education. *Specializations:* Ed.D. in Curriculum and Instruction with emphasis in educational technology. *Features:* Individually constructed program based on background and needs of student; 20 hours of microcomputer-related instruction available. *Admission Requirements:* Baccalaureate degree, 3.0 GPA or better in major; master's degree acceptable; GRE or MAT also required. *Faculty:* 5 full-time; 3 part-time. *Students:* 28 full-time; 6 part-time. *Assistance:* Some graduate assistantships available. *Doctoral Program Trends:* Specialization in technological areas. *Doctorates Awarded 1983-84:* 0.

OHIO

Kent State University. Kent, OH 44242. Barbara L. Martin, Asst. Prof. and Coord., Educational Technology Program, Curriculum and Instruction, College of Education. *Specializations:* Ph.D. and Ed.D. in curriculum and instruction with emphasis in educational technology with courses in instruction design and development, change strategies, research and evaluation, and media selection and design. *Features:* Program encourages students to take elective courses in relevant departments in the College of Education and across the university, e.g., in communications, psychology, and technology. *Admission Requirements:* Obtain a doctoral program application packet from the Graduate School of Education, 409 White Hall, Kent State University, Kent, Ohio 44242. Two completed copies of the application and a check or money order for the $10.00 application fee are required. Also required are: official transcripts from the registrar of each college or university (except KSU) in which at least eight semester hours or twelve quarter hours were earned – sent directly to the Graduate School of Education; five letters of recommendation for admission to either doctoral program including two from former or present professors who can speak to the applicants academic potential; an acceptable score from *one* of the following examinations – Miller Analogies Test, Terman Concept Mastery Test, GRE; 3.00 UGPA, 3.50 GPA; interview with Educational Technology faculty member plus a one-hour examination to assess applicant's writing ability. *Faculty:* 3

full-time; 4 part-time. *Students:* 10 full-time. *Assistance:* Assistantships are frequently available that include tuition and stipend. *Doctoral Program Trends:* The program in Educational Technology was recently moved from the department housing Curriculum and Instruction to the department housing educational psychology. One purpose of this change is to emphasize further the links between instructional design and educational technology and instructional psychology/learning theory. *Doctorates Awarded 1983-84:* 1.

Ohio State University. Columbus, OH 43210. Instructional Design and Technology Program. College of Education. Keith Hall; William D. Taylor, Chair. *Specializations:* Ph.D. in educational communications for preparation of individuals to teach in higher education, administer comprehensive media services, or engage in production/development leadership functions in higher education and related educational agencies. *Features:* Interdisciplinary work in other departments (photography, journalism, communications, radio and television, computer and information science); individual design of doctoral programs according to candidate's background, experience, and goals; and internships provided on campus in business and industries, and in schools; integrated school media laboratory, microcomputer and videodisc laboratory, videoproduction laboratory. *Admission Requirements:* Admission to graduate school and to the Faculty of Educational Foundations and Research in the College of Education; minimum 2.7 GPA (on 4.0 scale); and satisfactory academic and professional recommendations. *Faculty:* Regular faculty: 5 full-time in education; 1 part-time in another department. Adjunct faculty: 1 full-time in education; 2 part-time in other departments. *Students:* 6 full-time; 30 part-time. *Assistance:* Graduate fellowships and scholarships are often available, as well as departmental teaching and research assistantships and assistantship opportunities in media facilities on campus. *Doctoral Program Trends:* Increasing enrollments of students interested in position placements in business/industry, instructional design/development, and computer education. *Doctorates Awarded 1983-84:* 2 [1984 data]

University of Toledo. Toledo, OH 43606. L. Elsie, Chair, Dept. of Educational Technology, College of Education. *Program:* Research and theory in the areas of instructional design, development, evaluation, computers, video, and training. Emphasis is in the empirical study of systematic processes and procedures in instructional technology. *Requirements:* 135 quarter hours beyond the baccalaureate degree or 90 quarter hours beyond the master's degree, including tool skill courses and dissertation credit. Residency requirement of one year or three full-time summer quarters depending on Ph.D. or Ed.D. option. Option of one or two minor areas of study to be included in total program hours. *Admission Requirements:* Miller Analogies Test at or above fiftieth percentile, three letters of recommendation, official transcripts of undergraduate and graduate work, and autobiographical sketch. *Tuition and Fees:* $308.50 per quarter in-state; $793.50 out-of-state. *Assistance:* Graduate assistantships require 20 hours of work per week. Basic stipend for assistantships of $4,700 with full tuition remission. *Doctoral Program Trends:* Increasing enrollments of students seeking position placements in business/industry, health, government, college teaching, program administration, instructional design/development, media production, and computer education. *Doctorates Awarded 1983-84:* 1.

OKLAHOMA

Oklahoma State University. Stillwater, OK 74078. Douglas B. Aichele, Head, Dept. of Curriculum and Instruction, College of Education. *Specializations:* M.S. and Ed.D. programs in educational technology (microcomputers), media management/administration, materials production, utilization/application, theory and research, selection, college teaching, evaluation, instructional systems design, instructional development, curriculum foundations, and learning theory. *Admission Requirements:* Minimum of 3.0 GPA on undergraduate work (both programs); Miller Analogies Test and minimum of 1 year teaching experience (doctorate). *Faculty:* 3 full-time; 2 part-time. *Students:* 10 full-time, 6 part-time M.A. candidates; 5 full-time Ph.D. candidates. *Assistance:* 3 graduate assistantships. *Doctoral Program Trends:* Increasing enrollments of students interested in position placements in business/industry, college teaching, program administration, and instruc-tional design/development. *Doctorates Awarded 1983-84:* 2.

University of Oklahoma. Norman, OK 73019. Tillman J. Ragan, Prof., Area Coord. of Educational Technology, College of Education. *Specializations:* Ph.D. and Ed.D. leading to specializations for research, teaching, management, and consulting in instructional technology (including preparation in instructional materials development — computer, video, computer-assisted video instruction — and preparation in management of instructional systems and programs). *Features:* Programs are designed through the vehicle of an advisory conference in which the student's background and goals are translated into a program of study and research proficiencies; a practicum is included to provide experiences resembling those related to the individual's career objectives. Computer emphasis area now available. *Admission Requirements:* Evidence of potential for contribution to the field; satisfactory performance on the GRE aptitude test; satisfactory performance on TOEFL and other measures of English proficiency for international students; and satisfactory performance on Advisory Conference in second semester of post-master's work. *Faculty:* 3 full-time; 4 part-time. *Assistance:* Graduate assistantships involving teaching and service or research are available for capable students. *Doctoral Program Trends:* Increasing enrollments of students interested in position placements in college teaching and computer education. *Doctorates Awarded 1983-84:* 3.

OREGON

Oregon State University — Western Oregon State College. Monmouth, OR 97330. Richard Forcier, Prof. and Dir., Educational Communications and Technology Program, Dept. of Educational Foundations, School of Education. (This institution has a joint doctoral program offering with Western Oregon State College.) *Specializations:* Ph.D. in Education (with specialization in educational communications and technology); computer education; instructional systems. Offers advanced courses in media management, media production, instructional systems, instruction development, and computer technology. Some specialization in "distance delivery" of instruction. *Admission Requirements:* Bachelor's degree; minimum 2.75 GPA in undergraduate program; interview; satisfactory performance on GRE or Miller Analogies tests. *Faculty:* 5 full-time; 1 part-time. *Students:* 6 full-time; 4 part-time. *Assistance:* 3 graduate assistantships. *Doctoral Program Trends:* Increasing enrollments of students interested in position placements in health, government, instructional design/development, and computer education. *Doctorates Awarded 1983-84:* 2.

University of Oregon. Eugene, OR 97401. Judith Grosenick, Assoc. Dean, Division of Teacher Education. *Specializations:* Ph.D. or Ed.D. in Curriculum and Instruction leading to public school, junior college, college, and university supervision of media use and instructional development; higher education research and teaching, and positions in business, industry, and public and private agencies concerned with communications, instructional development, and training. *Features:* A flexible program designed to meet specific student needs. *Admission Requirements:* Admission to graduate school; masters degree or equivalent in field appropriate to the specialization; two years of successful teaching and/or related experience relevant to program focus. *Faculty:* Full-time. *Students:* In curriculum and instruction. *Assistance:* Graduate assistantships — 24 part-time, 5 full-time. *Doctoral Program Trends:* Increasing enrollments of students interested in position placements in business/industry, health, government, college teaching, media production, instructional design/development, and computer education. *Doctorates Awarded 1983-84:* 6.

PENNSYLVANIA

Pennsylvania State University. University Park, PA 16802. Paul W. Welliver, Division of Curriculum and Instruction. *Specializations:* Ph.D. and Ed.D. for individuals seeking professional pursuits in instructional systems design, development, management, evaluation and research in instructional endeavors within business, industrial, medical, health, religious, higher education, and public school settings. Present research emphases are on instructional development, dissemination, implementation and management; interactive video; computer-based education; and visual learning. *Features:* A common thread throughout all programs is that candidates have basic competencies in the understanding of human learning; curriculum; instructional design, development, and evaluation; and research procedures. Practical experience is available in mediated independent learning, research, and instructional development and dissemination projects. *Admission Requirements:* GRE; 2.75 GPA; and acceptance as a prospective candidate by a graduate faculty member. *Faculty:* 4 full-time; 1 part-time. *Students:* 25 full-time; 36 part-time. *Assistance:* Graduate assistantships in managing mediated independent study courses, operating media facilities, assisting in research projects, and participating in university instructional development projects. *Doctoral Program Trends:* Increasing enrollments of students interested in position placements in business/industry, program administration, instructional design/development, interactive video, and computer education. *Doctorates Awarded 1983-84:* 6.

Temple University. Philadelphia, PA 19122. Elton Robertson, Dept. of Educational Media. *Specializations:* Ed.D. in educational media for proficiency in employing instructional technology to enhance learning and teaching at elementary, secondary, and university levels, as well as in industrial training situations. *Features:* The program is designed to take into account the candidate's personal and professional goals. Practical experience is provided for those wishing to: (1) teach media related courses; (2) apply the newer interactive technology to enhance the instructional development process; and (3) function in various administrative roles in support of learning resource and instructional resource centers. *Admission Requirements:* Bachelor's degree from an accredited institution, a master's degree or 24 credits in educational media, admission to the graduate school, and a satisfactory interview with the faculty. *Faculty:* 3 full-time. *Students:* 7 full-time; 26 part-time. *Assistance:* 1 departmental teaching associateship; 3 departmental assistantships; fellowships. *Doctoral Program Trends:* Increasing enrollments of students interested in position placements in business/industry, government, instructional design/development, media production, and computer education. *Doctorates Awarded 1983-84:* 3.

University of Pittsburgh. Pittsburgh, PA 15260. Barbara Seels, Prof., Program Dir., Program in Educational Communications and Technology. *Specializations:* Ph.D., Ed.D., M.Ed., and M.A. programs for the preparation of generalists with skills in production, selection, utilization, instructional design, and computer-assisted and computer-managed instruction; certification programs for media specialists and supervisors of educational communications and technology. The principal program objective is to prepare people for positions in which they can effect educational change through educational communication and technology—individuals who have skills in interacting with people, analysis, and problem solving, knowledge of media, expressive skills, and broad knowledge of teaching-learning processes and ways of mediating them. *Features:* A very flexible curriculum permits student/advisor-designed major and minor subject areas. A post-master's Certificate of Advanced Studies program is also available for intensive specialization in selected areas. Candidates function in instructional development teams in a variety of organizations: public and private schools, inner city and suburban institutions, institutions of higher education, research institutions, hospitals, and industry. *Admission Requirements:* Submission of written statement concerning the applicant's professional goals and the applicant's expectations for the program's helping him or her to reach those goals; three letters of recommendation from former employers or educators; demonstration of English proficiency; satisfactory GPA; and personal interviews. Approximately 25 percent of the student body are from other countries and extra attention and special counseling is provided for foreign students. *Faculty:* 5 full-time; 5 part-time. *Students:* 25 full-time; 100 part-time. *Assistance:* 1 graduate assistant; 1 teaching assistant; and some tuition scholarships. *Doctoral Program Trends:* Increasing enrollments of students interested in position placements in business/industry, health, instructional design/development. Program is moving toward Instructional Design Doctorate, Instructional Technology Master's. *Doctorates Awarded 1983-84:* 19.

TENNESSEE

University of Tennessee. Knoxville, TN 37816. Alfred D. Grant, Chair, Dept. of Instructional Media and Technology, College of Education. *Specializations:* M.A. and M.Ed. in curriculum and instruction with emphasis in instructional media and technology and Ed.D., Ed.S., and Ph.D. programs in media management/administration materials production, utilization/application, theory and research, selection, training, teaching, evaluation, instructional systems design, and instructional development. *Admission Requirements:* GRE required; 3 years' full-time teaching experience (Ed.D.); minimum undergraduate GPA of 2.5 (M.A.) and graduate GPA of 3.25 (Ed.D.). *Faculty:* 2 full-time. *Students:* 2 part-time M.A. candidates; 5 full-time, 2 part-time Ed.D. candidates. *Assistance:* None reported. *Doctoral Program Trends:* Increasing enrollments of students seeking position placements in health fields; increased numbers of foreign doctoral students. *Doctorates Awarded 1983-84:* 0.

TEXAS

East Texas State University. Commerce, TX 75428. Inez G. Johnson, Prof. and Acting Head, Center for Educational Media and Technology. *Specializations:* Ed.D. is offered for individuals interested in specializing in educational technology within the broad area of supervision, curriculum, and instruction; master's degree with majors in educational technology or library science is offered. *Objectives:* Programs are designed to prepare professionals in various aspects of instructional technology, including management, instructional design, production of instructional materials, utilization, theory and research, and teaching in public schools and higher education. *Features:* Programs are tailored to fit professional goals of individuals. Opportunities are provided for practical applications through internships, practicums, and assistantships. *Admission Requirements:* Satisfactory GPA; GRE score; evidence of literary and expository skills and aptitudes; and recommendations. *Faculty:* 8. *Students:* 25 full-time; 150 part-time. *Assistance:* Graduate assistantships, which include stipends and waivers of out-of-state tuition. *Doctoral Program Trends:* Increasing enrollments of students interested in position placements in business/industry, college teaching, and computer education. *Doctorates Awarded 1983-84:* 7.

Texas A & M University. College Station, TX 77843. Ronald D. Zellner, Assoc. Prof., Coord., Educational Technology Program, College of Education. *Specializations:* Ph.D. and Ed.D. programs to prepare individuals to teach college and university courses in instructional technology; manage learning resource centers in schools, community colleges, higher education, and research and development organizations; perform instructional design activities in education, business, industry, and public and private agencies concerned with communication and instructional processes. *Features:* The doctoral programs are flexible and interdisciplinary in nature, emphasizing both theoretical and practical aspects of selecting instructional resources; both may include an internship, and the Ed.D. requires a field experience in the career area; the program also includes microcomputer courses with an emphasis in CAI, CMI, and interactive television, and a new microcomputer laboratory. *Admission Requirements:* A bachelor's degree; master's degree; admission to graduate college which includes satisfactory performance on the GRE. *Faculty:* 6 full-time; 2 part-time. *Students:* 9 full-time; 40 part-time. *Assistance:* Several graduate assistantships (apply by January 1) and a limited number of fellowships; part-time employment on university campus, local school districts (College Station and Bryan), and the College Station area. *Doctoral Program Trends:* Increasing enrollments of students interested in position placements in government, industry, and computer education. *Doctorates Awarded 1983-84:* 1.

University of Texas. Austin, TX 78712. DeLayne Hudspeth, Prof., Coord., Instructional Technology, Dept. of Curriculum & Instruction, School of Education. *Specializations:* Ph.D. program emphasizes research, design, and development of instructional systems and communications technology. *Features:* The program is interdisciplinary in nature, although certain competencies are required of all students. Programs of study and dissertation research are based on individual needs and career goals. Learning resources include a modern LRC, computer labs and classrooms, a color TV studio and access to a photo and graphics lab. *Admission Requirements:* Minimum 3.0 GPA; a score of at least 1,000 on the GRE aptitude test. *Faculty:* 3 full-time; many courses are offered cooperatively by faculty members of other departments (Radio-TV-Film, Computer Science, Educational Psychology, Library Science and others). *Students:* 15 full-time; 20 part-time. *Assistance:* Assistantships are available in planning and developing instructional materials and in teaching undergraduate media courses; there are also some paid internships. *Doctoral Program Trends:* Increasing enrollments of students seeking position placements in business/industry, health, program administration, instructional design/development, and computer education. *Doctorates Awarded 1983-84:* 5.

UTAH

Brigham Young University. Provo, UT 84602. James W. Dunn, Chair, Dept. of Curriculum and Instructional Science. The graduate programs of Instructional Science, Instructional Psychology, Elementary Education, and Secondary Education have been reorganized into a graduate department of Curriculum and Instructional Science. *Specializations:* M.S. and Ph.D. degrees are offered in Instructional Science and Technology. In the M.S. program, students may specialize in Instructional Design and Production, Computers in Education, or Research and Evaluation. In the Ph.D. program students may specialize in Instructional Design, Instructional Psychology, or Research and Evaluation. *Features:* Course offerings include principles of learning, instructional design, assessing learning outcomes, evaluation in education, empirical inquiry in education, project and instructional resource management, quantitative reasoning, microcomputer materials production, audiovisual production, naturalistic inquiry, and more. Students are required to participate in internships and projects related to development, evaluation, measurement, and research. *Admission Requirements:* For further information, write Dr. James Dunn, Chair, Dept. of Curriculum and Instructional Science, 201 MCKB, Brigham Young University, Provo, UT 84602. *Faculty:* Data not available. *Students:* Data not available. *Doctoral Program Trends:* Increasing enrollments of students interested in position placements in business/industry, health, college teaching, instructional design/development, and computer education. *Doctorates Awarded 1983-84:* 0.

Utah State University. Logan, UT 84322. Don C. Smellie, Chair, Dept. of Instructional Technology, College of Education. *Specializations:* Ed.D., with emphasis in educational technology. Offered for individuals seeking to become professionally involved in instructional development and administration of media programs in public schools, community colleges, and universities. Teaching and research in higher education is another career avenue for graduates of the program. *Features:* A relatively small program allowing individual attention. The doctoral program is built on a strong master's and specialist's program in instructional technology. All doctoral students complete a core with the remainder of the course selection individualized based upon career goals. *Admission*

Requirements: 3.0 GPA; successful teaching experience or its equivalent; satisfactory performance on the GRE test written recommendations; and a personal interview. *Faculty:* 7 full-time; 6 part-time. *Students:* 135 M.A. candidates; 22 Ed.S. candidates; 9 Ph.D. candidates. *Assistance:* Approx. 18 to 26 assistantships (apply by June 1). *Doctoral Program Trends:* Increasing enrollments of students seeking position placements in business/industry, college teaching, instructional design/development, and computer education. *Doctorates Awarded 1983-84:* 1.

VIRGINIA

University of Virginia. Charlottesville, VA 22903. John B. Bunch, Assoc. Prof. of Education, Dept. of Curriculum and Instruction, School of Education. *Specializations:* Ed.D. or Ph.D. program for well-qualified students seeking professional training in the design, production, and evaluation of instructional programs and materials in school or nonschool settings; graduates are placed as instructional developers or media specialists in education or as training developers in business, industry, or government agencies. *Features:* A relatively small program that enables the department to tailor programs to the needs and goals of individual students (including options of minor area concentrations in other professional schools); concentration in microprocessor technology available; student involvement in university faculty research activities; and support of program through course offerings in other departments. *Admission Requirements:* Satisfactory performance on GRE aptitude test; a master's degree; written recommendations; and a personal interview. *Faculty:* 2 full-time. *Students:* 15 full-time; 25 part-time. *Assistance:* Several graduate assistantships; and a limited number of fellowships available each year. (Applications for financial assistance must be made prior to April 1 each year.) *Doctoral Program Trends:* Increasing enrollments of students seeking position placements in business/industry, health, college teaching, instructional design/development, media production, and computer education. *Doctorates Awarded 1983-84:* 2.

Virginia Polytechnic Institute and State University. Blacksburg, VA 24060. Thomas M. Sherman, Program Area Leader, Science and Technology of Instruction, Learning and Evaluation, College of Education. *Specializations:* M.A., M.S., and Ed.D. programs in learning disabilities, instruction in higher education, evaluation, instructional design, media technology, school learning, and computers in education. *Admission Requirements:* Minimum undergraduate GPA of 2.75 (M.A. and M.Ed.), 3.3 (doctorate); master's degree and 3 letters of recommendation (Ed.D.). *Faculty:* 7 full-time. *Students:* 6 full-time; 3 part-time M.A. candidates; 8 full-time, 11 part-time Ph.D. candidates. *Assistance:* 2 graduate assistantships. *Doctoral Program Trends:* Increasing enrollments of students seeking position placements in health, instructional design/development, and computer education. *Doctorates Awarded 1983-84:* 3.

WASHINGTON

University of Washington. Seattle, WA 98195. Gerald M. Torkelson, Prof. of Education, College of Education. *Specializations:* Ph.D. and Ed.D. for individuals in public schools, higher education, business, industry, public and religious institutions concerned with communications and teaching processes. *Features:* Emphasis upon competencies in full range of technological devices and methods applied to instruction; additional competencies in management, supervision, research, evaluation, instructional design and development, curriculum, human learning, and computers in learning. *Admission Requirements:* Admission to Graduate School; master's degree or equivalent in field appropriate to the specialization; 3.5 GPA in master's program; two years of successful professional and/or related experience relevant to the program. *Faculty:* 3. *Students:* 2 full-time; 24 part-time. Increasing enrollments of students seeking position placements in computer education. *Doctorates Awarded 1983-84:* 1.

Washington State University. Pullman, WA 99164. John A. Davis, Dir. Instructional Media Services; Inga Kromann-Kelly, Chair, Dept. of Education. *Specializations:* Ph.D. in education and Ed.D. for development of learning resources and college instruction in curriculum-media. *Features:* Specialization in educational technology occurs within the curriculum-media area, with particular emphasis upon curriculum and instructional design and methodology. Individualized program may include teaching experience in media and learning resources courses, applications of microcomputers in education, and cooperation with the Instructional Media Center or Murrow Communications Center, including internships. *Admission Requirements:* Admission to graduate school; master's degree in appropriate area; admission to Dept. of Education doctoral program during first semester or summer session in residence. *Faculty:* 3 full-time; 3 part-time. *Students:* 41 full-time, 31 part-time (5 full-time in curriculum-media). *Admission Requirements:* 3.0 GPA; GRE and MAT scores. *Assistance:* Graduate assistantships are available for students with 3.0 GPA and teaching experience. *Doctoral Program Trends:* Increasing emphasis on computer literacy; moving toward educational leadership emphasis. *Doctorates Awarded 1983-84:* 17.

WEST VIRGINIA

West Virginia University. Morgantown, WV 26506. Paul DeVore, Prof., Chair, Technology Education, Communication and Information Systems Sequence of Study, College of Human Resources and Education. *Specializations:* M.A. and Ed.D. degree programs in media history and research, college teaching, instructional systems design, instructional development, and communication and information systems. *Admission Requirements:* GRE and Miller Analogies Test; minimum GPA (3.0 for doctorate). *Faculty:* 2 full-time; 4 part-time. *Students:* 5 full-time; 2 part-time. *Assistance:* 7 teaching assistantships, 1 research assistantship. *Doctoral Program Trends:* Increasing enrollments of students seeking position placements in business/industry, government, program management, educational delivery systems, and computer education. *Doctorates Awarded 1983-84:* 5.

WISCONSIN

University of Wisconsin. Madison, WI 53706. Ann Becker, Assoc. Prof., Dept. of Curriculum and Instruction, School of Education. *Specializations:* Ph.D. programs to prepare specialists in teacher education, and in instructional development. *Features:* The program is designed to provide broad understanding of the entire field with special emphasis upon relationships of media to learning theory, communication theory, perceptual theory, and instructional development. The program is coordinated with media operations of the university. *Admission Requirements:* Previous experience in instructional technology; previous teaching experience; minimum 2.75 GPA on all undergraduate work completed; acceptable scores on either the Miller Analogies Test or the GRE aptitude test; and a minimum 3.0 GPA on all graduate work. (Note: Some exceptions may be made on one of these requirements if all others are acceptable.) *Faculty:* 2 full-time; 5 part-time. *Students:* 25 Ph.D. candidates; 35 M.S. candidates. *Assistance:* Stipends of approx. $550/mo. (ann.) for 20 hours of work per week. *Doctoral Program Trends:* Increasing enrollments of students seeking position placements in business/industry, government, instructional design/development, media production, and computer education. *Doctorates Awarded 1982-83:* 4.

WYOMING

University of Wyoming. Laramie, WY 82071. James R. Collins, Prof., Department of Educational Foundations and Instructional Technology. *Specializations:* The College of Education offers both the Ed.D. and the Ph.D. Instructional Technology is not currently offered as a separate degree. The Ed.D. or Ph.D. may be earned with an emphasis in

Instructional Technology through programs in Curriculum Instruction, Educational Administration, Adult Education, or Educational Foundations. For additional information, contact James R. Collins.

Master's Degree Programs in
Instructional Technology

Edwin (Ned) Logan
Professor Emeritus of Instructional Technology
Towson State University
Baltimore, Maryland

This directory presents data obtained from representatives of more than 210 institutions of higher learning located in the various states and the District of Columbia.

Each entry in the directory contains the following information: (1) name and mailing address of the institution; (2) name, academic rank, and title of the program head; (3) name of the administrative unit offering the program; (4) the basis on which the program is offered, i.e., whether semester, quarter, or trimester; (5) minimum degree requirements; (6) the number of faculty in the following order: full-time men, full-time women, and equivalent part-time faculty; (7) the number of foreign nationals, the number of men (m), and the number of women (w) who graduated with master's degrees from the program during the one-year period between July 1, 1983 and June 30, 1984; and (8) identification of those institutions offering six-year specialist degree programs in instructional technology.

Because there are a number of master's degree-granting institutions in many states and users are likely to be interested in locating information about master's programs in their own or nearby states, the institutions in this section are arranged alphabetically by state and then alphabetically by the names of the institutions.

More specific information about listed programs, including instructions on filing for admission, may be obtained by writing to individual program coordinators. General or graduate catalogs will usually be furnished for a nominal charge, while specific program information will usually be sent free.

In our attempt to provide completeness in the listings that follow, we are greatly indebted to members of the staff of the Association for Educational Communications and Technology; all of the state departments of education throughout the United States; and especially the instructional technology/media representatives of the colleges and universities in the United States who contributed up-to-date information.

Several institutions have been listed twice since their computer technology programs are offered apart from their educational/instructional technology programs.

It should be noted that while considerable effort has been expended to ensure completeness of the listings, there may be institutions within the United States or its territories that have been omitted. Readers who know of such omissions are invited to provide information leads to the editors who will follow up on them for the next edition of *EMTY*.

ALABAMA

Alabama A&M University. Huntsville, AL 35672. Howard G. Ball, Chair, Dept. of Instructional Media. *Program Basis:* Semester. *Minimum Degree Requirements:* 36 semester hours including individualized number of media hours; thesis optional. *Faculty:* 4, 2, 1. *Graduates:* 6m, 26w. (School also offers a six-year specialist program in instructional technology.)

Alabama State University. Montgomery, AL 36195. Katie Bell, Assoc. Prof., Coord., Library Education and Media, School of Education. *Program Basis:* Quarter. *Minimum Degree Requirements:* 49 credit hours including 24 in media; thesis optional. *Faculty:* 2, 1, 0. *Graduates:* 1m, 8w. (School also offers a six-year specialist degree program in instructional technology.)

Auburn University. Auburn, AL 36849. C. Dan Wright, Assoc. Prof., Dept. Head, Educational Media. *Program Basis:* Quarter. *Minimum Degree Requirements:* 52 credit hours including 36 in media; thesis optional. *Faculty:* 5, 5, 0. *Graduates:* 0m, 10w. (School also offers a six-year specialist degree program in instructional technology.)

Jacksonville State University. Jacksonville, AL 36265. Alta Millican, Dean, College of Library Science, Communications, and Instructional Media. *Program Basis:* Semester. *Minimum Degree Requirements:* 30 credits including 21 in media; thesis optional. *Faculty:* 4, 2, 1. *Graduates:* 4m, 7w. (School also offers a six-year specialist degree program in instructional technology.)

University of Alabama. University, AL 35486. James D. Ramer, Prof., Dean of Graduate School of Library Service. *Program Basis:* Semester. *Minimum Degree Requirements:* 36 credit hours including 18 in media; thesis optional. *Faculty:* 10, 6, 0. *Graduates:* (including 2 foreign nationals) 9m, 32w. (School also offers a six-year specialist degree program in instructional technology.)

University of Alabama-Birmingham. Birmingham, AL 35294. Mary Sue McGarity, Assoc. Prof., Coord., Educational Leadership and Instructional Support, School of Education. *Program Basis:* Quarter. *Minimum Degree Requirements:* 39 semester hours including 30 in media; thesis optional. *Faculty:* 2, 2, 3. *Graduates:* 0m, 27w. (School also offers a six-year specialist degree program in instructional technology.)

University of South Alabama. Mobile, AL 36688. John G. Baylor, Asst. Prof., Chair, Dept. of Educational Media, School of Education. *Program Basis:* Quarter. *Minimum Degree Requirements:* 48 credit hours including 38 in media; thesis optional. *Faculty:* 4, 4, 0. *Graduates:* (including 1 foreign national) 1m, 6w. (School also offers a six-year specialist degree program in instructional technology.)

ARIZONA

Arizona State University. Tempe, AZ 85281. Karen Beyard-Tyler, Assoc. Prof., Chair, Dept. of Educational Technology and Library Science, College of Education. *Program Basis:* Semester. *Minimum Degree Requirements:* 30 credit hours including 18 in media; thesis optional. *Faculty:* 9, 9, 1. *Graduates:* 7m, 11w.

University of Arizona. Tucson, AZ 85721. Bruce R. Ledford, Assoc. Prof. of Secondary Education/Media, Media Dept., College of Education. *Program Basis:* Semester. *Minimum Degree Requirements:* 32 credit hours including 18 in media; thesis optional. *Faculty:* 5, 5, 0. *Graduates:* 8m, 7w. (School also offers a six-year specialist degree program in instructional technology.)

ARKANSAS

Arkansas Tech University. Russellville, AR 72801. Alex Carter, Asst. Prof., Dir. of Education Media Services, Dept. of Secondary Education. *Program Basis:* Semester. *Minimum Degree Requirements:* 30 credit hours including 18 in media; thesis optional. *Faculty:* 0, 0, 2. *Graduates:* 1m, 5w.

University of Arkansas. Fayetteville, AR 72701. David Loertscher, Assoc. Prof., Program Coord. for Instructional Resources, College of Education. *Program Basis:* Semester. *Minimum Degree Requirements:* 36 credit hours including 18 in media; thesis optional. *Faculty:* 5, 4, 0. *Graduates:* 1m, 15w. (School also offers a six-year specialist degree program in instructional technology.)

University of Central Arkansas. Conway, AR 73032. Selvin W. Royal, Assoc. Prof., Chair, Educational Media/Library Science Dept. *Program Basis:* Semester. *Minimum Degree Requirements:* 30 credit hours including 24 in educational media/library science. *Faculty:* 5, 3, 1. *Graduates:* 0m, 12w.

CALIFORNIA

California State College-San Bernardino. San Bernardino, CA 92407. R. A. Senour, Prof., Dir., Audiovisual and Instructional Television Center. *Program Basis:* Quarter. *Minimum Degree Requirements:* 45 credit hours including 15 in media: program in media required. *Faculty:* 1, 2, 9. *Graduates:* 6m, 5w.

California State University-Chico. Chico, CA 95929-0145. Henry T. Ingle, Dean, School of Communications. *Program Basis:* Semester. *Minimum Degree Requirements:* 30 credit hours including 18 in media; thesis required. *Faculty:* 2, 2, 0. *Graduates:* (including 3 foreign nationals) 6m, 4w.

California State University-Long Beach. Long Beach, CA 90840. Richard J. Johnson, Prof., Chair, Dept. of Instructional Media. *Program Basis:* Semester. *Minimum Degree Requirements:* 30 credit hours including 21 in media; thesis optional. *Faculty:* 4, 0, 1. *Graduates:* 7m, 9w.

California State University-Los Angeles. Los Angeles, CA 90032. Kathy Costintini, Asst. Prof., Coord. of the Instructional Media and Technology Program, Dept. of Education, School of Education. *Program Basis:* Quarter. *Minimum Degree Requirements:* 45 credit hours including 33 hours in media; thesis or thesis-related project required. *Faculty:* 2, 1, 15. *Graduates:* (including 6 foreign nationals) 39m, 34w. [1984 data]

California State University-Northridge. Northridge, CA 91330. Charles Lynch, Prof., Chair, Radio-TV-Film and Instruction Dept., School of Communications and Professional Studies. *Program Basis:* Semester. *Minimum Degree Requirements:* 36 credit hours including 36 hours in radio-TV-film with specialization in instructional technology. *Faculty:* 12, 1, 10. *Graduates:* 6m, 4w.

National University. San Diego, CA 92108. Gerry Ball, Prof., Dept. of Instructional Technology, School of Education. *Program Basis:* Monthly. *Minimum Degree Requirements:* The equivalent of 60 quarter hours with media courses tailored to meet student needs; thesis optional. *Faculty:* 5, 0, 3. *Graduates:* (including 3 foreign nationals) 26m, 9w.

Pepperdine University. Los Angeles, CA 90034. Terence R. Cannings, Assoc. Prof., Program Dir., M.S. in Educational Computing, School of Education and Psychology. *Program Basis:* Trimester. *Minimum Degree Requirements:* 30 unit hours in educational computing. *Faculty:* 4, 0, 2. *Graduates:* 21m, 42w.

San Diego State University. San Diego, CA 92182. Patrick Harrison, Prof., Chair, Dept. of Educational Technology. *Program Basis:* Semester. *Minimum Degree Requirements:* 30 credit hours including 27 in educational technology, instructional design, and training. *Faculty:* 6, 5, 0. *Graduates:* (including 8 foreign nationals) 14m, 25w.

San Francisco State University. San Francisco, CA 94132. James Laffey, Asst. Prof., Coord., Educational Technology Center. *Program Basis:* Semester. *Minimum Degree Requirements:* 30 credit hours, including 24 in educational technology; project required. *Faculty:* 4½, 3, 1. *Graduates:* (including 1 foreign national) 13m, 82. (School offers Graduate Certificate in Training Systems Development of which 18 units can be incorporated into M.A.)

San Jose State University. San Jose, CA 95192. Harold H. Hailer, Prof., Dept. of Instructional Technology, School of Education. *Program Basis:* Semester. *Minimum Degree Requirements:* 30 credit hours including 20 in media; thesis program. *Faculty:* 10, 10, 0. *Graduates:* (including 6 foreign nationals) 14m, 18w.

Stanford University. Stanford, CA 94305. Decker Walker, Prof., Interactive Educational Technology M.A. Program, School of Education. *Program Basis:* Quarter. *Minimum Degree Requirements:* 36 credit hours in education, psychology, and computer science with educational technology hours arranged to meet individual student needs; no thesis required but master's project is required. *Faculty:* 3, 0, 4. *Graduates:* (including 1 foreign national) 8m, 7w.

United States International University. San Diego, CA 92131. Dale G. Hamreus, Dean, School of Education. *Program Basis:* Quarter. *Minimum Degree Requirements:* M.A. program in computer education tailored to meet the computer programming needs of teachers and district level specialists as well as their needs for computer literacy, software selection, evaluation, and problem-solving applications; thesis optional. *Faculty:* 3, 4, 0. *Graduates:* (including 4 foreign nationals) 7m, 5w.

University of California-Los Angeles. Los Angeles, CA 90024. Aimee Dorr, Prof., Learning and Instruction, Graduate School of Education. *Program Basis:* Quarter. *Minimum Degree Requirements:* 36 credit hours with emphasis on all media of communication and instruction. *Faculty:* 2, 0, 6. *Graduates:* Program is rebuilding; initial program graduates include 1m, 2w.

University of California-Santa Barbara. Santa Barbara, CA 93106. Willis D. Copeland, Assoc. Prof., Program Leader, Instruction, Dept. of Education. *Program Basis:* Quarter. *Minimum Degree Requirements:* 40 credit hours including 28 required and 12 elective; thesis required. *Faculty:* 2, 4, 0. *Graduates:* 1m, 2w.

University of Southern California. Los Angeles, CA 90007-0031. Robert L. Baker, Prof., Dept. of Educational Psychology and Technology, School of Education. *Program Basis:* Semester. *Minimum Degree Requirements:* 28 credit hours including 12 in media; thesis optional. *Faculty:* 5, 11, 0. *Graduates:* (including 15 foreign nationals) 6m, 14w. (School also offers a six-year specialist degree program in instructional technology.)

COLORADO

University of Colorado-Boulder. Boulder, CO 80309. Richard L. Turner, Prof., Dean, Educational Technology and Instructional Computing Dept., School of Education. *Program Basis:* Semester. *Minimum Degree Requirements:* 30 credit hours including 21 in educational technology; no thesis required. *Faculty:* 2, 2, 4. *Graduates:* 2m, 6w. (Program to be replaced in late 1985 with courses in computer applications and related fields.)

University of Colorado-Denver. Denver, CO 80202. Bettie R. Helser, Assoc. Prof., Program Chair, Media Dept., Education Division. *Program Basis:* Semester. *Minimum Degree Requirements:* 36 credit hours including 24 in media; no thesis required. *Faculty:* 2, 2, 2. *Graduates:* 1m, 18w.

University of Denver. Denver, CO 90208. Bernard Franckowiak, Prof., Dean, Graduate School of Librarianship and Information Management (including Media). *Program Basis:* Quarter. *Minimum Degree Requirements:* 60 credit hours including 23 in media for school library media specialist certification; thesis optional. *Faculty:* 3, 2, 0. *Graduates:* 3m, 8w. (School, though offering an instructional technology program, places its major emphasis on library science and information management.) [Program terminated, 1985.]

University of Northern Colorado. Greeley, CO 80639. Andy Gibbons, Prof., Dept. of Educational Technology, College of Education. *Program Basis:* Quarter. *Minimum Degree Requirements:* 45 credit hours including 23 in media; thesis optional. *Faculty:* 2, 2, 0. *Graduates:* (including 3 foreign nationals) 5m, 15w. (School offers a six-year specialist degree program in instructional technology.) [1984 data]

CONNECTICUT

Central Connecticut State University. New Britain, CT 06050. Leroy E. Temple, Admin. Off. and Dir., Center for Instructional Media. *Program Basis:* Semester. *Minimum Degree Requirements:* 30 credit hours of which the number taken in media varies. *Faculty:* 5, 0, 1. *Graduates:* 4m, 2w. (School offers a six-year special degree program in instructional technology.)

Fairfield University. Fairfield, CT 06430. Ibrahim M. Hefzallah, Prof., Dir., Educational Technology Division, School of Graduate and Continuing Education. *Program Basis:* Semester. *Minimum Degree Requirements:* 33 credit hours including 24 in media and computers in education; thesis optional. *Faculty:* 4, 2, 1. *Graduates:* 8m, 10w. (School also offers a six-year specialist program in instructional technology.)

Southern Connecticut State University. New Haven, CT 06515. Rocco Orlando, Acting Dean and Prof., School of Library Science and Instructional Technology. *Program Basis:* Semester. *Minimum Degree Requirements:* For Instructional Technology only: 30 credit hours including 21 in media with comprehensive examination; 36 hours without examination. *Faculty:* 1, 2, 1. *Graduates:* 3m, 11w.

University of Connecticut. Storrs, CT 06268. Phillip J. Sleeman, Prof., Dir., Univ. Center for Instructional Media and Technology. *Program Basis:* Semester. *Minimum Degree Requirements:* 24 credit hours including 15 in media; thesis optional. *Faculty:* 2, 1, 6. *Graduates:* 5m, 7w. (School also offers a six-year specialist degree program in instructional technology.)

DISTRICT OF COLUMBIA

Catholic University. Washington, DC 20064. Carol Walker, Asst. Prof., Coord., Curriculum, Instruction, and Technology, School of Education. *Program Basis:* Semester. *Minimum Degree Requirements:* 36 credit hours including instructional design; comprehensives; thesis optional. *Faculty:* 6, 0, 2. *Graduates:* (including 5 foreign nationals) 1m, 2w.

Gallaudet College. Washington, DC 20002. Ronald Nomeland, Assoc. Prof., Chair, Dept. of Educational Technology, School of Education and Human Services. *Program Basis:* Semester. *Minimum Degree Requirements:* 36 credit hours including 33 hours in educational media and a related practicum. *Faculty:* 2, 0, 6. *Graduates:* 1m, 2w.

Howard University. Washington, DC 20059. Nancy Arnez, Chair, Dept. of Educational Leadership and Community Services, School of Education; John Greene, Coord., Educational Technology Program. *Program Basis:* Semester. *Minimum Degree Requirements:* 36 credit hours for M.Ed., including introduction to educational technology; computer-assisted instruction; individualized instruction; and instructional systems development; thesis required for M.A. degree. *Faculty:* 3, 3, 5. *Graduates:* 6m, 7w. (School also offers a six-year specialist degree program in instructional technology.)

University of the District of Columbia. Washington, DC 20001. Edith M. Griffin, Prof., Chair, Dept. of Media/Library and Instructional Systems, College of Education and Human Ecology. *Program Basis:* Semester. *Minimum Degree Requirements:* 36 credit hours of which 27 must be in media; thesis optional. *Faculty:* 6, 1, 0. *Graduates:* (including 2 foreign nationals) 4m, 3w.

FLORIDA

Barry University. Miami Shores, FL 33161. Robert L. Burke, Dean, School of Computer Science and Joel S. Levine, Prof. and Coord. of Computer Education. *Program Basis:* Four nine-week cycles plus one nine-week summer cycle and three intensive three-week cycles. *Minimum Degree Requirements:* 36 semester credit hours including 6 credits in one of the following: practicum, internship or thesis. *Faculty:* 4, 0, 0. *Graduates:* (including 3 foreign nationals) 7m, 7w.

Florida State University. Tallahassee, FL 32306. Ernest Burkman, Prof., Coord. of Instructional Systems Programs, M.S. Degrees in Educational Media and in Instructional Design. *Program Basis:* Semester. *Minimum Degree Requirements:* 32 semester hours. *Faculty:* 9, 7, 0. *Graduates:* 6m, 7w.

Jacksonville University. Jacksonville, FL 32211. Daryle C. May, Prof. and Dir., M.A. in Teaching Program in Computer Education, Div. of Education. *Program Basis:* Semester. *Minimum Degree Requirements:* 36 credit hours including 18 in computer related major. *Faculty:* 4, 3, 0. *Graduates:* 0m, 1w. (new program).

Nova University. Fort Lauderdale, FL 33314. Donald Stanier, Program Prof., M.S. and Ed.S. in Learning Resources, Center for the Advancement of Education. *Program Basis:* Modules. *Minimum Degree Requirements:* 36 credit hours including 24 in media; practicum required instead of thesis. *Faculty:* 5, 2, 2. *Graduates:* 3m, 25w.

University of Central Florida. Orlando, FL 32816. Donna Toler Baumbach, Assoc. Prof., Dept. of Educational Services, Educational Media/Instructional Technology Programs, College of Education. *Program Basis:* Semester. *Minimum Degree Requirements:* 33 semester hours including 21 in technology/media; thesis or project required. *Faculty:* 3, 3, 1. *Graduates:* (including 5 foreign nationals) 18m, 20w.

University of Florida. Gainesville, FL 32611. Lee J. Mullaly, Assoc. Prof., Educational Media and Instructional Design, Program Leader. *Program Basis:* Semester. *Minimum Degree Requirements:* 36 credit hours including 24 in educational media and instructional design; thesis optional. *Faculty:* 1, 1, 0. *Graduates:* (including 2 foreign nationals) 4m, 3w. (School also offers a six-year specialist degree program in instructional technology.)

University of Miami. Coral Gables, FL 33124. Charles E. Hannemann, Assoc. Prof., Area Coord. for Educational Technology, Dept. of Educational and Psychological Studies, School of Education and Allied Professions. *Program Basis:* Semester. *Minimum Degree Requirements:* 33 credit hours including 15 hours in media for M.S.Ed. program—Education Media Specialist; 33 credit hours including 12 hours in media for M.S.Ed. in Organizational Training; 30 credit hours for M.S.Ed. in Computer Education; no thesis required but comprehensive exam required. *Faculty:* 6, 5, 1. *Graduates:* 1m, 7w. (School offers a Specialist Degree in Professional Studies with an emphasis in Educational Technology.)

University of South Florida. Tampa, FL 33620. John A. McCrossan, Prof., Chair, Library, Media, and Information Studies. *Program Basis:* Semester. *Minimum Degree Requirements:* 39 credit hours including 33 in media, library or information studies; thesis optional. *Faculty:* 9, 8, 0. *Graduates:* 12m, 79w. (School also offers a six-year specialist degree program in library and educational media.)

GEORGIA

Georgia Southern College. Statesboro, GA 30460. Jack A. Bennett, Instructional Media Center, School of Education. *Program Basis:* Quarter. *Minimum Degree Requirements:* 60 credit hours including a varying number of hours of media for individual students. *Faculty:* 2, 2, 0. *Graduates:* 1m, 14w. (School also offers a six-year specialist program requiring 45 credit hours in the Ed.S. program in instructional technology.)

Georgia State University. Atlanta, GA 30303. Rosalind Miller, Assoc. Prof., Coord., Library Science/Media, Dept. of Curriculum and Instruction, School of Education. *Program Basis:* Quarter. *Minimum Degree Requirements:* 60 credit hours including 45 hours in media; thesis optional. *Faculty:* 3, 3, 0. *Graduates:* (including 3 foreign nationals) 1m, 21w. (School also offers a six-year specialist degree program in instructional technology.)

University of Georgia. Athens, GA 30602. Kent L. Gustafson, Prof., Chair, Dept. of Educational Media and Librarianship, College of Education. *Program Basis:* Quarter. *Minimum Degree Requirements:* 60 credit hours including 25 in media; thesis optional. *Faculty:* 9, 8, 0. *Graduates:* (including 3 foreign nationals) 9m, 16w. (School also offers a six-year specialist degree program in instructional technology.)

West Georgia College. Carrollton, GA 30118. Gerard Lentini, Prof., Chair, Media Education Dept. *Program Basis:* Quarter. *Minimum Degree Requirements:* 60 credit hours including 40 in media; thesis optional. *Faculty:* 3, 1, 0. *Graduates:* 1m, 82.

HAWAII

University of Hawaii-Manoa. Honolulu, HI 96822. Geoffrey Z. Kucera, Prof., Chair, Educational Communications and Technology Dept. *Program Basis:* Semester. *Minimum Degree Requirements:* 36 credit hours including 27 in educational communications and technology; thesis and nonthesis available. *Faculty:* 5, 5, 0. *Graduates:* (including 3 foreign nationals) 4m, 4w.

ILLINOIS

Chicago State University. Chicago, IL 60628. Marion W. Taylor, Prof., Chair, Dept. of Library Science and Communications Media. *Program Basis:* Trimester. *Minimum Degree Requirements:* 32 credit hours including 27 in media (plus prerequisites); thesis optional, but encouraged. *Faculty:* 5, 0, 0. *Graduates:* (including 1 foreign national) 1m, 11w.

Eastern Illinois University. Charleston, IL 61920. Donald W. Smitley, Chair, School Service Personnel. *Program Basis:* Semester. *Minimum Degree Requirements:* 32 credit hours including 18 in library/media; thesis optional. *Faculty:* 3, 3, 1. *Graduates:* (including 2 foreign nationals) 1m, 14w.

Governors State University. Park Forest South, IL 60466. Michael Stelnicks, Prof., Instructional and Training Technology, College of Arts and Sciences. *Program Basis:*

Trimester. *Minimum Degree Requirements:* 36 credit hours including all hours in educational technology. Faculty: 2-1/5, 2, 1/5. *Graduates:* 6m, 6w.

Illinois State University. Normal, IL 61761. George Tuttle, Prof., Chair, Dept. of Communications. *Program Basis:* Semester. *Minimum Degree Requirements:* 30 credit hours including 18 in media; thesis optional. *Faculty:* 3, 3, 1. *Graduates:* 5m, 7w.

National College of Education. Evanston, IL 60201. Patricia Breed, Program Dir., Library Science and Instructional Media, Graduate Program. *Program Basis:* Semester. (Note: Though this program is offered on a semester basis, the school operates on a quarter system.) *Minimum Degree Requirements:* M.Ed., 34 credit (semester) hours including 24 in media, thesis optional; C.A.S., 30 hours (semester) including 26 in media. *Faculty:* 3, 2, 0. *Graduates:* 3m, 8w.

Northeastern Illinois University. Chicago, IL 60625. Michael J. Belica, Prof., Coord. of Instructional Media. *Program Basis:* Trimester. *Minimum Degree Requirements:* 33 credit hours including 21 in media; thesis optional. *Faculty:* 2, 2, 0. *Graduates:* (including 3 foreign nationals) 13m, 33w.

Northern Illinois University. DeKalb, IL 60115. James Lockard, Assoc. Prof., Instructional Technology Programs, College of Education. *Program Basis:* Semester. *Minimum Degree Requirements:* 36 credits including 21 in media; thesis optional. *Faculty:* 8, 7, 0. *Graduates*: (including 2 foreign nationals) 10m, 11w.

Southern Illinois University-Carbondale. Carbondale, IL 62901. Pierre Barrette, Assoc. Prof., Coord., Educational Technology Program, Div. of Curriculum, Instruction, and Media, College of Education. *Program Basis:* Semester. *Minimum Degree Requirements:* 32 credit hours plus research paper; thesis optional. *Faculty:* 3, 1, 4. *Graduates:* (including 2 foreign nationals) 3m, 5w. (School offers a six-year specialist degree program in instructional technology.)

Southern Illinois University-Edwardsville. Edwardsville, IL 62026. Gary L. Hull, Prof., Chair, Dept. of Educational Administration and Instructional Technology, School of Education. *Program Basis:* Quarter. *Minimum Degree Requirements:* 52 degree credit hours including 36 in instructional technology; thesis optional. *Faculty:* 5, 5, 0. *Graduates:* (including 2 foreign nationals) 17m, 15w.

University of Illinois at Urbana-Champaign. Champaign, IL 61820. J. Richard Dennis, Assoc. Prof., Dept. of Secondary Education, College of Education. *Program Basis:* Semester. *Minimum Degree Requirements:* 32 credit hours with emphasis on media, educational psychology, and educational policy studies. *Faculty:* 7½, 0, 0. *Graduates:* (including 1 foreign national) 2m, 4w. (School also offers a five-year advanced certificate program in instructional technology.)

University of Illinois at Urbana-Champaign. Champaign, IL 61820. George W. McConkie, Prof., Div. of Learning and Instruction, Dept. of Ed. Psychology. *Program Basis:* Semester. *Minimum Degree Requirements:* 8 units of credit, at least 3 of which must be in 400-level courses, 2 of which in the major field (graduate courses are offered for 1 or ½ units each); thesis required. *Faculty:* 3, 1, 6. *Graduates:* 2m, 2w. (School also offers a six-year specialist degree program in instructional technology.)

Western Illinois University. Macomb, IL 61455. Don Crawford, Prof., Chair, Dept. of Learning Resources. (Offered in cooperation with Dept. of Educational Administration.) *Program Basis:* Semester. *Minimum Degree Requirements:* 32-36 credit hours including 18 in media; thesis optional. *Faculty:* 5, 5, 0. *Graduates:* 2m, 3w.

INDIANA

Ball State University. Muncie, IN 47306. Ray R. Suput, Prof., Chair, Dept. of Library and Information Science, College of Applied Sciences and Technology. *Program Basis:* Quarter. *Minimum Degree Requirements:* 45 credit hours including 24 hours of integrated educational media-library science courses tailored to meet the specific needs of individual students. *Faculty:* 9, 8, 0. *Graduates:* 3m, 21w. (Program to be terminated in August.)

Butler University. Indianapolis, IN 46208. Henriette Kaplan, Prof., Chair, Audiovisual and Library Science Dept., College of Education. *Program Basis:* Semester. *Minimum Degree Requirements:* 39 credit hours including 24 in media. *Faculty:* 3, 1, 0. *Graduates:* (including 2 foreign nationals) 3m, 8w. (Program has been discontinued.)

Indiana State University. Terre Haute, IN 47809. James E. Thompson, Prof., Chair, Dept. of Educational Foundations and Media Technology. *Program Basis:* Semester. *Minimum Degree Requirements:* 32 credit hours including 18 in media; thesis optional. *Faculty:* 10, 9, 1. *Graduates:* (including 9 foreign nationals) 9m, 3w. (School also offers a six-year specialist degree program in instructional technology.)

Indiana University. Bloomington, IN 47405. Dennis Pett, Prof., Chair, Dept. of Instructional Systems Technology (IST), School of Education. *Program Basis:* Semester. *Minimum Degree Requirements:* 37 credit hours including 18 in IST; thesis optional. *Faculty:* 13, 16, 0. *Graduates:* (including 31 foreign nationals) 40m, 37w. (School also offers a six-year specialist degree program in instructional technology plus a certificate in training and development.)

Purdue University. West Lafayette, IN 47907. James Russell, Prof., Educational Computing and Instructional Development, Dept. of Education. *Program Basis:* Semester. *Minimum Degree Requirements:* 30 credit hours including 20 in media; thesis optional. *Faculty:* 5, 4, 1. *Graduates:* 4m, 10w. (School also offers a six-year specialist degree program in instructional technology.)

Purdue University-Calumet. Hammond, IN 46323. John R. Billard, Assoc. Prof., Coord., Educational Media Program, Dept. of Education. *Program Basis:* Semester. *Minimum Degree Requirements:* 33 credit hours including 24 in media; thesis optional. *Faculty:* 2, 2, 2. *Graduates:* 5m, 15w.

IOWA

Clarke College. Dubuque, IA 52001. Judith Decker, Asst. Prof., Coord., Computer Applications in Education. *Program Basis:* Semester. *Minimum Degree Requirements:* 15-18 credit hours in computer applications; 9-12 hours in education; and 3-6 hours of electives. *Faculty:* 2¼, 1, 3. *Graduates:* 4m, 6w.

Iowa State University. Ames, IA 50011. Roger Volker, Prof., Professional Studies, College of Education. *Program Basis:* Semester. *Minimum Degree Requirements:* 30 credit hours including 15 in media; thesis optional. *Faculty:* 5, 6, 1. *Graduates:* (including 2 foreign nationals) 4m, 4w.

University of Iowa. Iowa City, IA 52242. Lowell A. Schoer, Prof., Chair, Instructional Design and Technology, College of education. *Program Basis:* Semester. *Minimum Degree Requirements:* 35 credit hours with or without thesis. *Faculty:* 6, 4, 0. *Graduates:* 3m, 9w. (School also offers a six-year specialist degree program in instructional technology.)

University of Northern Iowa. Cedar Falls, IA 50614. Robert R. Hardman, Prof. and Dir. of Educational Media, Dept. of Curriculum and Instruction. *Program Basis:* Semester.

Minimum Degree Requirements: For the Educational Media Degree—38 credit hours including 34 in media; thesis optional; for the Communications Media Degree—38 credit hours including 32 in media; thesis optional. *Faculty:* 8, 4, 0. *Graduates:* 2m, 7w in media; 2m, 5w in communications.

KANSAS

Kansas State University. Manhattan, KS 66506. John A. Hortin, Prof., Dept. of Curriculum and Instruction, College of Education. *Program Basis:* Semester. *Minimum Degree Requirements:* 30 credit hours including 21 in media; thesis optional. *Faculty:* 4, 4, 0. *Graduates:* (including 6 foreign nationals) 8m, 30w. (School offers a six-year supervisory certification program in instructional technology.)

University of Kansas. Lawrence, KS 66045. Walter S. Smith, Assoc. Prof., Chair, Curriculum and Instruction Dept., School of Education. *Program Basis:* Semester. *Minimum Degree Requirements:* 30 credit hours including 10 in media; thesis optional. *Faculty:* 0, 1, 1. *Graduates:* (including 1 foreign national) 1m, 3w. (School also offers a six-year specialist degree program in instructional technology.)

KENTUCKY

University of Kentucky. Lexington, KY 40506. Gary Anglin, Asst. Prof., Instructional Design, Dept. of Curriculum and Instruction, College of Education. *Program Basis:* Semester. *Minimum Degree Requirements:* 36 credit hours including 24 in instructional design and media; no thesis required. *Faculty:* 2, 2, 1. *Graduates:* 4m, 14w. [1984 data]

University of Louisville. Louisville, KY 40292. G. Keith Bayne, Jack C. Morgan, and Stanley I. Mour, Profs., Coords., Instructional Systems Technology Program, School of Education. *Program Basis:* Semester. *Minimum Degree Requirements:* 30 credit hours including 12 in instructional systems development; thesis optional. *Faculty:* 2, 2, 2. *Graduates:* 5m, 7w. (School offers a six-year specialist degree program in instructional technology.)

Western Kentucky University. Bowling Green, KY 42101. Robert C. Smith, Assoc. Prof., LME Coord., Dept. of Teacher Education. *Program Basis:* Semester. *Minimum Degree Requirements:* 33 credit hours including 21 in media; thesis optional. *Faculty:* 6, 3, 2. *Graduates:* 1m, 14w. (School offers a six-year specialist degree program in instructional technology.)

LOUISIANA

Louisiana State University. Baton Rouge, LA 70803. William F. Grady, Prof., Coord., Div. of Educational Technology, Administrative and Foundational Services, College of Education. *Program Basis:* Semester. *Minimum Degree Requirements:* 36 credit hours including 15 in media; thesis not required. *Faculty:* 7, 5, 2. *Graduates:* (including 2 foreign nationals) 7m, 15w. (School also offers a six-year specialist degree program in instructional technology.)

McNeese State University. Lake Charles, LA 70609. Elmer H. Wagner, Prof., Head, Dept. of Educational Technology. *Program Basis:* Semester. *Minimum Degree Requirements:* 30 credit hours including 15 in media; thesis not required. *Faculty:* 4, 2, 1. *Graduates:* 1m, 10w.

Northeast Louisiana University. Monroe, LA 71209. Bill L. Perry, Assoc. Prof., Dir., Educational Media Center, College of Education. *Program Basis:* Semester. *Minimum Degree Requirements:* 30 credit hours including 18 in media; thesis optional. *Faculty:* 1, 1, 0. *Graduates:* 5m, 14w.

Northwestern State University. Natchitoches, LA 71457. Dan Carr, Prof., Head, Div. of Educational Media, Dept. of Education. *Program Basis:* Semester. *Minimum Degree Requirements:* 33 credit hours including 15 in media; thesis optional. *Faculty:* 0, 2, 4. *Graduates:* 2m, 7w. (School also offers a six-year specialist degree program in instructional technology.)

Southern University. Baton Rouge, LA 70813. Arnold Crump, Asst. Prof., Chair, Dept. of Mass Communications, College of Arts and Humanities. *Program Basis:* Semester. *Minimum Degree Requirements:* 30 credit hours including 21 in mass communications and instructional technology; thesis optional. *Faculty:* 4, 3, 4. *Graduates:* (including 17 foreign nationals) 17m, 9w.

MARYLAND

The Johns Hopkins University. Baltimore, MD 21218. Dianne Tobin, Asst. Prof., Coord., Technology Training Program, Div. of Education. *Program Basis:* Semester. *Minimum Degree Requirements:* 33 credit hours, 12 required courses with remaining courses being electives in several broad areas. *Faculty:* 4, 0, 0. *Graduates:* 2m, 3w. (School also offers the equivalent of a six-year specialist degree program in instructional technology.)

Towson State University. Baltimore, MD 21204. Paul E. Jones, Asst. Prof., Chair, Dept. of Instructional Technology. *Program Basis:* Semester. *Minimum Degree Requirements:* 36 credits including 36 in media; thesis optional. *Faculty:* 5, 4, 0. *Graduates:* 3m, 13w.

University of Maryland. College Park, MD 20742. Claude E. Walston, Dean and Prof., College of Library and Information Services. *Program Basis:* Semester. *Minimum Degree Requirements:* 36 credit hours including majors in library media; no thesis required. *Faculty:* 8, 8, 0. *Graduates:* (including 4 foreign nationals) 97.

University of Maryland-Baltimore County. Catonsville, MD 21228. J. Marvin Cook, Assoc. Prof., Coord., Instructional Systems Development Program, Dept. of Education. *Program Basis:* Semester. *Minimum Degree Requirements:* 30 credit hours including 30 hours in systems development. *Faculty:* 6, 5, 3. *Graduates:* (including 11 foreign nationals) 9m, 16w.

Western Maryland College. Westminster, MD 21157. Margaret W. Denman-West, Assoc. Prof., Coord., Media/Library Science, Dept. of Education. *Program Basis:* Semester. *Minimum Degree Requirements:* 33 credit hours including 18 in media; thesis optional. *Faculty:* 2, 1, 2. *Graduates:* 0m, 4w.

MASSACHUSETTS

Boston College. Chestnut Hill, MA 02167. Walter M. Haney, Assoc. Prof., Dir., Educational Technology Program, Dept. of Education, Graduate School of Arts and Sciences. *Program Basis:* Semester. *Minimum Degree Requirements:* 36 credit hours including 30 in educational technology/media; thesis optional. *Faculty:* 4, 3, 1. *Graduates:* 3m, 3w. (School offers a certificate of advanced education studies degree [30 credit hours] beyond M.Ed. and a special fifth year M.Ed. program in instructional technology for Boston College undergraduates.)

Boston University. Boston, MA 02215. Gaylen B. Kelley, Prof., Program Dir. of Educational Media and Technology, Div. of Instructional Development, School of Education. *Program Basis:* Semester. *Minimum Degree Requirements:* 32 credit hours; thesis optional. *Faculty:* 7, 3, 4. *Graduates:* (including 3 foreign nationals) 11m, 15w. (School also offers a six-year specialist degree program in instructional technology.)

Bridgewater State College. Bridgewater, MA 02324. Alan Lander, Prof., Chair, Dept. of Media and Librarianship. *Program Basis:* Semester. *Minimum Degree Requirements:* 33 credit hours including 27 in media; thesis optional. *Faculty:* 4, 4, 0. *Graduates:* 6m, 8w.

Fitchburg State College. Fitchburg, MA 01420. Lee DeNike and David Ryder, Assoc. Profs., Communications/Media Dept. *Program Basis:* Semester. *Minimum Degree Requirements:* 36 credit hours of which all 36 hours are in media; thesis optional. *Faculty:* 4, 0, 3. *Graduates:* 2m, 1w.

Harvard University. Cambridge, MA 02138. Katherine K. Merseth, Prof., Coord., Interactive Technology in Education, Graduate School of Education. *Program Basis:* Semester. *Minimum Degree Requirements:* 32 credit hours including 16 in interactive technology; thesis optional. *Faculty:* 4, 4, 0. *Graduates:* 4m, 17w.

University of Massachusetts. Amherst, MA 01003. Patrick J. Sullivan, Prof., Member, Media Program, School of Education. *Program Basis:* Semester. *Minimum Degree Requirements:* 33 credit hours including 18 in media; thesis optional. *Faculty:* 1, 1, 1. *Graduates:* (including 1 foreign national) 2m, 3w.

MICHIGAN

Central Michigan University. Mt. Pleasant, MI 48859. John F. Jacobs, Prof., Chair, Library/Media, Div. of Teacher Education and Professional Development. *Program Basis:* Semester. *Minimum Degree Requirements:* 30 credit hours including 6 in media; thesis optional. *Faculty:* 2, 0, 3. *Graduates:* 1m, 7w.

Michigan State University. East Lansing, MI 48824. Joe L. Byers, Prof., Dir., Educational Systems Development, College of Education. *Program Basis:* Quarter. *Minimum Degree Requirements:* 45 credit hours with emphases in instructional design, computer-based education and media; thesis optional. *Faculty:* 7, 6, 4. *Graduates:* (including 6 foreign nationals) 14m, 15w. (School also offers a six-year specialist degree program in instructional technology.)

University of Michigan. Ann Arbor, MI 48109. Warren G. Palmer, Assoc. Prof., Dir., Office of Educational Communication, Div. of Curriculum and Instruction, School of Education. *Program Basis:* Trimester. *Minimum Degree Requirements:* 30 credit hours including 10 hours in media; thesis optional. *Faculty:* 1, 0, 1. *Graduates:* (including 1 foreign national) 2m, 3w. [1984 data]

Wayne State University. Detroit, MI 48212. John W. Childs, Prof., Instructional Technology Program, Area Coord., Div. of Administrative and Organizational Studies, College of Education. *Program Basis:* Semester. *Minimum Degree Requirements:* 30 credit hours including 21 in media; project required. *Faculty:* 3, 1, 7. *Graduates:* (including 5 foreign nationals) 10m, 13w. (School also offers a six-year specialist degree program in instructional technology.)

MINNESOTA

Mankato State University. Mankato, MN 56001. Frank Birmingham, Prof., Chair, Library Media Education. *Program Basis:* Quarter. *Minimum Degree Requirements:* 45 credit hours including 27 in media. *Faculty:* 4, 2, 0. *Graduates:* 2m, 5w. (School also offers a six-year specialist degree program in library media.)

St. Cloud State University. St. Cloud, MN 56301. John Berling, Prof., Dir., Center for Information Media, College of Education. *Program Basis:* Quarter. *Minimum Degree Requirements:* 51 credit hours including 33 in media; nonthesis, but research paper required.

Faculty: 6, 3, 0. *Graduates:* (including 1 foreign national) 1m, 8w. (School also offers a six-year specialist degree program in instructional technology.)

University of Minnesota. Minneapolis, MN 55455. Robert D. Tennyson, Prof., Dir., Instructional Systems. *Program Basis:* Quarter. *Minimum Degree Requirements:* 44 credit hours including 22 in instructional systems. *Faculty:* 8, 8, 1. *Graduates:* (including 1 foreign national) 8m, 92. (School also offers a six-year specialist degree program in instructional technology.)

MISSISSIPPI

Jackson State University. Jackson, MS 39217. Elayne Hayes-Anthony, Asst. Prof., Chair, Program of Educational Technology, School of Liberal Studies. *Program Basis:* Semester. *Minimum Degree Requirements:* 36 credit hours including 24 in media; thesis optional. *Faculty:* 1, 1, 1. *Graduates:* (including 1 foreign national) 3m, 3w.

University of Mississippi. University, MS 38677. Burl Hunt, Prof. of Educational Media, School of Education. *Program Basis:* Semester. *Minimum Degree Requirements:* 30 credit hours including 15 in media; thesis optional. *Faculty:* 2, 1, 0. *Graduates:* 4m, 5w. (School also offers a six-year specialist degree program in instructional technology.)

University of Southern Mississippi. Hattiesburg, MS 39406-5146. Onva K. Boshears, Jr., Prof., Dean, School of Library Service. *Program Basis:* Semester. *Minimum Degree Requirements:* 30 credit hours including 15 hours in media for M.Ed. degree and 39 credit hours including 15 hours in media for the M.L.S. degree; thesis or comprehensive required in both programs. *Faculty:* 12, 8, 2. *Graduates:* (including 2 foreign nationals) 5m, 32w for both programs.

MISSOURI

Central Missouri State University. Warrensburg, MO 64093. Kenneth Brookens, Assoc. Prof., Coord., Instructional Technology, Dept. of Library Science & Instructional Technology. *Program Basis:* Semester. *Minimum Degree Requirements:* 32 credit hours with emphasis on instructional technology, curriculum, and instruction; thesis optional. *Faculty:* 1, 1, 0. *Graduates:* 0m, 1w. (School also offers a six-year specialist degree program in learning resources.)

Northwest Missouri State University. Maryville, MO 64468. Phillip J. Heeler, Prof., Dir., School Computer Studies Program, Dept. of Computer Science. *Program Basis:* Semester. *Minimum Degree Requirements:* 32 credit hours including 20 hours of core computer courses. (Program is primarily a summer program.) *Faculty:* 4, 0, 0. *Graduates:* 3m, 6w.

University of Missouri-Columbia. Columbia, MO 65211. A. T. Dunathan, Prof., Area Coord., Curriculum and Instruction Dept., College of Education. *Program Basis:* Semester. *Minimum Degree Requirements:* 32 credit hours including 16 in media; thesis optional. *Faculty:* 2, 3, 2. *Graduates:* (including 2 foreign nationals) 2m, 4w. (School also offers a six-year specialist degree program in instructional technology.)

University of Missouri-St. Louis. St. Louis, MO 63121. Donald R. Greer, Assoc. Prof., Coord. of Educational Technology, Dept. of Administration, Foundations, and Secondary Education, School of Education. *Program Basis:* Semester. *Minimum Degree Requirements:* 32 credit hours including 18 in media. *Faculty:* 2, 1, ⅔. *Graduates:* 2m, 2w.

Webster University. St. Louis, MO 63119. Paul Steinman, Prof. and Assoc. Dean, Graduate Studies and Instructional Technology. *Program Basis:* Semester. *Minimum*

Degree Requirements: 33 credit hours including 24 in media; no thesis required. *Faculty:* 4, 1, 1. *Graduates:* (including 7 foreign nationals) 9m, 20w.

MONTANA

University of Montana. Missoula, MT 59812. Geneva T. Van Horne, Prof. of Library/ Media, School of Education. *Program Basis:* Quarter. *Minimum Degree Requirements:* 54 credit hours including 32 in media; thesis optional. *Faculty:* 2, 1, 0. *Graduates:* 3m, 6w.

NEBRASKA

Kearney State College. Kearney, NE 68847. Roger Hanson, Assoc. Prof., Coord., Media Program, Dept. of Educational Administration. *Program Basis:* Semester. *Minimum Degree Requirements:* 36 credit hours including 15 in media; thesis optional. (Since this is a cooperative program, the University of Northern Colorado provides the 15 hours required for media and the faculty.) *Graduates:* 1m, 1w. [1984 data]

University of Nebraska-Lincoln. Lincoln, NE 68588. R. Scott Grabinger, Asst. Prof., Educational Administration Dept., Teachers College. *Program Basis:* Semester. *Minimum Degree Requirements:* 36 credit hours including 24 in media; thesis optional. *Faculty:* 1, 1½, 0. *Graduates:* 3m, 2w. (School also offers a six-year specialist degree program in instructional technology.)

University of Nebraska-Omaha. Omaha, NE 68182. Verne Haselwood, Prof., Educational Media Program in Teacher Education. *Program Basis:* Semester. *Minimum Degree Requirements:* 36 credit hours including 27 in media; thesis optional. *Faculty:* 2, 3, 0. *Graduates:* 2m, 10w.

NEVADA

University of Nevada. Reno, NV 89557. Paul M. Hollingsworth, Prof., Chair, Curriculum and Instruction, College of Education. *Program Basis:* Semester. *Minimum Degree Requirements:* 36 credit hours including 20 or more in media; thesis optional. *Faculty:* 15, 15, 0. *Graduates:* 2m, 1w. (School also offers a six-year specialist degree program in instructional technology.)

NEW JERSEY

Glassboro State College. Glassboro, NJ 08028. Rinehart Potts, Asst. Prof., Coord. of Graduate Studies, Acting Program Advisor for School and Public Librarianship, Dept. of Curriculum and Instruction in Secondary Education. *Program Basis:* Semester. *Minimum Degree Requirements:* 36 credit hours including 12 hours in media; thesis or project required. *Faculty:* 2, 1, 2. *Graduates:* 2m, 8w.

Jersey City State College. Jersey City, NJ 07305. Mildred Goodwin, Prof., Chair, Div. of Administration, Curriculum and Instruction. *Program Basis:* Semester. *Minimum Degree Requirements:* 45 credit hours including 36 in media; thesis optional. *Faculty:* 7, 5, 2. *Graduates:* 2m, 2w.

Montclair State College. Upper Montclair, NJ 07043. Grosvenor C. Rust, Assoc. Prof., Graduate Media Advisor, Dept. of Media, Technology, and Educational Leadership. *Program Basis:* Semester. *Minimum Degree Requirements:* 39 credit hours including 15 hours in media; thesis optional. (Graduate Specialist Certification Program requires 30-33 media hours.) *Faculty:* 2, 1, 0. *Graduates:* (including 2 foreign nationals) 4m, 7w.

Rutgers-The State University of New Jersey. New Brunswick, NJ 08903. Patricia G. Reeling, Assoc. Prof., Chair, Library and Information Studies, School of Communication, Information and Library Studies. *Program Basis:* Semester. *Minimum Degree Requirements:* 36 credit hours in which the hours for media vary for individual students; thesis optional. *Faculty:* 20, 17, 0. *Graduates:* (including 4 foreign nationals) 18m, 96w.

Seton Hall University. South Orange, NJ 07079. Rosemary W. Skeele, Asst. Prof., Dir., Graduate Program in Educational Media, Div. of Educational Media. *Program Basis:* Semester. *Minimum Program Requirements:* 36 credit hours including 21 in media; mediated project instead of thesis. *Faculty:* 3, 1, 0. *Graduates:* 9m, 16w. (School also offers a six-year specialist degree program in instructional technology.)

William Paterson College. Wayne, NJ 07470. Lina Walter, Prof., Chair, Program in Library/Media, Elementary Education Dept., School of Education. *Program Basis:* Semester. *Minimum Degree Requirements:* 30 credit hours in media including research. *Faculty:* 0, 1, 4. *Graduates:* 4m, 13w. (Graduate program also offers certification for educational media specialists.)

NEW MEXICO

Eastern New Mexico University. Portales, NM 88130. Barbara Black, Asst. Prof., Dept. of Library Media Education, School of Education. *Program Basis:* Semester. *Minimum Degree Requirements:* 32 credit hours including 6 in media and 18 in library science; thesis optional. *Faculty:* 1, 1, 0. *Graduates:* 0m, 2w. (Program presently includes media courses for certification purposes only.)

University of New Mexico. Albuquerque, NM 87131. Guy Watson, Assoc. Prof., Dir., Learning Materials Laboratory, Educational Foundations Dept., College of Education. *Program Basis:* Semester. *Minimum Degree Requirements:* 32 credit hours including 24 in media; thesis optional. *Faculty:* 4, 2, 0. *Graduates:* 2m, 2w.

NEW YORK

Fordham University. Bronx, NY 10458. Trisha Curran, Assoc. Prof., Chair, Communication Dept. *Program Basis:* Semester. *Minimum Degree Requirements:* 30 credit hours including 12 in media; thesis optional. *Faculty:* 11, 9, 1. *Graduates:* (including 4 foreign nationals) 9m, 12w.

Ithaca College. Ithaca, NY 14850. Palmer Dyer, Prof., Chair, Graduate Communications, School of Communications. *Program Basis:* Semester. *Minimum Degree Requirements:* 30 credit hours including 24 in media; thesis or project required. *Faculty:* 5, 5, 0. *Graduates:* 9m, 9w.

The New School for Social Research. New York, NY 10011. Peter L. Haratonik, Dir., Media Studies Program. *Program Basis:* Semester. *Minimum Degree Requirements:* 36 credit hours including all 36 hours in media; thesis encouraged. *Faculty:* 3, 1, 10. *Graduates:* (including 3 foreign nationals) 17m, 19w.

New York Institute of Technology. Old Westbury, NY 11568. Felisa B. Kaplan, Assoc. Prof., Assoc. Dir., Media and Arts. *Program Basis:* Semester. *Minimum Degree Requirements:* 32 credit hours including 26 in media; thesis optional. *Faculty:* 14, 8, 9. *Graduates:* (including 1 foreign national) 13m, 11w.

New York University. New York, NY 10003. Francine Shuchat-Shaw, Assoc. Prof., Educational Communication and Technology, School of Education. *Program Basis:* Semester. *Minimum Degree Requirements:* 36 credit hours including 24 in media; terminal experience required; thesis optional. *Faculty:* 2, 2. *Graduates:* (including 4 foreign nationals) 4m, 11w. (School also offers an 18-point certificate and a six-year specialist certificate program in instructional technology.)

New York University-Tisch School of Arts. New York, NY 10003. Red Burns, Prof., Chair, The Interactive Telecommunications Program. *Program Basis:* Semester. *Minimum Degree Requirements:* 60 credit hours (in this two-year program) which include interactive telecommunications courses; thesis required. *Faculty:* 3, 2, 5. *Graduates:* (including 2 foreign nationals) 6m, 11w.

Rochester Institute of Technology. Rochester, NY 14623. Clint Wallington, Prof., Dir. of the Depts. of Instructional Technology and Career and Human Resource Development, College of Applied Science and Technology. *Program Basis:* Quarter. *Minimum Degree Requirements:* 48 credit hours including an instructional development project (noncredit). *Faculty:* 8½, 0, 1. *Graduates:* (including 1 foreign national) 3m, 4w.

St. John's University. Jamaica, NY 11439. Mildred Lowe, Assoc. Prof., Dir., Div. of Library and Information Science. *Program Basis:* Semester. *Minimum Degree Requirements:* 36 credit hours including 21 in media; no thesis required. *Faculty:* 8, 5, 0. *Graduates:* (including 4 foreign nationals) 9m, 34w. (School also offers a six-year specialist program in instructional technology on an individual basis.)

State University College at Oswego. Oswego, NY 13126. Richard D. Hubbard, Prof. and Coord. of the Unified Master's Track Program in Educational Communications, Dept. of Secondary Education. *Program Basis:* Semester. *Minimum Degree Requirements:* 36 credit hours including 18 hours in media for the nonthesis progra; 30 credit hours including 12 hours in media for the thesis program. *Faculty:* 2, 1, 0. *Graduates:* (including 2 foreign nationals) 3m, 2w.

State University College of Arts and Science. Potsdam, NY 13676. Norman Licht, Prof., Coord., Instructional Technology and Media Management, Dept. of Graduate Programs, School of Professional Studies. *Program Basis:* Semester. *Minimum Degree Requirements:* 33 credit hours including emphasis in instructional technology, media and computer education; thesis optional. *Faculty:* 6, 0, 0. *Graduates:* (including 3 foreign nationals) 2m, 3w.

State University of New York at Albany. Albany, NY 12222. Clarence O. Bergeson, Prof., Coord., Educational Communication. *Program Basis:* Semester. *Minimum Degree Requirements:* 30 credit hours including 15 in media; thesis optional. *Faculty:* 3, 3, 2. *Graduates:* (including 3 foreign nationals) 12m, 12w. (School also offers a six-year specialist degree program in instructional technology.)

State University of New York-Buffalo. Buffalo, NY 14260. George S. Bobinski, Dean, School of Information and Library Studies. *Program Basis:* Semester. *Minimum Degree Requirements:* 36 credit hours; thesis optional. *Faculty:* 9, 7, 0. *Graduates:* 28m, 56w. (School also offers a six-year specialist degree program in instructional technology.)

State University of New York-Buffalo. Buffalo, NY 14260. Taher Razik, Prof., Instructional Communications, Dept. of Education, Organization, and Policy, Faculty of Educational Studies. *Program Basis:* Semester. *Minimum Degree Requirements:* 33 credit hours including 21 hours in instructional communications; thesis or project required; comprehensive examination. *Faculty:* 3, 3, 0. *Graduates:* 3m, 3w. (School also offers a six-year specialist degree program in instructional technology.)

State University of New York-Stony Brook. Stony Brook, NY 11794. Thomas T. Liao, Prof., Dir., Dept. of Technology and Society. *Program Basis:* Semester. *Minimum Degree Requirements:* 30 credit hours with emphases in technology systems management and educational computer use. *Faculty:* 6, 0, 0. *Graduates:* (including 4 foreign nationals) 29m, 18w.

Syracuse University. Syracuse, NY 13210. Philip Doughty, Assoc. Prof., Chair, Instructional Design, Development and Evaluation Program, School of Education. *Program Basis:* Semester. *Minimum Degree Requirements:* 30 credit hours. *Faculty:* 6, 7, 5. *Graduates:* (including 7 foreign nationals) 8m, 9w. (School also offers a six-year specialist degree program in instructional technology.)

Teachers College, Columbia University. New York, NY 10027. Robert E. Holloway, Assoc. Prof., Dept. of Communication, Computing, and Technology in Education. *Program Basis:* Semester. *Minimum Degree Requirements:* M.A. — 32 credit hours including 18 in media, core courses in communication and computing, thesis optional; M.A. Media Specialist (Certification) — 36 credit hours, core in School of Library Service, internship; research paper. *Faculty:* 4, 2, 1. *Graduates:* (including 3 foreign nationals) 7m, 9w.

NORTH CAROLINA

Appalachian State University. Boone, NC 28608. James S. Healey, Prof., Chair, Dept. of Library/Media Studies, College of Education. *Program Basis:* Semester. *Minimum Degree Requirements:* 42 credit hours including selected courses in media; thesis optional. *Faculty:* 6, 0, 0. *Graduates:* (including 1 foreign national) 7m, 20w.

East Carolina University. Greenville, NC 27834. Emily S. Boyce, Prof., Chair, Dept. of Library Science. *Program Basis:* Semester. *Minimum Degree Requirements:* 30 semester hours, 18 hours in Library Science, 9 hours in media, 3 hours in electives. *Faculty:* 10, 7, 0. *Graduates:* 3m, 14w. (School also offers a six-year specialist degree program in instructional technology.)

North Carolina A&T State University. Greensboro, NC 27411. Tommie M. Young, Prof., Chair, Dept. of Educational Media. *Program Basis:* Semester. *Minimum Degree Requirements:* 30 credit hours including 18 in media; thesis optional. *Faculty:* 3, 2, 0. *Graduates:* (including 2 foreign nationals) 14m, 18w.

North Carolina Central University. Durham, NC 27707. Marvin E. Duncan, Prof., Dir., Learning Resources Center, Dept. of Education. *Program Basis:* Semester. *Minimum Degree Requirements:* 33 credit hours including 21 in media; thesis or project required. *Faculty:* 3, 1, 0. *Graduates:* (including 7 foreign nationals) 9m, 15w.

University of North Carolina. Chapel Hill, NC 27514. Ralph E. Wileman, Prof., Div. of Curriculum and Instruction. *Program Basis:* Semester. *Minimum Degree Requirements:* 36 credit hours including 21 in media; thesis optional. *Faculty:* 2½, 3, 1. *Graduates:* 4m, 5w.

University of North Carolina-Greensboro. Greensboro, NC 27412-5001. David H. Jonassen, Assoc. Prof., Library Science/Educational Technology Dept. *Program Basis:* Semester. *Minimum Degree Requirements:* 36 credit hours for supervision and instructional development tracks; comprehensive examination and instructional development project required. *Faculty:* 2, 2, 0. *Graduates:* New program.

Western Carolina University. Cullowhee, NC 28723. Paul S. Flynn, Prof., Coord., Dept. of Administration, Curriculum, and Instruction. *Program Basis:* Semester. *Minimum Degree Requirements:* 30 credit hours including 18 in media. *Faculty:* 5, 4, 0. *Graduates:* Data not available.

OHIO

Bowling Green State University. Bowling Green, OH 43403. Fred E. Williams, Prof., Coord. of Graduate Studies, Dept. of Library and Educational Media. *Program Basis:* Semester. *Minimum Degree Requirements:* 33 credit hours including 22 in media; thesis optional. *Faculty:* 4, 3, 0. *Graduates:* 5m, 5w.

John Carroll University. University Heights, OH 44118. James L. Dague, Assoc. Prof., Coord. of Educational Media, Education Dept. *Program Basis:* Semester. *Minimum Degree Requirements:* 30 credit hours including 15 in media; comprehensive examination required. *Faculty:* 8, 6, 1. *Graduates:* 0m, 4w.

Kent State University. Kent, OH 44242. Barbara Martin, Asst. Prof., Program contact person for Educational Technology Program. *Program Basis:* Semester. *Minimum Degree Requirements:* 32 credit hours including 14-20 hours in instructional development and media depending on type of certification desired, if any. *Faculty:* 5, 3, 5. *Graduates:* 6m, 5w. (School also offers a six-year specialist degree program in instructional technology.)

Miami University. Oxford, OH 45056. Edward F. Newren, Prof., Chair, Dept. of Educational Media, School of Education and Allied Professions. *Program Basis:* Semester. *Minimum Degree Requirements:* 30 credit hours; thesis optional. *Faculty:* 7, 8, 5. *Graduates:* 3m, 7w.

Ohio State University. Columbus, OH 43210. William D. Taylor, Assoc. Prof., Program contact person, Instructional Design and Technology, College of Education. *Program Basis:* Quarter. *Minimum Degree Requirements:* 50 credit hours including an individualized number of hours in media; thesis optional. *Faculty:* 5, 5, 0. *Graduates:* 4m, 13w. (School media certification available.)

Ohio University. Athens, OH 45701. Seldon D. Strother, Assoc. Prof., Dir. of Educational Media, School of Curriculum and Instruction. *Program Basis:* Quarter. *Minimum Degree Requirements:* 52 credit hours including 26 in media; thesis optional. *Faculty:* 1, 2, 0. *Graduates:* (including foreign nationals) 0m, 0w.

University of Toledo. Toledo, OH 43606. Amos C. Patterson, Prof., Chair, Dept. of Educational Technology. *Program Basis:* Quarter. *Minimum Degree Requirements:* 48 credit hours including 36 in media; master's project. *Faculty:* 5, 5, 1. *Graduates:* 9m, 17w. (School also offers a six-year specialist degree program in instructional technology.)

Wright State University. Dayton, OH 45434. Bonnie Mathies, Assoc. Prof., Program Coord., Div. of Library and Communication Science, College of Education and Human Services. *Program Basis:* Quarter. *Minimum Degree Requirements:* 48 credit hours including 30 in media; thesis optional. *Faculty:* 4, 2, 1. *Graduates:* 3m, 16w.

Xavier University. Cincinnati, OH 45207. John Pohlman, Asst. Prof., Dir., Graduate Programs in Educational Media, Dept. of Education. *Program Basis:* Semester. *Minimum Degree Requirements:* 30 credit hours including 18 hours in media; nonthesis but field practicum required. *Faculty:* 2, 1, 0. *Graduates:* 1m, 9w.

OKLAHOMA

Central State University. Edmond, OK 73034. Frances Alsworth, Assoc. Prof., Library Science and Instructional Media, Dept. of Curriculum and Instruction, College of Education. *Program Basis:* Semester. *Minimum Degree Requirements:* 32 credit hours including 15 in media; thesis optional. *Faculty:* 3, 2, 0. *Graduates:* 1m, 3w.

Northeastern State University. Tahlequah, OK 74464. Lorna Lair, Asst. Prof., Coord., Library Media Program, Div. of Psychology, Special Education, and Library Media. *Program Basis:* Semester. *Minimum Degree Requirements:* 32 credit hours including 19 hours in library media; nmonthesis, but project paper or media practicum required. *Faculty:* 3, 1, 2. *Graduates:* 1m, 10w.

Oklahoma State University. Stillwater, OK 74078. Douglas B. Aichele, Prof., Head, Curriculum and Instruction Dept. *Program Basis:* Semester. *Minimum Degree Requirements:* 30 credit hours including 18 in media; thesis optional. *Faculty:* 3, 3, 2. *Graduates:* 2m, 2w. (School also offers six-year specialist degree program in instructional technology.)

Southwestern Oklahoma State University. Weatherford, OK 73096. Jeffry A. Hurt, Asst. Prof., Coord. of Instructional Media, School of Education. *Program Basis:* Semester. *Minimum Degree Requirements:* 32 credit hours including 18 in media; thesis optional. *Faculty:* 2, 2, 0. *Graduates:* 2m, 4w.

University of Oklahoma. Norman, OK 73019. Tillman J. Ragan, Prof., Area Coord., Educational Technology Program Area. *Program Basis:* Semester. *Minimum Degree Requirements:* 32 credit hours including 21 in educational technology; no thesis required. *Faculty:* 3, 2, 4. *Graduates:* 2m, 3w.

OREGON

Oregon State University. Corvallis, OR 97331. Les D. Streit, Asst. Prof., Dept. of Educational Foundations, School of Education. *Program Basis:* Quarter. *Minimum Degree Requirements:* 45 credit hours including 21 in media; thesis optional. *Faculty:* 3, 3, 1. *Graduates:* 2m, 3w.

Portland State University. Portland, OR 97207. Joyce Petrie, Prof., Coord., Educational Media, School of Education. *Program Basis:* Quarter. *Minimum Degree Requirements:* 45 credit hours including 36 hours in media; thesis optional. *Faculty:* 6, 2, 2. *Graduates:* (including 2 foreign nationals) 15m, 22w.

University of Oregon. Eugene, OR 97403. Gary W. Ferrington, Coord., Instructional Technology, Teacher Education, College of Education. *Program Basis:* Quarter. *Minimum Degree Requirements:* 45 credit hours including 30 hours in media; thesis, internship, or field study. *Faculty:* 5, 4, 0. *Graduates:* (including 3 foreign nationals) 15m, 16w.

Western Oregon State College. Monmouth, OR 97361. Richard C. Forcier, Prof., Dir., Div. of Educational Communications and Technology, Dept. of Educational Foundations. *Program Basis:* Quarter. *Minimum Degree Requirements:* 45 credit hours including 36 in media; thesis optional. *Faculty:* 6, 5, 1. *Graduates:* 4m, 8w. A joint program is currently being conducted between Oregon State University and Western Oregon State College. (Schools also offer a six-year specialist degree program in instructional technology.)

PENNSYLVANIA

Clarion University of Pennsylvania. Clarion, PA 16214. Allan D. Larson, Prof., Chair, Dept. of Communication. *Program Basis:* Semester. *Minimum Degree Requirements:* 36 credit hours including 27 in media; nonthesis but research design and research study required. *Faculty:* 11, 6, 0. *Graduates:* 7m, 7w.

Edinboro University. Edinboro, PA 16444. Karl E. Nordberg, Assoc. Prof., Dir., Instructional Media Program, Educational Services Div. *Program Basis:* Semester. *Minimum*

Degree Requirements: 30 credit hours including 24 in media; thesis or project required. *Faculty:* 1, 0, 3. *Graduates:* 5m, 5w.

Indiana University of Pennsylvania. Indiana, PA 15701. William E. McCavitt, Assoc. Prof., Chair, Dept. of Communication and Media. *Program Basis:* Semester. *Minimum Degree Requirements:* 30 credit hours including 21 in media; thesis optional. *Faculty:* 10, 5, 0. *Graduates:* (including 3 foreign nationals) 5m, 4w.

Lehigh University. Bethlehem, PA 18015. Leroy J. Tuscher, Prof., Educational Technology Coord., Graduate School of Education. *Program Basis:* Semester. *Minimum Degree Requirements:* 30 credit hours including 6 in media; thesis optional. *Faculty:* 4, 2, 3. *Graduates:* (including 2 foreign nationals) 10m, 11w.

Pennsylvania State University. University Park, PA 16802. Paul W. Welliver, Prof., contact person, Instructional Systems Program, Div. of Curriculum and Instruction. *Program Basis:* Semester. *Minimum Degree Requirements:* 30 credit hours including either a thesis or project paper. *Faculty:* 4, 0, 1. *Graduates:* (including 2 foreign nationals) 3m, 4w.

Shippensburg University. Shippensburg, PA 17257. Stephen G-M. Shenton, Dept. of Communications and Journalism, College of Arts and Sciences. *Program Basis:* Semester. *Minimum Degree Requirements:* 30 credit hours including 18 in media; thesis or project in advanced communication problems. *Faculty:* 10, 4, 6. *Graduates:* 5m, 5w.

Temple University. Philadelphia, PA 19122. Elton Robertson, Prof., Chair, Educational Media Dept. *Program Basis:* Semester. *Minimum Degree Requirements:* 33 credit hours including 24 in media; thesis optional. *Faculty:* 2, 2, 3. *Graduates:* (including 3 foreign nationals) 10m, 2w.

University of Pittsburgh. Pittsburgh, PA 15260. Barbara Seels, Assoc. Prof., Program Dir., Educational Communication and Technology Div. *Program Basis:* Trimester. *Minimum Degree Requirements:* 36 credit hours including 18 in media; thesis optional. *Faculty:* 5, 6, 0. *Graduates:* (including 8 foreign nationals) 13m, 14w.

West Chester University. West Chester, PA 19380. Joseph Spiecker, Prof., Chair, Instructional Media Dept., School of Education. *Program Basis:* Semester. *Minimum Degree Requirements:* 34 credit hours including 28 in media; thesis optional. *Faculty:* 4, 1, 1. *Graduates:* 5m, 8w.

RHODE ISLAND

Rhode Island College. Providence, RI 02908. James E. Davis, Assoc. Prof., Chair, Dept. of Instructional Technology, Curriculum, and Administration. *Program Basis:* Semester. *Minimum Degree Requirements:* 30 credit hours including 21 in instructional technology; thesis optional. *Faculty:* 3, 2, 0. *Graduates:* 5m, 6w. (School also offers a six-year specialist degree program in instructional technology.)

SOUTH CAROLINA

University of South Carolina. Columbia, SC 29208. D. W. Felker, Prof., Chair, Educational Psychology Department. *Program Basis:* Semester. *Minimum Degree Requirements:* 33 credit hours including 3 each in administration, curriculum, and research, 9 in production, and 3 in instructional theory; no thesis required. *Faculty:* 3, 1, 2. *Graduates:* 1m, 1w.

Winthrop College. Rock Hill, SC 29733. George H. Robinson, Assoc. Prof., Educational Media Coord., School of Education. *Program Basis:* Semester. *Minimum Degree Requirements:* 30 credit hours including 12-30 in media depending on media courses a student has had prior to admission to this program; nonthesis. *Faculty:* 2, 0, 2. *Graduates:* (including 1 foreign national) 1m, 10w.

SOUTH DAKOTA

University of South Dakota. Vermillion, SD 57069. Wayne Bruning, Assoc. Prof., Convenor, Library/Media Dept., Div. of Specialized and Administrative Studies, School of Education. *Program Basis:* Semester. *Minimum Degree Requirements:* 32 credit hours including 18 in media; thesis optional. *Faculty:* 3, 3, 1. *Graduates:* 1m, 8w.

TENNESSEE

East Tennessee State University. Johnson City, TN 37614. Rudy Miller, Assoc. Prof. of Instructional Communication, College of Education. *Program Basis:* Semester. *Minimum Degree Requirements:* 36 credit hours including 18 in instructional communication; thesis optional. *Faculty:* 1, 1, 0. *Graduates:* Program being revised.

Memphis State University. Memphis, TN 38152. Rosestelle B. Woolner, Prof., Chair, Dept. of Curriculum and Instruction, College of Education. *Program Basis:* Semester. *Minimum Degree Requirements:* 33 credit hours including 15 in media; thesis optional. *Faculty:* 2, 1, 0. *Graduates:* 5m, 10w. (School also offers a six-year specialist degree program in instructional technology.)

Middle Tennessee State University. Murfreesboro, TN 37132. Ralph L. White, Prof. and Chair, Dept. of Young Education and School Personnel Services. *Program Basis:* Semester. *Minimum School Requirements:* 33 credit hours including 18 in media; no thesis required. *Faculty:* 2, 1, 0. *Graduates:* 3m, 11w. (School also offers a six-year specialist degree program in instructional technology.)

University of Tennessee. Knoxville, TN 37916. Alfred D. Grant, Assoc. Prof., Coord. of Academic Media and Technology Program, Dept. of Curriculum and Instruction, College of Education. *Program Basis:* Quarter. *Minimum Degree Requirements:* 51 credit hours including individualized number of media hours; thesis optional. *Faculty:* 2, 2, 2. *Graduates:* 1m, 1w. (School offers a six-year specialist program in curriculum and instruction with emphasis in instructional technology.)

TEXAS

East Texas State University. Commerce, TX 75428. Inez G. Johnson, Prof., Acting Head, Dept. of Educational Media and Technology. *Program Basis:* Semester. *Minimum Degree Requirements:* 30 credit hours with thesis; 36 nonthesis including 18 in media. *Faculty:* 8, 6, 1. *Graduates:* 11m, 26w.

North Texas State University. Denton, TX 76203-3857. Terry Holcomb, Asst. Prof., Prog. Coord., Educational Foundations, College of Education. *Program Basis:* Semester. *Minimum Degree Requirements:* 36 credit hours including 27 in media and related fields; thesis optional. (The computer-based educational systems program requires 38 credit hours including 17 hours in computer courses.) *Faculty:* 3 media and a "mix" of full-time and part-time interdisciplinary faculty. *Graduates:* 2m, 2w. (Relatively new program.)

Prairie View A&M University. Prairie View, TX 77446. Marion Henry, Prof., Chair, Educational Media and Technology Dept. *Program Basis:* Semester. *Minimum Degree Requirements:* 30 credit hours including 21 in media; thesis required. *Faculty:* 6, 2, 0. *Graduates:* 3m, 10w.

Texas A&M University. College Station, TX 77843. Ronald D. Zellner, Assoc. Prof., Coord., Educational Technology Program, College of Education. *Program Basis:* Semester. *Minimum Degree Requirements:* 37 credit hours including 19 in educational technology; nonthesis. *Faculty:* 4, 2, 2. *Graduates:* 1m, 4w.

Texas Tech University. Lubbock, TX 79409. Bettye Johnson, Assoc. Prof., Dir., Learning Resources Center, College of Education. *Program Basis:* Semester. *Minimum Degree Requirements:* 36 credit hours; nonthesis. *Faculty:* 2, 2, 1. *Graduates:* 0m, 1w.

Texas Woman's University. Denton, TX 76204. Teddy B. Palmore, Assoc. Prof., Coord., Media Programs, College of Education. *Program Basis:* Semester. *Minimum Degree Requirements:* 36 credit hours including tailored media programs for individual students; thesis optional. *Faculty:* 5, 5, 0. *Graduates:* Male students are welcome to all graduate programs, including media. School also offers a Learning Resources Specialist Program leading to a master's degree. (Program being terminated.)

University of Texas. Austin, TX 78712. De Layne Hudspeth, Assoc. Prof., Dept. of Curriculum and Instruction, College of Education. *Program Basis:* Semester. *Minimum Degree Requirements:* 36 credit hours including 18 in media; thesis optional. *Faculty:* 6, 0, 0. *Graduates:* 6m, 9w.

University of Texas, Health Science Center. Dallas, TX 75235. Mike Sheridan, Chair, Instructional Development Programs, Biomedical Communications Dept. *Program Basis:* Semester. *Minimum Degree Requirements:* 30 credit hours including 24 in media; thesis required. *Faculty:* 7, 5, 0. *Graduates:* (including 1 foreign national) 5m, 4w.

UTAH

Brigham Young University. Provo, UT 84602. James W. Dunn, Prof., Chair, Curriculum and Instructional Science Dept. *Program Basis:* Semester. *Minimum Degree Requirements:* 37 including 20 in core; thesis optional. *Faculty:* 13, 13, 0. *Graduates:* (including 1 foreign national) 6m, 6w.

University of Utah. Salt Lake City, UT 84112. L. F. Beatty, Assoc. Prof., Advisor, Education Studies Dept. — Microcomputer/Media Specialty. *Program Basis:* Quarter. *Minimum Degree Requirements:* 50 credit hours including 21 in microcomputer/media; M.A., M.S., and M.Ed. offered; thesis or nonthesis. (Research project required for M.Ed.) *Faculty:* 4, 3, 0. *Graduates:* (including 3 foreign nationals) 8m, 6w.

Utah State University. Logan, UT 84322. Don C. Smellie, Prof., Head, Instructional Technology Dept. *Program Basis:* Quarter. *Minimum Degree Requirements:* 54 credit hours including 45 in media; thesis or practicum encouraged. *Faculty:* 9, 4, 3. *Graduates:* 14m, 9w. (School also offers six-year specialist degree program in instructional technology.)

VIRGINIA

James Madison University. Harrisonburg, VA 22801. Raymond Ramquist, Assoc. Prof., Coord., School Library Program, Dir., Ed. Media Laboratories and Coord. of Library/ Media Services. *Program Basis:* Semester. *Minimum Degree Requirements:* 33 credit hours including 21 hours in media; thesis optional. *Faculty:* 2, 2, 1. *Graduates:* (including 2 foreign nationals) 1m, 8w.

Old Dominion University. Norfolk, VA 23508. Charles Smith, Assoc. Prof., Dir., Learning Resources Center, Dept. of Educational Curriculum, Instruction, and Educational Leadership. *Program Basis:* Semester. *Minimum Degree Requirements:* 33 credit hours including 18 in media; thesis or project encouraged. *Faculty:* 3, 2, 0. *Graduates:* 4m, 6w.

Radford University. Radford, VA 24142. Gary Ellerman, Assoc. Prof., Academic Advisor, Educational Media, Human Services. *Program Basis:* Semester. *Minimum Degree Requirements:* 48 credit hours including 26 in media; thesis optional. *Faculty:* 3, 2, 0. *Graduates:* 2m, 3w.

University of Virginia. Charlottesville, VA 22903. Shirl S. Schiffman, Asst. Prof., Coord., Instructional Technology Program, Dept. of Curriculum and Instruction, Curry School of Education. *Program Basis:* Semester. *Minimum Degree Requirements:* 36 credit hours including 12 in media and computers; thesis optional. *Faculty:* 2, 2, 0. *Graduates:* 1m, 1w. (School also offers a six-year specialist degree program in instructional technology including an internship.)

Virginia Commonwealth University. Richmond, VA 23284. Fred Schneider, Asst. Prof., Core Coord. of Educational Technology, Div. of Teacher Education. *Program Basis:* Semester. *Minimum Degree Requirements:* 36 credit hours including 18 in media plus externships; thesis optional. *Faculty:* 2, 0, 0. *Graduates:* 3m, 12w.

Virginia Polytechnic Institute and State University. Blacksburg, VA 24061. Thomas M. Sherman, Assoc. Prof., Program Area Leader, Science and Technology of Instruction, Learning, and Evaluation, Curriculum and Instruction Division, College of Education. *Program Basis:* Quarter. *Minimum Degree Requirements:* 45 credit hours including 21 in media; thesis optional. *Faculty:* 7, 0, 2. *Graduates:* 2m, 3w.

Virginia State University. Petersburg, VA 23803. Vykuntapathi Thota, Prof., Chair, Dept. of Library Information Science and Instructional Media, School of Education. *Program Basis:* Semester. *Minimum Degree Requirements:* 30 semester hours plus thesis for Master of Science; 36 semester hours plus project for the Master of Education. *Faculty:* 5, 3, 0. *Graduates:* (including 2 foreign nationals) 9m, 15w.

WASHINGTON

Central Washington University. Ellensburg, WA 98926. Lillian Canzler, Assoc. Prof., Dept. of Education. *Program Basis:* Quarter. *Minimum Degree Requirements:* 45 credit hours including 30 in media; thesis optional. *Faculty:* 1, 2, 0. *Graduates:* 2m, 2w. (School has developed a six-year specialist degree program for implementation in instructional technology.)

Eastern Washington University. Cheney, WA 99004. Donald R. Horner, Prof., Computer Science, School of Mathematical Sciences and Technology. *Program Basis:* Quarter. *Minimum Degree Requirements:* 45 credit hours with emphasis in computer science. *Faculty:* 4, 2, 2. *Graduates:* 6m, 2w.

Saint Martin's College. Lacey, WA 23068. Pat McIntyre, Prof., Dir. of Microcomputer Resource Center, Dept. of Education. *Program Basis:* Semester. *Minimum Degree Requirements:* 30 credit hours with emphasis in computer science. *Faculty:* 1, 0, 1. *Graduates:* 4m, 2w.

University of Washington. Seattle, WA 98195. John P. Driscoll, Prof., Acting Head, Dept. of Educational Communication, School of Education. *Program Basis:* Quarter. *Minimum Degree Requirements:* 45 credit hours including 24 in media; thesis optional. *Faculty:* 3, 3, 0. *Graduates:* 3m, 5w.

Washington State University. Pullman, WA 99164-2110. Inga Kromann-Kelly, Prof., Chair, Area of Curriculum and Media, Dept. of Education. *Program Basis:* Semester. *Minimum Degree Requirements:* 30 credit hours including 10 in media; thesis or project required. *Faculty:* 5, 3, 2. *Graduates:* (including 1 foreign national) 3m, 2w.

Western Washington University. Bellingham, WA 98225. Leslie Blackwell, Assoc. Prof., Area Head, Div. of Educational Technology, Dept. of Educational Administration and Foundations. *Program Basis:* Quarter. *Minimum Degree Requirements:* 52 credit hours including 22 in media; thesis optional. *Faculty:* 3, 3, 8. *Graduates:* (including 2 foreign nationals) 5m, 5w.

WEST VIRGINIA

Marshall University. Huntington, WV 25701. Virginia D. Plumley, Prof., Chair, Dept. of Educational Media. *Program Basis:* Semester. *Minimum Degree Requirements:* 36 credit hours including 30 hours in media; thesis optional. *Faculty:,* 3, 5, 0. *Graduates:* 4m, 6w. (School also offers a six-year specialist degree program in instructional technology.)

West Virginia University. Morgantown, WV 26506. Paul De Vore, Prof., Chair, Technology Education Program. *Program Basis:* Semester. *Minimum Degree Requirements:* 36 credit hours including 15 hours in communication technology; thesis optional. *Faculty:* 0, 5, 0. *Graduates:* (including 1 foreign national) 2m, 3w.

WISCONSIN

University of Wisconsin-La Crosse. La Crosse, WI 54601. Clyde L. Greve, Dir., Educational Media Program, College of Education. *Program Basis:* Semester. *Minimum Degree Requirements:* 30 credit hours including 15 in media; thesis optional. *Faculty:,* 3, 0, 0. *Graduates:* 3m, 7w.

University of Wisconsin-Madison. Madison, WI 53706. Ann Becker, Assoc. Prof., Coord., Instructional Media and Educational Technology, Dept. of Curriculum and Instruction, School of Education. *Program Basis:* Semester. *Minimum Degree Requirements:* 32 credit hours including 22 hours in media; thesis or project required. *Faculty:* 3, 3, 2. *Graduates:* (including 2 foreign nationals) 6m, 82. [1984 data]

University of Wisconsin-Milwaukee. Milwaukee, WI 53201. Will Roy, Assoc. Prof., Dept. of Curriculum and Instruction, School of Education. *Program Basis:* Semester. *Minimum Degree Requirements:* 30 credit hours including 12 in media; thesis encouraged. *Faculty:* 2, 1, 0. *Graduates:* 3m, 1w.

University of Wisconsin-River Falls. River Falls, WI 54022. Clifford C. Fortin, Prof., Library Science/Media Education, College of Education. *Program Basis:* Quarter. *Minimum Degree Requirements:* 45 credit hours including 18 hours in media; thesis optional. *Faculty:* 1½, 1, 0. *Graduates:* 1m, 1w.

University of Wisconsin-Stout. Menomonie, WI 54751. David L. Graf, Assoc. Prof., Program Dir., Media Technology Dept. *Program Basis:* Semester. *Minimum Degree Requirements:* 32 credit hours including 15 in media; thesis optional. *Faculty:* 4½, 2, 4. *Graduates:* (including 5 foreign nationals) 10m, 8w.

WYOMING

University of Wyoming. Laramie, WY 82071. James Collins, Prof., Head of Instructional Technology, College of Education. *Program Basis:* Semester. *Minimum Degree Requirements:* 32 credit hours including 24 in media; project or thesis option. (For students pursuing instructional development or media generalist master's degrees, thesis required; for master's degrees in media production, 22 hours of media production required.) *Faculty:* 1, 3, 2. *Graduates:* 1m, 1w.

Part Four

Directory of Funding Sources

Introduction

Media-related projects have often been supported with funding from foundations or from granting agencies within the government or elsewhere.

Although funds from these sources have become much more difficult to obtain because of current economic and government conditions, resources are available to the producer or researcher who has patience and who will work at making enough contacts to find funding sources.

Media professionals should look at their own institutions as appropriate places to start a search for funding. Most educational and training organizations have funding offices who specialize in assisting the producer with such a search for support.

An additional place to begin a search is to contact some of the organizations listed in the following "Sources of Information" portion of the *Yearbook*.

Foundations

Foundations listed in this section of the *Yearbook* were selected after all foundations listed in the 1984 edition were sent written descriptions and invited to edit and/or change the listings to meet 1985 conditions. Other entries were selected from readings and other sources available to media professionals.

Foundations are listed alphabetically according to the name of the organization or the last name of the individual for which the foundation is named. Necessary contact information is included in the individual listings.

Academy of Motion Picture Arts and Sciences Foundation. 8949 Wilshire Blvd., Beverly Hills, CA 90211. (213) 278-8990. James M. Roberts, Exec. Dir. *Grants Distribution:* National. *Media Grants:* Scholarships to encourage students interested in creative and technological cinematic developments; cooperates with American Film Institute and Society of Motion Picture and Television Engineers in administering young filmmaker internship programs. No direct grants are given with the exception of cash grants to winners of annual Student Film Awards.

American Council of Learned Societies (ACLS). 228 E. 45th St., New York, NY 10017. (212) 697-1505. John William Ward, Pres. *Grants Distribution:* National. *Chief Interests:* Promotes postdoctoral research in humanities and humanistic aspects of the social sciences. Funds approximately 120 individuals doing research each year.

The Annenberg/CPB Project. 1111 16th St. NW, Washington, DC 20036. (202) 955-5251. A fifteen-year, $150 million dollar project will provide funds to develop college-level materials and to demonstrate use of telecommunications systems to enhance higher education. Write to above address for further information, application, formats, and guidelines.

Apple Education Affairs. 20525 Mariana Ave., Cupertino, CA 95014. (408) 973-2105. *Grants Distribution:* National. *Chief Interests:* A corporate educational contributions group established in 1979 by Apple Computer, Inc., to support and develop new methods of learning through innovative use of small computers. *Media Grants:* For specific project in response to guidelines. Contact for current guidelines. Grants consist primarily of hardware equipment for computer-based projects.

The Asia Foundation. Box 3223, 550 Kearny St., San Francisco, CA 94119. (415) 982-4640. This foundation works with Asian organizations, institutions, and individuals dedicated to furthering social and economic progress within their societies; maintains representation in ten Asian countries and administers programs elsewhere in Asia from its headquarters office. It also provides small grant assistance in the fields of human resource development; public administration and law; rural and community development; communications, books, and libraries; Asian region cooperation; food and nutrition; population and community health; and human rights and Asian-American understanding. Since its founding in 1954, it has provided over twenty million books and journals, through its Books for Asia program, to all levels of society in Asia wherever English is used.

Bell and Howell Foundation. 7100 McCormick Rd., Chicago, IL 60645. (312) 262-1600. Lois H. Robinson, Pres. *Grants Distribution:* Local communities where facilities are located. *Chief Interests:* Health and human services, youth charities.

Benton Foundation. 1776 K St. NW, Suite 900, Washington, DC 20006. (202) 429-7350. Carolyn Sachs, Exec. Dir.; Karen Menichelli, Prog. Off. *Grants Distribution:* National. *Chief Interests:* The relationship of communications to public affairs and the political process. Program priorities include communications policy research, innovative uses of the electronic media for public policy dialogue, and efforts to increase public understanding and use of media.

The Buhl Foundation. Four Gateway Center, Room 1522, Pittsburgh, PA 15222. (412) 566-2711. Doreen E. Boyce, Dir. *Grants Distribution:* Emphasizes educational institutions in the southwestern Pennsylvania area. *Chief Interests:* All levels of education. *Media Grants:* None specified.

The Commonwealth Fund. One E. 75th St., New York, NY 10021. (212) 535-0400. J. Robert Moskin, Editorial Dir. Programs focus on health and medical fields where grants are made to U.S. institutions or through institutions to qualified individuals. Harkness Fellowships for citizens of the United Kingdom, Australia, and New Zealand are given to those who wish to study and travel in the United States.

The Dow Jones Newspaper Fund, Inc. Box 300, Princeton, NJ 08540. (609) 452-2820. Thomas Engleman, Exec. Dir. A nonprofit foundation supported by Dow Jones and Co., publishers of *The Wall Street Journal*, to encourage careers in journalism. Sponsors teacher fellowships, newspaper editing internships for college juniors and college minority senior students, provides grants to colleges and universities for the operation of high school urban workshop programs, and publishes the *Journalism Career and Scholarship Guide* for aspiring journalists.

Eastman Kodak Company. Rochester, NY 14650. (716) 724-4000. S. C. Wright, Secy., Financial Aid Committee. *Grants Distribution:* National. *Chief Interests:* To support excellence in higher education with undergraduate and graduate scholarships to company-selected schools and departments. Kodak has a fourfold grant program in education that includes: Kodak Scholars Program, Fellows Program, Kodak Minority Academic Awards Program, and Presidential Young Investigator Awards.

The Film Fund. 80 E. 11th St., Suite 647, New York, NY 10003. (212) 475-3720. Margaret-Carmen Ashhurst, Exec. Dir. *Grants Distribution:* National. *Media Grants:* Support for the production of films, videotapes, and slide shows on pressing social issues. Priority is given to applications for completion grants and to projects that deal with issues on which there are few media in existence.

Edward E. Ford Foundation. 84 Nassau St., Princeton, NJ 08542. (609) 921-1126. Lawrence L. Hlavacek, Dir. *Grants Distribution:* National. Grants limited to secondary schools holding membership in the National Association of Independent Schools (NAIS). *Chief Interests:* Independent secondary education.

Foundation for Exceptional Children. Bill Geer Minigrant Award Fund, 1920 Association Dr., Reston, VA 22091. *Grants Distribution:* National. *Chief Interests:* Projects that benefit gifted or handicapped children and are education related. In 1984-85 offered twenty-one minigrants of up to $500 each for projects that fostered greater understanding between parents and handicapped children.

Charles Hayden Foundation. One Bankers Trust Plaza, 130 Liberty St., New York, NY 10006. (212) 938-0790. William Wachenfeld, Pres. *Grants Distribution:* New York City and Boston areas. *Chief Interests:* Physical facilities of well-established institutions concerned with mental, moral, and physical development of youth.

The Hearst Foundation: Appeals from east of Mississippi River to: 888 7th Ave., New York, NY 10106. (212) 584-5404. Robert Frehse, Jr., Exec. Dir. Appeals from west of Mississippi River to: 690 Market St., Suite 502, San Francisco, CA 94104. (415) 781-8418. *Chief Interests:* Education, health, culture, social programs, religion.

The Hyde and Watson Foundation. 507 Westminster Ave., Elizabeth, NJ 07208. (212) 867-2420. Robert W. Parsons, Jr., Pres. *Grants Distribution:* National. A consolidation of the former Lillia Babbitt Hyde Foundation and the John Jay and Eliza Jane Watson Foundation. *Chief Interests:* Support of developmental projects (rather than operational programs) of a wide range of institutions in the fields of health, education, religion, social services, and the humanities. Because of heavy current commitments, priorities likely to be given dire emergency needs, the satisfaction of previous support agreements, and institutions serving the disadvantaged.

The Inglewood Foundation. Box 906, Little Rock, AR 72203. (501) 372-1333. B. Frank Mackey, Jr., Dir. *Grants Distribution:* National. *Chief Interests:* Grants to improve community interrelationships among various groups of people. Such grants frequently are given through public school districts.

Inter-American Foundation. 1515 Wilson Blvd., Rosslyn, VA 22209. (703) 841-3800. Media-related inquiries should be sent to Stephen N. Abrams, Gen. Counsel. The foundation is an independent public corporation that makes grants to private organizations in Latin America and the Caribbean carrying out development projects to improve the economic and social conditions of poor people in the region. Most grants support organizations in agricultural and rural development, small urban-based enterprises, community services, nonformal education, and research. The foundation publishes an annual report and semiannual journal, *Grassroots Development.*

The Jerome Foundation. W-2090 First National Bank Bldg., St. Paul, MN 55101. (612) 224-9431. Cynthia Gehrig, Exec. Dir. *Grants Distribution:* New York City and the Midwest. *Chief Interests:* Arts, humanities. *Media Grants:* Emerging film and video artists.

W. K. Kellogg Foundation. 400 North Ave., P.O. Box 3425, Battle Creek, MI 49016-3425. (616) 968-1611. Chief Programming Off. *Grants Distribution:* United States, Latin America, and Caribbean. *Media Grants:* No grants are provided for capital facilities, equipment, conferences, publications, films, or television or radio programs unless they are an integral phase of a project being funded. Areas of major concentration for grantmaking include: adult continuing education; betterment of health (health promotion/disease prevention and public health); communitywide, coordinated cost-effective health services; a wholesome food supply; broadening leadership capacity of individuals; economic development in Michigan; and opportunities for youths in Michigan.

The Kerr Foundation, Inc. 6301 N. Western, Oklahoma City, OK 73118. (405) 842-1510. Robert S. Kerr, Jr., Pres. *Grants Distribution:* Oklahoma, Texas, Arkansas, Missouri, Kansas, New Mexico, Colorado. *Chief Interests:* Charitable and educational grants, research and development, and improvement of social and economic factors. *Media Grants:* Higher education, the arts, and historic preservation; grants to university libraries for collection development in Americana, philosophy, music, and art.

Knight Foundation. One Cascade Plaza, Akron, OH 44308. (216) 253-9301. C. C. Gibson, Pres. *Grants Distribution:* In circulation areas covered by Knight newspapers. *Chief Interests:* General.

KIDS Fund (Knowledge, Independence, Decision-Making, Sensitivity). 535 Cordova Rd., #428, Santa Fe, NM 87501. Mary Pinto, Dir. *Grants Distribution:* National. *Chief Interests:* Parent-child communications. Nonprofit organizations may apply for grant support (seed money) for projects. Deadline for applications: April 15th. Revenues come from royalties from the sale of *The Judy Blume Diary* (Dell Books, 1981).

The Kresge Foundation. 3215 W. Big Beaver Rd., Box 3151, Troy, MI 48007-3151. (313) 643-9630. Alfred H. Taylor, Jr., Pres. *Grants Distribution:* National. *Chief Interests:* Challenge grants are made only toward projects involving construction of facilities, renovation of facilities, purchase of a major item of equipment or an integrated equipment system (provided the cost involved is at least $75,000), and the purchase of real estate. Grants are made to well-established, financially sound, fully accredited, tax-exempt charitable organizations operating in the fields of four-year college and university education, health care, social services, science and conservation, the arts and humanities, and public affairs. *Deadlines:* Applications are accepted only from January 1 through February 15 of each year.

The John and Mary R. Markle Foundation. Suite 940, 50 Rockefeller Plaza, New York, NY 10020. (212) 489-6655. Lloyd N. Morrisett, Pres. *Grants Distribution:* National. *Chief Interests:* The improvement of the media of mass communications, including services growing out of new technologies for the processing and transfer of information. In its effort to improve the mass media, the foundation supports projects that expand research on the role of mass communications in society; analyze public policy issues and questions of public interest; improve the performance of professionals involved in the mass communications industry; explore the relationship between the media and politics; and enrich the quality of print and electronic journalism. The foundation has a general interest in all aspects of the media and supports a wide range of efforts to improve mass communications. *Media Grants:* Computers as a medium for mass communication; standards and ethics in journalism; research in radio, television, and other media; development of a qualitative television ratings system; media commentary and criticism. The foundation does not normally support production of a specific program.

Fay McBeath Foundation. 1020 N. Broadway, Milwaukee, WI 53202. (414) 272-5805. David M. G. Huntington, Secy. *Grants Distribution:* Wisconsin, primarily Milwaukee. *Chief Interests:* Medical education and services; promotion of good health in Wisconsin; increasing understanding of needs and wants of older persons; promoting the welfare of children. *Media Grants:* Facilitation of information dissemination techniques in higher education; community education; the shaping of zoo-related learning experiences for young children; and others.

Milwaukee Foundation. 1020 N. Broadway, Milwaukee, WI 53202. (414) 272-5805. David M. G. Huntington, Dir.-Secy. *Grants Distribution:* Wisconsin, greater Milwaukee area. *Chief Interests:* Varied, to meet community needs. *Media Grants:* Video equipment to strengthen English programs; construction of new library; scholarships; construction of art gallery; outdoor education; and others.

Research Corporation. 6840 E. Broadway Blvd., Tucson, AZ 85710. (602) 296-6400. W. S. Bacon, Dir. of Communications. *Grants Distribution:* National. *Chief Interests:* Support of basic academic research in the natural and physical sciences; evaluation, patenting, and licensing to industry of inventions made at educational and scientific institution.

Z. Smith Reynolds Foundation. 101 Reynolds Village, Winston-Salem, NC 27106. (919) 725-7541. Thomas W. Lambeth, Exec. Dir. *Grants Distribution:* North Carolina. *Chief Interests:* Education, cultural resources, health and human services, criminal justice. *Media Grants:* Computerized instruction laboratories; Cued Speech Center for the Deaf; faculty development, and facilities grants for the performing arts.

Rockefeller Brothers Fund. 1290 Ave. of the Americas, New York, NY 10104. (212) 397-4800. Benjamin R. Shute, Jr., Secy. *Grants Distribution:* National; international. *Chief Interests:* The Fund's program is in a period of transition, and it is anticipated that the emerging program interests of the Fund will center on the following areas: sustainable global resources (including conservation and development) and global security (including arms control and international relations). The Fund will continue a special interest in New York City, and in the well-being of the private nonprofit sector in the United States.

Short Film Showcase/Foundation for Independent Video and Film (FIVF). 625 Broadway, New York, NY 10012. (212) 473-3400. Sol Horwitz, Project Admin. *Grants Distribution:* National. *Chief Interests:* Stimulates theatrical distribution of high-quality independent films of fifteen minutes or less duration. Each producer whose film is selected receives $3,000 and he or she supervises the blowup to 35mm. Films must qualify for a Motion Picture Association of America (MPAA) rating of G or PG and must have not been accepted yet for theatrical distribution.

Social Science Research Council. 605 3rd Ave., New York, NY 10158. (212) 557-9500. Apply to Fellowship and Grants Office. *Grants Distribution:* National. *Chief Interests:* Established for the advancement of research in the social sciences; fellowships and grants given for international dissertation and postdoctoral research in the social sciences and humanities. Funds are received from other foundations and agencies.

Spencer Foundation. 875 N. Michigan Ave., Chicago, IL 60611. (312) 337-7000. Marion M. Faldet, V.P. *Grants Distribution:* National. *Chief Interests:* Research in the behavioral sciences aimed at the improvement of education. *Grants:* To universities to support research in biological bases of learning; cognitive studies; affective studies; early childhood development; effects of schooling; and educational organization and administration.

University Film and Video Foundation (UFVF). Dept. of Photography and Cinema, The Ohio State Univ., Columbus, OH 43210. (614) 422-4920/1766. Robert W. Wagner, Pres. of Board. *Grants Distribution:* National. *Chief Interests:* Promotes university film and video production, the improvement of education of filmmakers and video producers, research, exchange of student work both in the United States and abroad; encourages film and video events; assists in funding scholarships and grants for the University Film and Video Association.

Weyerhaeuser Company Foundation. Tacoma, WA 98477. (206) 924-3159. Mary Hall, V.P. *Grants Distribution:* National. *Chief Interests:* Gives priority to special education programs. *Media Grants:* Some recent grants made to aid in the school purchase of computer equipment for a "linked computer" project.

H. W. Wilson Foundation. 950 University Ave., Bronx, NY 10452. (212) 588-8400. *Grants Distribution:* National. *Chief Interests:* Scholarships in support of education for librarianship. *Grants:* To sixty-nine U.S. and Canadian graduate library schools on a sequential basis from 1982 to 1986.

Sources of Information

Various sources and leads for foundations and granting agencies, as well as suggested sources to assist in finding funds, are included in this section. Current conditions in 1985 in the granting and funding arena make it necessary for the educator to be both persistent and creative in order to find and secure funds for worthwhile projects. A visit to an academic library to study many of these suggested sources should be of some assistance.

Actionfacts. International Communications Industries Association, bi-mo., pna. Devoted to providing information about federal grants programs for purchase of audiovisual materials and equipment. Informs readers as to what money is currently available for the purpose and offers lists of grants for specific programs. It is tied closely to the *A-V Connection* (ICIA guide to federal programs for audiovisual users) with articles keyed to *Connection* pages.

Annual Register of Grant Support (17th ed.). Marquis Professional Publications, 1983-1984. Book, 826 pp., $75.00. Over 2,800 entries detailing the type, purpose, and duration of the grant; amount of funding available for each award and for the entire program or all programs of the organization; data concerning the organization's areas of interest, cooperative funding programs, and consulting or volunteer services; also includes eligibility requirements, application instructions, address and telephone as well as names and titles of persons to whom proposals should be submitted.

Art of Winning Corporate Grants. Howard Hillman. Vanguard Press, 1980. Book, 188 pp., $10.95. Lists and explains ten steps in the grants process; includes sample proposals, typical questions asked, and information sources.

Art of Writing Business Reports and Proposals. Howard Hillman. Vanguard Press, 1981. Book, 238 pp., $12.95. Lists and explains four steps in report and proposal writing, including graphic aids, common English errors and other writing guidelines, information sources, and samples.

Awards, Honors, and Prizes (5th ed.). Paul Wasserman. Gale Research Co., 1982. Book (2 vols.): vol. 1, 900 pp., $110.00; vol. 2, 727 pp., $125.00. Volume 1 covers awards issued in the United States and Canada; Volume 2 covers international awards; entries provide full descriptions of the sponsoring groups; completely indexed.

Careers in the Arts: A Resource Guide. Center for Arts Information, 1981. Book, 48 pp., $6.75. A guide to sources of information such as professional unions, associations, and training programs to help in career choices in the arts.

Casebook of Grant Proposals in the Humanities. William Coleman, David Keller, and Arthur Pfeffer, eds. Neal-Schuman Publishers, Inc., 1982. Book, 300 pp., $29.95. Reproduces the actual narratives of fifteen successfully funded humanities grants proposals with an accompanying text that emphasizes the strategy, construction, and dynamics behind each.

Catalog of Federal Domestic Assistance: 1983. Government Printing Office, 1983. Book, 1,288 pp., $32.00 domestic; $40.00 foreign. Looseleaf compendium of federal programs, projects, services, and activities that provide assistance or benefits to the U.S. public. (COFA) S/N 041-001-81001-3.

Challenge Grant Guidelines. National Endowment for the Humanities, Office of Challenge Grants, 1983. Booklet, n.p., free. A list of provisions for the Challenge Grant Program administered by the NEH; includes information on program criteria and procedures for application.

The Complete Fund Raising Guide. Howard R. Mirkin. Public Service Materials Center, 1981. Book, n.p., $13.50. How to raise funds from business and labor, foundations, government, memorials, bequests, and the general public.

Corporate 500: The Directory of Corporate Philanthropy (2nd ed.). Research Staff of the Public Management Institute, eds. and comps. Gale Research Co., 1983. Book, 1,000 pp., $225.00. A single source of information on contributions programs of the five hundred U.S. corporations most active in supporting nonprofit organizations and public agencies; each entry includes areas of interest, geographic areas receiving funds, activities funded, eligible organizations, sample grants, and application procedures. Eight indexes give complete and alternative access points.

Corporate Philanthropy. Council on Foundations, 1982. Magazine-format report, 160 pp., $12.00. Comprehensive descriptions of the background, philosophy, trends, management, and future of corporate philanthropy, now the largest and still-growing segment of the philanthropic community.

Directory of Financial Aids for Minorities. Gail Schlachter. ABC-Clio Information Services, 1983. Book, apkprox. 400 pp., $35.00 plus $2.00 postage/handling. A comprehensive guide to funding sources for minorities. Each listing includes program title; sponsor name, address, and telephone number; program purpose, eligibility, financial data, duration, special features, limitations, number of awards and application deadline. Indexed by program title, sponsoring organization, geographic location, subject, and calendar (month of application deadline).

Directory of Financial Aids for Women (2nd ed.). Gail Schlachter. ABC-Clio Information Services, 1982. Book, 368 pp., $26.00 plus $2.00 postage/handling. A comprehensive guide to funding sources for women; nearly nine hundred entries, arranged alphabetically. Lists scholarships, fellowships, loans, grants, internships, awards, and prizes with complete information on application procedures. Also includes over one hundred other assistance programs open to both men and women. Indexed by subject, geographical area, and sponsoring organization.

Directory of Research Grants. William K. Wilson and Betty L. Wilson, eds. Oryx Press, ann. Book., 368 pp., $52.50. An annual directory of more than two thousand grants programs in ninety academic disciplines; includes grants from government agencies, private foundations, corporations, and professional organizations. Lists all pertinent information for application, including *Catalog of Federal Assistance* program numbers.

ELHI Funding Sources Newsletter. William K. Wilson and Betty L. Wilson, eds. Oryx Press, mo., $125.00/yr. Services elementary, secondary, and special education fields by annotating government, foundation, and other sources of grant funds for educational projects.

Federal Fast Finder. Washington Researchers Ltd. (6th ed.). Book, 53 pp., $10.00. Lists addresses for eighty-six major federal government offices and telephone numbers for over one thousand departments; includes sixty-six recorded messages and some fifty toll-free hotlines.

Federal Register. Office of the Federal Register, d., $300.00/yr. A daily publication listing changes in government regulations, proposed regulations, and deadlines for submission for specific grant/contract programs. Order from the Superintendent of Documents, Government Printing Office.

FEDfind: Your Key to Finding Federal Government Information. ICUC Press, 1983. Book, n.p., $8.95. A comprehensive guide to the U.S. government's "bureaucratic maze." Includes list of useful government publications.

Film Service Profiles. Center for Arts Information, 1980. Booklet, 68 pp., $5.00. Detailed descriptions of fifty-seven national and local organizations that offer services to independent filmmakers and film users.

The Financial Aids File. TSC/A Houghton Mifflin Company, 1983. Database, pna. Part of the Guidance Information System (GIS) produced for use on the Apple III personal computer; contains up-to-date information on financial aid possibilities from the federal government, foundations, business, industry, the military, labor organizations, and religious and charitable groups.

Financial Assistance for Library Education, Academic Year 1984-85. Standing Committee on Library Education (SCOLE). American Library Association, 1983. Booklet, n.p., $1.00. Information on scholarships and assistantships in the library field.

Financial Choices for Public Libraries. American Library Association, 1980. Booklet, 89 pp., $5.50. Proceedings of the Public Library Association conference at ALA 1980.

The Foundation Center. 888 Seventh Ave., New York, NY 10106. Thomas R. Buckman, Pres. A not-for-profit organization dedicated exclusively to the gathering, analysis, and dissemination of factual information on philanthropic foundations. The center has two main purposes: (1) to be a useful resource for anyone interested in applying for funds to grant-making foundations and (2) to compile reliable descriptive data and statistics on the foundation field for use by foundations, government agencies, and other organizations and individuals. The center's national library collections in New York and Washington, DC are open to the public. The center also has field offices in San Francisco and Cleveland and over one-hundred cooperating library collections in public, academic, and foundation libraries throughout the country. Through an Associates Program, individuals and organizations can, for an annual fee and service charges, gain access to the center's computerized data bank and request reference and research service from the professional library staff. Free pamphlets on foundations, proposals, and the services of the Foundation Center are available on request. Its principal publications are: *Foundation Center Source Book Profiles; The Foundation Directory; Foundation Grants Index Annual Volume; Foundation Grants Index* (bi-mo.); *COMSEARCH Printouts; National Data Book; Foundation Grants to Individuals; Foundation Fundamentals;* and *Corporate Foundation Profiles.* (*See* these and other entries in this section for descriptions and ordering data.) Call (800) 424-9836 toll-free for additional information about publications, library locations, or to place credit card orders.

Foundation Center National Data Book. The Foundation Center, ann. (2 vols.). Identifies all active foundations; indexed by state, foundation name, and subject.

Foundation Center Source Book Profiles. The Foundation Center, q. service, $250.00. New analytical profiles of more than five hundred foundations provided each year. The "top" one thousand foundations are profiles on a two-year cycle with quarterly updates and quarterly cumulated indexes to all.

The Foundation Directory (8th ed.). Marianna O. Lewis, ed. The Foundation Center, 1981. Book, 672 pp., $60.00. Updated information on the 3,363 largest foundations having assets of $1 million or more, or awarding more than $100,000 annually in grants. Indexed by subject, personnel, and geographic location.

Foundation Fundamentals: A Guide for Grantseekers. (rev. ed.). Carol M. Kurzig. The Foundation Center, 1981. Book, 148 pp., $6.50. A guide to foundations and to foundation research — instructions for researching foundation grants by foundation name, subject interest, or geographic location. Describes resources and services of the Foundation Center. Includes forty-six illustrations, worksheets, and checklists.

The Foundation Grants Index Annual Volume. The Foundation Center, 1982. 590 pp., $35.00. Summarizes about twenty-three thousand grants made by approximately four hundred major foundations. Each entry includes amount of the grant, names and location of recipients, and description of the grant. Four indexes: names of recipients, names of foundations, fields of interest, and key word.

The Foundation Grants Index Bimonthly. The Foundation Center, bi-mo. $20.00. Each issue describes more than two thousand recent foundation grants. Formerly appeared as part of the Foundation Center's *Foundation News*.

Foundation Grants to Individuals (3rd ed.). The Foundation Center, 1981. Book, 236 pp., $15.00. Profiles of programs of about one thousand foundations making grants to individuals. Arranged by program categories.

Foundations Today — 1983: Current Facts and Figures on Private Foundations. Foundation Center, 1983. Book, n.p., $2.00. Information on foundations grants: size, geographic location, type of foundation, date of establishment, and type of grant awarded.

Foundation Funds for Education: A Guide to Grants for Elementary, Secondary, and Post-Secondary Schools. NAVA, 1983. Book, n.p., $11.50. Lists eighty-two foundations that have either funded classroom and library projects that included AV, video, and microcomputers or are willing to consider a proposal for a project that includes these purchases.

Fund Sources in Health and Allied Fields. William K. Wilson and Betty L. Wilson, eds. Oryx Press, mo., $125.00/yr. Designed for use by health administrators, scientists, doctors, researchers, health educators, and others seeking financial support for programs and special projects.

Funding Opportunities at the National Institute of Education: FY 1984. National Institute of Education, 1984. Booklet, n.p., free. Lists grants competitions and requests for proposals for three NIE divisions: Teaching and Learning, Educational Policy and Organization, and Dissemination and Improvement of Practice.

Gadney's Guide to 1800 International Contests, Festivals & Grants in Film & Video, Photography, TV-Radio Broadcasting, Writing, Poetry, Playwriting & Journalism. Alan Gadney. Festival Publications, 1980. Book, 610 pp., $15.95 PB; $22.95 HB plus $1.75

postage. A reference directory with complete information on millions of dollars in world-wide contests, festivals, grants, loans, scholarships, fellowships, residencies, apprentice-training-intern programs, and more in various media-related fields. Alphabetical and subject category indexes, cross-referenced. Awarded "outstanding reference book of the year" by the American Library Association.

Getting Grants. Craig W. Smith and Eric W. Skjei. Public Service Materials Center, 1982. Book, n.p., $14.00. Describes the grantmaking process from the corporate or foundation point of view; gives complete directions and sample forms of letters for winning grant funds.

Grant Information System. Oryx Press, mo., $475.00/yr. Available online with Dialog and SDC; a comprehensive source to more than two thousand private and public grant programs; all information needed for applications is covered.

Grant Money and How to Get It: A Handbook for Librarians. Richard W. Boss. R. R. Bowker, 1980. Book, 138 pp., $19.95. Offers sources of grant money and advice regarding the preparation of proposals to increase chances of funding; with glossary of terms, bibliography, illustrations, and index.

Grant Proposals That Succeeded. Virginia White, ed. Plenum Publishing Co., 1983. Book, approx. 230 pp., $22.50. Reviews grant proposals and gives advice on writing and presenting grants for funding; covers successful grants in training, the arts, humanities, foundations and corporations, and federal contracts.

Grants for Libraries: A Guide to Public and Private Funding Programs and Proposal Writing Techniques. Emmett Corry. Libraries Unlimited, Inc., 1982. Book, 240 pp., $22.50. Describes funding sources for school media programs, colleges and universities, public libraries, and library science programs; also details instructions for proposal writing; lists available grants and sources of funding in government agencies and private foundations.

Grants for Scientific and Engineering Research. National Science Foundation, 1983. Booklet, 32 pp., free. An information booklet pertaining to National Science Foundation grants, what they are for, and how to prepare proposals to obtain them.

Grants in the Humanities: A Scholar's Guide to Funding Sources. (2nd ed.). William Coleman. Neal-Schuman Publishers, Inc., 1984. Book, 152 pp., $24.95. Devoted to securing postgraduate study grants in the humanities. Proposal writing, including requirements and format. Also lists over one hundred funding sources, including information type, purpose, areas of support, conditions, deadlines, and addresses for inquiries. Completely updated with new listings of funding sources.

Grants Register 1983-85 (8th ed.). Craig Alan Lerner, ed. St. Martin's Press, 1983. Book, 866 pp., $35.00. A directory of fellowships, scholarships, and awards in the arts, sciences, and professions; updated every two years, providing current information on opportunities and application procedures.

Handbook on Private Foundations. Council on Foundations, 1981. Book, 448 pp., $22.95. Lists names and addresses of various foundations in the United States; discusses reasons for establishing foundations; making grants; administering foundation business, including investments; sources of further information and assistance.

How to Enter and Win Film Contests. Alan Gadney. Facts on File, Inc., 1981. Book, 224 pp., $14.95. Revised every other year; lists information for some 350 film contests, festivals, screenings, and grants sources.

How to Enter and Win Video/Audio Contests. Alan Gadney. Facts on File, Inc., 1981. Book, 224 pp., $14.95. Revised every other year. Covers the field of video and television, with more than 500 entries on contests, festivals, and grants open to television and video producers.

The Independent Film & Videomaker's Guide. (rev. and exp. ed.). Michael Wiese, 1984. Book, approx. 250 pp., $16.15. Describes how to raise money for independent films; equitable distribution agreements; available film and videotape markets; other financial considerations.

The Individual's Guide to Grants. Judith B. Margolin. Plenum Publishing Co., 1983. Book, 290 pp., $15.95. Designed specifically to assist individuals (as opposed to institutions or organizations) seeking grant support for their projects.

International Cultural Exchange. Center for Arts Information, 1983. Booklet, 12 pp., $3.50. A guide to sixty-three organizations that facilitate or fund international cultural exchange programs.

International Foundation Directory (3rd ed.). H. V. Hodson. Gale Research Co., 1983. Book, approx. 450 pp., $78.00. Over one thousand entries detailing international foundations, trusts, and other nonprofit organizations; names, addresses, purpose, activities, and publications given.

Literary Publishing: Assistance to Literary Magazines, Small Press Assistance, Distribution Projects. National Endowment for the Arts, Literature Program, 1985. Booklet, n.p., free. Includes legal requirements, how to apply, and instructions for completing applications for grants, as well as a list of what is and is not funded.

Millions for the Arts: Federal & State Cultural Programs. Washington International Arts Letter, 1979. Book, 64 pp., $20.00 (includes update). Results of a survey taken fro the U.S. Senate by the Congressional Research Service; lists authorities under which money is available in federal and state cultural activities; both funds and facilities available are recorded.

Mini-Grants for Classroom Teachers. Leo McGee. Phi Delta Kappa, 1983. Booklet, 34 pp., $0.75. no. 200. A PDK fastback written for classroom teachers showing how they can develop grant proposals for classroom needs that can be funded in their own communities. Includes three sample proposals.

Money for Artists. Center for Arts Information, 1980. Booklet, 6 pp., $3.00. A guide to grants, awards, fellowships, and artist-in-residence programs primarily for New York State artists; bibliographic references useful nationally.

National Directory of Arts and Education Support by Business Corporations (3rd ed.). Daniel Millsaps and editors of *Washington International Arts Letter*. Washington International Arts Letter, 1984. Book, 240 pp., $75.00. Lists over eight hundred business corporations and thousands of their subsidiaries that have contributed to arts and education; includes officers, contacts, addresses, and analyses of giving pattern.

National Directory of Arts Support by Private Foundations (vol. 5). Daniel Millsaps, ed. Washington International Arts Letter, 1980. Book, 336 pp., $79.95. Includes over 2,200 foundations, with addresses, officers, typical grants, and areas of interest; updated and indexed.

National Directory of Grants and Aid to Individuals in the Arts (International) (5th ed.). Daniel Millsaps, ed. Washington International Arts Letter, 1983. Book, 256 pp., $15.95. Includes complete categories of government grants, private organizations, and association sources; cross-reference, index.

National Educational Audio Visual Festival. Box 4135, Ormond Beach, FL 32075. (904) 677-7190. Joseph J. Dougherty, contact person. A national recognition program to acknowledge outstanding media production achievements of high school students (grades 9-12) throughout the United States. Write for further information.

Preparing Contract-Winning Proposals and Feasibility Studies. Tim Whalen. Pilot Books, 1982. Booklet, 48 pp., $5.00. Explains the processes involved in writing proposals primarily for industrial or government projects.

Private Foreign Aid. Landrum R. Bolling with Craig Smith. Council of Foundations, 1982. Book, 339 pp., $14.95. A history of the involvement of U.S. private foundations in development abroad. Reviews nature and extent of private voluntary organizations and their role in relief and development undertakings.

Process of Grant Proposal Development. Gerald V. Teague and Betty S. Heathington. Phi Delta Kappa, 1980. Booklet, 46 pp., $0.75. no. 143. A PDK fastback giving step-by-step procedures for writing and submitting grant proposals; describes projects likely to be granted funding from government agencies or private foundations.

The Process of Grantsmanship and Proposal Development. Century Planning Associates, Inc., n.d. Book, 191 pp., $24.00. Contains information and directions for writing and processing proposals; a working guide, a model proposal, reference sections included.

Proposal Writing Guide. Norman T. Bell and Frank Jackson. Radio Shack, n.d. Book, 96 pp., $10.00. A guide for educators seeking funds for computer-related education projects; includes examples and how-to information for writing winning grant proposals.

Publishing in the Arts: Assistance to Literary Magazines, Small Press Special Assistance, Small Press Development Grants. National Endowment for the Arts, Literature Program, 1983. Booklet, n.p., free. Includes legal requirements, how to apply, and instructions for completing applications for grants, as well as a list of what is and is not funded.

A Quick Guide to Loans and Emergency Funds. Center for Arts Information, 1982. Booklet, 8 pp., $2.00. Describes six free or low-cost loan funds for organizations in New York, two special bank programs, four grant programs for performance or works in progress, and fourteen loan or emergency funds for artists.

Stalking the Large Green Grant: A Fundraising Manual for Youth Serving Agencies (3rd ed.). National Youth Work Alliance, 1980. Book, 78 pp., $8.50. Examines in detail the funding opportunities provided by federal, state, and local government agencies as well as those by foundations and other private sources of support. Chapters on writing a successful proposal and on how youth workers can influence legislative and administrative funding decisions.

United States Government Manual (1983-84 ed.). Office of the Federal Register, ann., 908 pp., $9.00. Primary source of information on the organization, functions, activities, and principal officials of the federal government; also provides detailed information to aid the public in obtaining specifics on employment, government contracts, environmental programs, publications and films, and other matters of citizen interest. Order from the Superintendent of Documents, Government Printing Office.

Video Service Profiles. Center for Arts Information, 1983. Booklet, 40 pp., $6.75. Provides detailed descriptions of sixty-eight national and local organizations and funding agencies that offer services to independent video artists.

Washington International Arts Letter. 10/yr., $48.00 inst.; $24.50 indiv. Covers the practical aspects of grants and other forms of assistance to the arts and humanities; includes information, advance data and reports of congressional actions, authorizations and appropriations; personalities in the arts, scholarship and job information, cultural exchanges, financial information, and tax changes.

World Dictionary of Awards and Prizes (1st ed.). Europa Publications Ltd./Gale Research Co., 1979. Book, 380 pp., $60.00. Covers artistic, scientific, and intellectual achievements; a comprehensive guide to more than two thousand awards, prizes, and medals given in countries throughout the world.

Part Five

Mediagraphy
Print and Nonprint Resources

Introduction

The "Mediagraphy" section of *EMTY* 85 has been revised and reorganized as well as updated. Periodicals published by associations and organizations are no longer listed here; they now are listed in part 3. In addition, items now are listed alphabetically under main entries rather than under function. The items are divided into two groups under each main entry, either "Media-related Periodicals" or "Reference Tools and Recommended Media."

The items listed in the mediagraphy reflect a selected list rather than a general compilation. A favorable review source is cited whenever possible in the "Reference Tools and Recommended Media" section. New periodicals also have a favorable review citation. All items include annotations and ordering information. A "Directory of Producers, Distributors, and Publishers," the last section of the mediagraphy, provides names and addresses for items for which such information is not provided in the annotation.

Magazines, newsletters, and other media-related periodicals from the United States and abroad are listed in the "Media-related Periodicals" section under each main entry. Any recently available item that provides organized source information about media-related resources, services, activities, or individuals has been included under "Reference Tools and Recommended Media" as has any other new item of possible interest to those in the instructional media and technology, library, training, or other media-related fields.

How Data Were Obtained

Data for entries in the "Mediagraphy" section were obtained from scanning articles, news columns, and reviews found in magazines and newsletters related to the fields of educational/instructional technology, computers, librarianship, information science, and training. Issues checked were published between January 1, 1984, and December 31, 1984 (the closing date for *EMTY* 85). In addition, *American Reference Books Annual* 1985 was reviewed for items of interest to *EMTY* users as were abstracts of ERIC documents provided by the staff of the Educational Clearinghouse on Information Resources.

Ordering information was checked with the publisher, in *Books in Print*, or in *Ulrich's International Periodical Directory* whenever possible. Ordering information often changes on short notice, however, and it should be checked before ordering an item. Users are reminded that in the annotated entries, names of publishers or producers that are identical to the titles of the periodicals themselves have not been repeated.

The publications that were reviewed for items to be included in the mediagraphy are listed on page 249. The abbreviation that precedes each publication shows how it is cited in the annotations. The abbreviation EMTY indicates a review by the editors.

Using the "Mediagraphy"

Ordering Information

The names of publishers or producers that are identical to the titles of the periodicals have not been repeated. Users are reminded that name and address data are provided in the "Directory of Producers, Distributors, and Publishers" appearing at the end of this section. It is suggested that users refer directly to the index in cases where names of individuals or organizations are known but specific titles are not.

Obtaining ERIC Documents

All entries in this section carrying "EDRS" identifying numbers are in the ERIC microfiche collection and available in that format from the ERIC Document Reproduction Service (EDRS), Box 190, Arlington, VA 22210, (703) 841-1212. When ordering, use the ED number and state that the microfiche format is desired. Enclose the amount of money indicated in ED entries plus postage. Small numbers of microfiche are sent by first-class mail; 1-3 microfiche require $0.22 postage. Paper copies may also be ordered at higher prices. Consult the latest *Resources in Education* (*RIE*) for up-to-date information about costs and ordering procedures. Several hundred colleges and universities, as well as other institutions and organizations, maintain ERIC microfiche collections where education documents (EDs) may be consulted (usually without charge) and paper copies obtained for a fee.

Main Entries

The items are classified according to major subject emphasis and listed under a main entry. Journals, newsletters, and other periodically published items are listed alphabetically in the "Media-related Periodicals" section. All other items are listed alphabetically in the "Reference Tools and Recommended Media" section. The majority of these items were published in 1984 and are new to the mediagraphy. Both print and nonprint items, they help the user find information about the subject, refer the user to other sources, or provide definitions, short descriptions, or a general introduction. The review source, if any, is cited after the annotation. The main entries for this year's *EMTY* are listed below.

Publications Cited

Form of Citation	Journal Title
A+	A+
ARBA	American Reference Books Annual
BL	Booklist
CA	Calico
C	Choice
C!	Compute!
CUE	Computer Using Educators
CT	The Computing Teacher
CC	Creative Computing
ECTJ	Educational Communications and Technology Journal
ET	Educational Technology
EE	Electronic Education
EL	Electronic Learning
ERIC	ERIC/IR Update
HT	High Technology
II	Instructional Innovator
JCBI	Journal of Computer-Based Instruction
JID	Journal of Instructional Development
LJ	Library Journal
OT	Online Today
PI	Performance and Instruction
PCP	Personal Computing "Plus"
PDK	Phi Delta Kappan
RA	Robotics Age
TS	Telescan
THE	T.H.E. Journal
T	Training
TD	Training and Development Journal
VO	Videodisc and Optical Disk
VT	Videodisc/Videotex

Mediagraphy

CLASSIFIED LIST

Adult, Continuing, Distance Education
Artificial Intelligence (AI) and Robotics
Audio (Records, Audiocassettes and Tapes, Radio); Listening
Audiovisual/Instructional Media (General)
Computers/General; Computer-assisted Instruction; Computer-managed Instruction; Computer Literacy
Computers—Hardware
Computers—Software
Databases; Networking
Education and Research

Films/Filmstrips—Educational and Theatrical
Information Science
Instructional Technology/Design/Development; Training
Libraries/Media Centers
Microforms; Micrographics
Photography
Print—Books/Magazines
Selection; Free/Inexpensive Materials
Video (Broadcast, Cable, Interactive, Satellite, Telecommunications, Television, Videodisc, Videotex)

ADULT, CONTINUING, DISTANCE EDUCATION

Media-related Periodicals

Adult and Continuing Education Today. 1221 Thurston, Manhattan, KS 66502. bi-wk., $40.00/yr. Covers news, professional development, teaching tips, book reviews, events, and jobs.

Appropriate Technology. Intermediate Technology Publications, Ltd. q., $15.00/yr. indiv.; $20.00/yr. inst. Articles are on low-cost, small-scale technology, particularly for developing countries.

Development Communication Report. Clearinghouse on Development Communication. q., free to readers in developing countries; $10.00/yr. to others. Applications of communications technology to international development problems such as agriculture, health, and nutrition are covered.

Reference Tools and Recommended Media

Audio Tapes for Distance Education. (ED 246 849). E. David Mecham and Brian A. Butler. EDRS, 1984. Microfiche, 48 pp., $0.97. Offers planning, production, and evaluation advice about preparation of audiotapes for distance learning.

Distance Learning: A Review for Educators. (ED 246 872). Heather E. Hudson and Charles H. Boyd. EDRS, 1984. Microfiche, 75 pp., $0.97. Provides an overview of experiences with application of communication and computer technology to distance education. Includes a summary of potential distance technologies, evaluation factors, and projects.

Independent Learning in Higher Education. Euan S. Henderson and Michael B. Nathenson, eds. Educational Technology Publications, 1984. Book, n.p., $29.95. Discusses both distance learning and student autonomy as experienced at the Open University in Britain. Includes literature reviews and case studies. (EMTY)

Strategies for Strengthening Student-Teacher Contact in Distance Education: Results of an Evaluation of Distance Education in Swedish Universities. (ED 243 444). Birgitta Willen. EDRS, 1984. Microfiche, 58 pp., $0.97. The background, history, development, and evaluation of distance education in Sweden since 1973 is described.

Survey on Uses of Distance Learning in the U.S. (ED 246 874). Diane E. Downing. EDRS, 1984. Microfiche, 53 pp., $0.97. Twenty-eight states responded to a survey about the extent to which distance learning techniques were used in public education.

Telecommunications-based Distance Learning. (ED 246 873). Michael B. Goldstein. EDRS, 1984. Microfiche, 92 pp., $0.97. Examines the constraints of federal and state laws and their implications for the present and future use of telecommunications-based delivery.

ARTIFICIAL INTELLIGENCE (AI) AND ROBOTICS

Media-related Periodicals

Robotics Age. 174 Concord St., Peterborough, NH 03458. mo., $24.00. Features several articles each month on current and future trends and projects in robotics. Also, has a calendar, book reviews, and classified advertising.

Reference Tools and Recommended Media

AI Trends '84. DM Data Inc., 6900 E. Camelback, Suite 1000, Scottsdale, AZ 85251. 1984. Book, $195.00 PB. A sourcebook on artificial intelligence (AI) that includes definitions, current information on the AI industry and developments, government involvement, and companies involved in AI. (EMTY)

Artificial Intelligence. O. Firschein, ed. AFPIS Press, 1899 Preston White Dr., Reston, VA 22091. 1984. Book, 252 pp., $29.95 PB. Selected papers presented at recent computer-related conferences, symposia, and so forth that deal with the technical aspects of AI. Not for the novice. (EMTY)

The Fifth Generation: Artificial Intelligence and Japan's Computer Challenge to the World. Edward Feigenbaum and Pamela McCurduck. Addison-Wesley, 1983. Book, 275 pp., $15.55. Describes the competition between the United States and Japan in the development of AI in computers that can reason and make conclusions. (LJ, Mar 84)

Industrial Robots and Robotics. Edward Kafrissen and Mark Stephans. Reston (Prentice-Hall), 1984. Book, 396 pp., $25.95. Reviews history of robotics before describing the economics and new developments of robots. Terms are defined and manufacturers, journals, and bibliographies listed. (C, July-Aug 84)

The International Robotics Yearbook. Ballinger, 1983. Book, 336 pp., $150.00. Provides summary data for the current state of the art. Contains a directory of manufacturers, research and development activities, and funding sources. (ARBA, 85)

Learning and Teaching with Computers. Tim O'Shea and John Self. Prentice-Hall, 1983. Book, 307 pp., $12.95. Suggests to educators who have some experience with computers that ideas and examples from AI need to be incorporated into computer-assisted instruction. (ET, Apr 84)

The Robot Revolution. Tom Logsdon. Simon & Schuster, 1984. Book, 208 pp., $17.95 HB; $9.95 PB. Traces the development and use of robots in industry, military, games, and so forth and suggests future trends. Includes sources of robot building supplies, information. (LJ, July 84)

Robotics, 1960-1983: An Annotated Bibliography. Andrew Garoogian. CompuBibs/Vantage Information Consultants, 298 State St., Brooklyn, NY 11201. 1984. Book, 119 pp., $10.00 PB. An annotated, nontechnical bibliography of articles on applications of robotics. Lists organizations, periodicals, and directories. (ARBA, 85)

Robotics Explained. Bergwall Productions, P.O. Box 238, Garden City, NY 11530. 1983. 4 sound filmstrips, 12-16 min. each, $219.00. Community college-level filmstrips that cover robotic terms and classification, robots in the workplace, and the teachmover robot. (C, July-Aug 84)

Robotics Sourcebook and Dictionary. David F. Tver and Roger W. Bolz. Industrial Press, 1983. Book, 258 pp., $29.95. Describes robots, tasks successfully managed by robots, robotics and computer terms, and lists manufacturers and addresses. (ARBA, 85)

Turing's Man. David J. Bolter. The University of North Carolina Press, 1984. Book, n.p., pna. Discusses AI and its implications for society from both a science and a humanities perspective. Compares the computer age to the ancient world and the Enlightenment. Suggests new ways of looking at society. (EMTY)

AUDIO (RECORDS, AUDIOCASSETTES AND TAPES, RADIO); LISTENING

Media-related Periodicals

Audio. CBS Publications. mo., $15.94/yr. A consumer publication containing current hi-fi news and data, trends, and reviews of hardware, software, equipment, and books.

Audio-Cassette Newsletter. Cassette Information Services. q., $15.00/yr. prepaid. Supplements the *Audio-Cassette Directory* with information about new educational, training, and motivational programs available in audiocassette. Contains bibliographic information.

Broadcasting. Broadcasting Publications. wk., $60.00/yr. All-inclusive newsweekly for radio, television, cable, and allied businesses.

Gramophone. General Gramophone Publications, Ltd. mo., $33.20/yr. Reviews of new records, audio-related books, cassettes, and discs; articles also.

High Fidelity. ABC Leisure Magazines, Inc. mo., $13.95/yr. Aimed at people interested in stereo equipment, home recording, playback systems, and video.

Historical Journal of Film, Radio, and Television. Carfax Publishing Co. 2/yr., $51.00/yr. indiv.; $102.00/yr. inst. Articles by international experts in the field, news and notices, and book reviews.

It's on Tape. Audio-Forum. q., free on request. A newsletter from Jeffrey Norton Publishers, Inc. and its divisions: Audio-Forum, Video-Forum, and Sound Seminars. News, reviews of new audio and videotapes, equipment, and supplies are covered.

Journal of College Radio. Intercollegiate Broadcasting System, Inc. 5/yr., free with membership, $12.50/yr. nonmembers. Includes the latest news of the field, book reviews, and articles by practicing experts.

Radio-Electronics. Gernsback Publications, Inc. mo., $14.97/yr. Covers all aspects of the fast moving electronics field featuring video, stereo, technology, service, communications, and projects.

Radio y Television. Intertec Publishing Corp. 6/yr., $20.00/yr. Includes articles on management and application of broadcast technology, operation of facilities, technical production techniques, and other developments of special interest to the Spanish-speaking markets.

Schwann-1 Record & Tape Guide. Schwann. mo., $25.00. Selective reference guide to recorded music on records and tapes for dealer, librarian, and consumer. Two supplements per year included.

Stereo Review. Ziff-Davis Publishing Co. mo., $10.00. Articles related to the field of serious and popular music; reviews of current productions.

Voicespondent. Voicespondence Club. q., $7.00/yr. News of exchanges of tapes among individuals, especially the blind, plus directory of membership.

Reference Tools and Recommended Media

The Acquisition and Cataloging of Music and Sound Recordings: A Glossary. Suzanne E. Thorin and Carole Franklin Vidali, comps. Music Library Association (MLA Technical Report, No. 11), 1984. Book, 40 pp., $14.00 PB. A guide for music librarians with limited backgrounds. Also contains definitions. (ARBA, 85)

Big Sounds from Small Peoples: The Music Industry in Small Countries. Roger Wallis and Krister Malm. Pendragon Press, 162 W. 13th St., New York, NY 10011. 1984. Book, 419 pp., $18.50. Analyzes the impact of the Western-dominated music recording business on small countries. Discusses ways to prevent loss of the local music culture. (C, Oct 84)

AUDIOVISUAL/INSTRUCTIONAL MEDIA (GENERAL)

Media-related Periodicals

Audio-Visual Communications. United Business Publications, Inc. mo., $13.50/yr. Covers production and use of film, slides, tape, video, audiovisual, and other telecommunications systems and techniques in business, industry, government, and education.

Audiovisual Notes from Kodak. Eastman Kodak Co. 3/yr., free on request. Information regarding communication industry trends and techniques, plus specific details on using Kodak hardware and software more effectively.

Biomedical Communications. United Business Publications, Inc. bi-mo. free. Production and use of media in medical education, continuing education, patient/public education, and health care delivery.

Educational Media International. Modino Press, Ltd. q., $25.00/yr. Covers all aspects of educational technology theory, practice, and new developments.

Electronic Education. 9/yr., $18.00/yr. For educators at the middle school through college levels; articles on the current technology and its use as well as hardware, software, and book reviews.

Electronic Learning. Scholastic, Inc. 8/yr., $19.00/yr. Stresses nontechnical information about uses of computers, videocassettes, educational television, and other electronic devices that can be used in education.

HOPE Reports Perspective. HOPE Reports. bi-mo., $40.00/yr. Newsletter giving analyses and opinions, forecasting on a specific medium of visual and audio communications each issue, plus other audiovisual topics not covered in major HOPE Reports publications.

International Journal of Instructional Media. Baywood Publishing Co., Inc. q., $24.00/yr. indiv.; $50.00/yr. inst. Current information on the applications of educational media; reports of research; media reviews.

Kidstuff. Guidelines Press. mo., $24.00/yr. A variety of ideas with educational goals including storytime programs, puppet plays, songs, creative dramatics, and reading lists.

Puppetry Journal. George Latshaw and Pat Latshaw, 8005 Swallow Dr., Macedonia, OH 44056. q., with membership; inst. rates on request. Articles of interest to puppeteers.

Simulation & Games. Sage Publications, Inc. q., $25.00/yr. indiv.; $56.00/yr. inst. An international journal of theory, design, and research devoted to the study of games and computer simulations; reviews books and products.

Studies in Visual Communication. Annenberg School Press. 4/yr., $20.00/yr. Focuses on problems and issues of importance in the study of visual communications.

Young Viewers. Media Center for Children. q., $20.00/yr. Articles, interviews, and reports on making and using media (film, video, television, radio) with children. Gives reviews and teaching suggestions.

Reference Tools and Recommended Media

Audio-Video Market Place 1984. R. R. Bowker Co., 1984. Book, 450 pp., $45.00. Formerly *AudioVisual Market Place*; a guide to audiovisual products or services. Includes names and addresses of AV companies, professionals, producers, distributors, production companies, and equipment manufacturers. Arranged by state and with subject classifications. (EMTY)

Development Communication Report No. 45. (ED 243 457). Agency for International Development. EDRS, 1984. Microfiche, 17 pp., $0.97. Innovative uses of media in international development are covered.

Media Review Digest. Pierian Press, P.O. Box 1808, Ann Arbor, MI 48106. 1984. Book, 800 pp., $198.00. Over forty thousand citations to reviews and descriptions of media found in more than 145 periodicals. (EMTY)

COMPUTERS/GENERAL; COMPUTER-ASSISTED INSTRUCTION; COMPUTER-MANAGED INSTRUCTION; COMPUTER LITERACY

Media-related Periodicals

A+. Ziff-Davis Publishing Co. mo., $24.97. A magazine for all levels of users of any Apple product; reviews new developments in software and hardware and provides how-to articles. (EMTY)

Apple Orchard. International Apple Core. mo., $24.00/yr. Articles and lists of current literature on Apple computer products, programs, and peripherals.

Basic Computing. mo., $19.97/yr. Articles and reviews covering all models of the TRS-80 microcomputer.

Byte Magazine. mo., $21.00/yr. Current articles on computer hardware, software, applications, and reviews of computer products.

Calico Journal. Brigham Young University Press, 229 KMB, BYU, Provo, UT 84602. q., $25.00/yr. indiv.; $60.00/yr. inst. Covers all aspects ranging from trends and issues to teaching tips for using computers to teaching language in school and in business/industry. Also includes reviews. (EMTY)

The Catalyst. Western Center for Microcomputers in Special Education, Inc. bi-mo., $12.00/yr. indiv.; $20.00/yr. inst. A newsletter with the latest information on microcomputer products, applications, and research for special educators.

Classroom Computer Learning. Learning Periodicals Group. 9/yr., $22.50/yr. Deals with potentials and applications of microcomputers in classroom learning; includes news on products, grants, research, and so forth.

Collegiate Microcomputer. Rose-Hulman Institute of Technology, Terre Haute, IN 47803. q., $28.00/yr. Features articles about instructional uses of microcomputers in college and university courses. Topics range from establishing computer literacy programs to software issues and reviews to computer simulations for science classes. (EMTY)

Compute! Compute! Publications, Inc. mo., $24.00/yr. Specifically designed for Apple, Atari, VIC, PET/CBM, and other microcomputer users; contains educational columns, programs, and information.

Computer Book Review. bi-mo., $15.97/yr. Reviews books on computers and computer-related subjects.

Computer Decisions. Hayden Publishing Co. 16/yr., $35.00/yr. Features articles and reviews on using computer hardware and software for management. (EMTY)

Computer Law Journal. Center for Computer/Law. q., $66.00/yr. Contains book reviews, bibliographies, articles, and reference materials on computer and telecommunications law worldwide.

Computer News Audio Digest. Rabcom Corp. bi-wk., $195.00/yr. Reviews the best articles digested from the leading computer magazines; four special issue cassettes produced each year.

Computers and Education: An International Journal. Pergamon Press. q., $120.00/yr. A theoretical refereed journal that emphasizes research project reports.

Computers and Electronics. Ziff-Davis Publishing Co. mo., $16.00/yr. Informative columns on computers and computer applications.

Computers and People. Berkeley Enterprises, Inc. mo., $14.50/yr. Covers all aspects of information processing systems with articles, reviews, games, and so forth.

Computers, Reading, and Language Arts. q., $14.00/yr. indiv.; $18.00/yr. schools and libraries. Focuses on the relationship of computers to reading, language arts, and related issues.

Creative Computing. mo., $24.97/yr. Application of the computer to education, home, and business is emphasized. Includes tutorials, reviews, resources.

CS/HI. P.O. Box 7991, Haledon, NJ 07538. mo., $60.00/yr. Indexes software, hardware, and book reviews and programs found in more than thirty magazines.

Datapro Reports. Datapro Research Corp., 1805 Underwood Blvd., Delran, NJ 08075. Base volumes and monthly updates range from $385.00-$460.00/yr. depending on the topic (such as microcomputers, software, or minicomputers). The updates provide evaluations as well as descriptions of new products. Includes directories to vendors, companies, and so forth.

Desktop Computing. Wayne Green, Inc. mo., $25.00/yr. Stresses articles and news of interest to microcomputer users.

Dr. Dobb's Journal. People's Computer Co. mo., $25.00/yr. Articles on the latest in operating systems, programming languages, hardware design and architecture, data structures, and telecommunications; in-depth hardware and software reviews.

Educational Computer Magazine. Educational Computer. 10/yr., $25.00/yr. Features articles on computer literacy and use of computers in the classroom, by administration, and in the media center. Lists free/inexpensive software.

Educational Electronics. mo., $60.00/yr. Uses and availabilities of computer hardware and software in schools and colleges.

Electronic Education. *See* Audiovisual listings.

Electronic Learning. Scholastic, Inc. 8/yr., $19.00/yr. Professional magazine for media specialists, teachers, and administrators that stresses nontechnical information about uses of computers, video equipment, and other electronic devices.

Family Computing. Scholastic, Inc. mo., $17.97/yr. This periodicals explains to parents what their children are doing with microcomputers and gives suggestions for what they can do. (LJ, 15 Apr 84)

Incider. Wayne Green, Inc. mo., $25.00/yr. Features Apple computer programs, software uses, announcements, and reviews.

Infoscan. Syncom, Inc. mo., free. Indexes more than four hundred articles from twelve leading personal computer magazines.

Infoworld. CW Communications, Inc. 51/yr., $31.00/yr. News of the information and microcomputer field including some software reviews.

Interface Age. mo., $21.00/yr. Business computer applications, tutorials, hardware and software reviews, programming, book reviews, and new product information.

Macworld. PC World Communications, Inc. mo., $30.00/yr. Describes software, tutorials, and applications for users of the Macintosh microcomputer. (EMTY)

Micro Publications in Review. Vogeler Publications. mo., $56.00/yr. Reproduces tables of contents of some forty journals in the field.

The Micro Review. P.O. Box 14394, Austin, TX 78761. mo., $36.00/yr. Formerly *Educational Micro Review*; reviews software and hardware and features microcomputer-related articles.

Microcomputer Index. Microcomputer Information Services. q., $22.00/yr. A guide to articles and reviews in twenty-three popular microcomputer magazines. Also available online with DIALOG.

Microcomputer Industry Update. mo., $175.00/yr. Briefly summarizes articles and new products announcements from eight microcomputer publications.

Microzine. Scholastic, Inc. bi-mo., $149.00/yr. A magazine on a computer disk with interactive programs. For users of Apple II in grades four and up.

The National Logo Exchange. 9/yr., $25.00/yr. Newsletter containing book and software reviews, program evaluations, and news.

PC Home Computing. Ziff-Davis Publishing Co. mo., $19.97/yr. Covers home applications of the IBM PC such as word processing, accounting, self-study.

PC World. PC World Communications, Inc. mo., $24.00/yr. Contains new reports on hardware, software, and applications of the IBM PC.

Peelings II. 9/yr., $21.00/yr. Contains evaluative reviews of software and hardware for Apple equipment.

Personal Computer News. bi-mo., $24.00/yr. A newspaper aimed at beginning and intermediate computer users; includes articles, interviews, reviews.

Personal Computing. Hayden Publishing Co. mo., $18.00/yr. For everybody who wants to use, understand, and maximize personal computer capabilities. General overview of new developments and techniques.

Popular Computing. Byte Publications. mo., $15.00/yr. Reviews software and hardware and features tutorials, educational uses of the computer, and new programming.

Student Computer News. mo., $14.00/yr. A newsletter listing software and hardware, articles on programming, and a question-and-answer column.

Teaching and Computing. Scholastic, Inc. 8/yr., $15.95. For the elementary/junior high school teacher with articles that clearly explain software, hardware, and the mechanics of a computer. Includes reviews. (LJ, 15 Apr 84)

T.H.E. Journal (Technological Horizons in Education). Information Synergy, Inc. 9/yr., free to administrators and trainers. Describes the application and administration of technology in education and training. Reviews use of new or alternative learning delivery systems and research studies on applicability.

Whole Earth Software Review. Point, 150 Gate Five Rd., Sausalito, CA 94965. q., $18.00. Guides personal computer users through software, hardware, books, online services, and so forth.

Window. Window, Inc. 5/yr., $120.00/yr. Published on a disk for the Apple computer, which includes programs, games, reviews, and so forth.

Word Processing News: A Writer's POV on Word Processing. bi-mo., $24.00/yr. A newsletter written by writers for computerists who work with words. Includes equipment reviews, user reviews, and idea exchanges.

Reference Tools and Recommended Media

Book Bytes: The User's Guide to 1200 Microcomputer Books. Cris Popenoe. Pantheon, 1984. Book, 233 pp., $9.95 PB. Suggests books for a core collection and how to find the right books for users. Evaluative reviews are provided. (BL, July 84; ARBA, 85)

Bowker's Complete Sourcebook of Personal Computing 1985. R. R. Bowker, 1984. Book, 1050 pp., $19.95. A revised version of the 1984 edition; contains 3,300 review citations for hardware, software, peripherals, and books. Lists more than 750 computers, 2,500 peripherals, 1,800 user groups, 545 computer-related magazines, and 6,300 books about microcomputers. (EMTY)

CAD/CAM: Computer-aided Design and Manufacturing. Mikell P. Groover and Emory W. Zimmers. Prentice-Hall, 1984. Book, 489 pp., $32.95. Provides full coverage of CAD/CAM, robotics, and automated computer-aided manufacturing. Describes systems, applications, and techniques. (C, July-Aug 84)

The Complete Computer Compendium. Michael Edelhart and Douglas Garr. Addison-Wesley, 1984. Book, 276 pp., $12.95 PB. Describes a variety of topics from different viewpoints that include predictions. (BL, 1 Sept 84)

The Complete Guide to Microsystem Management. Steven K. Roberts. Prentice-Hall, 1984. Book, 184 pp., $16.95 PB. Discusses in understandable detail all aspects of buying, troubleshooting, and setting up a microcomputer system. (OT, Nov 84)

Computer-assisted Instruction: Its Use in the Classroom. Jack A. Chambers and Jerry W. Sprecher. Prentice-Hall, 1984. Book, 232 pp., $12.95 PB. A guide for administrators and teachers to designing, developing, and using CAI programs. Also describes how to evaluate, buy, and integrate courseware into the curriculum. (ET, Aug 84)

Computer Books and Serials in Print 1984. R. R. Bowker Co., 1984. Book, 1,500 pp., $49.50. Provides bibliographic and subscription information about the over 20,000 current U.S. and foreign books, serials, and pamphlets. Indexes by title, subject, and author. (ARBA, 85)

Computer Buyer's Protection Guide: How to Protect Your Rights in the Microcomputer Marketplace. L. J. Kutten. Prentice-Hall, 1984. Book, $19.95 HB; $12.95 PB. Describes hardware, software, and what to know before buying a microcomputer, including contract law. (BL, 1 May 84)

The Computer Cookbook. William Bates. Doubleday/Anchor, 1984. Book, 399 pp., $14.95. A handy one-volume encyclopedia of computing. Provides many lists and addresses. (BL, 1 Sept 84)

Computer Dictionary. Patricia Conniffe. Scholastic, 1984. Book, 96 pp., $4.95 PB. Defines more than five hundred computer-related terms for children and young adults. Includes biographical entries for some famous computer pioneers. (ARBA, 85)

Computer Education: A Catalog of Projects Sponsored by the U.S. Department of Education, 1983. (ED 244 624). Susan S. Klein, ed. EDRS, 1984. Microfiche, 310 pp., $0.97. Summarizes 275 computer education projects and Department of Education computer-related activities.

The Computer Graphics Glossary. Oryx Press, 1984. Book, 95 pp., $24.50. Defines the technical terms related to computer-aided manufacturing. Includes some commercial product names. (BL, Aug 84)

Computer Publishers & Publications: An International Directory and Yearbook, 1984 Edition. Efrem Sigel and Frederica Evan, eds. Gale, 1984. Book, 379 pp., $90.00. Comprehensive listing of publishers and journals that includes advertising rates, editorial policy, and important personnel. (C, June 84; ARBA, 85)

Computer Tutor: [A] Picture Is Worth 1,000 Words. Film Ideas, 1983. 60 min. ½-inch video, $140.00; video, $168.00; all rental, $15.00. A step-by-step guide to creating both low- and high-resolution graphics on an Apple computer. (BL, 1 May 84)

The Computer: What It Can – and Can't – Do. The Center for Humanities, 1984. 4 sound filmstrips, $169.50. An overview that demonstrates specific applications of computers, such as in banks, for weather prediction, for heat sensors, and for robots. (BL, Aug 84)

Computers & Learning: A Compendium of Papers. (ED 239 591). Alfred Bork. EDRS, 1983. Microfiche, 167 pp., $0.97. The fifteen papers cover computer-assisted instruction, software design, and course organization as well as practical suggestions for implementing computer-oriented instruction.

Computers Plus: A Program to Develop Computer Literacy among Educators. (ED 246 852). Peter J. Gray and Jon Tafel. EDRS, 1984. Microfiche, 55 pp., $0.97. The development and implementation of a workshop series are described.

Computers: What They're All About. January Productions, Inc., 1224 Rea Ave., Hawthorne, NJ 07506. 5 sound filmstrips, $105.00. Describes the workings and uses of the microcomputer and the BASIC language to give elementary school children some computer literacy. (ET, Feb 84)

Dictionary of Computers, Data Processing, and Telecommunications. Jerry M. Rosenberg. John Wiley & Sons, 1983. Book, 614 pp., $29.95 HB; $14.95 PB. Contains more than ten thousand entries related to computers, information transmission, telecommunications, and so forth. Sources are listed and a French and Spanish glossary of equivalent terms is included. (BL, 1 June 84; ARBA, 85)

The Handbook of Computers and Computing. Arthur H. Seidman and Ivan Flores, eds. Van Nostrand Reinhold, 1984. Book, 874 pp., $77.50. Contains fifty technical articles on new developments written by experts in components, devices, hardware, software, languages, and procedures. (ARBA, 85)

How to Do Computer Graphics in Your Classroom. Educational Dimensions Corp., Box 126, Stamford, CT 06904. 1984. 4 sound filmstrips, $146.00. Overviews low resolution graphics on the Apple including examples, procedures, and use of a light pen, digitizing tablet, and Koala Pad. (BL, 1 Sept 84)

Microprocessor Systems: Software and Hardware Architecture. Stephen Evanczuk, ed. McGraw-Hill, 1984. Book, 389 pp., $38.00. Contains state-of-the-art reports from the 1981-83 issues of *Electronics*, which highlight major trends, techniques, and benchmark developments. (C, July-Aug 84)

Personal Computers A-Z. Joel Makower. Doubleday, 1984. Book, 185 pp., $14.95 HB; $8.95 PB. Defines 350 terms related to hardware, software, and peripherals and gives advice about all aspects of computing. (ARBA, 85; BL, July 84)

The Reader's Guide to Microcomputer Books. Michael Nicita and Ronald Petrusha. Golden-Lee, 100 Dean St., Brooklyn, NY 11238. 1984. Book, 409 pp., $9.95 PB. An annotated bibliography of four hundred books published between 1979 and 1983. (LJ, Mar 84)

School Uses of Microcomputers: Reports from a National Survey. Issue No. 5. (ED 246 886). Johns Hopkins University. EDRS, 1984. Microfiche, 14 pp., $0.97. Data from the National Survey of School Uses of Microcomputers; indicates the impact of school location of microcomputers on their use.

The Second Self. Sherry Turkle. Simon & Schuster, Inc., 1984. Book, 362 pp., $17.95. Discusses the effects of the computer on the way we think and on the development of a computer culture—from the view of a humanist. (EMTY)

The Sybex Personal Computer Dictionary. Sybex, 1984. Book, 121 pp., $3.95 PB. Introduces the common microcomputer terms, acronyms, and jargon. Also lists some EIA and IEEE standards of microcomputer systems and component suppliers. (ARBA, 85)

What's in Print: The Subject Guide to Microcomputer Magazines. W. H. Wallace. TAB Books, 1984. Book, 461 pp., $14.95 PB. Indexes articles in more than seventy microcomputer-related magazines from 1981 to 1983. (C, Oct 84)

COMPUTERS—HARDWARE

Media-related Periodicals

Color Computer Magazine. New England Publications, Inc. mo., $24.00/yr. News, general information, reviews, surveys of color computer developments.

Computer Equipment Review. Meckler Publishing. bi-ann., $185.00/yr. Evaluates computer equipment for library applications, emphasizing online bibliographic searching and conversion of catalog data to machine-readable form.

Microcomputing. Wayne Green, Inc. mo., $25.00/yr. Contains reviews, program applications, and articles for the major microcomputing machines.

PC: The Independent Guide to IBM Personal Computers. Ziff-Davis Publishing Co. mo., $26.97/yr. Objective product reviews for IBM personal computer users, including user reports.

PC World. PC World Communications, Inc. mo., $24.00/yr. Articles on using the IBM PC, reviews of software and hardware, PC compatibility ratings, and so forth.

Personal Computer Age. mo., $24.00/yr. A journal geared to the IBM PC with technical and nontechnical articles on applications, programming, hardware, and so forth.

Reference Tools and Recommended Media

The Atari User's Encyclopedia. Gary Phillips and Jerry White. Book Co., 1984. Book, 267 pp., $19.95. Answers questions for the novice Atari computer user and acts as a guide to vendors and user groups. (ARBA, 85)

Busy Person's Guide to Selecting the Right Word Processor: A Visual Shortcut to Understanding and Buying. Alan Gadney. Festival Publications, 1984. Book, $24.95 HB; $14.95 PB. Uses many illustrations to compare word processing hardware and software systems. Also covers installation, training, and financing. (BL, 1 Sept 84)

Here Come the Clones!: The Complete Guide to IBM PC Compatible Computers. Melody Newrock. McGraw-Hill, 1984. Book, 200 pp., $18.95 PB. Discusses good and bad points of major IBM PC-compatible computers. Warns about hidden costs, software incompatibilities, and other problems. Includes a directory of manufacturers. (ARBA, 85)

The Personal Computer Handbook: A Complete Practical Guide to Choosing and Using Your Micro. Peter Rodwell. Barron's, 1983. Book, 208 pp., $14.95 PB. Summarizes for novices how computers work and how to select one. Also discusses artificial intelligence. (LJ, Mar 84)

The Plain English Repair and Maintenance Guide for Home Computers. Henry F. Beechhold. Simon & Schuster, 1984. Book, 265 pp., $14.95 PB. Begins with basic repairs and tools and moves to advanced troubleshooting, enhancement techniques, and custom building. Contains many drawings. (OT, Oct 84; BL, 1 Sept 84)

Terminals & Printers Buyer's Guide. Tony Webster. McGraw-Hill, 1984. Book, 345 pp., $19.95 PB. A guide to over 500 products with reviews and explanations of 270 visual display models. (C, Sept 84)

Word Magic: Evaluating and Selecting Word Processing. Michael Scriven. Lifetime Learning Publications, 1983. Book, 282 pp., $25.00 HB; $18.95 PB. Explains and compares word processing technologies and includes terms, vendors, and checklists. (BL, 1 May 84)

Your Apple Computer: A User's Guide. Center for Humanities, Inc. 6 sound filmstrips, $209.50; sound/slide version, $229.50. Provides a general introduction to the Apple II computer and to application programs and programming languages. Includes questions and follow-up activities. (ET, Aug 84)

COMPUTERS—SOFTWARE

Media-related Periodicals

Compendium. EPICUROUS Publishing, P.O. Box 129, Lincolndale, NY 10540. $22.00/yr.; disk for $250.00/yr. Indexes with synopses of over eight hundred articles from the major microcomputer magazines each issue and cross references by subject.

The Digest of Software Reviews: Education. The Digest of Software Reviews: Education, 1341 Bulldog Ln., Suite C, Fresno, CA 93710. q., $52.95/yr. Compiles software reviews from over sixty journals and magazines. The reviews emphasize critical features of the instructional software for grades K-12. Grade level, price, system requirements, and instructional mode are reported. (ET, Apr 84)

Nibble. MicroSPARC, Inc., 45 Winthrop St., Concord, MA 01742. mo., $26.95. Reviews Apple software and has how-to articles on using and enhancing the software.

Personal Computing "Plus". Hayden Publishing Co., Inc. mo., $10.00/yr. Describes new software packages and evaluates best ones as well as features articles on related topics. (EMTY)

School Courseware Journal. School & Home CourseWare Inc. 5/yr., $75.00/yr. A journal of microcomputer software designed for educational use; four versions are available (Apple II, PET, ATARI, and TRS-80 level II); machine-readable programs for K-12 in various subject areas.

Small Computer Program Index. ALLM Books. bi-mo., $45.00/yr. A guide to program listings in personal and small computer magazines and books from the United States, the United Kingdom, and other countries; includes printed programs.

Softline. Softalk Publishing Co. 6/yr., $12.00/yr. A serious yet entertaining publication covering the broad range of microcomputer applications including role playing, simulation, and exploratory learning.

Softside. Softside Publications. mo., $30.00/yr. Written especially for Apple, TRS-80, and Atari programmers; emphasizes games and graphics.

Software Digest. Software Digest, Inc., 1 Wynnewood Rd., Wynnewood, PA 19096. Now divided into *Ratings Book* ($175.00/yr.) and *Ratings Newsletter* ($135.00/yr.). Information about easy-to-use computer software.

Software Review. Meckler Publishing. 4/yr., $58.00/yr. Reviews computer programs and other software, books, and publications for library and educational applications.

Software Supermarket. mo., $18.00/yr. Ratings, reviews, and previews of new microcomputer software by experts in health, finance, small business, and entertainment fields.

Reference Tools and Recommended Media

The Art of Computer Game Design. Chris Crawford. Osborne/McGraw-Hill, 1984. Book, 113 pp., $14.95. Overviews the purposes of computer games and uses examples to describe how to design them. (BL, July 84)

Book of Apple Software, or **Book of Atari Software,** or **Book of IBM Software.** Book Company, 11223 S. Hindry Ave., Los Angeles, CA 90045. 1984. Books, $19.95 PB each. Each directory has long and thorough reviews of software for the identified microcomputer. Each review includes a grade for the software. The directories are updated each year. (LJ, 15 Mar 84)

Choosing Educational Software: A Buyer's Guide. Carol Truett and Lori Gillespie. Libraries Unlimited, 1984. Book, 202 pp., $18.50 PB. Discusses the criteria and processes for evaluating software; includes fourteen evaluation forms and describes major sources of commercial software. (C, July-Aug 84; ARBA, 85)

The Directory of Software Publishers: How and Where to Sell Your Program. Eric Balkan, ed. Van Nostrand Reinhold, 1983. Book, 310 pp., $25.50. Provides a directory of eight hundred software publishers and other companies. Gives suggestions to software authors regarding copyright, documentation, marketing, and so forth. (ARBA, 85)

The Free Software Catalog and Directory: The What, Where, Why, and How of Selecting, Locating, Acquiring, and Using Free Software. Robert A. Froehlich. Crown, 1984. Book, 475 pp., $9.95 PB. This lists free CP/M software sources and describes technical information about the CP/M operating system. Describes user groups, bulletin boards, documentation, and programming. (ARBA, 85)

Free Software for the IBM PC. Bertram Gader and Manuel V. Nodar. Warner Books, 1984. Book, 466 pp., $8.95 PB. A directory of over six hundred programs in the public domain for the IBM and compatibles that can be found on electronic bulletin boards. A variety of programs are listed, from games to utilities to education. (OT, Oct 84)

Hively's Choice: School Year 1983-4. Wells Hively, ed. Hively's Choice Publications, Inc., and The Continental Press, Inc., Elizabethtown, PA 17022. 1983. Book, 241 pp., $19.95. Describes good computer programs that teachers can use in the classroom; each two-page description includes the objectives, curriculum areas, time needed, and examples. Each program was field tested. (ET, July 84)

How to Buy Software: The Master Guide to Picking the Program. Alfred Glossbrenner. St. Martin's, 1984. Book, 600 pp., $14.95 PB. Good for both the novice and the experienced user; lists software guides, newsletters and magazines, and online databases; describes different types of computer programs and how to choose software. (BL, 1 May 84; LJ, Mar 84)

Microcomputer Software Buyer's Guide. Tony Webster and Richard Champion. McGraw-Hill, 1984. Book, 422 pp., $19.95. Describes the types of software packages available as well as which software works with which computer system and peripherals; advises how to select the best software for your own needs. (ARBA, 85)

Microprogrammer's Market 1984. Marshall Hamilton. TAB Books, 1984. Book, 229 pp., $18.95 HB; $13.50 PB. Describes how to sell software programs to publishers, lists contact people, and describes details about each publisher. (ARBA, 85)

Microsift Courseware Evaluations. (ED 239 606 and ED 245 666). Northwest Regional Educational Lab. EDRS, 1984. Microfiche, $0.97 each. Microcomputer software packages are evaluated on twenty-one criteria and include descriptive information.

PC Telemart/Vanloves IBM Software Directory: Yellow Pages to the World of Micro Computers. R. R. Bowker, 1984. Book, 934 pp., $24.95 PB. A well-organized and readable directory; lists over three thousand software packages that run on the IBM PC and other MS DOS computers; includes lists of vendors, producers, bulletin boards, and a glossary of terms. (ARBA, 85)

The Software Marketplace: Where to Sell What You Program. Suzan D. Prince. McGraw-Hill, 1984. Book, 201 pp., $16.95. Describes the software marketplace, trends, legal problems, and includes a directory of publishers, magazines, and agents. (ARBA, 85)

Software Quality & Copyright: Issues in Computer-assisted Instruction. Virginia Helm. AECT, 1984. Book, 128 pp., $16.00. Reviews copyright issues as related to educational software. Also examines the problems of producing quality programs and how to select good software. (EMTY)

Swift's Educational Software Directory for Corvus Networks. Sterling Swift, 1984. Book, 219 pp., $14.95. This directory, along with Swift's other directories for software, includes extensive annotations on software and a listing of software publishers. The other directories describe software for the Apple and for the IBM PC. (ARBA, 85)

T.E.S.S.: The Educational Software Selector. EPIE Institute, 1984. Book, 593 pp., $49.95 PB. Describes about six thousand software programs for all educational levels and includes two thousand citations to software reviews. (ARBA, 85; EMTY)

DATABASES; NETWORKING

Media-related Periodicals

Data Sources. Ziff-Davis Publishing Co. q., $120.00/yr. A guide to the information processing industry; covers equipment, software, services, companies, and systems.

Database Update. Newsletter Management Corporation. mo., $219.00/yr. Covers all types of databases and search services; gives the latest information and happenings in the online database field. Also available online with the NEWSNET online newsletter service.

EMMS: Electronic Mail & Message Systems. International Resource Development, Inc. semi-mo., $275.00/yr. Up-to-the-minute coverage of new technological products and market trends in facsimile, office communications, and record and graphic communications.

Information Today. Learned Information, Inc. mo., $19.50/yr. Covers news and trends; reviews of hardware, software, and databases; job listings. Has online service buyer's guide and a calendar of events.

Infotecture. Espial Productions. 18/yr., $210.00/yr. in the United States. A news publication covering the online information industry in Canada.

Link-Up: Communications and the Small Computer. 3938 Meadowbrook Rd., Minneapolis, MN 55426. Mo., $23.95. Covers small computer communications news, projects, people, databases, hardware, and software. Includes tutorials and how-to's for beginners and experts.

Modem Notes. Modem Notes, P.O. Box 408472, Chicago, IL 60640. mo., $24.00/yr. Published by the information brokerage firm of Katherine Ackerman and Associates, this newsletter provides information on everything accessible by computer and phone. It compares systems, reviews new databases, and gives tips for using databases.

Online Review. Learned Information, Inc. bi-mo., $70.00/yr. An international journal of online information systems featuring articles on using and managing online systems, training and educating online users, developing search aids, and creating and marketing databases.

Online Today. P.O. Box 20212, Columbus, OH 43220. mo., $30.00/yr. A CompuServe publication; gives current news about computer communication and information retrieval; in-depth articles on issues and techniques; and software and book reviews. Also available online through CompuServe.

Resource Sharing and Information Networks. Haworth Press. q., $33.00/yr. indiv.; $60.00/yr. inst. Practical aspects of using various types of network services, training, cost-effectiveness, and user access to public terminals.

Reference Tools and Recommended Media

Communications & Networking for the IBM PC. Larry E. Jordan and Bruce Churchill. Robert J. Brady Co., 1983. Book, 237 pp., $18.95. All aspects of communications among personal computers are covered in nontechnical language. Accurate details are provided about both hardware and software. (OT, Oct 84)

The Complete Handbook of Personal Computer Communications: Everything You Need to Go Online with the World. Alfred Glossbrenner. St. Martin's, 1984. Book, 325 pp., $14.95 PB. Shows how to access hundreds of databases and discusses topics such as electronic bulletin boards and teleconferencing. (LJ, Mar 84)

Computer-Security Technology. James Cooper. Lexington Books, 1984. Book, 166 pp., $25.00. Introduces computer security technology for those who use computer networks and databases. Includes vendors, glossary, and references for further reading. (C, May 84)

Computerized Literature Searching: Research Strategies and Databases. Charles L. Gilreath. Westview Press, 1984. Book, 177 pp., $22.00. Warns of potential search problems with computer-based bibliographic services and suggests thesauri for each subject area. (ARBA, 85)

Designing and Implementing Local Area Networks. Dimitris N. Chorafas. McGraw-Hill, 1984. Book, 354 pp., $32.95. A comprehensive source of information about local area networks in general and about different types of systems. For nontechnical readers, it includes a glossary. (C, May 84)

Dictionary of New Information Technology Acronyms. Michael Gordon, Alan Singleton, and Clarence Rickards. distr., Gale, 1984. Book, 217 pp., $56.00. Acronyms associated with information technology terms and organizations are identified and explained, including company names and countries for products. (ARBA, 85)

Directory of Online Databases. Cuadra Associates, $75.00/yr. subscription. Grouped into reference and source types, 1,878 databases and files are described with bibliographic information. Includes directory of producers and online services, telecommunications systems, and master index. (BL, 1 Sept 84)

A Guide to Searching Ontap ABI/INFORM. (ED 245 691). Data Courier, Inc. EDRS, 1983. Microfiche, $0.97. Suggests cost-effective techniques for searching ABI/INFORM, a database that provides worldwide coverage of management trends, tactics, and techniques.

Handbook of Data Communications. John D. Lenk. Prentice-Hall, 1984. Book, 308 pp., $24.95. Discusses hardware, software, and principles of data communications. Explains how to use test equipment to diagnose and correct problems with data transfer. Not for the novice. (C, Sept 84)

How to Get the Most out of CompuServe. Charles Bowen and David Peyton. Bantam Books, 1984. Book, 278 pp., $12.95 PB. Provides useful, timely information about the complete range of CompuServe activities. (OT, Oct 84)

Information Resource/Data Dictionary Systems. Henry C. Lefkovits, Edgar H. Sibley, and Sandra L. Lefkovits. QED Information Sciences, 1983. Book, $30.00 looseleaf in binder. Surveys the field of information resource management and analyzes in-depth seven commercially available systems.

Omni Online Database Directory. Mike Edelhart and Owen Davies. Macmillan, 1984. Book, 292 pp., $19.95 HB; $10.95 PB. Describes the contents of more than one thousand online, public access databases and tells how to select equipment and software, and how to search. Indexes databases by subject and provides user evaluation. (BL, 15 Sept 84)

Subject Thesaurus for Bowker Online Databases. R. R. Bowker, 1984. Book, 700 pp., $25.00. Lists eighty-five thousand headings used for the bibliographic and biographical records in Bowker's online databases.

EDUCATION AND RESEARCH

Media-related Periodicals

American Education. Government Printing Office. mo., $20.00/yr. Covers preschool to adult education, new research and demonstration projects, major education legislation, bond data, grants, loans, contracts, and fellowships.

Chronicle of Higher Education. Corbin Gwaltney. wk., $40.00/yr. News and trends in higher education, current legislation, statistical surveys, meetings, book reviews, and classified advertising.

The COINT Reports. (Communication and Information Technology: A Multidisciplinary Approach). AD Digest. 6/yr., $12.00/yr. Syntheses of research findings in the fields of data processing, audiovisual/video/TV technology, library technology, and related fields.

Current Index to Journals in Education (CIJE). Oryx Press. mo., $150.00. A guide to articles published in some 780 education and education-related journals. Each ERIC clearinghouse compiles monthly resumes of journal articles including complete bibliographic information. (ARBA, 85)

Education Index. H. W. Wilson. mo. (except July and August); variable costs. Provides easy access to information in 319 educational periodicals, yearbooks, monographs, and other publications. Offers quarterly cumulations and permanent bound annual cumulations.

Educational Research. Carfax Publishing Co. 3/yr., $22.50/yr. indiv.; $45.00/yr. inst. A journal of educational research reporting on current research, evaluation, and applications.

History of Higher Education Annual. Alan Karp, ed. State University of New York at Buffalo, Faculty of Educational Studies, 367 Balky, Buffalo, NY 14260. ann., $5.00. A refereed journal for teachers and administrators that covers the international history of higher education. (C, July-Aug 84)

Instructor Magazine. Instructor Publications, Inc. mo. (August-May), $18.00/yr. Teaching and class content/activity suggestions including some for audiovisual applications and uses of computers in the classroom.

Research in Science and Technological Education. Carfax Publishing Co. 2/yr., $70.00/yr. Publication of original research in the science and technological fields; articles on psychological, sociological, economic, and organizational aspects as well.

Resources in Education (RIE). Government Printing Office. mo., $95.00. Abstracts and indexes by subject, author, and institution; recently completed research-related reports, books, and other documents. Cumulative semiannual indexes must be purchased separately. A service of the ERIC Information Clearinghouse System, sponsored by the National Institute of Education.

Teacher. Instructor Publications. 10/yr., $18.00/yr. Teaching tips and resources; discussion of teaching problems and procedures, learning center development, and books.

Teachers & Writers Magazine. Teachers and Writers. 5/yr., $12.50/yr. New ideas and teaching strategies based on classroom experiences; articles on projects involving writing, filmmaking, video production, visual arts, other activities.

Reference Tools and Recommended Media

Directory of State Education Agencies 1983-1984. Washington, DC, Council of Chief State School Officers, 1984. Book, 195 pp., $8.00 PB. Contains a directory of state and national agencies concerned with education. Also includes NEA officers, U.S. Congress committees, and U.S. Department of Education employees. To be published annually. (ARBA, 85)

DRG: Directory of Research Grants 1984. Oryx Press, 1984. Book, 416 pp., $55.00 PB. Provides information about more than two thousand grants available from government agencies, professional organizations, corporations, and private foundations and covers eighty-five subject areas including "Grants for Women," "Library Programs," and "Publishing Support." (ARBA, 85)

1984 Directory of Resources for Technology in Education. Far West Laboratory, 1984. Book, n.p., $19.95 HB; $12.95 PB. A directory of national and state associations, resources organizations, computer camps, periodicals, databases, degree programs, and so forth that can help in the implementation of technology programs. (EMTY)

Televised Higher Education: Catalog of Resources. Jo Ann Green, ed. Western Interstate Commission for Higher Education, 1984. Book, 349 pp., $65.00 PB. Describes over 1,100 videocourses beyond high school produced by over two hundred colleges, universities, businesses, associations, and television stations. To be included, a production had to be produced after 1976, not exceed four hours, and be purchasable or leasable. (ARBA, 85)

Thesaurus of ERIC Descriptors. James E. Houston. Oryx Press, 1984. Book, 614 pp., $45.00. A thesaurus, with 680 changes since the last edition, for those who search the ERIC indexes and database. Lists 9,076 terms, both main entry and nonindexable *use* references or invalid terms. (ARBA, 85)

FILMS/FILMSTRIPS — EDUCATIONAL AND THEATRICAL

Media-related Periodicals

CINEASTE: A Magazine on the Art and Politics of the Cinema. CINEASTE Magazine. q., $8.00/yr. indiv.; $11.00/yr. inst. Book and film reviews, articles, interviews; social and political perspective on international and domestic cinema.

Film Comment. bi-mo., $12.00/yr. An illustrated commentary on film developments around the world; reviews, interviews with important filmmakers, and trends in the cinema.

Film Quarterly. q., $11.00/yr. indiv.; $19.00/yr. inst. Scholarly articles on films and television and critiques of productions in those media.

Film Review. mo., $14.00/yr. Reviews and featured articles on films, books, and records.

Film Video News. Open Court (Carus) Publishing Co. q., $12.00/yr. An international review of nontheatrical films, video, filmstrips, and AV materials and equipment.

Films, Etc. National Audiovisual Center. mo., free. Highlights notable additions to the U.S. film and video distribution unit.

Historical Journal of Film, Radio, and Television. Carfax Publishing Co. 2/yr., $51.00/yr. indiv. Articles by international experts in the field, news and notices, and book reviews.

Journal of Popular Film and Television. Heldref Publications. q., $20.00/yr. Articles on film and television, book reviews, theory and criticism, filmographies, and bibliographies covering many aspects of these media.

Landers Film Reviews. Landers Associates. bi-mo. (September-May), $45.00. Reviews and evaluations of films for schools and libraries; cumulative title and subject indexes available.

Literature/Film Quarterly. Salisbury State College. q., $8.00/yr. indiv.; $16.00/yr. inst. Articles on film presentations of published literary works, with special attention to comparisons of the two media. Interviews with directors and screenwriters.

Media Profiles: Audiovisual Marketing Newsletter. Olympic Media Information. bi-mo., $48.00/yr. Deals with marketing nontheatrical films, video, filmstrips, and slide sets.

Media Scene Prevue. Supergraphics. bi-mo., $15.00/yr. News, photos, and features on upcoming developments in the worlds of film, fiction, television, art, and media entertainment.

Quarterly Review of Film Studies. Redgrave Publishing Co. q., $21.00/yr. indiv.; $34.00/yr. inst. This journal contains scholarly articles and critical review essays of current books and film journals.

Sight & Sound: International Film Quarterly. Eastern News. q., $16.00/yr. Reviews of films and TV programs, historical articles, current developments in film and television, news of actors, producers, and new publications.

Reference Tools and Recommended Media

Creative Writing through Films: An Instructional Program for Secondary Students. Bruce McDonald, Leslie Orsini, and Thomas J. Wagner. Libraries Unlimited, 1984. Book, 224 pp., $23.50. Films that illustrate storywriting techniques provide the basis for teaching students both the elementary and advanced skills of fiction writing. Indexes and suggested student activities also are included. (ARBA, 85)

Fifty Years of Serial Thrills. Scarecrow, 1983. Book, 210 pp., $15.00. Five hundred American movie serials from the pretelevision era are described. Includes general commentary and some photos. (C, Apr 84)

Film Directors: A Complete Guide. Michael Singer, ed. Lone Eagle Productions, 1984. Book, 392 pp., $32.95. This second edition is a reference for finding out who directed what and vice versa. About 1,200 current international and domestic directors are covered. Includes interviews, addresses, and indexes. (LJ, 1 May 84)

Films and Filmmakers. Christopher Lyon and Susan Doll, eds. Gale, 1984. Book, 4 vols., 2,600 pp., $50.00/vol., $200.00/set. The volumes cover films, directors/filmmakers, actors and actresses, and writers and production artists throughout the world. The focus is on those who have influenced films. (EMTY)

Magill's Cinema Annual: 1984. Frank N. Magill, ed. Salem Press, Inc., 1984. Book, n.p., pna. Essay reviews of films released in the United States in 1984. (EMTY)

Selected Film Criticism: Foreign Films, 1930-1950. Anthony Slide, ed. Scarecrow, 1984. Book, 207 pp., $17.50. Part of an ongoing series that selects reviews from about nineteen periodicals. Not always critical or informative. (C, Oct 84)

Turning Mirrors into Windows: Teaching the Best Short Films. Marion Bue. Libraries Unlimited, 1984. Book, 287 pp., $21.50. For secondary level educators to find films for teaching. Includes suggestions of how to use specific films as well as annotations and reviews of others. Has a directory of film distributors. (ARBA, 85)

Who Was Who on Screen. Evelyn Mack Truitt, comp. R. R. Bowker, 1984. Book, 438 pp., $18.95 PB. Profiles of about 3,300 film personalities are covered, including biographies and film credits. (EMTY)

INFORMATION SCIENCE

Media-related Periodicals

Datamation. Technical Publishing Co. mo., $50.00/yr. Covers semitechnical news and views, such as hardware, software, and databases, for data and information processing professionals.

Electronic Publishing Review. Learned Information, Inc. q., $66.00/yr. An international journal of the transfer of published information via videotex and online media. Also has advice, articles, and news from the fields of communications, information transfer, publishing, and computers.

Information Retrieval and Library Automation. Lomond Publications, Inc. mo., $48.00/yr. Includes new techniques, equipment, software, and publications; covers events, meetings, international developments, networks and communications, media innovation, technology transfer, and federal policies.

Information Services and Use. Elsevier Science Publishing Co., Inc. bi-mo., $72.00. An international journal for those in the information management field; includes online and offline systems, library automation, micrographics, videotex, telecommunications, and so forth.

The Information Society. Crane Russak & Co., Inc. q., $60.00/yr. Provides a forum for discussion of the world of information—transborder data flow, regulatory issues, the impact of the information industry.

Journal of Documentation. Aslib Publications. q., $87.00/yr. Describes how technical, scientific, and other specialized knowledge is recorded, organized, and disseminated.

INSTRUCTIONAL TECHNOLOGY/DESIGN/DEVELOPMENT; TRAINING

Media-related Periodicals

Educational Technology. Educational Technology Publications. mo., $49.00/yr. Learning and instruction, systems, computer-assisted instruction, instructional design and development, and evaluation are some of the topics covered. Also reviews literature, software, audiovisual materials.

High Technology. mo., $21.00/yr. Covers all aspects of emerging technology and science, such as genetic engineering, communications, energy, robotics, and the electronic office.

Holosphere. Museum of Holography. q., $30.00/yr. Reports on research, applications, patents, innovations in techniques, equipment, and other world news of holography.

International Journal of Instructional Media. *See* Audiovisual listings.

Journal of Educational Technology Systems. Baywood Publishing Co., Inc. q., $51.00/yr. In-depth articles on completed and ongoing research in all phases of educational technology and its application and future within the teaching profession.

Journal of Technical Writing and Communication. Baywood Publishing Co., Inc. q., $27.00/yr. indiv.; $53.00/yr. inst. Expresses the views of communicators, records their problems and successes, promotes their research, and acts as a forum.

Machine-Mediated Learning. Crane Russak & Co., Inc. 4/yr., $86.00/yr. Focuses on the scientific, technological, and management aspects of the application of machines to instruction and training. Evaluates economic and educational effectiveness, analyzes computer, telecommunication, videodisc, and other technological developments.

Training. Lakewood Publications, Inc. mo., $36.00/yr. News, how-to features, case studies, and opinions on managing training and human resources development activities.

Reference Tools and Recommended Media

Basic References on Instructional Development. (ED 239 579). Roberts A. Braden and Steven G. Sachs. EDRS, 1983. Microfiche, 15 pp., $0.97. More than three hundred instructional developers were surveyed about books they would recommend for personal use, textbook, reference, and for nondevelopers.

Countering Educational Design. Ted Nunan. Nichols Publishing Co., 1983. Book, 131 pp., $22.50. Opposes professional educational design and emphasizes need for classroom teacher to control design. (ET, Feb 84)

Directory of Resources for Technology in Education, 1984. Donna Lloyd-Kolkin, Sharon Taylor, and Guiselle Maffioli-Hesemann. Far West Laboratory, 1984. Book, 243 pp., $19.95 HB; $12.95 PB. Lists organizations using microcomputers in education, some organizations promoting instructional television, and eighteen national associations. Also has a directory of companies, funding sources, databases, and so forth. (ARBA, 85)

Educational Consulting: A Guidebook for Practitioners. Fenwick W. English and Betty E. Steffy. Educational Technology Publications, 1984. Book, $26.95. Talks about consulting from both the external and internal viewpoints based on the authors' experiences and their survey of educational consulting firms.

Elementary Teacher's New Complete Ideas Handbook. Iris McClellan Tiedt and Sidney Willis Tiedt. Prentice-Hall, 1983. Book, $16.50. Describes instructional strategies for K-8 classes. Covers each discipline and has book lists, exercises, lesson plans, and so forth. (ARBA, 85)

Guide to Nonsexist Teaching Activities (K-12). Northwest Regional Educational Laboratory Center for Sex Equity. Oryx Press, 1983. Book, 99 pp., $22.50. Materials were selected from an ERIC search for nonsexist teaching activities and by reviewing catalogs and other sources. The guide is divided into eight subject areas and broken down by activities with grade level indicated. (ARBA, 85)

Instructional Design Theories and Models: An Overview of Their Status. Charles Reigeluth, ed. Lawrence Erlbaum Associates, 1983. Book, n.p., pna. A collection of essays written by some of the leaders in the educational technology field. Awarded the outstanding book award by Division of Instructional Development of AECT during the 1985 convention. (EMTY)

Proceedings of Selected Research Paper Presentations Made at the 1984 Convention of the Association for Educational Communications and Technology and Sponsored by the Research and Theory Division. (ED 243 411). Michael R. Simonson, ed. EDRS, 1984. Microfiche, 664 pp., $0.97. The thirty-one papers cover current issues in educational communications and technology such as computer anxiety, learning strategies, and instructional design.

Processes of Skill Performance: A Foundation for the Design and Use of Training Equipment. (ED 239 583). William D. Spears. EDRS, 1983. Microfiche, 167 pp., $0.97. Dimensions of skill performance and cognitive and motor skills are analyzed to guide the design and effective use of low-cost training devices.

A Review of the Literature on Training Simulators: Transfer of Training and Simulator Fidelity. (ED 246 864). Yuan-Liang David Su. EDRS, 1984. Microfiche, 84 pp., $0.97. Summarizes current research issues on simulation and the training effectiveness of simulators.

Selecting Media for Instruction. Robert A. Reiser and Robert M. Gagne. Educational Technology Publications, 1983. Book, 126 pp., $24.95. Describes a media selection model based on principles of learning while accounting for practical considerations. User is guided through a series of choices by questions. (ET, Dec 83)

Training and Technology: A Handbook for HRD Professionals. Greg Kearsley. Addison-Wesley, 1984. Book, 208 pp., $25.95. General description of audiovisual and other electronic materials and hardware that can be used in training. Provides references after each chapter. (ET, July 84)

Training by Contract: College-Employer Profiles. College Board, 1983. Book, 82 pp., $8.95 PB. Training programs offered by colleges and universities to businesses and government agencies are described. Training includes such topics as management development, international finance, and problem solving. (ARBA, 85)

Using Technology for Education and Training. Information Dynamics, Inc., 111 Claybrook Dr., Silver Spring, MD 20902. 1984. Book, 242 pp., $27.00. The proceedings of the Fifth National Conference on Communications Technology in Education and Training cover topics such as cost-effectiveness and adequacy of communications technology and practical applications in training, military, and education.

LIBRARIES/MEDIA CENTERS

Media-related Periodicals

Access: Microcomputers in Libraries. DAC Publications. q., $11.00/yr. Theory and practice of microcomputer usage in libraries.

Braille Book Review. Library of Congress. National Library Service for the Blind and Physically Handicapped. bi-mo., free. In braille or in print. Announces braille books and magazines available to readers and includes information about developments and activities in library services to the handicapped.

Computer Equipment Review. *See* Computers — Hardware listings.

Journal of Academic Librarianship. bi-mo., $22.00/yr. indiv.; $38.00/yr. inst. Results of significant research; issues and problems facing academic libraries; book reviews; and innovations in academic libraries.

Journal of Librarianship. Library Assn. Publishing. q., $63.00/yr. Deals with all aspects of library and information work in the United Kingdom and reviews literature from everywhere.

Library and Information Science Abstracts. Library Assn. Publishing. mo., $303.00/yr. includes annual name and subject indexes. Over five hundred abstracts per issue from over five hundred periodicals, reports, books, and conference proceedings.

Library Hi Tech Journal. Pierian Press. q., $19.50/yr. indiv.; $39.50/yr. inst. Covers new technology in the library field including feature articles, software and database reviews, book reviews, and conference highlights.

Library Hi Tech News. Pierian Press. 11/yr., $39.50/yr. indiv.; $59.50/yr. inst. News and ideas about technology related to library operations; database developments; annotated bibliographies.

Library Journal. R. R. Bowker Co. 20/yr., $59.00/yr. A professional periodical for librarians with current issues and news, professional reading, lengthy book review section, classifieds.

Library Quarterly. Univ. of Chicago Press. q., $20.00/yr. indiv.; $30.00/yr. inst. Scholarly articles of interest to librarians.

Library Trends. Univ. of Illinois, Graduate School of Library and Information Science. Univ. of Illinois Press. q., $20.00/yr. Each issue is concerned with one aspect of library and information science, analyzing current thought and practice and examining ideas that hold the greatest potential for the field.

Public Library Quarterly. Haworth Press. q., $32.00/yr. indiv.; $48.00/yr. inst. Serves as a forum for discussion of issues relating to library administration, research, and practice.

School Library Journal. R. R. Bowker Co. 10/yr., $38.00/yr. For school and youth service librarians, it contains about 2,500 critical book reviews annually.

Small Computers in Libraries. Univ. of Arizona, Graduate School Library. mo. (except July and August), $20.00/yr. This newsletter serves as a clearinghouse for information on microcomputers in small libraries. Includes reviews of programs and books.

The U*N*A*B*A*S*H*E*D Librarian: The "How I Run My Library Good" Letter. Marvin H. Scilken. q., $20.00/yr. Down-to-earth library items: procedures, forms, programs, cataloging, booklists, software reviews.

Wilson Library Bulletin. H. W. Wilson Co. mo. (except July and August), $25.00/yr. Significant articles on librarianship; news, reviews of films, books, and professional literature.

Reference Tools and Recommended Media

Automation in Libraries: A LITA Bibliography, 1978-1982. Anne G. Adler et al., comps. Pierian Press, 1983. Book, 177 pp., $18.95. This sixth bibliography of library automation includes over 2,500 citations divided into 45 sections including networks and utilities, telecommunications, and computers. Selective coverage of journals and some monographs, annuals, and so forth. (ARBA, 85)

The Bowker Annual of Library & Book Trade Information 1984. 29th ed. Julia Ehresmann, comp. and ed. R. R. Bowker Co., 1984. Book, 683 pp., $60.00. Covers librarianship, publishing, bookselling, and other information activities such as publishing awards. Includes a bibliography for the publisher and book trade and a directory of book trade associations as well as a section on foundation grants. (ARBA, 85)

Children's Magazine Guide. Children's Magazine Guide. mo., with semi-ann. cumulations, $22.50. Authoritative guide directed toward needs of elementary and junior high school students; indexes some sixty children's magazines.

Directory of Government Collections & Librarians. 4th ed. Barbara Kile and Audrey Taylor, eds. Congressional Information Service, 1984. Book, 690 pp., $40.00 PB. The directory is arranged by state, then by city and name of the library. Information includes subject specialties, depository designations, names of government document staff members, notes on public access, and so forth. (ARBA, 85)

Directory of Special Libraries and Information Centers. 8th ed. Brigitte T. Darnay, ed. Gale, 1983. 2 vols. Vol. 1, $260.00; vol. 2, $230.00. Provides information on subject coverage, holdings, and services of special libraries and other holdings that are defined by subject or form. Over 80 percent responded to a questionnaire. (BL, July 84)

A Guide to Sources of Information in Libraries. James G. Olle. Gower Publishing, 1984. 178 pp., $32.95. Looks at nonprint media as well as print in terms of form—a continuous composition or an arrangement for easy access—and describes how information can be found. (ARBA, 85)

Guide to the Production and Use of Audio-Visual Aids in Library and Information Science Teaching. (ED 243 486). Anthony H. Thompson. EDRS, 1983. Microfiche, 133 pp., $0.97. For use in developing countries by teachers of librarianship and information science who make audiovisual materials. Illustrations may be duplicated or adapted.

Introduction to Library Automation. James Rice. Libraries Unlimited, 1984. Book, 209 pp., $28.00 HB; $18.50 PB. Introduces all aspects of library automation from subsystem needs to participants; presents pro-con explanations of different approaches. (BL, July 84)

Library Automation: Issues and Applications. Dennis Reynolds. R. R. Bowker Co., 1984. Book, 304 pp., $37.50. Serves as a guidebook to the applications, trends, systems, vendors, and terms related to library automation.

Library Literature. H. W. Wilson Co. bi-mo., sold on service basis. A cumulative author and subject index to materials in library and information science published in the United States and abroad.

Media and Microcomputers in the Library: A Selected, Annotated Resource Guide. Evelyn H. Daniel and Carol I. Notowitz. Oryx Press, 1984. Book, 157 pp., $24.95. Acts as a resource guide to notable audio, film, slide, photographic and video media, toys, and microcomputers. Includes use of computers and computer-related materials in education. Provides information about copyright and about telecommunications and technological forecasts. (ARBA, 85)

Media Center Management with an Apple II®. Janet Noll Naumer. Libraries Unlimited, 1984. Book, 250 pp., $19.50. Describes how to set up a management system for the media center with an Apple II microcomputer.

The Media Specialist, the Microcomputer, and the Curriculum. Joanne Troutner. Libraries Unlimited, 1983. Book, 181 pp., $19.50. Uses examples and checklists to explain how a microcomputer can fit into the curriculum. Includes suggestions for evaluating hardware and software and for training. (BL, July 84)

Popular Periodical Index. Robert M. Bottorff, ed. and pub. semi-ann., $20.00/yr. A basic index to thirty-seven periodicals; supplements *Readers' Guide to Periodical Literature.*

Readers' Guide to Periodical Literature. H. W. Wilson Co., variable publishing, $80.00 (bound annual cumulations). A cumulative author and subject index to 174 general-interest periodicals published in the United States.

Reference Service: An Annotated Bibliographic Guide. Supplement 1976-1982. Marjorie E. Murfin and Lubomyr R. Wynar. Libraries Unlimited, 1984. Book, 353 pp., $35.00. Includes 1,668 annotated entries for books, articles, chapters, theses, dissertations, and conference proceedings and papers that are related to the reference process. (ARBA, 85)

School Library Media Annual. Volume Two. Shirley L. Aaron and Pat R. Scales, eds. Libraries Unlimited, 1984. Book, 508 pp., $35.00. Covers events, issues, programs, collections, research, and trends for the future in school libraries. (ARBA, 85)

Stacks of Ideas: Activities for Library Media Center and Classroom K-12. (ED 239 659). Oklahoma State Department of Education. EDRS, 1983. Microfiche, 292 pp., $0.97. The combination of library media skills with the regular instructional program is described. Fifteen elementary and junior high school units and twelve high school units are presented.

Training Users of Online Public Access Catalogs. Marsha Hamilton McClintock, comp. and ed. Council on Library Resources, 1983. Book, 122 pp., $10.00 PB. Reports on a conference that focused on ways to train the public to use online catalogs. (LJ, Jan 84)

Ulrich's International Periodicals Directory. R. R. Bowker Co., 1984. Book (or online through BRS or DIALOG), $110.00. Lists and classifies more than 64,000 periodicals of all kinds throughout the world. Provides essential data about each, including ordering notes.

Where to Find What: A Handbook to Reference Service. James M. Hillard. Scarecrow, 1984. Book, 357 pp., $22.50. About 2,000 titles are arranged in 595 subject areas that best help the librarian find answers to questions. Bibliographical information and a brief annotation is supplied. (ARBA, 85)

MICROFORMS, MICROGRAPHICS

Media-related Periodicals

Micrographics Newsletter. Microfilm Publishing, Inc. semi-mo., $95.00/yr. Information on everything of interest to microfilm users and suppliers.

Reference Tools and Recommended Media

International Micrographics Source Book, 1984-85. Microfilm Publishing, 1984. Book, 328 pp., $65.00 PB. Lists directory information on micrographics equipment, products, manufacturers, dealers, consultants, associations, service bureaus, and storage centers. Also describes four hundred leading commercial and educational publishers and books and periodicals. (ARBA, 85)

PHOTOGRAPHY

Media-related Periodicals

Aperture. A Division of Silver Mountain Foundation, Inc. q., $32.00/yr. A forum for criticism and appreciation of contemporary photography.

Industrial & Commercial Photography. Globe Publishing Co. bi-mo., $30.00/yr. For professional photographers; includes audiovisual and film production.

Industrial Photography. United Business Publications, Inc. mo., $15.00/yr. Organizational applications of photography, audiovisuals, motion pictures, and video.

Junior Education. Scholastic Publications, Ltd. mo., $20.00/yr. Book reviews, pictures, articles, visualized education information.

Montage. Eastman Kodak Co. 3/yr., free. A newsletter sponsoring "imagination in learning," with emphasis on using various photographic processes in the curriculum. Stresses the impact of visual elements on communication.

Petersen's Photographic. Petersen Publishing Co. mo., $11.94/yr. Monthly columns provide information about darkroom work, medium-format photography, electronics, professional tips, and new equipment.

Technical Photography. PTN Publishing Corp. mo., $10.00/yr. Profiles individuals and in-plant departments, techniques, new products, and current literature of interest to educators and other professionals.

Reference Tools and Recommended Media

American Photography: A Critical History, 1945 to the Present. Jonathan Green and James Friedman. Abrams, 1984. Book, 247 pp., $35.00. The key roles of select photographers, curators, and critics are explained in this history of photographs. (C, Sept 84)

Art of Black-and-White Enlarging. David Vestal. Harper, 1984. Book, 320 pp., $24.95. Explains the production of black-and-white prints for an intermediate-level photographer. (LJ, July 84)

Great Action Photography. Bryn Campbell, ed. Watson-Guptill/Amphoto, 1983. Book, 160 pp., $24.95. A collection of pictures from eight well-respected sports photographers is discussed in technical detail. (BL, Apr 84)

International Photography Index, 1981. William S. Johnson and Susan E. Cohen, eds., Stuart Alexander et al., comps. G. K. Hall, 1984. Book, 299 pp., $95.00. Indexes about 7,000 articles from 111 U.S. and foreign journals published in 1981 that focus on different aspects of photography. (C, Sept 84)

McGraw-Hill's Handbook for Professional Photographers. Ted Schwarz. McGraw-Hill, 1983. Book, 308 pp., $24.95. Provides an overview of a career in photography, for the novice. (LJ, Jan 84)

Photographer's Market: 1985. Robert D. Lutz, ed. Writer's Digest, 1984. Book, n.p., pna. Lists and provides contact data for three thousand buyers of freelance photography; articles on successful photography.

The Wildlife and Nature Photographer's Field Guide. Michael Freeman. Writer's Digest, 1984. Book, 223 pp., $14.95. Covers camera techniques, fieldwork, and photographing in different environments. Introductory level for the novice or review for the experienced photographer. (LJ, July 84)

PRINT — BOOKS/MAGAZINES

Media-related Periodicals

Book & Author Magazine. Profiles Partners, 232 S. Meramec, St. Louis, MO 63105. mo., $10.00 yr. Covers a variety of subjects and styles to create interest in reading for relaxation. Features several commercial writers and books each month. (C, July-Aug 84)

EPB: Electronic Publishing and Bookselling. Oryx Press. bi-mo., $60.00/yr. Provides current information on computer systems that are working for publishers, booksellers, and other information professionals.

Small Press. The Magazine of Independent Book Publishing. R. R. Bowker Co. bi-mo., $18.00/yr. A how-to magazine for independent publishers covering information vital to distribution, production, marketing, and contractual arrangements for publishing books.

Reference Tools and Recommended Media

American Book Trade Directory. 30th ed. R. R. Bowker Co., 1984. Book, 1,511 pp., $99.50. This is the guide to the book business from wholesale to retail books and magazines in the United States and Canada. It lists 534 more retailers than the last edition. Includes a summary of booksellers' statistics. (ARBA, 85)

Book Publishing Annual. Editors of Publishers Weekly. R. R. Bowker Co., 1984. Book, 300 pp., $42.50. Covers current data related to publishing, selling, and distributing books in the United States and abroad.

Book Review Digest. H. W. Wilson Co. ann., sold on service basis only. Book. Extracts of reviews from eighty-one periodicals; lists more than six thousand books.

Books in Print Supplement 1983-1984. 2 vols. R. R. Bowker Co., 1984. Book, $85.00. Indexes over 40,000 new titles and provides 160,000 price, binding, and other changes in backlisted titles. Contains ordering information.

Forthcoming Books. R. R. Bowker Co. 6/yr., $80.00. Provides complete, current information on adult trade books, technical and science books, juvenile, El-Hi and college textbooks, paperbacks, imports, and revised editions and reprints.

International Literary Marketplace 1984/85. R. R. Bowker Co., 1984. Book, 600 pp., $65.00. Provides profiles and contact data for publishers, literary agents, booksellers, major libraries, and organizations. Includes three hundred new entries among its ten thousand listings.

Kirkus Reviews. Kirkus Service, Inc. semi-mo., $225.00/yr. Critical, chiefly staff-developed, reviews of fiction and nonfiction books, many of them six to eight months in advance of publication date. Reviews four thousand to five thousand titles each year.

Magazine Industry Market Place 1984. R. R. Bowker Co., 1984. Book, 720 pp., $45.00. Some 2,500 trade, consumer, religious, scholarly, and specialized publications are described. Includes directories to companies and individuals.

Oxford Companion to Canadian Literature. William Toye, ed. Oxford Univ. Press, 1984. Book, 843 pp., $49.95. Covers both English- and French-Canadian writings in 750 entries on authors, titles, periods, and subjects. (LJ, 1 May 84)

Paperbound Books in Print. R. R. Bowker Co., 1984. Book, 2 vols. (April and October), $125.00. Indexes new paperbacks; updates backlisted titles; provides a directory of publishers and distributors.

The Poet's Marketplace: The Definitive Sourcebook on Where to Get Your Poems Published. Joseph J. Kelly, ed. Running Press, 1984. Book, 174 pp., $19.80 HB; $9.95 PB. Surveyed publishers to develop list of three hundred magazines that feature poetry. Describes other markets as well as how to submit poems. (BL, Aug 84; LJ, July 84)

The Private Press. 2nd ed. Roderick Cave. R. R. Bowker Co., 1983. Book, 389 pp., $59.95. Updates a general survey of private printing including new scholarship, terms, and presses active now in English-speaking countries. (C, Sept 84)

Writer's Market: 1985. Writer's Digest Books, 1984. Book, pna. An annotated list of more than four thousand buyers of freelance writing.

SELECTION; FREE/INEXPENSIVE MATERIALS

Media-related Periodicals

Free! The Newsletter of Free Materials and Services. Dyad Services. bi-mo., $18.00/yr. Materials selected and evaluated by teachers and librarians; brief descriptions.

Horn Book Magazine. The Horn Book, Inc. bi-mo., $27.00/yr. Journal of children's and young people's literature containing articles, reviews of books and recommended book-related records, films, and filmstrips, and paperbacks.

Media Review. mo., $89.00/yr. K-8 ed.; $89.00/yr. 9-College ed. In-depth evaluations of educational audiovisual materials and microcomputer software based on field testing; intended for library/media specialists.

New York Review of Books. New York Review, Inc. 22/yr., $25.00/yr. A major source of book reviews; fairly long essays; scholarly.

Publishers Weekly. R. R. Bowker Co. wk., $78.00/yr. News, developments, and trends in books throughout the world. Contains over five thousand book reviews.

Reference Tools and Recommended Media

American Reference Books Annual 1984. Bohdan S. Wynar, ed. Libraries Unlimited, Inc., 1984. Book, 793 pp., $65.00. Reviews reference books published in the United States during the calendar year and those received too late to be included in the previous edition. Organized in broad subject categories. Strengths and weaknesses are discussed in signed reviews.

Bibliography: Books for Children. Bibliography of Books for Children Committee, 1980-83. Sylvia Sunderlin, ed. Association for Childhood Education International, 1984. Book, 112 pp., $10.00 PB. Three ACEI Committees selected the books and periodicals for 3-14 year olds. The entries are annotated. Also lists recommended magazines, newspapers, and selection tools. (ARBA, 85)

A Bibliography of Navajo and Native American Teaching Materials. T. L. McCarty et al., comps. Navajo Curriculum Center, Rough Rock, AZ. 1983. Book, 104 pp., $7.50 PB. Evaluates curriculum material as well as ethnic literature. Provides a directory of major print and nonprint resources of use to teachers of Navajo students. (ARBA, 85)

Bibliography of Nonsexist Supplementary Books (K-12). Northwest Regional Educational Laboratory Center for Sex Equity. Oryx Press, 1984. Book, 108 pp., $22.50 PB. Books were analyzed for sex, race, and career bias. Some bibliographic data are provided for the 595 titles as is grade-level readability. (ARBA, 85)

Bilingual Educational Publications in Print 1983: Including Audio-Visual Materials. R. R. Bowker Co., 1983. Book, 539 pp., $45.00. Lists about thirty thousand books, learning and teaching materials, and audiovisual aids related to bilingual education and to teaching English as a second language. (ARBA, 85)

Choices: A Core Collection for Young Reluctant Readers. Carolyn Flemming and Donna Schatt, eds. John Gordon Burke Publisher, 1983. Book, 554 pp., $45.00. Annotates 360 general books for readers who are reading at or below grade level. Includes bibliographic citation and plot summary or critique as well as interest levels, readability levels, and related subjects. (ARBA, 85)

Educators Guide to Free Audio and Video Materials, 1984. 31st ed. James L. Berger, comp. and ed. Educators Progress Service, 1984. Book, 390 pp., $19.50 PB. The 1,602 entries fall under 15 subjects and have been checked for availability. (ARBA, 85)

Educators Guide to Free Health, Physical Education and Recreation Materials 1984. 17th ed. Foley A. Horkheimer. Educators Progress Service, 1984. Book, 625 pp., $25.25 PB. The 799 new multimedia items, out of 2,842, are starred; the other items have been checked for availability. (ARBA, 85)

Educators Guide to Free Science Materials, 1984. 25th ed. Mary H. Saterstrom, comp. and ed. Educators Progress Service, 1984. Book, 330 pp., $21.75 PB. The majority of 1,650 items are films and printed materials. Entries show the scope, purpose, and use. (ARBA, 85)

Educators Guide to Free Social Studies Materials, 1984. 24th ed. Steven A. Suttles and Sharon F. Suttles, comps. and eds. Educators Progress Service, 1984. Book, 617 pp., $25.50 PB. Includes 669 new titles among the 3,185 multimedia items. Arranged by format and then subject. Bibliographic information included. (ARBA, 85)

Elementary Teachers Guide to Free Curriculum Materials 1984. 41st ed. Kathleen Suttles Nehmer, ed. Educators Progress Service, 1984. 417 pp., $22.75 PB. Over half of the 1,885 items are new. Items were selected for their appropriateness, timeliness, style, and suitability. (ARBA, 85)

Exceptional Free Library Resource Materials. Carol Smallwood. Libraries Unlimited, 1984. Book, 233 pp., $18.50. Bibliographic and order information with annotations are included for 850 items in 27 curriculum-related subject areas. (ARBA, 85)

Field Guide to Alternative Media: A Directory to Reference and Selection Tools Useful in Accessing Small and Alternative Press Publications and Independently Produced Media. Patricia J. Case. American Library Assoc., 1984. Book, 44 pp., $6.00 PB. Published within the last five years, 164 sources that list, index, or review small and alternative press publications and independently produced media are annotated. Includes a selective bibliography. (ARBA, 85; LJ, Aug 84)

High Interest, Easy Reading for Junior and Senior High School Students. 4th ed. Hugh Agee. National Council of Teachers of English, 1984. Book, 96 pp., $5.00 PB. All new titles, this annotated bibliography consists of books selected for their readability and interest to teenagers who are not interested in reading. Includes a directory of publishers. (ARBA, 85)

Literacy Resources: An Annotated Check List for Tutors and Librarians. Jane-Carol Heiser, comp. Enoch Pratt Free Library, 1984. Book, 144 pp., $5.00 PB. An annotated bibliography of useful resources that includes some specialized materials such as workbooks, teachers' guides, newspapers, and audiovisual materials. Reading levels and instructional areas are identified. (ARBA, 85)

Magazines for Young Adults: Selections for School and Public Libraries. Selma K. Richardson. American Library Assoc., 1984. Book, 329 pp., $22.50 PB. Included are six hundred entries indexed in *Readers' Guide* and a few major newspapers. Each entry is annotated and has bibliographic information. (ARBA, 85)

New Books. U.S. Government Printing Office, Mail Stop: MK, Washington, DC 20401. bi-mo., free. Contains bibliographic and ordering information for new titles published by federal agencies and offered for sale by the GPO.

Online Database Search Services Directory: A Reference and Referral Guide to Libraries, Information Firms, and Other Sources Providing Computerized Information Retrieval and Associated Services Using Publicly Available Online Databases. John Schmittroth, Jr. and Doris Morris Maxfield, eds. Gale, 1984. Book, 2 vols., $75.00 PB/set. Describes the online database search services available at 634 institutions in the United States and Canada. Includes six indexes and a directory. (ARBA, 85)

Outstanding Books for the College Bound. Mary Ann Paulin and Susan Berlin, comps. American Library Assoc., 1984. Book, 92 pp., $5.95 PB. An annotated bibliography of fiction, nonfiction, biography, theater, and other performing arts books. (ARBA, 85)

Recommended Reference Books for Small and Medium-sized Libraries and Media Centers. Bohdan S. Wynar, ed. Libraries Unlimited, 1984. Book, 287 pp., $27.50. Contains 506 titles with reviews from *ARBA 84*. Strengths and weaknesses are pointed out. Review focuses on reference books to fit the libraries' needs. (ARBA, 85)

Reference Sources in Library and Information Services: A Guide to the Literature. Gary R. Purcell, with Gail Ann Schlachter. ABC-Clio, 1984. Book, 359 pp., $45.00. The one thousand sources cover all major types of reference works, international and multilingual as well. Includes bibliographies, directories, and glossaries. (ARBA, 85)

Teaching English as a Second Language: An Annotated Bibliography. 2nd ed. Wallace L. Goldstein. Garland, 1984. Book, 323 pp., $37.00. The 935 annotated entries of books, articles, and dissertations from 1974 to 1982 are divided into 16 subject areas. (ARBA, 85)

The Vocational-Technical Core Collection. Volume 2: Films and Video. Jack Hall and Victoria Cheponis Lessard. Neal Schuman, 1984. Book, 250 pp., $22.95. Selected 16mm films and ¾-inch videotapes are arranged by subject, related to trade areas such as business, graphics, construction. Bibliographic information and annotations are given. (ARBA, 85)

VIDEO (BROADCAST, CABLE, INTERACTIVE, SATELLITE, TELECOMMUNICATIONS, TELEVISION, VIDEODISC, VIDEOTEX)

Media-related Periodicals

Access. Telecommunications Research and Action Center (TRAC). mo., $40.00/yr. Aid to groups and individuals in the broadcast reform movement. Provides such information as license renewals, legislative developments, regulatory policies, and strategies for reform.

Broadcasting. Broadcasting Publications. wk., $60.00/yr. All-inclusive newsweekly for radio, television, cable, and allied business.

Cablevision. Titsch Communications, Inc. wk., $64.00/yr. A newsmagazine for the cable television industry; covers programming, marketing, advertising, business, and other topics.

Communication Abstracts. Sage Publications, Inc. q., $50.00/yr. indiv.; $90.00/yr. inst. Abstracts communication-related articles, reports, books; cumulative annual index.

Communication Booknotes. Center for Telecommunication Studies, George Washington University. mo., $20.00/yr. Newsletter that reviews books and periodicals about mass media, telecommunications, and information policy.

Communications News. mo., $25.00/yr. Up-to-date information from around the world regarding voice, video, and data communications.

E*ITV. Tepfer Publilshing Co. mo., $15.00/yr. Reviews and evaluates video equipment for industrial and educational use; includes news in the field of video production, teleconferencing reports, and reviews of new products and literature.

Electronic Publishing Review. Learned Information, Inc. q., $66.00/yr. An international journal of the transfer of published information via videotex and online media. Features articles, how-to advice, and news in the fields of communications, information transfer, publishing, and computer professionals.

Federal Communications Commission Reports. Government Printing Office. wk., $86.85/yr. Decisions, public notices, and other documents pertaining to FCC activities.

Historical Journal of Film, Radio, and Television. Carfax Publishing Co. 2/yr., $102.00/yr. Articles by international experts in the field, news and notices, and book reviews.

International Videotex Teletext News. Arlen Communications, Inc. mo., $225.00/yr. Includes reports and analyses of legislation, standards, marketing, software developments, products, and people in the fields of home information, videotex, and teletext.

Journal of Broadcasting. q., $17.50/yr. Includes articles, book reviews, research reports, and analyses; provides a forum for research relating to telecommunications and related fields.

Journal of Popular Film and Television. Heldref Publications. q., $25.00/yr. Articles on film and television, book reviews, theory and criticism, bibliographies.

Media International. Alain Charles House, mo., $50.00/yr. Contains features on the world's major media developments and regional news reports from the international media scene.

Prime Time School Television. mo., $15.00/yr. Subscribers receive monthly outlines of television programs of special value in schools. Each outline contains activities, discussion questions, a bibliography, and background information on the broadcast.

Radio y Television. *See* Audio listings.

Sight & Sound: International Film Quarterly. *See* Film listings.

Telematics and Informatics. Pergamon Press, Inc. q., $95.00. Intended for the specialist in telecommunications and information science; covers the merging of computer and telecommunications technologies worldwide. (C, July-Aug 84)

Video. Reese Publishing Co., Inc. mo., $15.00/yr. Devoted to video equipment, videotapes, video recordings, and the video environment. Includes reports on product testing, equipment reviews, how-to articles.

Video Computing. P.O. Box 3415, Indialantic, FL 32903. mo., $130.00/yr. A newsletter for trade people and others interested in interactive video. Covers specific and practical information related to new developments in applications, equipment, or service.

Video Review. mo., $18.00/yr. Emphasizes how-to articles; also reviews news items and equipment test reviews.

Video Systems. Intertec Publishing Corp. mo., $20.00/yr. Edited for video professionals and contains articles such as state-of-the-art audio and video technology reports, how-to ideas on equipment and facilities, and production techniques.

Video User. Knowledge Industry Publications. mo., $24.00/yr. Gives creative ideas for uses of video as well as current information on hardware, programs, and services.

Videodisc News. mo., $144.00/yr. Reports on new products and services, software and hardware reviews, addresses of producers and distributors, and new ideas for videodisc use.

Videodisc Update. Meckler Publishing. mo., $96.00/yr. A newsletter with news and facts about technical, software, courseware developments, calendar, conference reports, and job listings.

Videodisc/Videotext. Meckler Publishing. bi-mo., $75.00/yr. Features articles on the applications of videodisc and teletext systems; future implications; system and software compatibilities, and cost comparisons. Also tracks videodisc projects and covers world news.

Videography. United Business Publications, Inc. mo., $15.75/yr. For the video professional; covers techniques, applications, equipment, technology, and video art.

Videoprint. International Resource Development, Inc. semi-mo., $234.00/yr. Follows video and print communications fields; emphasizes videotex, teletext, and database publishing markets.

Reference Tools and Recommended Media

AIT Catalog of Educational Materials, 1984: Elementary, Secondary, Post-secondary, In-Service Broadcast Videotape, Videocassette, 16 mm Film. Agency for Instructional Television, 1984. Book, 158 pp., pna. The American-Canadian Agency for International Television describes television series and programs in broadcast, film, videocassette, and videokit formats. (ARBA, 85)

Broadcast Regulation: Selected Cases and Decisions. Marvin R. Bensman. University Press of America, 1983. Book, 136 pp., $19.50. Summarized briefly are 564 FCC and court cases that were landmark cases in radio and television broadcasting. Legal citations and a subject index are provided. (C, Apr 84)

Cable for Information Delivery: A Guide for Librarians, Educators, and Cable Professionals. Brigitte L. Kenny, ed. Knowledge Industry Publications, Inc., 1984. Book, n.p., $34.50 HB; $27.50 PB. A resource that explains cable technology, discusses trends, and describes various ways to use cable.

Cable Programming Market Place 1984/85. R. R. Bowker, 1984. Book, 350 pp., $39.95. A source for contacts and business information about cable programming. Also describes firms and networks and annotates program content.

Children and Television ... A Primer for Parents. (ED 243 466). Boys Town, NE, EDRS, 1984. Microfiche, 16 pp., $0.97. Summarizes results of research findings on the impact of television on children and advises parents about moderating the influence of television. Lists eleven publications containing information and names and addresses of television networks and other organizations.

The Complete Guide to Satellite TV. Martin Clifford. TAB Books, 1984. Book, 250 pp., $17.95 HB; $10.95 PB. A guide to satellite technology that includes extensive technical notes. Includes a glossary and a directory. (BL, 15 Sept 84)

Designing and Producing Videotex Instruction. (ED 244 595). Gwen Nugent et al. EDRS, 1983. Microfiche, 106 pp., $0.97. Summarizes videotex technology and its educational applications, the development process for videotex instruction, and cost and manpower data. Includes a bibliography.

Index to Educational Videotapes. 6th ed. NICEM, P.O. Box 40130, Albuquerque, NM 87196. 1985. Book or microfiche, $185.00. Lists over sixty thousand entries of educational videotapes that are available and producers and distributors. (EMTY)

Issues in International Telecommunications Policy: A Sourcebook. Jane H. Yurow, ed. Center for Telecommunications Studies, George Washington University, 1983. Book, 260 pp., $49.95 PB. Contains essays on current topics and annotated lists of laws, regulations, organizations, and citations. Covers telecommunications policy worldwide. Has selected bibliographies. (C, June 84)

Off-Air Videotaping in Education: Copyright Issues, Decisions, Implications. Esther R. Sinofsky. R. R. Bowker Co., 1984. Book, 163 pp., $27.50. Explains copyright laws and how they apply to educators, based on court decisions; possible penalties as well as legal taping are covered. Includes bibliography, directory, and glossary. (EMTY)

A Practical Guide to Interactive Video Design. Nicholas V. Iuppa. Knowledge Industry Publications, Inc., 1984. Book, 133 pp., $34.95. Gives step-by-step explanations and suggestions for using instructional design techniques to make an interactive video lesson more effective. Compares and contrasts interactive video strategies with those of linear video, both for production and for design. Provides checklists, flow charts, and practice exercises. (EMTY)

Telecommunications and the Schools. (ED 245 668). Designs for Education. EDRS, 1983. Microfiche, 152 pp., $0.97. Problems and possibilities associated with production and use of various technological delivery systems, such as radio, computers, and TV, are evaluated.

Telecommunications in the Information Age: A Nontechnical Primer on the New Technologies. Loy A. Singleton. Ballinger, 1984. Book, 239 pp., $19.95. Describes background of each technology ranging from cable to videotex to satellites and summarizes future applications and trends. (LJ, 1 Feb 84)

Telecommunications Systems and Services Directory. John Schmittroth and Martin Connors, eds. Gale, 1983. Book, 218 pp., $150.00 for a three-issue subscription. Describes, in the first issue, 242 companies and 500 terms related to telecommunications. Covers voice, data, teleconferencing, facsimile, satellite services, and so forth. (C, Mar 84)

Television and the School. Joseph R. Amatuzzi. R&E Publishers, P.O. Box 2008, Saratoga, CA 95070. 1983. Book, 135 pp., $14.95. Describes how TV can be better used in instruction, at home, and for school productions. Focuses on skills and suggests activities. (ET, July 84)

U.S. Television Network News: A Guide to Sources in English. Myron J. Smith. McFarland, 1984. Book, 233 pp., $29.95. A well-organized and wide-ranging bibliography that lists 3,215 sources covering network news from the late 1940s to 1983. Aids search for published literature on news. (C, July-Aug 84)

The Video Encyclopedia. Larry Langman. Garland, 1983. Book, 179 pp., $19.00. Defines video terms; describes history, scientific concepts, and equipment for the home video reader. (C, Apr 84; BL, 15 Sept 84)

Video Source Book. 5th ed. Gale, 1984. Book, 1,500 pp., $125.00. Contains information on thirty-five thousand program titles available on videocassette and videodisc. Includes audience ratings.

The Videodisc Book. Rod Daynes and Beverly Butler, eds. John Wiley & Sons, Inc., 1984. Book, 480 pp., $89.95. Covers how to design and develop interactive programs; equipment capabilities; a directory of individuals, organizations, and companies involved with interactive videodisc. (EMTY)

Video Discs: The Technology, the Applications & the Future. 2nd ed. Efrem Sigel et al. Knowledge Industry Publications, 1984. Book, $34.95. Describes information and other uses of videodiscs, production and cost comparisons, production, and consumer and international markets.

The Videotex Marketplace. Phillips Publishing Inc., Suite 1200N, 7315 Wisconsin Ave., Bethesda, MD 20814. 1984. Book, $67.00. A directory that lists videotex and teletext equipment manufacturers, distributors, developers, consultants, and associations. Also describes federal regulations.

Who's Who in Television and Cable. Facts on File, 1984. Book, 579 pp., $49.95. More than twenty-five hundred entries cover the broadcast and cable television industries. Several indexes included. (LJ, July 84)

Directory of Producers, Distributors, and Publishers

This directory provides, in one alphabetical listing, the names and addresses of the producers, distributors, and publishers whose media-related products are mentioned in the *Educational Media and Technology Yearbook 1985*.

This arrangement saves space that would otherwise be required for duplications of addresses. At the same time, a useful directory is provided for quick reference by those requiring address information.

The directory itself is arranged alphabetically, by principal name. Foreign and U.S. entries are interfiled.

Users of this list are reminded that addresses of this type change often. Accuracy of addresses was carefully checked, however, and is believed to be correct as of 1 January 1985.

ABC-Clio Information Services
Riviera Campus
2040 A.P.S.
Box 4397
Santa Barbara, CA 93103

ABC Leisure Magazines, Inc.
825 Seventh Ave., 6th Floor
New York, NY 10019

ABC Schwann Publications
535 Boylston St.
Boston, MA 02116

Harry N. Abrams, Inc.
110 E. 59th St.
New York, NY 10022

AD Digest
Information and Communication
Box 165
Morton Grove, IL 60053

Addison-Wesley Publishing Co.
General Books Division
Reading, MA 01867

AECT. *See* Association for Educational
Communications and Technology

Agency for Instructional Television (AIT)
Box A
Bloomington, IN 47402

ALA. *See* American Library Association

ALLM Books
21 Beechcroft Rd.
Bushey, Watford
Herts WD2 2JU, England

American Library Association
50 E. Huron St.
Chicago, IL 60611

Amphoto/Watson Guptill
1515 Broadway
New York, NY 10036

Annenberg School Press
Box 13358
Philadelphia, PA 19101

Aperture
Elm St.
Millerton, NY 12546

Arlen Communications, Inc.
Box 40871
Washington, DC 20016

**Aslib (Association of Special Libraries
and Information Bureaus)**
Three Belgrave Sq.
London SW1X 8PL, England

**Association for Childhood Education
International (ACEI)**
3615 Wisconsin Ave. NW
Washington, DC 20016

**Association for Educational Communica-
tions and Technology**
1126 16th St. NW
Washington, DC 20036

Audio Forum
On-the-Green
Guilford, CT 06437

Ballantine Books
(Division of Random House)
201 E. 50th St.
New York, NY 10022

Ballinger Publishing Co.
54 Church St.
Box 281
Harvard Square
Cambridge, MA 02138

Bantam Books
666 Fifth Ave.
New York, NY 10103

Barron's
113 Crossways Park Dr.
Woodbury, NY 11797

Basic Computing
3838 S. Warner St.
Tacoma, WA 98409

Baywood Publishing Co., Inc.
120 Marine St., Box D
Farmingdale, NY 11735

Berkeley Enterprises, Inc.
815 Washington St.
Newtonville, MA 02160

The Book Company
11223 S. Hindry Ave.
Los Angeles, CA 90045

R. R. Bowker Co.
1180 Avenue of the Americas
New York, NY 10036

Robert J. Brady Co. (Prentice Hall)
Rtes. 197 and 450
Bowie, MD 20715

Broadcasting Publications
1735 DeSales St. NW
Washington, DC 20036

John Gordon Burke
Box 1492
Evanston, IL 60204

Byte Publications
70 Main St.
Peterborough, NH 03458

Carfax Publishing Co.
Hopkinton Office and Research Park
35 South St.
Hopkinton, MA 01748

Cassette Information Services
Box 9559
Glendale, CA 91206

CBS Educational and Professional
 Publications
1515 Broadway
New York, NY 10036

Center for Computer/Law
Box 54308 T.A.
Los Angeles, CA 90054

Center for Telecommunication Studies
George Washington University
2000 L St. NW, Suite 301
Washington, DC 20052

Center for the Humanities, Inc.
Communications Park, Box 1000
Mount Kisco, NY 10549

Alain Charles House
27 Wilfred St.
London SW1E 6PR, England

Children's Magazine Guide
7 N. Pinckney St.
Madison, WI 53703

CINEASTE Magazine
200 Park Ave. S.
New York, NY 10003

Clearinghouse on Development
 Communication
1414 22nd Ave. NW
Washington, DC 20015

The College Board
888 Seventh Ave.
New York, NY 10106

Collegiate Microcomputer
Rose-Hulman Institute of Technology
Terre Haute, IN 47803

Communications News
124 S. First St.
Geneva, IL 60134

COMPUTE! Publications, Inc.
505 Edwardia Dr.
Greensboro, NC 27409

Computer Book Review
735 Ekekela Pl.
Honolulu, HI 96817

Computers, Reading, and Language Arts
Box 13247
Oakland, CA 94661

Congressional Information Service
4520 East-West Hwy.
Bethesda, MD 20814

Consortium of University Film Centers
330 Library
Kent, OH 44242

Corporation for Public Broadcasting
1111 16th St. NW
Washington, DC 20036

Council of Chief State School Officers
400 N. Capitol St. NW
Washington, DC 20001

Council on Foundations
1828 L St. NW
Washington, DC 20036

Council on Library Resources
1785 Massachusetts Ave. NW
Washington, DC 20036

Crane, Russak & Co.
3 E. 44th St.
New York, NY 10017

Creative Computing
39 E. Hanover Ave.
Morris Plains, NJ 07950

Creative Computing Press
Box 789M
Morristown, NJ 07960

Crown Publishers, Inc.
1 Park Ave.
New York, NY 10016

Cuadra Associates
2001 Wilshire Blvd., Suite 305
Santa Monica, CA 90403

CW Communications, Inc.
530 Lytton Ave., Suite 303
Palo Alto, CA 94301

DAC Publications
Box 764
Oakridge, OR 97463

Doubleday
245 Park Ave.
New York, NY 10017

Dyad Services
Department 284
Box C34069
Seattle, WA 98124

Eastern News
111 8th Ave.
New York, NY 10011

Eastman Kodak Co.
343 State St.
Rochester, NY 14650

EDRS (ERIC Document Reproduction Service)
Box 190
Arlington, VA 22210

Educational Computer
Box 535
Cupertino, CA 95015

Educational Electronics
One Lincoln Plaza
New York, NY 10023

Educational Software Evaluation Consortium
Ann Lathrop
SMERC Library
San Mateo County Office of Education
333 Main St.
Redwood City, CA 94063

Educational Technology Publications, Inc.
140 Sylvan Ave.
Englewood Cliffs, NJ 07632

Educator's Progress Service, Inc.
214 Center St.
Randolph, WI 53956

Electronic Education
1311 Executive Center Dr., Suite 220
Tallahassee, FL 32301

Elsevier North-Holland, Inc.
52 Vanderbilt Ave.
New York, NY 10017

Elsevier Science Publishing Co., Inc.
Box 1663 Grand Central Sta.
New York, NY 10163

Enoch Pratt Free Library
400 Cathedral St.
Baltimore, MD 21201-4484

EPIE Institute
Educational Products Information Exchange
Box 839
Water Mill, NY 11976

ERIC/ChESS
855 Broadway
Boulder, CO 80302

ERIC Clearinghouse on Educational Management
University of Oregon
Eugene, OR 97403

ERIC Clearinghouse on Elementary and Early Childhood Education
University of Illinois
805 W. Pennsylvania Ave.
Urbana, IL 61801

ERIC Clearinghouse on Higher Education
One Dupont Cir. NW, Suite 630
Washington, DC 20036

ERIC Clearinghouse on Information Resources
Syracuse University
030 Huntington Hall
Syracuse, NY 13210

ERIC Clearinghouse on Urban Education
Teachers College
Columbia University
Box 40
New York, NY 10027

ERIC/ESSCE. *See* ERIC Clearinghouse on Elementary and Early Childhood Education

Lawrence Erlbaum Assoc.
365 Broadway
Hillsdale, NJ 97642

Espial Productions
Box 624, Sta. K
Toronto, M4P 2H1, Canada

Facts on File, Inc.
460 Park Ave. S.
New York, NY 10016

Far West Educational Laboratory
1855 Folsom St.
San Francisco, CA 94103

Festival Publications
Box 10180
Glendale, CA 91209

Film Comment
140 W. 65th St.
New York, NY 10023

Film Ideas
1155 Laurel Ave.
Deerfield, IL 60015

Film Quarterly
2120 Berkeley Way
Berkeley, CA 94720

Film Review
30-31 Golden Sq.
London W1, England

The Foundation Center
888 Seventh Ave.
New York, NY 10106

Gale Research Co.
Book Tower
Detroit, MI 48226

Garland Publishing
136 Madison Ave., 2nd Floor
New York, NY 10016

General Gramophone Publications, Ltd.
177-179 Kenton Rd.
Harrow MSHA 3 0HA, England

Gernsbach Publications, Inc.
200 Park Ave. S.
New York, NY 10003

Globe Publishing Co. *See* Photo Publishing Co.

Goddard & Case Publishers, Inc.
108 Oregon Ave.
Bronxville, NY 10708

Golden-Lee Book Distributor's, Inc.
1000 Dean St.
Brooklyn, NY 11238

Government Printing Office (GPO)
Superintendent of Documents
Washington, DC 20402

Gower Publishing
Old Post Rd.
Brookfield, VT 05036

GPO. *See* Government Printing Office

Grantsmanship Center
1031 S. Grand Ave.
Los Angeles, CA 90015

Wayne Green, Inc.
80 Pine St.
Peterborough, NH 03458

GuideLines Press
1307 S. Killian Dr.
Lake Park, FL 33403

Corbin Gwaltney
1333 New Hampshire Ave. NW
Washington, DC 20036

G. K. Hall
70 Lincoln St.
Boston, MA 02111

Harmony Books
One Park Ave.
New York, NY 10016

Harper and Row
10 E. 53rd St.
New York, NY 10022

Haworth Press
28 E. 22nd St.
New York, NY 10010

Hayden Publishing Co.
50 Essex St.
New York, NY 10010

Heldref Publications
4000 Albemarle St. NW
Washington, DC 20016

High Technology
38 Commercial Wharf
Boston, MA 02110

HOPE Reports, Inc.
1600 Lyell Ave.
Rochester, NY 14606

The Horn Book, Inc.
Park Square Bldg.
31 St. James Ave.
Boston, MA 02116

IBM (International Business Machines)
Information Systems Group
900 King St.
Rye Brook, NY 10573

ICUC Press
Box 1447C
Springfield, VA 22151

Indiana University Audio-Visual Center
Indiana University
Bloomington, IN 47405

Industrial Press
200 Madison Ave.
New York, NY 10157

Information Synergy, Inc.
2922 S. Daimler St.
Santa Ana, CA 92705

Instructor Publications, Inc.
757 3rd Ave.
New York, NY 10017

Intercollegiate Broadcasting System
3107 Westover Dr. SE
Washington, DC 20020

Interface Age
Box 1234
16704 Marquardt Ave.
Cerritos, CA 90701

Intermediate Technology Publications, Ltd.
Nine King St.
London WC2E 8HN, England

International Apple Core
908 George St.
Santa Clara, CA 95050

International Communications Industries Association
3150 Spring St.
Fairfax, VA 22031

International Resource Development, Inc.
30 High St.
Norwalk, CT 06851

Intertec Publishing Corporation
Box 12901
Overland Park, KS 66212

January Productions
124 Rea Ave.
Hawthorne, NJ 07506

Johns Hopkins University Press
Baltimore, MD 21218

Journal of Academic Librarianship
Box 8330
Ann Arbor, MI 48107

Journal of Broadcasting
1771 N St. NW
Washington, DC 20036

Kirkus Service, Inc.
200 Park Ave. S.
New York, NY 10003

Knopf/Pantheon
201 E. 50th St.
New York, NY 10022

Knowledge Industry Publications
701 Westchester Ave.
White Plains, NY 10604

Lakewood Publications, Inc.
731 Hennepin Ave.
Minneapolis, MN 55403

Landers Associates
Box 27309
Escondido, CA 92027

Learned Information, Ltd.
Besselsleigh Rd.
Abingdon OXON OX13 6LG, England

Learned Information, Inc.
143 Old Marlton Pike
Medford, NJ 08055

Learning Corporation of America
1350 Avenue of the Americas
New York, NY 10019

Learning Periodicals Group
19 Davis Dr.
Belmont, CA 94002

Learning Publications, Inc.
Box 1326
Holmes Beach, FL 33509

Lexington Books
Division of D. C. Heath
125 Spring St.
Lexington, MA 02173

Libraries Unlimited, Inc.
Box 263
Littleton, CO 80160-0263

Library Association Publishing
7 Ridgmont St.
London WC1E 7AE, England

Library of Congress
Information Office
Box A
Washington, DC 20540

Life-Time Learning Publishing
10 Davis Dr.
Belmont, CA 94002

Lomond Publications, Inc.
Box 88
Mt. Airy, MD 21771

Lone Eagle Productions
9903 Santa Monica Blvd., No. 204
Beverly Hills, CA 90212

Macmillan Publishing Co.
866 Third Ave.
New York, NY 10022

Marquis
200 E. Ohio St.
Chicago, IL 60611

McFarland Publications
Four Stuyvesant Oval
New York, NY 10009

McGraw-Hill Book Co.
1221 Avenue of the Americas
New York, NY 10020

Meckler Publishing
520 Riverside Ave.
Westport, CT 06880

Media Center for Children
Three W. 29th St.
New York, NY 10001

Media Review
346 Ethan Allen Hwy.
Box 425
Ridgefield, CT 06877

Microcomputer Industry Update
Box 681
Los Altos, CA 94022

Microcomputer Information Services
2464 El Camino Real, Suite 247
Santa Clara, CA 95051

Microfilm Publishing, Inc.
Box 313, Wykagyl Sta.
New Rochelle, NY 10804

Microsparc, Inc.
Box 325
Lincoln, MA 01773

Minnesota Educational Computing Consortium (MECC)
3490 Lexington Ave. N.
St. Paul, MN 55112

Modino Press Ltd.
Keswick House
3 Greenway
London N20 8EE, England

Museum of Holography
11 Mercer St.
New York, NY 10013

Music Library Association
2017 Walnut St.
Philadelphia, PA 19103

National Audio-Visual Association. *See*
NAVA/International Communications
Industries Association

National Audiovisual Center
National Archives and Records Service
General Services Administration
Washington, DC 20409

National Center for Audio Tape Archives
University of Colorado
Campus Box 379
Boulder, CO 80309

National Council of Teachers of English
1111 Kenyon Rd.
Urbana, IL 61801

National Education Association
1201 16th St. NW
Washington, DC 20036

National Endowment for the Arts
2401 E St. NW
Washington, DC 20506

National Endowment for the Arts
Literature Program
806 15th St. NW
Washington, DC 20506

National Endowment for the Humanities
Office of Challenge Grants
806 15th St. NW, Room 429
Washington, DC 20506

National Endowment for the Humanities
The Old Post Office, Room 426
1100 Pennsylvania Ave. NW
Washington, DC 20004

National Film Board of Canada
1251 Avenue of the Americas, 16th Floor
New York, NY 10020

National Institute of Education
1200 19th St. NW
Washington, DC 20208

National Logo Exchange
Box 5341
Charlottesville, VA 22905

National Public Radio
2025 M St. NW
Washington, DC 20036

National Science Foundation (NSF)
Washington, DC 20550

National Society for Performance and Instruction
1126 16th St. NW, Suite 315
Washington, DC 20036

National Youth Work Alliance
1346 Connecticut Ave. NW
Washington, DC 20036

NAVA. *See* International Communications Industries Association

Neal-Schuman Publishers, Inc.
23 Cornelia St.
New York, NY 10014

New England Publications, Inc.
Highland Mill
Camden, ME 04843

New York Review, Inc.
250 W. 57th St.
New York, NY 10107

Newsletter Management Corporation
10076 Boca Entrada Blvd.
Boca Raton, FL 33433

NICEM
Box 40130
Albuquerque, NM 87196

Nichols Publishing Co.
Box 96
New York, NY 10024

Northwest Regional Educational Laboratory
300 SW 6th Ave.
Portland, OR 97204

OCLC (Online Computer Library Center, Inc.)
6565 Frantz Rd.
Dublin, OH 43017

Office of the Federal Register
National Archives and Records Service
Washington, DC 20408

Olympic Media Information
70 Hudson St.
Hoboken, NJ 07030

Open Court (Carus) Co.
1500 8th St.
LaSalle, IL 61301

Oryx Press
2214 N. Central at Encanto, Suite 103
Phoenix, AZ 85004

Osborne/McGraw-Hill
630 Bancroft Way
Berkeley, CA 94710

Oxford University Press
200 Madison Ave.
New York, NY 10016

Pantheon
201 E. 50th St.
New York, NY 10022

PC World
Box 6700
Bergenfield, NJ 07621

PC World Communications, Inc.
555 De Haro St.
San Francisco, CA 94107

Peelings II
Box 188
Las Cruces, NM 88004

Pendragon Press
162 W. 13th St.
New York, NY 10011

People's Computer Co.
Box E
Menlo Park, CA 94025

Pergamon Press
Maxwell House
Fairview Park
Elmsford, NY 10523

Personal Computer Age
Box 70725
Pasadena, CA 91107

Personal Computer News
Box 848
Point Reyes, CA 94956

Petersen Publishing Co.
8490 Sunset Blvd.
Los Angeles, CA 90069

Phi Delta Kappa
Box 789
8th and Union Sts.
Bloomington, IN 47402

Photo Publishing Co.
Box 4689 G.P.O.
Sydney, Australia 2001

Pierian Press
Box 1808
Ann Arbor, MI 48106

Pilot Books
103 Cooper St.
Babylon, NY 11702

Plenum Publishing Corp.
233 Spring St.
New York, NY 10013

Popular Periodical Index
Box 2157
Wayne, NJ 07470

Prentice-Hall, Inc.
200 Old Tappan Rd.
Old Tappan, NJ 07675

PTN Publishing Corporation
101 Crossways Park W.
Woodbury, NY 11797

Public Broadcasting Service
475 L'Enfant Plaza SW
Washington, DC 20024

Public Service Materials Center
111 N. Central Ave.
Hartsdale, NY 10530

The Puppetry Journal
George and Pat Latshaw
8005 Swallow Dr.
Macedonia, OH 44056

QED Information Sciences
170 Linden St.
Wellesley, MA 02181

Rabcom Corporation
Box 10266
Stamford, CT 06904

Radio Shack. *See* Tandy Corporation

Recording for the Blind, Inc.
215 E. 58th St.
New York, NY 10022

Redgrave Publishing Co.
89 Danbury Rd.
Ridgefield, CT 06877

Reese Publishing Co., Inc.
235 Park Ave. S.
New York, NY 10003

Research Technology International
4700 Chase Ave.
Lincolnwood, IL 60646

Reston Publishing
11480 Sunset Hills Rd.
Reston, VA 22090

Running Press
125 S. 22nd St.
Philadelphia, PA 19103

Sage Publications, Inc.
275 S. Beverly Dr.
Beverly Hills, CA 90212

St. Martin's Press, Inc.
175 5th Ave.
New York, NY 10010

Salem Press, Inc.
Box 1097
Englewood Cliffs, NJ 07632

Salisbury State College
Salisbury, MD 21801

Scarecrow Press
Box 656
Metuchen, NJ 08840

Scholastic, Inc.
Box 7501
2931 E. McCarty St.
Jefferson City, MO 65102
or
730 Broadway
New York, NY 10003
or
902 Sylvan Ave.
Englewood Cliffs, NJ 07632

School & Home CourseWare, Inc.
1341 Bulldog Ln., Suite C
Fresno, CA 93710

Marvin H. Scilken
The U*N*A*B*A*S*H*E*D Librarian
Box 2631
New York, NY 10116

Simon and Schuster
1230 Avenue of the Americas
New York, NY 10020

Softalk Publishing Co.
Box 60
North Hollywood, CA 91603

Softside Publications, Inc.
6 South St.
Milford, NH 03055

Software Supermarket
Box 4004
Sidney, OH 45365

Student Computer News
Box 87H
Kickapoo, IL 61528

Supergraphics
Box 48
Reading, PA 19603

SYBEX, Inc.
2344 6th St.
Berkeley, CA 94710

Syncom, Inc.
1000 Syncom Dr.
Box 130
Mitchell, SD 57301

TAB Books, Inc.
Blue Ridge Summit, PA 17214

Tandy Corporation/Radio Shack
1800 One Tandy Center
Fort Worth, TX 76102

Teachers and Writers
84 Fifth Ave., Room 307
New York, NY 10011

Technical Publishing Co.
875 Third Ave.
New York, NY 10022

Telecommunications Research and Action Center
Box 12038
Washington, DC 20005

Tepfer Publishing Co.
51 Sugar Hollow Rd.
Danbury, CT 06810

Titsch Communications, Inc.
Box 5400-TA
Denver, CO 80217

TSC/Houghton Mifflin
Box 683
Hanover, NJ 03755

United Business Publications, Inc.
475 Park Ave. S.
New York, NY 10016

University of Arizona
Graduate Library School
College of Education
Tucson, AZ 85721

University of Chicago Press
5801 Ellis Ave.
Chicago, IL 60637

University of Illinois Press
Box 5081 Sta. A
54 E. Gregory Dr.
Champaign, IL 61820

University of North Carolina Press
Box 2288
Chapel Hill, NC 27514

University Press of America
4720 Boston Way
Lanham, MD 20706

Van Nostrand Reinhold Co.
135 W. 50th St.
New York, NY 10020

Vanguard Press
424 Madison Ave.
New York, NY 10017

Video Review
350 E. 81st St.
New York, NY 10028

Videodisc News
Box 6302
Arlington, VA 22206

Vogeler Publications
455 Crossen Ave.
Elk Village, IL 60007

Voicespondence Club
Box 259
Trexlertown, PA 18087

Warner Books, Inc.
666 Fifth Ave.
New York, NY 10103

Warner Press Pubs.
Box 2499
1200 E. Fifth St.
Anderson, IN 46018

Washington International Arts Letter
Box 9005
Washington, DC 20003

Washington Researchers, Ltd.
918 16th St. NW
Washington, DC 20006

Watson-Guptill Publications
1515 Broadway
New York, NY 10036

Western Center for Microcomputers in
  Special Education, Inc.
1259 El Camino Real, Suite 275
Menlo Park, CA 94025

Western Interstate Commission for Higher
  Education
Drawer P
Boulder, CO 80302

Westview Press
5500 Central Ave.
Boulder, CO 80301

Michael Wiese
Box 406
Westport, CT 06881

John Wiley & Sons
605 Third Ave.
New York, NY 10158

H. W. Wilson Co.
950 University Ave.
Bronx, NY 10452

Window, Inc.
469 Pleasant St.
Watertown, MA 02172

Word Processing News
211 E. Olive Ave., Suite 210
Burbank, CA 91502

Writer's Digest
205 W. Center St.
Marion, OH 43302

Writer's Digest Books
9933 Alliance Rd.
Cincinnati, OH 45242

Ziff-Davis Publishing Co.
One Park Ave.
New York, NY 10016

Index

This index gives page locations of names and associations and organizations, authors, titles, and subjects. Subject entries are in boldface. In addition, acronyms for all organizations and associations are cross-referenced to the full name, so that this index may also serve as a directory of acronyms.

Please note that a classified list of U.S. organizations and associations appears on pages 89 to 96.